Mantegna to Rubens

The Weld-Blundell Drawings Collection

THE
PAUL HAMLYN
LIBRARY

DONATED BY
THE PAUL HAMLYN
FOUNDATION
TO THE
BRITISH MUSEUM

opened December 2000

MANTEGNA TO RUBENS

THE WELD-BLUNDELL DRAWINGS COLLECTION

Xanthe Brooke

MERRELL HOLBERTON
PUBLISHERS LONDON

This book accompanies the exhibition
'Mantegna to Rubens:
Drawings from the Liverpool Weld-Blundell Collection Revealed'
at the Walker Art Gallery, Liverpool,
26 June – 20 September 1998,
and the British Museum, London,
10 October 1998 – 10 January 1999

First published in 1998 by
Merrell Holberton Publishers Ltd
Willcox House, 42 Southwark Street, London SE1 1UN

British Library Cataloguing in Publication Data
Brooke, Xanthe, 1960–
Mantegna to Rubens: the Weld-Blundell drawings collection
1.Drawings, European
I.Title
741.9 4

ISBN 1 85894 052 4 (hardback)
ISBN 1 85894 053 2 (paperback)

Designed by Roger Davies
Produced by Merrell Holberton Publishers

Printed and bound in Italy

Front jacket/cover Peter Paul Rubens, *God creating Adam, after Michelangelo*, detail (exh. cat. 77)
Back jacket/cover Andrea Mantegna, *Three studies for a figure of St John the Baptist* (exh. cat. 36)
Half title Luca Giordano after Domenichino, *St Mark*, detail (exh. cat. 31)
Frontispiece Domenichino, *Portrait of a young girl* (exh. cat. 23)

Contents

Preface

In 1995 the Walker Art Gallery made one of the most important acquisitions in its history, the Weld-Blundell collection of over 300 European Old Master drawings, at a stroke transforming our holdings in this field. To the small group of drawings already in the gallery, including some major works such as Primaticcio's *Ulysses winning the archery contest* (purchased in 1991 also from the Weld-Blundell collection), we have added notable works by Mantegna, Correggio, Fra Bartolommeo, the Carracci, Parmigianino, Vasari, Tintoretto, Domenichino, Reni and Rubens. As can be seen from this list, the bias is in favour of Italy but the collection also contains some striking works by Dutch and Flemish artists.

Such a purchase, even with the tax concessions involved in a private treaty sale, placed excessive demands on our acquisition funds, and we could not have contemplated it without outside assistance. We are deeply grateful to those who helped: the National Heritage Memorial Fund, which gave us an outstandingly generous grant; the National Art Collections Fund, for substantial support; Sir Denis Mahon, whose donation was made through the NACF; and British Nuclear Fuels.

The acquisition for Liverpool of the Weld-Blundell collection is especially apt – 161 items formerly belonged to William Roscoe of Liverpool, botanist, lawyer, banker, anti-slavery campaigner, poet, historian and biographer of Lorenzo de' Medici. Roscoe's dream was to make Liverpool a cultural and artistic centre: his Italian and Flemish pictures are much admired as the basis of the Walker's paintings collection and a number of drawings with Roscoe provenance have been acquired since. The acquisition of such a large group of his drawings keeps faith with his wish for his collection to be publicly available in his native city.

The connection of the Weld-Blundell family with Liverpool is also strong. The Blundells were an old Lancashire Catholic family residing at Ince Blundell Hall, north of Liverpool. In the eighteenth century Henry Blundell visited Italy on the Grand Tour and formed a collection of antique and contemporary Italian sculpture which his descendant Colonel Joseph Weld presented to Liverpool in 1959: it is now divided between the Antiquities Gallery of the Liverpool Museum and the European Sculpture Gallery at the Walker. Henry also bought drawings, as did his son Charles, who was responsible for buying the Roscoe drawings when Roscoe was forced to sell his collection at auction after the failure of his bank. The drawings were kept at Ince Blundell until the Weld family moved to Dorset in 1960.

In Dorset the drawings stayed, largely unseen, apart from a very small number of Italian works lent to Edinburgh Festival exhibitions in 1969 and 1972 and an exhibition in Venice in 1980. These exhibitions picked out some of the exceptional items, as indeed does the exhibition this book accompanies, but we are delighted to have acquired the Weld-Blundell drawings as a whole collection. This has great historical interest in itself, as a document of the history of collecting, quite apart from the intrinsic aesthetic value of individual items. This is the first publication devoted to the collection; in addition to the exhibited items, an illustrated checklist of the remainder is included with provisional attributions so that the collection can be studied in its entirety.

The catalogue has been written by Xanthe Brooke, Curator of European Art at the Walker. The drawings have been meticulously conserved, mounted and prepared for exhibition by Sally Ann Yates, Ann Stewart, Caroline Cotgrove, Alison Readey, Gerald Regan, Keith Oliver and Roy Irlam. After its inaugural showing in Liverpool the exhibition travesl to the British Museum, London, where Antony Griffiths and his colleagues have overseen the arrangements. We are grateful to all the above, and to everyone else who has worked on the project.

We would also like to thank all those who have given financial assistance to this project. Xanthe Brooke's research for the catalogue has been supported by a grant from the Getty Trust. Derald H. Ruttenburg has generously contributed to publication costs. Support for the exhibition has also been received from Phillips, International Auctioneers and Valuers, and the Hon. Andrew Bigham. Finally, particular thanks are due to Rathbones, the investment management group, for sponsoring the exhibition, a particularly happy collaboration in view of the close friendship between the Liverpool merchant William Rathbone (1757–1809) and William Roscoe himself.

RICHARD FOSTER
Director of National Museums and Galleries on Merseyside

JULIAN TREUHERZ
Keeper of Art Galleries

Introduction

The Weld-Blundell Collection

Fig. 1 Sir Martin Archer Shee, *William Roscoe*, 1822, oil on canvas, 233 × 166.5 cm, National Museums and Galleries on Merseyside (Walker Art Gallery), Liverpool

Throughout the months of August and September in 1816 Liverpool witnessed the sale of the collections of the lawyer and sometime banker William Roscoe – over 150 paintings, more than 1300 prints, an extensive library of books, many related to Italian literature, history and art history and 1045 drawings.[1] The sale was partly the result of the economic slump which followed the Napoleonic Wars and led to political discontent, riots to promote Parliamentary reform and the stoning of the Prince Regent in St James's Park. In Liverpool merchants engaged in the American trade were badly affected and the bank of which Roscoe was a temporary partner suffered a run on its capital. The sale was Roscoe's ultimately futile attempt to stave off personal bankruptcy, which came in 1820. On a more personal level the sale was supposed to have been brought about at the insistence of two of his creditors, one of whom was the South Lancashire Catholic landowner Charles Robert Blundell of Ince Blundell Hall (some ten miles north of Liverpool), the estranged son of Henry Blundell, Roscoe's friend, fellow founder of Liverpool cultural societies and major collector of Roman and Greek antiquities.[2] It was Charles Blundell's purchase of 161 of Roscoe's drawings from the 1816 sale, supplemented by those of his father, which formed the core of what is now called the Weld-Blundell collection.

Together with Charles Blundell's later additions the collection remained at Ince Blundell until 1960, and then moved with the Weld family to Lulworth, Dorset, until its purchase by National Museums and Galleries on Merseyside (NMGM) for the Walker Art Gallery in the autumn of 1995. The superb quality of many of the drawings makes the collection outstanding. But the fact that it has remained essentially intact from its creation at the beginning of the nineteenth century to this day – a rare achievement considering the pressure to break up landed estates over the last five decades – ensures that the Weld-Blundell collection is also a fascinating and revealing document of the interests and passions of the two men, from such contrasting social backgrounds, who created it, William Roscoe (1753–1831) and Charles Robert Blundell (1761–1837).

ROSCOE'S COLLECTION

When the American writer Washington Irving met Roscoe during his visit to Europe in 1815, he was prompted to pen a paean of praise to this "self-prompted, self-sustained, almost self-educated scholar and a gentleman" who had without "fortune, family connections or patronage" become eminent and used his influence to "embellish his native town".[3] In America Roscoe was particularly admired for setting a personal example as the archetypal self-made man whose

Fig. 2 Ebony-veneered cabinet with brass inlay, made by George Bullock for William Roscoe to house portfolios and medals, National Museums and Galleries on Merseyside (Sudley House), Liverpool

activities demonstrated the benefits of uniting commercial and intellectual pursuits. He provided what was considered a peculiarly appropriate role model for its citizens.[4] Roscoe, by nature a retiring family man, father to seven sons and three daughters, would no doubt have been embarrassed by this eulogy. He was nevertheless accomplished in many fields. Without the benefits of any formal education beyond the age of twelve, let alone of a university career or a Grand Tour, he had grown, from beginnings in his father's inn-keeping and market-garden business, where he first dug and bagged potatoes, to become the leader of Liverpool's cultural life and the internationally acknowledged cultural historian of the Florentine Medici family.

From 1773, when at the age of twenty he played a leading role in the formation of a society for the encouragement of the arts of painting and design, Roscoe helped found most of Liverpool's artistic and learned societies and academies, of which the impact extended abroad. The constitution he helped write in 1799 for Liverpool's Athenaeum Library was used as model for its equivalent in Boston, Massachusetts. Most of these cultural societies encouraged the membership of men from his own business and professional class rather than the nobility and gentry. In his old age he became the city's cultural icon, constantly cited by contemporaries and successors as an example of the union of business and culture. He was a successful lawyer, sometime banker, political campaigner and essayist, who saluted the early stages of the French Revolution, corresponded with the American Presi-

dent Thomas Jefferson and as a radical Whig was briefly MP for Liverpool in 1806 on a controversial anti-slavery platform which ensured that he was not re-elected. After his semi-retirement from the law in 1796 his correspondence with leading botanists led him to establish the Liverpool Botanic Garden in 1802, and in 1807 he published the children's verse classic *The Butterfly's Ball and the Grasshopper's Feast,* which he had written for his youngest son Robert. But he was to find international fame as an "author of celebrity ... the elegant historian of the Medici", who in 1796 published *The Life of Lorenzo de' Medici, called the Magnificent,* followed by *The Life and Pontificate of Leo X* in 1805.[5] His first purchases of paintings and drawings were probably stimulated by the research for the first of these biographies.

During the 1780s and the first half of the 1790s Roscoe built up a lucrative legal practice representing Liverpool Whig interests in London, which gave him opportunities to view the burgeoning drawings sales in the capital. His semi-retirement in 1796 ensured fewer visits to London, apart from the brief period in 1806–07 when he was a Liverpool MP, and thereafter he relied instead on London-based collector-dealers, such as William Young Ottley and the auctioneer Thomas Philipe, to keep an eye on the sales and buy on his behalf. However, the evidence we have of Roscoe's purchases is distorted by the fact that only the accounts for 1807–14 survive, and few of his surviving letters contain aesthetic comments or references to them.

From comments in his son's biography of his father we learn that Roscoe's first loves were books and prints, which he had begun collecting by 1782, shortly after his marriage.[6] The first evidence of his buying drawings is found in a note in his own sale catalogue which states that he bought a Reynolds copy after an *Old man's head* by Guercino at the auction of Thomas Hudson's studio in 1785.[7] By 1798 he was buying numbers of drawings from major sales, including that of Hudson's pupil Sir Joshua Reynolds, a priced copy of whose catalogue was in Roscoe's own sale as lot 1682. The following year, after the death of his brother-in-law Daniel Daulby, the author of one of the first English catalogues of Rembrandt's work (*A Descriptive catalogue of the works of Rembrandt ... compiled from original etchings,* Liverpool 1796), he bought a Rembrandt school drawing (Appendix: WAG1995.69) and many prints. It was probably his close friendship with Daulby that stimulated Roscoe's prime interest in prints and printmaking.

The growth and quickening of Roscoe's purchase of drawings in the 1790s was more likely the result of his publication in 1795 of the *Life of Lorenzo de' Medici ...,* without which Roscoe might have remained an obscure Liverpool lawyer

Fig. 3 After Samuel Austen, *William Roscoe's study at Lodge Lane*, probably 1820s, watercolour, 233 × 166.5 cm, National Museums and Galleries on Merseyside (Walker Art Gallery), Liverpool

with a few literary and artistic contacts in London and Edinburgh. As Roscoe never left British shores the biography was based on six years of intermittent documentary research among the Medici manuscripts of the Palazzo Vecchio and the Library of the Marchese Riccardi by his banking partner William Clarke.[8] Its publication thrust Roscoe into the national and international limelight, immediately attracted the attention of the London arts world, including the support of Horace Walpole, and earned him an advance of 1200 guineas for a second edition.[9] A request for another Medici biography, that of Pope Leo X, was soon forthcoming (1805) and both books went into multiple multilingual editions.

Roscoe and the Medici: the influence on his collecting habits
What was distinctive about Roscoe's biographies, as Francis Haskell has pointed out, was that he approached the study of them as historic figures essentially out of enthusiasm for them as patrons and then considered their other activities in that light.[10] What he attempted to write was a cultural history of the Medici – though the results were somewhat hindered by his reliance on second-hand visual and documentary evidence. He devoted a whole chapter of his *Lorenzo* to the progress of the arts from Giotto to Raphael – the fullest account of the topic in English – integrating it into the political narrative. For Roscoe the politician the cultural and commercial activities of the Medici family and the Florentine city-state were a blueprint for the successful development of Liverpool under the guiding hand of bankers and lawyers like himself. Roscoe's own fascination with the Medici bordered on obsession. He even acquired leaves from trees in Lorenzo's villa to paste into his personal copy of *Lorenzo the Magnificent* along with other Medici memorabilia. His self-identification with Lorenzo in particular became a major influence on Roscoe's collecting pattern. He favoured artists, such as Bandinelli (exh. cat. 3), whose careers developed through Medici patronage. Other drawings of his were directly related to Medici commissions and projects in Florence, Tuscany and Rome. The one with the closest links to both of Roscoe's literary projects is the copy after Franciabigio's fresco of the *Return of Cicero* for the Great Hall at Poggio a Caiano commissioned by Leo X in honour of Lorenzo, his father.[11] Vasari's *Triumph of the goddess Cybele* (exh. cat. 62) was for a room in the Palazzo Vecchio, the Sala degli Elementi, commissioned by Duke Cosimo. Its iconography, with the

goddess of Plenty riding in triumph above the fruits of the months' labours, was related to the room directly below, which eulogized Lorenzo the Magnificent with scenes from his life just as Roscoe praised Lorenzo in his biography. Roscoe may well have thought that his other Vasari (exh. cat. 61) was also for another Medici commission. He certainly believed that the architectural design (exh. cat. 27) was intended for a temporary façade created to celebrate the entry of Pope Leo X into Florence in 1515. In fact the design proved to be related to the tomb monument for another, non-Medici, pope. However, one of his drawings by Peruzzi (exh. cat. 42) was intended to commemorate the Jubilee Year of Clement VII, Lorenzo's grandson.

For Roscoe, the cultured lawyer-banker turned poet-historian, the Medici and their role in the rise of Florence provided an inspiring lesson for Liverpool's commercial élite. He saw the cultural revival of the Italian Renaissance as largely the result of the Medici's direction and liberal artistic patronage. His idolization of the Medici led him to ignore the uglier, despotic elements of their regime which should have been anathema to Roscoe the politician, as was caustically pointed out by his friend the painter Fuseli, who thought Roscoe had forsaken his principles as a fighter for liberty by publishing the *Life of Lorenzo*.[12] A similar point was made more academically and extensively in the *Histoire des Républiques Italiennes du Moyen Âge* by his Swiss opponent Simonde de Sismondi, who otherwise shared Roscoe's liberal political views. Roscoe was willing to turn a blind eye to a failing in the Medici which in others, such as Admiral Nelson, he was to criticize bitterly in verse.[13] His belief that his art collection could be used as an instrument in the cultural progress and economic development of Liverpool also lay behind his patronage of living artists. By encouraging such artists, sometimes native-born locals such as the sculptor John Gibson, often exiles from abroad, he also consciously or not followed in the path of the Medici.

Friends and fellow collectors

At least one of the artists Roscoe supported, the English-based Swiss artist Henry Fuseli, may also have provided influential advice on Roscoe's collecting activities. His collection's bias towards late sixteenth-century Mannerism was almost certainly reciprocally stimulated by his close friendship with the painter, whose own work was influenced by art of that period, and whom he first met in 1779 when Fuseli visited Liverpool. Thereafter a correspondence was struck up and mutual visits made, during one of which Fuseli copied Roscoe's drawing of *Venus and Cupid* by Cambiaso, inscribing it *Allerton Hall September 1799*.[14] Fuseli's knowledge as

an art historian was of great use to the self-educated Roscoe. His radical pro-French revolutionary politics, which had led to his exile from Switzerland, must also have appealed to Roscoe, who was always willing to support political refugees from the Continent – whether artists or academics such as the Italian Panizzi, who went on to become the British Library's first cataloguer and designer of its Round Reading Room.[15] Roscoe's acquisition of drawings attributed to Michelangelo may also have been influenced by Fuseli. Fuseli was one of a group of northern artists who from the 1770s onwards did much to rekindle Michelangelo's reputation. His own drawings were often influenced by Michelangelo's frescos in the Sistine Chapel, where he made studies of *The Brazen Serpent*, of which Roscoe also owned a sixteenth-century copy-drawing.[16]

Another artist who was allowed to view and copy from Roscoe's art works was his protégé the young sculptor John Gibson.[17] And not only artists benefited from Roscoe's willingness to share his collection. Once he had published his Medici biographies his house became part of the tourist trail for any visitor to Liverpool with cultural pretensions. In 1813 he and his "hearty", broadly accented wife provided hospitality for the Anglo-Irish author Maria Edgeworth, and Roscoe willingly showed off to her his pictures and drawings. She was suitably impressed with the portfolio of "Michelangelo" drawings, which included a "*Dream of Michelangelo*", but was horrified by the array of paintings by Fuseli on Medicean and Shakespearean themes which lined Roscoe's dining-room walls.[18] Thus his collection performed a social function. The friends and acquaintances from the literary and artistic discussion groups he frequented would almost certainly have been allowed access to it. Once he had retired from active business and political life he enjoyed leafing through his albums in the quiet of his study, as his son described: "The attraction of Mr Roscoe to works of art contributed greatly to his happiness. When fatigued with business and with the literary employments which generally succeeded to the engagements of the day, he was accustomed to amuse his mind with turning over the leaves of his portfolios – an occupation that always seemed to beguile his fatigue and to revive his spirits."[19]

Roscoe's friendship with the MP Thomas William Coke of Holkham, Norfolk (1754–1842), with whom he shared an interest in political and agricultural reform, led to Coke's commissioning in 1822 the splendid full-length portrait of Roscoe seated beside a bust of his hero Charles Fox, the Whig politician and fellow campaigner for the abolition of slavery, and in front of a view through to the library at Holkham [see fig. 1]. Coke had inherited an impressive collection of drawings from his great-uncle the 1st Earl of Leicester (1697–1759). Roscoe's awareness of it might also have affected his collecting pattern, although his familiarity with it and its owner deepened only after Roscoe's sale in 1816 when he began work on (but never published) an illustrated catalogue of Holkham's manuscript collection. During the enforced retirement brought on by his bankruptcy he used prints after Coke's drawings to interleave and illustrate his proof copies of the *Life of Leo X* and Lanzi's *La storia pittorica della Italia* as translated by his son Thomas Roscoe in 1828.[20] The Holkham collection represented an earlier eighteenth-century taste, but its roll-call of sixteenth-century artists – Bedoli, Casolani, Peruzzi, Parmigianino, Giulio Romano, Giuseppe della Porta, Francesco Salviati, Taddeo Zuccaro and Veronese – all found echoes in Roscoe's own. More compelling influences, however, were those of William Young Ottley (1771–1836), collector-dealer and future Keeper of Prints and Drawings at the British Museum, and the London auctioneer Thomas Philipe.

By the mid 1790s Philipe was already sending lists of prints and drawings he had for sale to Roscoe and his brother-in-law Daniel Daulby. Their relationship soon developed. Philipe would not only buy drawings on commission from Roscoe, but also research possible acquisitions and sometimes buy batches of drawings speculatively, sending them up to Liverpool on approval for purchase or return. The drawings were always carefully packed in solander boxes so as to "avoid their being affected by the motion of conveyance".[21] Roscoe bought not only from the sales Philipe held at his premises in Golden Square, London, but also from those he organized in Scotland. In 1804 he bought Elisabetta Sirani's *Madonna and Child* (exh. cat. 51) from a Philipe sale in Edinburgh of the collection put together over the previous fifty years by the Fellow of the Royal Society of Edinburgh John MacGowan (died 1803).[22] One of Roscoe's largest purchases from a single sale conducted by Philipe was that from the sale of 899 drawings owned by George John, 2nd Earl Spencer, which took place 10–17 June 1811. Roscoe commissioned Philipe to bid for 63 lots and was successful in buying 39. Later Philipe offered Roscoe a further 77 and 82 lots bought speculatively over the last two days of the sale.[23] At least twenty of Philipe's speculative purchases passed into Roscoe's collection and one, a Ghirlandaio workshop drawing (exh. cat. 30), was bought by Charles Blundell from Roscoe's sale. Despite Philipe's bulk-buying there is evidence that he also took Roscoe's taste into account when making his speculative purchases. The Spencer sale had a large number of landscape drawings by Claude and northern artists, none of which he bought for Roscoe. Roscoe's

deep interest in nature was more practical – promoting the agricultural improvement of the 'mosses' that lay between Liverpool and Manchester and establishing in 1802 Liverpool's first botanical gardens. In the prospectus for these gardens he wrote: "Even the cultivation of the fine arts, however alluring in its progress, and dignified in its object, must yield the superiority to the study of nature; for who will venture to compare the most finished productions of the painter and the sculptor, with the originals, whence they derived their ideas of beauty and proportion?"[24]

The collector-connoisseur Ottley had acquired many of his drawings and paintings in 1798–99 by taking advantage of the chaos caused by the French invasion of Italy. In Florence he obtained drawings from, amongst other family collections, that of Lamberto Gori, including a copy after Michelangelo's figures of *Joram and Jehosophat* from the Sistine Chapel (Appendix: WAG1995.204). Once settled back in London in 1799 he established himself as an art expert and advisor to others whilst continuing to buy drawings from most of the important sales of the first decade of the nineteenth century, including part of the collection gathered in Florence by J.-B.-J. Wicar, the French painter in charge of the official looting of art.[25] He financed his acquisitions through very active dealing as well as by arranging at least three sales from his own holdings in 1804, 1807 and 1814. From the last of these, arranged by Philipe, Roscoe bought a number of drawings – his final major purchases before bankruptcy forced his own sale, in which there were over sixty drawings from Ottley, including Domenichino's *Portrait of a little girl* and *Caricature study of a head* (exh. cats. 22, 24) and Peruzzi's *Design for a papal medal* (exh. cat. 42).[26] Both Ottley and Roscoe pioneered the interest in Britain in early Italian painting of the fourteenth and fifteenth centuries – amongst the paintings Roscoe owned were Simone Martini's *Christ discovered in the Temple* and Ercole de' Roberti's *Pietà* (WAG 2787 and 2773). They may also have shared similar feelings towards slavery, as in 1833, on its abolition in the British colonies, Ottley refused, on principle, the compensation due for the losses incurred by freeing the slaves on his family's West Indian plantations. But the closest comparison between the two men lay in their attitudes towards their respective collections. Between 1808 and 1823 Ottley published about eighty of his drawings in a lavishly illustrated book entitled *Italian Schools of Design*. It was part of an ambitious scheme to treat the history of drawing in Italy as a chronological progression up to the eighteenth century, and may well have inspired Roscoe's similarly unfulfilled idea of writing a history illustrating the rise, progress and vicissitudes of the arts, which might have included a section

'On Painters' Drawings'.[27] John Gere characterized Ottley's collection as being neither a carefully chosen cabinet of masterpieces nor a miscellaneous accumulation but as "complete and impersonal as a museum", formed as much from an historical as an aesthetic point of view.[28] Roscoe revealed the same cast of mind in the introduction to his sale catalogue when he wrote: "... the following works have been collected ... chiefly for the purpose of illustrating ... the rise and progress of the arts in modern times .... They are therefore not wholly to be judged of by their positive merits, but by a reference to the age in which they were produced. Their value chiefly depends on their authenticity, and the light they throw on the history of the arts."

The distinctive character of Roscoe's collection
By the time Roscoe began to collect at the end of the eighteenth century there was a tradition in England more than a century and a half old of collecting Old Master drawings. In Charles I's reign aristocrats and courtiers such as the Earl of Arundel (1585–1646) and Nicholas Lanier (1558–1666) and at the court of Charles II painters such as Sir Peter Lely (1618–1680) and his assistant Prosper Henry Lankrink (*ca.* 1628–1692) made and subsequently sold major collections. Early eighteenth-century England saw a rapid rise in the acquisition of drawings, fed by an influx of large collections from Italy such as the many albums collated by Padre Sebastiano Resta for the Bishop of Arezzo, which were acquired by Lord John Somers in 1710 and later reorganized by the portrait painter and art commentator Jonathan Richardson Senior (1667–1745). Richardson amassed what was probably the finest and certainly the largest collection, totalling almost 5000 drawings, which contemporaries praised for its quality, completeness and orderly arrangement. Richardson had a lasting influence on the way drawings were mounted and displayed over the next two centuries, for he created a mount design widely copied by later collectors which combined ruled lines with wash borders in colours chosen to harmonize with the drawing they framed (exh. cats. 6, 7, 8, 15, 39, 49, 63, 64, 77). Richardson's connoisseurship and his writings laid the foundations for the study of Old Master drawings in England. His influence also spread through the advice he gave major collectors of his own and the next generation. By the time his collection was finally broken up with the death of his son Jonathan Junior in 1771 Roscoe was just over a decade away from beginning his own and a number of Roscoe's drawings have a Richardson provenance.[29]

The second large influx of drawings to come on to the English market occurred in the 1760s when the combined collections of Niccolò Gabburri (1676–1742), the Florentine connoisseur and custodian of the Uffizi's self-portrait collection, and more than 19,000 drawings amassed by Pierre Crozat (1665–1740) filtered into England and were snapped up by a new type of collector with different social status from his predecessors. The growth of specialist dealers in the first half of the eighteenth century changed the art market, so that apart from aristocrats and artists one starts to see as collectors professional men such as doctors, lawyers and government office-holders as well as merchants involved in commerce. Amongst the wealthy circle who surrounded the artist and collector Arthur Pond (1701–1758), whose mentor had been Richardson Senior, there were Richard Houlditch (died 1736), a former linen-draper and director of the South Sea Company; the merchant Nathaniel Hillier (1707–1783) and the businessman's son John Barnard (died 1784), one of the keenest buyers from Pond's sale in 1759. Such men constituted the generation immediately previous or nearly contemporary to Roscoe's, and he acquired drawings from all their collections.[30]

Perhaps the collector closest in rank to Roscoe was the customs officer Charles Rogers (1711–1784). Like Roscoe, Rogers was self-taught, an administrator who spent his leisure hours improving his taste and cultivating his mind and whose scholarly status as a member of the Society of Antiquaries and Fellow of the Royal Society gave credibility to his publication in 1778 of *A Collection of Prints in Imitation of Drawings, To Which are Annexed the Lives of the Authors, with Explanatory Notes* after drawings in his own and other collections, including that of the Royal family. It was an innovative work which may well have influenced Roscoe, for, although Rogers's book did not feature in Roscoe's library sale, prints from it were used to interleave Roscoe's 'graingerized' copy of Lanzi's *La storia pittorica della Italia*. Whether or not Roscoe ever intended to reproduce his own collection in imitation of Rogers, he certainly knew of his collection as he bought at least one drawing from its sale, organized by Philipe, in 1799.[31]

Roscoe may seem to have shared many attributes of social class with his near contemporaries, but as a collector he was distinguished from them by various factors, not the least of which was his identity as an outsider, geographically – Liverpool, not London, was his base – and politically – a radical reformer, not a government-paid officer. Indeed his collection holds an important if not unique position in that it was one of the first in England to be created outside London and intended to benefit the citizens of a provincial city.

As so many drawings came from previous English collections it is not surprising that overall the artists whose work was represented in Roscoe's collection varied little from those owned by other English collectors – unlike his paintings collection, a greater proportion of which had been directly and recently imported from the Continent. The majority of his drawings were by Italian masters of the sixteenth and seventeenth centuries, a lesser number by northern artists of the same period from Flanders, the Netherlands and Germany. Even though he owned a total of nineteen drawings attributed to Rubens, one of the largest groups by a single artist, he believed they all had been created whilst the Flemish painter was in Italy. Like many other British collections his seventeenth-century works were dominated by drawings by or after Bolognese artists, from the Carracci family onwards through Domenichino, Guercino, Reni to Canuti, Sirani and, more unusually, Tiarini.[32]

In addition to those subjects with Medici links Roscoe's Italian collection was dominated by drawings from the second half of the sixteenth century; twenty-eight attributed to the Genoese artist Cambiaso (the largest single number by one artist); and a group by or after central Italian artists such as Cavaliere d'Arpino, Giorgio Vasari, the Zuccaro brothers, Perino del Vaga and Polidoro da Caravaggio, all of whom played dominant roles in the culture of central Italy and Rome at a time of great activity particularly executing important artistic commissions for papal patrons such as Paul III (1534–49), Pius IV (1559–65), Gregory XIII (1572–85), Sixtus V (1585–90) and Clement VIII (1592–1655).[33] Nowadays their works tend to be less well known, partly because they lived in the shadow of the great artistic achievements of Michelangelo and Raphael but also, more banally, for physical reasons. Most of their works were either large-scale, immovable fresco commissions for palaces, churches and private chapels, or temporary structures celebrating court festivities and theatrical performances such as Vasari's *River-gods* (exh. cat. 61). Sometimes they were inaccessible to the casual visitor or only viewable by a privileged few and sometimes they had simply disappeared, faded away owing to the action of weather, damp and pollution like, for example, Farinati's fresco of *Agriculture* (exh. cat. 25) or Federico Zuccaro's *Conversion of the Magdalene* (exh. cat. 79). So the easiest way in which someone such as Roscoe, who never travelled outside his native country yet who was fascinated with Italian culture and by the Medici and their patronage, could indulge his interest was to collect their drawings. Moreover, as such artists' large-scale works were always the result of collaborative workshop activity their drawings were much the best way to see the artist's own hand and mind at work. In any case the finished drawings and *modelli* of Italian Mannerists and Counter-Reformation artists of 1550–1600 often proved to be more immediately attractive than their finished easel paintings, altarpieces and frescos.

An analysis of his collection suggests that Roscoe overwhelmingly favoured highly finished whole-figure studies or compositional narratives over partial, unfinished sketches or anatomical and drapery studies. On the rare occasions when the latter appear in Roscoe's part of the Weld-Blundell collection they are always attributed to prestigious artists such as Leonardo, Parmigianino or Annibale Carracci. His sales catalogue often referred approvingly to "highly finished", "beautifully designed", "capital" studies although he also appreciated those drawings which were freely sketched or showed a "strong" or "free" pen. Such finished compositional studies may also have been chosen for their appeal to the audience who Roscoe expected might view them in Liverpool – essentially a visually illiterate public, who, rather like himself, were more attuned to literary and narrative imagery than visual aesthetics.

Roscoe considered himself first and foremost a literary historian, whose interest in art derived from the Italian poetry which he enjoyed reading. He often treated his drawings less as aesthetic objects than as historical documents, and the historian in him always stimulated the collector. Thus he inscribed on the mount of a caricature depicting *A Bacchanalian procession of monks* the title *I beoni*, the name of a satirical piece of Italian literature which he mentions in his *Life of Lorenzo*.[34] His art connoisseurship was limited and he usually refrained from making aesthetic judgements. As the novelist Maria Edgeworth commented, Roscoe's conversation was "not too literary ... [but] a happy mixture of anecdote and facts" – marred for her by the strong regional accent with which he spoke and which she felt undermined the elegant, gentlemanly impression created by his height, expression and physical bearing.[35] Roscoe relied heavily on printed sources, from Vasari and other sixteenth- and seventeenth-century Italian and northern artists' *Lives* through to Luigi Lanzi's illustrated history of Florentine art, *L'Etruria pittrice* (1791 and 1795), copies of which were all in his library. His devotion to fine arts stemmed less from connoisseurship than from his belief in the moral, civilizing influence it could exert on society – a society which, in Liverpool, according to Maria Edgeworth, was obsessed with money-making ventures ("If you ask a question you must *buy* an answer") and whose fortune was partly based on the slave-trade which Roscoe so abhorred.[36] For Roscoe the arts could educate, humanize and ennoble and it was this idea that gave his collection its distinctive character.

Roscoe's firm belief in the educational and civic value of art and his pride in his native city was reflected in his preface to the 1816 sale catalogue, which stated his wish that his entire collection might be kept together and be of some use to his native city by being put on display there. In order to further this hope he had originally intended to sell all the drawings as one lot. The unusual location of his sale, in Liverpool not London, and the nature of its catalogue with extensive descriptive entries are a further expression of his belief in Liverpool as an autonomous cultural centre and of the essentially didactic nature of his collections. As his son commented, when his father was preparing his sale catalogues for the press he was constantly aware "that they should bear a higher character than the generality of mere sale catalogues, even in form and appearance he wished them to be such as might be placed with credit on the shelves of a library".[37]

Roscoe's sale as a didactic memorial

The uncommon character of the sales catalogues stemmed partly from their being the result of an earlier project. Roscoe's decision to add a capacious new library to his villa at Allerton on the southern outskirts of Liverpool, to house his now large collection of books, manuscripts, prints and drawings, had prompted him to begin taking an inventory of his collection. Once the library was finished in the autumn of 1812 the original task soon changed to a much more ambitious scheme to write a catalogue of the collection that would illustrate the revival, rise, "vicissitudes" and establishment of literature and art. The catalogue was indeed published in 1815 but Roscoe's bank failure ensured that the information gathered for it was used in the different format of a sale catalogue intended almost as a didactic memorial to Roscoe himself.[38]

The didactic intent is evident in the high factual standard set by the catalogue, which included sizes of drawings, details of previous ownership and occasional quotations from books, none of which was common in London sales of the period. The catalogue's preface carefully explained why, unlike prints intended for publication, drawings – even highly finished ones – were rarely signed: hence the importance of the attributions provided by respected collectors such as Jonathan Richardson, referred to as "that very worthy man and excellent connoisseur ... who formed the finest collection of drawings ever brought together in this country". Each artist's name was also accompanied by a reference to Luigi Lanzi's *La storia pittorica della Italia*, first published in Italy in 1792 and translated into English in 1828 by one of Roscoe's sons, Thomas. In his old age Roscoe interleaved pages of his copy of the translated Lanzi with drawings, engravings and artists' portraits, either the remnants of his original collection or the results of an attempt to build up a secondary one.

Admittedly the extensive information provided in the auction catalogues would also have helped talk up the collection, increasing its commercial value. Such promotion for financial ends was sometimes hidden under a veneer of principle, as Roscoe's friend the auctioneer Philipe knew. When Philipe had sold Rogers' prints in March 1799 he had prided himself on introducing "better methods of arrangement and description than have hitherto been practised, and thereby contributing to excite a more general taste for collecting works of merit than is at present the fashion", for he believed that such collecting was too limited in London "whose prosperity depends, in no small degree, on the good taste of the manufactures of the country, and their reputation at foreign markets". This is a sentiment which would have chimed well with Roscoe's belief in the merits of promoting the arts amongst business men and manufacturers, but self-interest was irresistibly mixed in with it.

Roscoe's appreciation of his drawings extended to the care he took over their physical treatment. He commissioned two cabinets, which he kept in his study one either side of the fireplace, from the Liverpool-based furniture designer George Bullock to house portfolios of some of his drawings along with his medals [see figs. 2 and 3]. Some time between 1814 and the sale in September 1816 he had special card mounts made with tissue paper attached as a protective cover for many if not all of his drawings.[39] These integrated tissue-paper and card mounts may well have been devised for him by Mr Jones the bookbinder and librarian at the Liverpool Athenaeum, on whose skills Roscoe was later to call when conserving the parchment of manuscripts lent to him from Holkham by his friend Thomas Coke.[40]

Unlike previous collectors Roscoe left no indelible mark, inscription or stamp on his drawings or their mounts. Nor did he arrange his collection according to a complex system like that of Richardson's, whose shelfmarks combining letters and numbers associated comparable drawings in the collection. Roscoe's ownership is shown merely by a lot number on the back of his mounts (pencilled in the lower right corner) and occasionally by a pencilled attribution and comment on the tissue paper. This typical reticence as to his ownership has meant that over the years, as old tissue-paper and card mounts have been discarded by later owners, the evidence of Roscoe's ownership of drawings now in other collections has often disappeared.

When the sale of Roscoe's collection took place his friends and local supporters concentrated on trying to save the paintings collection for public display in Liverpool. Only a small number of drawings were bought by local collectors and landowners such as Lord Stanley of Knowsley (who bought thirty-seven lots) and Richard Heber of Hodnet, Shropshire; or by friends such as Coke who purchased five lots to add to the Holkham collection, including Parmigianino's *Woman balancing a vase on her head*.[41] Others were acquired by the Manchester bookseller and dealer William Ford and the print collector William Esdaile (1757–1837), whose London banking firm had close contacts with Roscoe's.[42] The core of Esdaile's collection seems to have been formed from his purchases at Roscoe's sale, which pre-date his first visit to Italy in 1825. At the sale he was repeatedly willing to pay the highest prices for drawings of quality attributed to artists such as Correggio, Dürer and Michelangelo.[43] However, the biggest single buyer of drawings at the Roscoe sale was the Lancashire landowner Charles Blundell, one of Roscoe's main creditors and supposedly the part instigator of his bankruptcy. He also put together most of the Weld-Blundell print collection (sold by Christie's in 1976) from his purchases at the sale. He used a fellow Liverpool-born Catholic, the Benedictine priest Dom Edward B. Slater (1774–1832), to make his bids at the auction, perhaps in an attempt to hide his activity.[44] Charles Blundell certainly showed persistence in acquiring as many drawings as possible from the sale. Annotations in different copies of Roscoe's sale catalogue suggest that a number of times Charles Blundell was prepared to buy from the Manchester dealer Ford drawings that had evaded his own bidder Slater at the auction.

THE BLUNDELL COLLECTION

Charles Blundell's interest in art was inherited from his father Henry Blundell (1724–1810; fig. 4), who had used his Catholic education in France and his Grand Tour connections to form an impressive collection of more than five hundred pieces of antique and eighteenth-century Italian sculpture, including works by Canova, and at least 197 paintings. The sculpture was displayed in and affixed to a classical-style temple in the grounds and a specially built rotunda, based on Rome's Pantheon, attached to Ince Blundell Hall [figs. 5 and 6].[45] On his death the collection of sculpture, gems and mosaics was the largest in England in private hands, exceeding in size that of his friend Charles Townley (1737–1805), with whose advice it had been formed. Henry Blundell was conservative in religion and politics, upholding the monarchy and the Catholic Church's hierarchy whilst opposing Fox and the abolition of the slave trade.[46] His Catholic faith prevented him from holding any political or public office. One of the few ways in which he could participate in society was by belonging to Liverpool's agricultural, learned and cultural associations, which usually

Fig. 4 George Bullock, *Henry Blundell*, exhibited 1804, National Museums and Galleries on Merseyside (Walker Art Gallery)

excluded religious matters from their debates. Many of them had been established by William Roscoe whose liberal political views, except in so far as they favoured Catholic emancipation, Blundell would not naturally have supported. However, cultural ties between the two proved stronger than any political differences. According to Roscoe's own inscription, Henry Blundell presented him with a portrait medal of Lorenzo de' Medici which Roscoe later had drawn by John Gibson and pasted into his copy of *Lorenzo the Magnificent*. Unlike Charles Townley, a fellow Lancashire Catholic, who cultivated London society, Blundell was quite happy to remain in Lancashire, leading the life of a country squire worried as much about planting, farming and livestock as the arts. Although he obviously enjoyed the pursuit of collecting he admitted to Townley that he "often lays aside the object once acquired".[47] He had no great intellectual pretensions and, if anything, was slightly prudish, to judge by his treatment of his sculpture – ordering the removal of genitals and the application of fig-leaves to their illustrations. He published a descriptive *Account* of his collection in 1803, followed in 1809 by over one hundred and fifty engraved plates illustrating the antiquities. The *Account* concentrated

Fig. 5 Exterior of Pantheon at Ince Hall, built between 1802 and 1810

heavily on the sculpture and paintings and barely mentioned drawings. Those few that were catalogued were by or after Continental artists, including two French genre works of a lady drinking coffee and a servant girl with a pot of beer.[48] The only other drawings that can definitely be linked to Henry Blundell are those of the so called Baths of Titus which he commissioned from Vincenzo Brenna but which were confiscated by the police in Rome in 1777 and are now in Krannert Art Museum, Illinois.[49] None of the very few drawings referred to in the *Account* remains in the Weld-Blundell collection. Drawings were mentioned, however, though not itemized, in Blundell's will of 1808. Some of these drawings may have been amongst those he dismissively described in 1799 as "a heap of rubbish, sketches of things I have not, many not fit to be seen &c.; They were tuck'd round my bedroom closet, and gathered dust, so I put them all in a book".[50] Although it is also possible that these were merely copy-drawings of antiquities that he had or had not purchased they may also have included ones in the Weld-Blundell collection.

We know that one drawing in the Weld-Blundell collection was owned by Henry Blundell because the printed inscription on the distinctive brightly coloured label stuck on to its mount reads, "A Mythological Bas-Relief, lately belonging to Pope Pius VI, and now in the Collection of Henry Blundell of Ince, Esq." (Appendix: Italian School (?), WAG1995.122). It illustrates one of Blundell's most celebrated pieces, a relief from a late second-century AD sarcophagus depicting *Phaeton imploring his father Phoebus to lend him his sky chariot* which he bought for the second time

on 31 May 1800 for £260 at Christie's sale of antiquities pillaged from the papal apartments by the French and intercepted at sea.[51] He had first bought the relief some ten years before, for only £10, when it had been found at the Villa d'Este heavily encrusted with mineral salts because it had been used as a fountain. Its cleaning revealed it to be so splendid that the Pope "requested" that it should stay in Rome and gave Blundell five marble-topped tables in return.[52] The drawing is marked out in dotted red lines with what would seem to be possible repairs to the relief. It could, therefore, date from the time when Blundell originally acquired the sarcophagus, as we know Fr John Thorpe, his art advisor and buyer in Rome until his death in 1792, habitually sent drawings of likely purchases back home to Henry.[53]

As similar printed coloured labels are attached to about 34 other Weld-Blundell drawings one might assume that they, too, were bought by Henry Blundell. If so, his interest in graphic art is represented by a mysterious group of 77 drawings previously owned by an anonymous collector dubbed "Pseudo-Crozat" by Frits Lugt because his brash mark, a large capital C stamped prominently on all his drawings, seemed to relate them to the major eighteenth-century French collector-connoisseur Pierre Crozat (1665–1740).[54] The Blundells kept the bulk of their 'Pseudo-Crozat' collection (one of which is exh. cat. 42) in two leather-covered albums, in which the drawings were pasted sometimes alongside a few reproductive etchings. The sarcophagus drawing was in the middle of Album I, and a small number of additions from the Roscoe and West sales were found at the beginning or near the end of the albums. With a few notable exceptions such as a Taddeo Zuccaro (exh. cat. 64), a Parmigianino (exh. cat. 42) and a Turchi (Appendix: WAG1995.175) this large group of 'Pseudo-Crozat' drawings is not rich in examples of the finest quality, suggesting that its collector may have been wealthy, but not primarily interested in amassing prime examples of the draughtsman's art. However, its size as the largest single block of 'Pseudo-Crozat' works and the inclusion of drawings stamped with other known collectors' marks means that it is now possible, by analysing the collection, to identify the previously anonymous owner.[55]

Henry Blundell was not the only collector to own examples from this collection. So also did Roscoe, although on a much reduced scale. This suggests that the collection was on the market at a time when Blundell was buying but perhaps Roscoe was not fully ready to purchase, in other words before the mid 1790s. Of the two Roscoe drawings that have this mark in the Weld-Blundell collection one has an eighteenth-century French provenance and the other is described in

Fig. 6 Interior of Pantheon at
Ince Hall, as photographed in 1959

Roscoe's sale catalogue, lot 419, as "From Count Caylus's and Mr. Hone's Collection".[56]

"Count Caylus" can be easily identified as the French aristocrat Anne-Claude-Philippe de Tubières (de Grimoard de Pestels de Lévis), comte de Caylus (1692–1765), but how substantial parts of his collection could have ended up in England and especially in the hands of an obscure landed gentleman in Lancashire is less clear. Caylus was an author, patron of Watteau, amateur engraver and wealthy collector who from the 1720s maintained a close friendship with the connoisseurs Pierre Crozat (1665–1740) and Pierre-Jean Mariette (1694–1774), creators of the largest and finest assembly of drawings in eighteenth-century Europe. Partly through his friendship with Crozat and Mariette he was in close contact with other collectors, for example in Italy the Venetian connoisseur Count Antonio Maria Zanetti and in Spain the Marquis de la Cañada, who in 1765 sent him drawings of antiquities dug up on his estate near Cadiz.[57] Caylus's supposedly overbearing patronage of French artists, his publication of erotic short stories and his support for Egyptian antiquities brought him criticism and derision from philosophers and art critics such as Voltaire, Diderot and their friends. In Francis Haskell's succinct though not entirely correct summary Caylus's reputation suffered from his "having

been despised by one genius (Diderot), patronised by another (Winckelmann) and heartily disliked by almost every contemporary who wrote about him".[58]

It is evident from his letters, Italian diary and his own publications that Caylus was essentially an antiquarian, fascinated by what ancient artefacts could reveal about the cultures of Egypt and of Etruscan and Roman Italy and interested in amassing sometimes newly excavated sculpted friezes, bronze statuettes, cameos, medals and minerals. He probably viewed his Old Master drawings as a secondary collection, stimulated mainly by his friendship with Crozat and Mariette. Unlike his friends he did not acquire drawings primarily for their own intrinsic qualities. Unless they reproduced ancient art or antiquities they barely feature in his lengthy correspondence with the Duke of Parma's librarian-antiquarian, Paciaudi, nor even with Mariette, who by contrast admitted to Caylus that he was devoted to drawings alone and "totally indifferent to even the most beautiful Etruscan vase".[59] In this respect Caylus was rather like Henry Blundell but on a much grander and more learned scale. Moreover, Blundell would have had an opportunity to meet Caylus in Paris in the mid 1740s and the early 1760s, for Caylus was one of the circle of scholars and literary figures who associated with the antiquarian and natural scientist the

Revd John Turberville Needham, Charles Townley's private tutor. Blundell's friendship with Townley, his education in Paris at the time of the 1745 Stuart uprising in Britain and his subsequent visits to the city would have brought him into contact with Caylus if only in a peripheral way.[60]

Caylus did take enough of an interest in the graphic arts to offer a lecture, *On Drawings (Reflexions on the utility of their study)*, to the Académie Royale in 1732, at which he revealed his attitude to the art form.[61] Stressing that he was an amateur, not a professional in such matters, he first flirted with the romantic notion that an original drawing gave particular insight into the artist's vision, enabling one to read the artist's intimate thoughts and "complete" such unfinished objects with the help of one's own imagination. But he soon reverted to the adage that a good copy, particularly one judged so by painters and connoisseurs, was as good as an original in conveying the artist's invention.[62]

On Caylus's death in 1765 part of his collection, notably four volumes of his own etchings made after drawings in his own and others' collections, including that of the French king, were given to the Bibliothèque Royale and the royal print cabinet. The rest, along with his fortune, passed to a nephew who took the title duc de Caylus and later became a commanding officer in the English-backed royalist forces during the French Revolution.[63] Despite Caylus's riches and perhaps because of his notoriety with the *encyclopédistes* he and his collection were soon forgotten.[64] In 1773 the nephew sold Caylus's natural history collection and in 1784 some drawings along with paintings, prints and sculpture were sold in Paris by Joullain.[65]

Some drawings stamped with the 'Pseudo-Crozat' mark were definitely in London by 1793, when they were in the hands of Charles-Paul-Jean-Baptiste de Bourgevin Vialart, comte de Saint-Morys (1743–1795), who etched and published them possibly as a way of advertising them for sale.[66] Some of these prints signed with the monograms of the comte de Saint-Morys and others and inscribed *London 1793* or *1794* are stuck into the Blundell albums along with the drawings they reproduce.[67] Another drawing etched, although not published, by Saint-Morys is Parmigianino's *Antique sacrifice* (exh. cat. 41). Saint-Morys's collection had been the most important in eighteenth-century France after those of Crozat and Mariette and was put together from purchases in France in the 1770s and 1780s. As a staunch royalist he could well have known the duc de Caylus. In 1790 he fled Revolutionary France. His country estate and the huge art collections there were seized for the state and so entered the Louvre.[68] Before fleeing, first to Cologne and then in 1792 to London, he had negotiated the smuggling via St Peters-

burg of some more portable items of his collection, including presumably some of his drawings. In London he was one of those in charge of the royalist counter-attack against France, using his etching skills to help flood the French market with fake banknotes and in 1795 commanding the invasion of Quiberon off the French mainland, during which he died. Some of his collection may have been sold on his death, as none of the 41 drawings sold by his son in 1814 included those illustrated in his 1793 publication.[69]

The character of the 'Pseudo-Crozat' drawings in the Weld-Blundell collection provides further support for the assumption that 'Pseudo-Crozat' can be identified as the comte de Caylus. A number have French provenances, attributions or inscriptions written on their mounts, including a trio by Michel Corneille the younger, son-in-law of Caylus's friend Mariette. One of Corneille's drawings is a copy of another in the French royal collection which Caylus also etched.[70] Like several others in the 'Pseudo-Crozat' part of Blundell's collection the Corneille drawings are copies after original compositions by or attributed to major artists of the sixteenth and seventeenth centuries: Raphael, Michelangelo, Parmigianino, Rubens and the Carracci family. All of these artists are either mentioned in Caylus's lecture *On Drawings* or designs by them were used as a source for his own etchings.[71]

The unexceptional calibre of the drawings in the group overall is occasionally raised by a study of the quality of Taddeo Zuccaro's *Alexander and Bucephalus* (exh. cat. 64). However, it was probably the nature of the collection as a whole, biassed as it was towards themes drawn from classical antiquity and with a number of drawings copying ancient and modern sculpture, that attracted the attention of Henry Blundell, who could have acquired the bulk of it in Paris in the 1770s when he is known to have been buying pictures, or whilst on his travels in the 1780s.[72]

Charles Robert Blundell
Compared to our knowledge of Henry Blundell, with his publications and frequent correspondence with Townley, our information about Charles Blundell, as a man and as a collector, is almost non-existent, and what we do know is vague, piecemeal and contradictory. In his father's letters his only son appears solitary and unsociable, refusing countless invitations to balls, assemblies and parties (where his father hoped he might meet suitable marriage partners), preferring his horses and a "rambling" life-style touring the country, hunting and staying at inns. Furthermore, his refusal to marry endangered the family succession and by the early 1800s he was barely in touch with his father.[73] Yet in the 1830s

Cardinal Wiseman credited Charles Blundell with being the main source of funding (£78,000) for a major campaign of Catholic pro-cathedral building in England.[74] Charles's later reputation amongst his own family was clouded by the long and bitterly fought Chancery court case (1837–48) brought by his two sisters and their husbands, in which they unsuccessfully challenged his will bequeathing the bulk of the Blundell inheritance not to his sisters but to his cousin Thomas Weld of Lulworth, who thereupon added the name Blundell to his surname.[75] The will specifically mentioned the collection of "busts, casts, statues, pictures, paintings, models, drawings, coins, medals, cameos, intaglios and other articles of vertue, works of art, statuary and curiosities with his library and books of every kind ... and also all plate", which, along with household furniture, linen, china, glass and carriages, formed a crucial part of the dispute, for in his own will Henry Blundell had in an unusual legal move deemed these items heirlooms: they were not to be sold by his son either in part or in whole, they were to be replaced by objects of equivalent value if any should be destroyed, and they were to remain at Ince.[76] The Court of Chancery ordered that an inventory be drawn up of the entire collection of antiquities and fine and decorative arts, a copy of which survives in the Weld archives. However, the inventory does not itemize all Charles's drawings: 68 of them are described as "A portfolio containing 67 drawings pasted on 1 loose", valued at sixteen guineas (presumably the 'Pseudo-Crozat' collection), and others as "a Ditto containing fine Italian drawings from West's Collection", valued at £40. Neither does it distinguish between drawings acquired by Charles Blundell or by his father.[77] Charles seems not to have continued his father's interest in antiquity, indeed after his father's death lawyers were worried that he might sell off the sculpture. Instead he showed a desire to enlarge the collection by buying large numbers of fine Old Master drawings from other collectors, and possibly the occasional early Netherlandish painting, to add to the sizeable group of mainly Italian pictures put together by Henry, whose picture collection had included works by Tiarini, Turchi and Romanelli, artists whose drawings were also to feature in Charles's acquisitions.

After his purchase of 161 drawings from the Roscoe sale Charles Blundell's next most important acquisition was the block of 61 drawings formerly owned by Benjamin West (1738–1820), the American artist who succeeded Sir Joshua Reynolds as President of the Royal Academy in 1792 and was from 1772 historical painter to King George III. West had begun collecting in the 1770s and by 1789 his collection was such that it merited illustration in C.M. Metz's *Imitations of Ancient and Modern Drawings ...*, which reproduced drawings

Fig. 7 Higgins, *Charles Robert Blundell*, 1803, private collection

by famous artists from celebrated English collections. West had picked up some choice items whilst on his trips abroad. In Paris in 1791 he bought a Bandinelli (exh. cat. 4) from Mariette's friend the Abbé Campion de Tersan, who, though he claimed not to be as knowledgeable as Mariette, nevertheless amassed a large collection of drawings, antiquities, medals, books and prints while travelling around France.[78]

The artists whose works West chose and the way he had their drawings mounted for display also reflected his connection from the 1770s onwards with the Royal Collection. It is possible that at least one drawing, Romanelli's *Laocoön attacked by the serpent* (exh. cat. 48), may originally have been in the Royal Collection. In 1765 it appeared in a publication engraved by Bartolozzi along with many other royal drawings, and the design of its wash-border mount seems to imitate those placed around drawings in George III's collection in the 1770s and 1780s. The same mount style appears around a few other West drawings, including the *Angler fish* (exh. cat. 1), Tintoretto's *Head of Vitellius* (exh. cat. 57) and those attributed to Annibale Carracci (exh. cats. 12, 13), so it seems likely that he took his style from that of the Royal Collection. Certainly the mounting card he used often bears the same watermarks as those found on the Royal Collection's mounts, suggesting that he might have borrowed for his own drawings from a stock of card produced by the company D. & C. Blauw for the Royal Collection.

Of Charles Blundell's 'West' drawings some had been dry-stamped with the initials B.W., presumably after the artist's death by his executors in preparation for the sale at auction of his collection by Christie's in June and July 1820. Many others in the Blundell collection merely have a pencilled inscription on the mount stating "Mr. West's" or "West's Collection", possibly added either by Charles Blundell himself or by a member of his household. The disposal of West's collection had itself been shrouded in difficulties and confusion. The auctions in 1820 did not go well, many items were bought in, and so the family determined on private sales once the collection had been exhibited.[79] Identification of drawings from West's collection is further hindered by the fact that the sales catalogues have no detailed descriptions of the drawings, as they were supposedly so well known that none was needed.[80] Of the 61 'West' drawings in Blundell's hands only three or four can be definitely identified in the sales and one of those is not stamped.[81] In 1826 West's family tried to sell 150 of his own paintings to the United States government as a foundation for a national gallery, and Old Master drawings were still for sale as late as 1836.[82] It seems likely, therefore, that many of Charles Blundell's drawings came from private sales. West had been secretive about his drawing collection and sales from it even during his lifetime, according to the dealer Samuel Woodburn, because he had copied so much from the drawings for poses in his own paintings.[83] As he had not had an academic training West's secrecy may well have been due to a lack of self-confidence as a draughtsman. As recent biographers have commented, his "ability to make an apt quotation became a crutch which he could substitute for more technical proficiency".[84] Looking at some of the 'West' drawings one can see that he might well have drawn inspiration from a figure such as that of Eustache Le Sueur's hunched old man (exh. cat. 71) for the patriarchal figures peopling his illustrations of ancient history, although it is admittedly harder to see the link between the stunning watercolour study of an *Angler fish* (exh. cat. 1) and West's paintings.

The subsequent history of the Weld-Blundell collection

It was the West connection that attracted the German art historian Gustav Waagen's attention when he visited Ince in 1850, although on the whole the Weld-Blundell collection was little noticed in the nineteenth century. No doubt its being overlooked was due partly to its geographical location, but it was mainly a consequence of the large size and overwhelming nature of the rest of the collection, which demanded and received the exhaustive and exhausting attention of visiting scholars. Waagen, who spent two and a half days at Ince, concluded his nineteen-page entry of detailed comments on its sculpture and pictures with the sentence: "Finally I saw a number of drawings from the collection of the late Benjamin West, of which, however, but few were worthy of note".[85] It is not even clear from this dismissive comment whether he actually saw the whole collection. His handwritten and initialled notes appear on only a few mounts, not all of them formerly owned by West.[86] He knew of Roscoe's activities as a collector, having noted the important paintings from his collection when he had visited the Liverpool Royal Institution, and would surely have mentioned Roscoe's part in the creation of the Weld-Blundell collection had he been made aware of it. But even a discerning art historian such as Waagen might devote little time to a drawings collection if it meant going through portfolios of unidentified or unprovenanced works, as would have been the case at Ince Blundell.

It was not until the twentieth century that interest grew in the collection. It benefited particularly from the attention of a succession of curators from the Prints and Drawings Department of the British Museum, A.E. Popham, Philip Pouncey, John Rowlands and John Gere, all of whom gave of their time and connoisseurship in identifying or attributing drawings. Even a brief study of the provisional attributions given in this catalogue's Appendix shows the especial debt owed to Popham, the staying-power of whose comments confirms the depth and scope of his knowledge. The author should also like to thank and acknowledge the help of friends and colleagues from Britain and Europe, curators, scholars and dealers, all of whom left their comments, sometimes useful, sometimes contradictory, amusing or vituperative, clear or obscure, for they made my task in cataloguing the collection so rewarding and enjoyable.

Collectors' Marks and Biographies

MIRANDA STACEY

John, 4th Duke of Argyll
(1693–1770)

 A (L45)

Heir of the great bibliophile Archibald Campbell, Duke of Argyll (1682–1761), a peer for Scotland, 1761–70, a general in the Army and MP respectively for Bute, for Elgin and for Co. Dumbarton (1715–61). He may have used the pseudonym 'General Campbell' when buying extensively at the second sale of Richard Houlditch (*q.v.*) in 1760 and so appears in a list of collectors drawn up by Horace Walpole. Lugt cites a collection of drawings "which formed the reserved part of the late Duke of Argyle's" belonging to Lord Frederick Campbell (1729–1816), which was probably dispersed or destroyed. Lugt had not then come across the Argyll coat of arms which has been carefully drawn in pen and ink on the mount of the Ghirlandaio drawing (exh. cat. 30), although he did hesitantly suggest a mark (L45) as the 4th Duke's. Argyll's drawings, prints, books and engravings were sold 21–23 May 1798 (T. Philipe).

Thomas Howard, Earl of Arundel
(1585-1646)

Politician and diplomat to Charles I, patron and collector, Arundel formed, together with his wife Aletheia Talbot, Countess of Arundel (*ca.* 1590–1654), a collection of Greek and Roman sculpture and of Renaissance and Baroque paintings unprecedented in England. He was especially interested in the drawings of Leonardo and Parmigianino and the work of Holbein. He was a patron of living artists such as Mytens, Van Dyck, Hollar, Van der Borcht and Rubens. In the years 1613–14 the Earl made an extensive and instructive tour of Italy in the company of Thomas Coke, Inigo Jones and William Petty; he also travelled as a diplomat. In 1635 his chief preoccupation is said to have been with drawings and Petty, acting as the Earl's agent in Italy for most of the 1630s, may have acquired drawings including those which had belonged to the Florentine Niccolò Gaddi; Vasari's *Libro del disegno* may also have belonged to the Earl. The collection included three large volumes, one each of Raphael, Leonardo and Michelangelo drawings, as well as two others of various artists. Despite the size of Arundel's collection (over 600 paintings and drawings are listed in the incomplete 1655 inventory), only a small percentage of his works has been positively identified. The collection began to be broken up when the Earl became bankrupt in 1639. There is no Arundel collector's mark as such, but detection of an Arundel provenance is assisted by the drawn and engraved copies by artists such as Wenceslaus Hollar, who was employed by Arundel from 1636. The Earl allowed his drawings to be exhibited to the public in the cabinet-room designed by Inigo Jones at Arundel House. The series of drawings by Leonardo da Vinci now at Windsor Castle is generally thought to have belonged to the Earl of Arundel, as well as the Codex Arundel now in the British Library.

John Barnard
(1685-1724)

J.B. (L1419)

The son of a rich merchant and politician, Sir John Barnard, Barnard bought prints and drawings on a lavish scale over a period of more than fifty years. He employed the artist Crone as one of his agents. He also collected paintings, which passed on his death to his nephew Thomas Hankey of Bedford Square (sold by Christie's, 7-8 June 1799). Barnard's mark on a drawing seems to have been considered a sign of quality and he had an especially fine eye for Rembrandt's prints, owning no fewer than 449 attributed to him. Barnard often signed his drawings and sometimes added the date of acquisition, dimensions, notes on the artist and a number (up to 1100). The drawings were sold in over 800 lots, 16–23 February 1787 (John Greenwood). The catalogue contains a print by Bartolozzi after Benjamin West's portrait of Barnard but most notably it includes a list of collectors' marks with short descriptions for each collection – the first of its kind.

Pierre Crozat
(1665-1740)

Friend of Watteau and Rosalba Carriera and treasurer of France from 1704, famous for his collection of paintings, prints, sculpture, engraved gems, ceramics and, above all, drawings which numbered some 19,201 at his death, the largest collection in Europe at the beginning of the 18th century. He enriched his collection when between 1714 and 1721 he was in Rome on behalf of the Regent, Philippe II, duc d'Orléans, negotiating to buy the collection originally formed by Queen Christina of Sweden; two thirds of the drawings in his collection were Italian. As well as buying extensively in France under unique market conditions, Crozat also sent agents to foreign sales, including that of John, Lord Somers, in London in 1717. Between 1720 and 1725 Crozat initiated his famous project to publish the most famous Italian paintings and drawings in France, the 'Recueil Crozat' (2 vols., Paris 1729 and 1742). The impetus for this came from the Regent, with the encouragement of Pierre-Jean Mariette (q.v.) and the comte de Caylus. Crozat originally wanted Louis XV to purchase his collection of drawings so that it would remain in France as a resource for artists and connoisseurs. However, his offer was refused and the collection was dispersed following his death, the drawings being sold 10 April–13 May 1741 at the Grands Augustins, Paris (expert P.J. Mariette) and the prints and remainder of his collection in February 1773. Mariette, who produced a remarkably detailed catalogue of the drawings for the 1741 sale, modified many of Crozat's attributions as well as providing full descriptions and, in many cases, provenances. Crozat did not use a collector's mark but small numbers in pen and ink inscribed on the sheets, along with annotations in his hand, help to identify the provenance.

William Esdaile (1758–1837)

 (L2617)

Fourth son of Sir James Esdaile of Great Gains, Essex, some time Lord Mayor of London, Esdaile joined the family bank of Esdaile, Hammet & Co. on its foundation (ca. 1780), from which time he began collecting prints. He visited Italy for the first time in 1825, returning in 1827 and 1835–36. To his prints he added drawings, paintings, marbles and bronzes, books and manuscripts, coins and ceramics. However, drawings were his prime interest and the broad range of his acquisitions can be seen from his posthumous sales, which took place in London 2 March

1838 (G. Jones), 19–21 March 1838 (Christie's) and 11–30 June 1840 (Christie's). There was also one anonymous sale during his lifetime of Old Master and modern drawings of various schools which took place on 2 March 1819. The collection included important original and reproductive graphic works from all the major schools from the 15th century onwards. Of particular note were the series of 100 drawings each by Rembrandt and Claude Lorrain (from the collection of Thomas Lawrence) and a comprehensive group of Rembrandt etchings. Esdaile often wrote the provenance and date of acquisition on the verso of his most important drawings and his calligraphic pen monogram is well known. He was a buyer at William Roscoe's sale and probably knew Roscoe, having been his London banker.

Alfonso IV d'Este (1634-1662)

 (L106)

Ninth Duke of Modena and Reggio, son of Francesco I d'Este, Alfonso IV continued his father's policies as an ally of France and as a patron and collector. The artist Pietro da Cortona served as the Duke's advisor, and sketches of potential acquisitions in Rome, drawn by Pietro's students, were sent to Modena for ducal consideration. Alfonso was also an eminent collector of Venetian paintings. The Duke founded the celebrated picture gallery of Modena, although his collection of over 2300 drawings remained separate from it. The miniature painter and engraver Bonaventura Bisi, known as Padre Pittorini, acted as the Duke's artistic advisor from until his death in 1659. The collection was organized by Giovanni Donzi, custodian, curator and 'cicerone' of the ducal gallery of drawings and medals. Inventories compiled by him are datable to 1669.

The 'Griffier Fagel' Collection

The collection, belonging to a Dutch family of government officials, was described by Joshua Reynolds in 1763 as "walls hung round with thoughts". At that time it belonged to Griffier Hendrick Fagel (1706–1790), who had been appointed

registry clerk at the Dutch States General in 1728 following the resignation of his uncle, Griffier François Fagel (1659–1746), who was the most powerful politician of the 'second stadholderless era' (1702–47). Hendrick was the owner of the collection described in a catalogue of 1752, though it may well have contained some pieces acquired by his uncle and father. On his death in 1790 he was succeeded as clerk by his great-grandson Hendrick Fagel (1765–1838), who was in England when the French invaded the Northern Netherlands in 1795. As a result his possessions in Holland were confiscated, including the substantial library (now mostly in Trinity College, Dublin) and the collection of prints, drawings and paintings by Italian, early Netherlandish and numerous 17th-century Dutch masters. On 22–23 May 1801, 106 paintings from the Fagel collection were sold at auction in London. The drawings were sold (Philipe) in two sales, of 20–25 May 1799 (586 lots) and 27–30 May 1801 (392 lots), under the name of the better known François, though they belonged by now to Hendrick.

William Ford (1771–1832)

A nationally known book and printseller based in Manchester. His first catalogue was published in 1805 and was followed by two others of 1807 and 1810-11 – all were admired for their accurate descriptions and detailed bibliographical notes. This *Bibliotheca Fordiana* brought Ford into contact with many leading bibliophiles, including William Roscoe. He brought together books, manuscripts, tracts, engraved portraits and illustrations of Lancashire history and biography. He also had a lively interest in painting, and an unusual manuscript of 1827 in Ford's handwriting in Manchester City Library, entitled *Characters of the different Picture Collectors in and about Manchester faithfully and impartially delineated*, is a series of often less than flattering portraits of the leading collectors of Manchester, taking note of their Old Master paintings and often malicious delight in the fact that many of the shrewdest businessmen had been duped by "Picture Jockeys". Connoisseurship was of prime importance to Ford, who, although principally interested in books and prints, seems to have dabbled in Old Master drawings, buying extensively at Roscoe's sale (some 125 lots of drawings as well as at least

27 paintings). His role was that of a dealer rather than a collector and many of the drawings which he bought were passed on to Charles Blundell and Richard Heber among others. From a letter dated December 29 1818 (Roscoe Papers 1560) from Ford to Roscoe it seems that Ford wished to act as an agent on Roscoe's behalf, consulting him on the dispersal of the books, prints *etc* which Ford had bought at the sale. Like Roscoe, Ford went bankrupt in 1816 and Winstanley auctioned his books and prints in sales of December 1816, January and March 1817. However, he resumed business soon after and transferred to Liverpool. In the British Library there is a copy of his last catalogue, printed in Liverpool the year he died, 1832. It consists mainly of books but appended at the end is a "*Collectio Selecta*: ... containing a selection from his general collection of Rare English Portraits and Amateur Engravings, Choice Drawings (Ancient and Modern) and Original Portraits, in Oil (Principally English)". There are only 39 lots of Old Master drawings, both framed and unframed; few are of any distinction, among these works by Schongauer, Veronese, Bourdon and Campagnola, all with detailed and connoisseurly descriptions.

Francesco Maria Niccolò Gabburri (1676–1742)

Florentine nobleman, diplomat in the service of Grand Duke Cosimo III de' Medici, painter, art historian and collector of drawings, prints, paintings and sculpture. Two inventories in the Biblioteca Nazionale, Florence (*Descrizione dei disegni della Galleria Gabburri in Firenze 1722 and Descrizione della Galleria e Gabinetto dell'Ill:mo Cav:re Gabburrj*), list sections of his collection of works on paper – some 632 drawings and 8620 prints. Inspired by Mariette's visit to Florence in 1719, Gabburri embarked on an ambitious encyclopaedic dictionary of artists' lives, from the primitives to his contemporaries. This *Vite di pittori* (manuscript in the Biblioteca Nazionale, Florence) was modelled on Orlandi's *Abecedario pittorico* of 1704. In line with this biographical tradition, Gabburri was particularly fascinated by drawn self-portraits and portraits of artists (including that by Elisabetta Sirani, exh. cat. 52) and he formed an extensive collection, latterly owned by Charles Rogers (*q.v.*), with which he no doubt intended to illustrate his *Vite*. He was, further,

at one time the custodian of Cardinal Leopoldo de' Medici's remarkable collection of artists' self-portraits (now in the Uffizi, Florence). To those drawings which he prized above all Gabburri gave elegant, exquisitely drawn mounts, usually oval, with an elaborate architectural framework. Between 1706 and 1737 he lent 284 works to exhibitions organized regularly by the Accademia del Disegno at SS. Annunziata, Florence. In 1725 he made an outstanding purchase of 600 drawings by Fra Bartolommeo, which he discovered in the convent of Santa Caterina di Siena (two of the three volumes were later owned by Benjamin West, then by Thomas Lawrence and are now in the Boymans-van Beuningen Museum, Rotterdam). In 1743 Horace Walpole, 4th Earl of Orford, purchased drawings from Gabburri's collection, acquiring two examples of each artist's work. Most of Gabburri's collection was purchased by the dealer William Kent from his heirs in 1758 and then brought to England to be sold. They may have been sold at an anonymous sale held at Langford's, London, between 8 and 11 December 1762, or at subsequent sales of Kent's property in 1766 and 1767. It is possible to reconstruct some of Gabburri's vast holdings from surviving inventories as well as from the mounts, numerical sequences and inscriptions on the drawings which he owned.

Lamberto Gori (died ca. 1757)

Florentine historian and collector from whose family William Young Ottley (*q.v.*) bought drawings. He was in contact with Mariette (*q.v.*) from whom, in 1746, he asked through Gabburri (*q.v.*) for notes on the life and work of Michelangelo so that he could prepare a new edition of Condivi's *Life* of Michelangelo.

Nicola Francesco Haym (ca. 1679–1729)

NH (L1971)

Musician of German origin and Roman birth working in London from *ca.* 1701–02. He translated or adapted several operas from the Italian, published tragedies and songs and worked for Handel. He published a fine edition of *Gerusalemme liberata* by Tasso as well as his bibliographical *Notizia de' libri rari*

nella lingua italiana (1726). In his spare time he enjoyed reproducing medals, bronzes and marbles which he had seen in aristocratic collections. Encouraged and assisted by his friends and by his benefactors, Lord Halifax and Lord Carnarvon, he decided to engrave these documents for a work entitled *Tesoro Britannico delle Antichità greche e latine* (1749), composed of four parts. Only two volumes of the first part were ever completed. Haym collected paintings as well as some 1100 drawings, which were sold prior to his death. His mark, of which there are three other variants (L1970, L1972–73), can occasionally be seen on some 18th-century engravings of drawings in his collection.

Richard Heber (1773–1833)

A collector of books who corresponded with William Roscoe (*ca.* 1791–1819) and was a purchaser from Roscoe's 1816 sale. He travelled extensively in France, Belgium and the Netherlands in search of books and when he died he possessed some 146,827 volumes dispersed in houses in London, Oxford, Hodnet (Shropshire), Paris, Brussels, Antwerp and Ghent. His enormous collections were dispersed in sales lasting from 1834 to 1836. The drawings, paintings and prints were sold 15–19 May 1834 (Stanley). Prints predominated with just 73 lots of drawings and four of paintings. All the drawings and three of the paintings were bought from Roscoe's 1816 sale (14 via William Ford [*q.v.*] and 59 directly). Heber wrote to Roscoe in July 1819 following the bankruptcy of the auctioneer Winstanley asking him to retrieve the purchases which he had left in the auction rooms ever since the sale (Roscoe Papers 1986). He mentions that the books were packed in strong cases while the drawings were carefully tied up in one, possibly two, portfolios. It is likely that Heber purchased drawings as a favour to Roscoe rather than in pursuance of his own interest.

Nathaniel Hillier (1707–1783)

Printseller and merchant of Pancras Lane and collector of drawings, who was elected Fellow of the Society of Antiquaries in 1755. He corresponded with Horace Walpole between May 1761 and October 1780, largely on the subject of Walpole's *Anecdotes*. There were two sales of prints and drawings (Christie's): 16–24 February 1784, including 338 lots of drawings and 753 of prints, and 15–22 March 1784, including 177 lots of drawings, 697 of prints, 81 of drawings and prints, and 25 of miscellaneous portfolios. Lugt proposes a mark of NH (L1974) similar but smaller than that used by Nicola Francesco Haym as Hillier's. The British Museum Prints and Drawings library possesses the complete manuscript catalogue of the Hillier collection (M.8.3), which describes in detail 330 sheets and mentions 776 less important drawings.

Nathanial Hone RA (1718-1784)

 (L2793)

Hone was born in Dublin, but transferred to London in the 1740s, becoming well known as a painter of miniatures on enamel as well as of portraits and occasional genre scenes. He exhibited regularly at the Society of Artists and in 1768 became a founder-member of the Royal Academy. He sold his drawings within his lifetime, 4–7 April 1781 (Christie's), and he is said to have had sales in 1765 and 1787 although no catalogues have been found. A posthumous sale, 7–14 February 1785 (Hutchins), included drawings, prints, engravings and some painted studies.

Richard Houlditch Senior (died Hampstead 1736)

R H. (L2214)

Houlditch, a director of the South Sea Company, was ruined by its collapse in 1720. Both he and his son, Richard Houlditch Junior, were important collectors of drawings. His son's "genuine, entire and valuable collection of drawings" was sold 12–14 February 1760 (Langford's) in 211 lots of summary description. There was perhaps a second sale, of paintings, 5–6 March 1760.

Thomas Hudson (1701–1779)

TH. (L2432)

Highly successful portraitist, the pupil and son-in-law of Jonathan Richardson and the master of Joshua Reynolds and Joseph Wright of Derby. Among his friends were Hogarth, Francis Hayman and the drapery painter Joseph van Aken (q.v.), with whom he collaborated extensively in his portraits. He travelled to France, Holland and Flanders in the company of Van Aken in 1748 and in 1752 to Italy with Roubiliac. He collected Old Master drawings and paintings throughout his career, although few of his paintings can be traced, many of the drawings can be identified by his collector's mark. He also owned large numbers of drawings by contemporaries such as Thornhill, Vanderbank and Rysbrack. He was one of the earliest collectors to prefer drawings of the Low Countries – Rubens, Van Dyck and Rembrandt – and he had more works by Guercino than by any other Italian artist. His earliest recorded purchase was in 1741, and he began collecting on a large scale in 1747 at Richardson's posthumous sale, where he apparently bought certain lots in conjunction with Van Aken. Hudson again bought extensively at the sale of Van Aken's collection in 1750. The collection was dispersed in sales after Hudson's death, 15–26 March 1779 (Langford's), and after the death of his wife, 25–26 February 1785 (Christie's).

Henry Constantine Jennings (1731-1818)

 (L2771)

A virtuoso and amateur who travelled extensively in Italy during his youth. While in Rome he purchased antiquities from the sculptor and art-dealer Cavaceppi and is famous for his discovery of an antique marble figure of a crouching dog which fetched 1000 guineas at his 1778 sale. He inherited the family estate at Shiplake in Oxfordshire and at one stage seems to have been wealthy, buying on a large scale. Following horseracing debts he was forced to sell his collections, styled his "Museum", at Christie's, 15 April 1778. About 1792, Jennings went to London, where he began to form a new collection until about 1816, when he went bankrupt. His drawings were sold on 6 August 1816 (Phillips). There were posthumous sales of miniatures, prints, bronzes, cameos and coins *etc* 22–26 June 1818; of paintings, drawings (62 lots) and prints 22–23 July 1818, and of paintings, drawings and the rest of his curiosities 12–13 May 1819 (all Phillips).

Nicholas Lanier (1558–1666)

 (L2885) ✱ (L2886)

A composer at the Stuart court, dealer and painter. As one of the earliest connoisseurs of prints and drawings in England, Lanier acted as an agent for the Earl of Arundel (q.v.) and also made purchases for the Royal collections. By the 1630s he had become one of the most important dealers in Europe. As principal picture agent to Charles I he, with Daniel Nys, negotiated the purchase of the collection of Ferdinando Gonzaga, 6th Duke of Mantua. He visited Italy on numerous occasions, basing himself in Venice, where he purchased works of art for English courtiers, whenever possible taking the opportunity to build up a collection of his own. Passes were issued to him on a number of occasions allowing him to import works of art into England. In his autobiography, published in 1660, Roger North wrote that drawings "… were not esteemed in England until Nicholas Laniere was employed by Charles I to go abroad and buy pictures", which were sometimes accompanied by "a good parcel of waste paper drawings, that had been collected, but not much esteemed" and which Lanier kept for himself. He purchased not only drawings by distinguished 16th-century Italian artists, but also owned a few 15th-century sheets, suggesting a pioneering interest in earlier Italian art, otherwise unrepresented at the Stuart court. Lanier's travels in Italy also made it possible for him to obtain drawings by contemporary artists such as Bartolomeo Cesi, Palma Giovane and Guido Reni. Lanier's marks were long confused with those of his patrons, Charles I and the Earl of Arundel. There are at least six star marks associated with Lanier. According to Richardson (*Traité de la peinture*) the 8-pointed star was Lanier's and the 5-pointed star that of Lanier's cousins, Jerome and Clement Lanier, who were also dealers. Lanier's attributions and prices paid appear alongside the star, although it is not known exactly when these stars were added as there was no grand sale of the drawings, as was the case with Lely's collection (q.v.). Although he did make mistakes with his attributions, Lanier's inscriptions are powerful evidence of his knowledge in a pioneering field. It seems that a large part of his drawings were sold in London in 1720–21, producing £6525.

Prosper Henry Lankrink
(ca. 1628–1692)

PH. (L2090)

Flemish painter and collector of German origin, active in England. As well as producing his own landscape and decorative works, he acted as an assistant to Peter Lely (*q.v.*). After Lely's death in 1680, Lankrink took part in finishing his paintings and compiling the inventory of his works of art. He made extensive purchases at the sale of Lely's studio and especially at the first sale of his drawings, adding to his own already extensive collection, which was particularly strong in 16th- and 17th-century Dutch and Flemish drawings, including Van Dyck's Antwerp and Italian sketchbooks. Drawings bearing only Lankrink's mark, that is, bought independently of Lely's sale, include a large number of drawings by Rubens, copies by him after other artists and drawings by others retouched by him, all probably acquired in Flanders at or immediately after Rubens's studio sale of 1657. Like many collectors Lankrink may have occasionally acted as a dealer, selling items from his collection. His collections were dispersed in three sales: 23 January 1692 (published *Burlington Magazine*, LXXXVI, February 1945, pp. 29–35), 8 May 1693 and following days and 22 February 1694 and following days, all London.

Sir Peter Lely
(1618-1680)

P.L (L2094)

Leading artist, fine draughtsman and portraitist working in England at the Restoration under Charles II. He began to form a collection of paintings, drawings and prints in the 1640s, buying from the collections of Charles I, Arundel (*q.v.*) and Nicholas Lanier (*q.v.*) and also from the studio of Van Dyck after its dispersal. Given the quality of his collection, it is also likely that Lely used agents abroad to buy on his behalf. Lely's collection of paintings was strongest in 16th- and 17th-century Italian, Dutch and Flemish works, although some 16th-century German and 17th-century French artists were represented. His collection of prints and drawings (at his death he owned about 10,000 drawings) was one of the first to be formed in England by a painter–collector and was of extremely high quality. The

enormous number of figurative and drapery studies suggests that the collection might have served as a pattern book for Lely and his studio. At his death it was auctioned in order to pay his debts. Copies of the descriptive catalogue, compiled by one of his executors, the writer and lawyer Roger North, were sent to the Netherlands, France and Italy. The administration of Lely's estate is recorded in an account book kept by his executors, now in the British Library, which notes the titles of works purchased, prices realised and the names of almost a hundred buyers at the 1682 sale. Unfortunately the book contains far less information relating to Lely's prints and drawings, which were sold over six years later in two mixed sales of 11 April 1688 and 15 November 1694. Individual buyers and the prices they paid were recorded but these lists have not survived. Roger North arranged the prints and drawings into alphabetically labelled portfolios, each drawing marked with the letter of the portfolio and an individual number. He stamped each sheet with the distinctive PL stamp.

Willem Anne Lestevenon
(born 1750)

Statesman and collector of The Hague, holding public offices both in Haarlem and in the states of Holland from 1768. Lugt mentions Lestevenon in relation to the formation of the drawings collection of the Teylers Museum, Haarlem (founded in 1778). He acted as an intermediary in the purchase of the collection of Italian drawings originally belonging to Queen Christina of Sweden when it was purchased *en bloc* in Rome in 1791.

John MacGowan
(died 1803)

An obscure figure. Sales of the collection of "John M'Gowan Esq. F.R.S., Edin[burgh], lately deceased" took place 13–18 May 1803 and 26 January 1804 and seven following days (T. Philipe). *The Gentleman's Magazine* of 1803, I, p. 90, contains an obituary for John MacGowan, "a gentleman well-known for his classical learning and for his taste in the fine arts", who died in Edinburgh on 6 January. Not only a Fellow of the Royal Society of Edinburgh but probably also a member of the English Society of Antiquaries, MacGowan gave a number of zoological specimens to the

museum of the Edinburgh Royal Society and numerous gems, cameos and intaglios from his collection are mentioned in R.E. Raspe's 1791 *Descriptive catalogue of a general collection of ancient and modern engraved gems, cameos as well as intaglios, taken from the most celebrated cabinets in Europe*. While the 1803 sale contained prints and portfolios, the 1804 sale was exclusively of Old Master drawings, containing notable Italian, Flemish and Dutch works as well as a few French, "collected with superior taste and judgement during more than half a century".

Pierre-Jean Mariette
(1694–1774)

Ⓜ (L1852)

Print dealer, publisher, collector and writer. The Mariette family were established printsellers in the rue St-Jacques, Paris, their principal shop being the Librarie des Colonnes d'Hercules. Pierre-Jean Mariette travelled in Italy between 1719 and 1720, making notes on works of art, and until 1736 acted as agent to Prince Eugene of Vienna. He became known and respected for his expertise in drawings and prints. His father's vast collection of notes on artists and original and reproductive prints provided the foundation for his own careful observations, to which he added information from his many correspondents throughout Europe, who included the abbé Barthélemy, Anton Maria Zanetti and Niccolò Gabburri (*q.v.*). His reputation was based above all on his catalogue for the 1741 sale of Pierre Crozat's drawings (*q.v.*), which was the first publication to use provenances to verify attributions. At the sale he himself bought many hundreds of drawings, including 132 of the 149 studies by Annibale Carracci for the ceiling of the Palazzo Farnese in Rome. Although he lacked the great wealth of Crozat he collected drawings of consistently high quality. At his death he owned over 3400 mounted drawings and approximately 6000 drawings in portfolios. His posthumous sale included 1600 Italian and 500 Flemish, Dutch and German drawings and more than 1000 by French artists. He also possessed an important collection of engravings, a few paintings, numerous sculptures and a valuable library of art books. Mariette's mounts are characteristically of thick blue paper trimmed with black lines surrounding a pattern of gold and grey and ornamented with a cartouche bearing the name of the artist and sometimes information regarding the provenance (see exh. cat. 3). In his will Mariette stipulated that his collections should be sold, preferably to the King. Although Louis XVI's offer of 300,000 livres was refused by the family, about 1000 drawings were bought for the Royal Collection at the sale. His collections were sold in Paris, 15 November 1775–30 January 1776 (F. Basan).

Cardinal Leopoldo de' Medici 1617–1675)

 (L2712) dry stamp

Son of Cosimo II de' Medici and energetic patron of literature, the natural sciences and the fine arts, presiding over the Accademia del Cimento (active 1657–67), Europe's first academy of experimental science. His celebrated collections, housed primarily in his apartment in the Palazzo Pitti, were composed of classical antiquities (including coins, engraved gems and sculptures), paintings, drawings, ivories, ceramics and a noted library of books. Leopoldo left an enormous quantity of letters and correspondence, almost all of which is preserved in the Archivio di Stato of Florence. One volume known as the 'Carteggio d'Artisti', consisting of artists' correspondence, offers an extraordinary overview of the formation of Leopoldo's collections and above all his network of 'agenti–correspondenti'. Between 1650 and 1675 Leopoldo corresponded with more than eighty agents dispersed throughout Italy and sometimes abroad, who were employed to research any opportunities for acquisitions of particular interest to his various collections. About thirty were concerned primarily with the research and acquisition of drawings. Authenticity, quality and subject-matter were important criteria for the acquisition of a drawing and emphasis was placed on compositional studies (see exh. cat. 5, Barocci). Some time around 1665, Filippo Baldinucci was employed to complete the chronological arrangement of the drawings within albums started by Leopoldo. In 1673 Leopoldo had 8143 drawings, and within two years this had grown to over 11,000 drawings, organized into 105 volumes. In 1662 Leopoldo circulated to his agents lists of the works collected to date so that they could fill any gaps in the chronological arrangement.

Leopoldo's famous gallery of artists's (painted) self-portraits was set up in 1664; it was strong in works by 16th- and 17th-century Italian artists, including specially commissioned self-portraits by Guercino and Pietro da Cortona. After Leopoldo's death the collection of self-portraits was augmented and is now housed in the Uffizi. The drawings collection was continued by his nephew, the Grand Duke Cosimo III (1642–1723), until 1700, when it was transferred to the Gabinetto dei Disegni of the Uffizi.

William Young Ottley (1771–1836)

𝒲𝒴𝒪. (L2664)

English writer, collector and amateur artist, who formed his outstanding collection of drawings and paintings while travelling in Italy from 1791 to 1799. His acquisitions were made principally in 1798–99, largely thanks to unprecedented market conditions following the French invasion of 1796. He is known to have bought drawings from the Martelli collection and that of Lamberto Gori (q.v.) in Florence; of Antonio Cavaceppi in Rome; of the Neapolitan royal family; and of the Zanetti family in Venice (an important group by Parmigianino). He also 'weeded' 120 drawings from the Galleria degli Uffizi in Florence and acquired major groups of Raphael and Michelangelo drawings from the collection of the French painter Jean-Baptiste Wicar, who was in charge of the official looting of pictures in Italy. As Ottley also acted as a dealer in drawings and in fact subsequently sold most of his Italian purchases in London, he rarely used his collector's mark (of which Lugt gives five variants: L2642, L2642–65). However, he is known to have used a particular style of mount, of yellowish unglazed cartridge paper with thin ruled lines, usually one black and two red, surrounding the drawing. The artist's name, and sometimes a short description of him, was inscribed below in italics. Ottley described and engraved about eighty of his drawings in The Italian School of Design (1808), which was part of an ambitious project to publish "a chronological sequence of designs of the most eminent artists of Italy". The work (completed with a further two volumes in 1823) is pioneering in its historical approach and outstanding in the quality of its facsimiles. Ottley also published

A series of Plates Engraved After the Paintings and Sculptures of the Most Eminent Masters of the Early Florentine School (1811?), a work which was instrumental in the reassessment of 14th- and 15th-century Italian painting and to which William Roscoe subscribed. Ottley even advised Roscoe, it seems, on possible purchases of early works (Roscoe Papers 2845A). Ottley's collection of drawings, dominated by the Italian schools, was historical in its approach, with every Italian artist of any importance from the 15th to the 18th century represented. Roscoe was a significant purchaser at Ottley's 1814 sale and in Roscoe's own 1816 sale over 60 of the drawings originated from Ottley's collection. In 1833 Ottley became Curator of Prints and Drawings at the British Museum. He held several anonymous drawings sales during his lifetime: 14–21 April 1803 (Philipe and Scott); 11–14 April 1804 (T. Philipe) and 6–13 July 1807 (T. Philipe). He sold 1781 drawings in a sale of 6–23 June 1814 (T. Philipe), and Sir Thomas Lawrence purchased Ottley's entire cabinet in 1823 for £8000. His paintings were sold in 1801, 1803 and 1811; like Roscoe, he failed to sell his earliest Italian pictures, thus retaining a small gallery of Italian 'primitives'. After his death, Old Master drawings and drawings by Ottley himself were sold 10 May 1838 (Sotheby's).

Cornelis Ploos van Amstel (1726–1798)

Dutch timber merchant, collector, printmaker, print publisher, draughtsman and art theorist, one of the most important Dutch dilettanti of the 18th century. He assembled a vast collection of drawings, unprecedented in Holland (numbering over 7000 at his death), as well as prints (including works by Rembrandt), paintings, sculptures, enamels, medals, coins, scientific instruments and optical tools, manuscripts and printed books. From 1771 he acted as a connoisseur–expert at many important art sales, from which he also purchased works for his own collection. His drawings collection consisted principally of works by Dutch artists of the 17th and 18th centuries, although he also bought contemporary graphic works. Between 1765 and 1787 he published, in several parts, his Prentwerk, a series of 46 colour facsimiles after drawings predominantly from his own collection. His Prenttekeningen ('printed drawings') after Dutch genre scenes and landscapes etc appeared in 350 impressions, enabling those who could not afford collections of their own to acquire an intimate knowledge of Old Master drawings. In 1746 Ploos became a working member of the Stadstekenacademie in Amsterdam, playing an important role in the reorganization of the drawing school in 1765. His posthumous sale took place on 3 March 1800 and following days (Ph. van der Schley *et al.*, Amsterdam). The catalogue was in two volumes, the first for the drawings and the second for the rest of his collection.

Arthur Pond
(1701–1758)

English painter, engraver, printseller, dealer and collector from the 1730s and Fellow of the Royal Society from 1752, perhaps best known for his *40 Prints in Imitation of Drawings*, which he etched and published in 1734–36 in collaboration with the landscape painter Charles Knapton. These imitated or reproduced Old Master drawings in local collections, as had their French prototype, the *Recueil Crozat* (Paris 1729). He also etched caricature drawings (1737–42) by Annibale Carracci, Ghezzi and others and helped to produce *Heads of Illustrious Persons of Great Britain* (London 1747 and 1752). He collaborated with booksellers John and Paul Knapton on several projects, including *Italian Landscapes* (1741–6), *Roman Antiquities* (1744–48) and *Scenes from British History* (1751). Every publication enhanced Pond's formidable reputation for connoisseurship, increased by his purchases from Jonathan Richardson's collection of Old Master drawings at his sale in 1747 and his own collection of prints and drawings. Pond occasionally wrote his guarantee of authenticity on the verso of his drawings, which were sold 25 April and seven following days 1759 (Langford's).

Padre Sebastiano Resta
(1634/35–1714)

Member of the Order of St Filippo Neri in Rome from 1665, an ardent collector and dealer in both contemporary and Old Master drawings, renowned for his connoisseurial approach to the ordering of his collection. He amassed some 3500 sheets in over thirty albums by Italian and Northern European artists, ranging from the early masters to the late 17th century, many of very high quality.

The drawings were glued on to sheets, bordered in ink and accompanied by a series of explanatory notes in a distinctive handwriting. Each volume was given a specific title and aimed to deal with one period of Italian art, the ambition being to trace a history of art through drawing. A few albums remain intact: the so called *Codice Resta* which Resta called the '*Galleria Portatile*', covering drawings from the 13th to the 17th centuries (Ambrosiana Library, Milan); the *Piccolo Preliminare al Grande Anfiteatro Pittorico* (Biblioteca Centrale, Rome); the small album entitled *Aggiunta e supplemento al Correggio in Roma* (British Museum, London) and a further small volume of drawings by Ambrogio Figino (Pierpont Morgan Library, New York). The mass of Resta's unpublished notes show consistent, though sometimes fallible, patterns of enquiry. His ideas reflected the theory of connoisseurship that developed during the late 17th and early 18th centuries and he was obsessed with the continuity between the work of a pupil and his master, which was expressed in the form of artistic genealogies, or *alberi*. Resta's most important patron was Giovanni Mattei Marchetti, Bishop of Arezzo, who bought a total of nineteen albums from Resta between 1698 and 1702. In 1710 Marchetti's heirs sold the Resta volumes to Lord John Somers (*q.v.*) through his agent in Italy, John Talman (*q.v.*). On their arrival in England, Jonathan Richardson Senior (*q.v.*) was employed to supervise the dismantling of the albums and to reorganize the collection, transcribing Resta's notes into the manuscript known as Lansdowne 802 (British Museum, London).

Sir Joshua Reynolds
(1723–1792)

 (L2364)

First President of the Royal Academy and successful portrait and history painter, who also owned a vast collection of Old Master prints, drawings, sculpture and paintings. He had been the student of Thomas Hudson (*q.v.*), from whose collection he bought and who most likely introduced him to auctions of Old Masters. The ample income which his fashionable portraits produced allowed him to start collecting in earnest from 1752. Apart from buying in London, he travelled abroad,

visiting Paris in 1771 specifically to attend the Thiers-Crozat sale. Reynolds seems to have supplemented his income with a moderate amount of dealing from 1755 and distinguished collectors often sought his advice. He considered his collection partly as an investment and also as a source of study for students. His collection of drawings included a few carefully finished studies but slight sketches, or "*primi pensieri*", predominated, reflecting his interest in the question of artistic 'invention' elaborated upon in his *Eighth Discourse*. His interest centred on Italian drawings of the 16th and 17th centuries, but he also owned many drawings by Van Dyck and Rembrandt. Reynolds was also a keen collector of prints, which provided him with a store of poses and compositional ideas. After his death, aside from a few bequests to friends, 2253 drawings were sold 26 May 1794 (Poggi) and a further 4000 were sold 5–22 March 1798 (Phillips). Each drawing was stamped by the executors with the collector's mark, those of higher quality and value on the recto and those considered "of inferior merit" on the verso.

Jonathan Richardson Senior
(1665–1745)

 (L2183)   (L2184)

Portrait painter, perhaps best known for his collection of some 5000 Old Master drawings and his important and influential writings on art theory. His main works are *An Essay towards the Theory of Painting* (1715) and *Two Discourses* (1719) which examine the art of connoisseurship. In collaboration with his son, he also wrote the famous *Account of Some of the Statues, Bas-reliefs, Drawings and Pictures in Italy* (1722). His works appeared in a three-volume French translation published in Amsterdam in 1728 under the title *Traité de la peinture*. In his writings, the artist whom Richardson praised most was Raphael, closely followed by Michelangelo. His own magnificent collection of drawings, partly inherited from his painting master John Riley and added to by judicious purchases from such sales as those of Sir Peter Lely and Lord Somers, included works by both these masters. The majority of his drawings were 16th- and 17th-century Italian, but the collection also included important works by Rubens, Van Dyck and Rembrandt. In line with his art historical theories about 'the Progress of the Art', he organized his collection chronologically according to both school and date (possibly derived from the albums formed by Padre Resta, *q.v.*). Typically, Richardson wrote multiple shelfmark references on his drawings, consisting of several sets of letters and numbers, indicating a complex system of classification. Unfortunately the catalogues of Richardson's collection, which were included in the 1772 sale of his son's collection (*q.v.*), have not survived, and thus it is not possible to decipher these marks. He also occasionally inscribed attributions and general information on the mounts. The collection was sold 22 January 1747 and following 17 nights (Christopher Cock).

Jonathan Richardson Junior (1694–1771)

R (L.2170)

Like his father (*q.v.*), a collector and connoisseur and probably an amateur portrait painter. He formed a far more modest collection of drawings than his father. He travelled to Holland, Flanders, Germany and France and in 1721 embarked on a tour of Italy to study ancient and Italian art. Although he failed to visit Venice, Naples and Genoa he was generally very diligent and made detailed notes which formed the basis of *An Account of Some of the Statues, Bas-reliefs, Drawings and Pictures in Italy* (1722), completed jointly with his father. This work was praised by scholars and became a *vade mecum* for the Grand Tourist. His collection of drawings and prints was auctioned in 616 lots, 5–12 February 1772 (Langford's); the catalogue notes, "On the Back of many of the Drawings are historical Explanations by Mr Richardson jun.".

Jan van Rijmsdijk (died after 1783–84, possibly 1788–89)

Little known Dutch portrait painter and engraver who lived in England, where he was known as Remsdyke. Along with his son Andreas (1754–1786) Jan produced aquatints of antiquities and natural history items in the British Museum, published in *Museum Britannicum* in 1778. He seems to have had an important collection of drawings inscribed either *Rymsdyk's Museum* or *M*.

Charles Rogers (1711–1784)

Collector, connoisseur and officer in the Customs House who, on inheriting the collection of his benefactor, William Townson, in 1740, created an outstanding library and collection of sculpture, coins, medals, paintings and, above all, prints and drawings. He was elected a Fellow of the Society of Antiquaries in 1752 and became a Fellow of the Royal Society in 1757. Although he never travelled abroad, friends purchased drawings for him on the Continent. His collection included a large series of self-portraits of artists, most of which had come from the collection of Niccolò Gabburri (*q.v.*). His pioneering two-volume *A Collection of Prints in Imitation of Drawings* (1778) reproduced 112 drawings and contained 463 pages of text. Forty-two of the drawings reproduced belonged to Rogers; the rest belonged to George III, George Knapton, Hudson (*q.v.*), the Duke of Marlborough, Earl Spencer (*q.v.*), Lord Cholmondeley, Lord Frederic Campbell, J.M. Rysbrack, Reynolds (*q.v.*), Richardson (*q.v.*), Hone (*q.v.*), Hillier (*q.v.*) among others. On his death the collection passed to his sister's husband, William Cotton, and then to his son William Cotton II, who sold a considerable portion of the drawings 18 March 1799 and 20 following days (T. Philipe). The remaining part of the collection passed to William Cotton III, who donated it to Plymouth Public Library in 1853; it is now housed in the Plymouth City Museum and Art Gallery.

Comte de Saint-Morys (1743–1795)

Amateur draughtsman and engraver who, thanks to his marriage to a wealthy heiress, was able to accumulate, between 1779 and 1789, a vast collection of paintings, drawings, prints and works of art, housed in his Paris hôtel in the rue Vivienne and in the Château d'Hondainville near Beauvais. On 6 February 1786 he sold part of it and in the wake of the Revolution emigrated to London, taking some items with him. The remainder, including some 12,600 drawings, was seized by the authorities in 1793 and incorporated into the Musée National (now the Louvre). Although the Saint-Morys collection has neither marks nor mounts, some drawings can be identified through etchings which he himself produced and by Revolutionary inventories of the rue

Vivienne hôtel and lists of paintings, drawings and prints seized at the Château. More than half the collection consisted of works by Italian artists, the other half being divided about equally between the French and Northern schools.

Paul Sandby (1725–1809)

P+S (L.2112)

Painter, draughtsman, printmaker and drawing-master, initially employed as a military draughtsman. Excelling in panoramic landscapes in watercolour and pen and ink, Sanby was the first to use the aquatint process in England. A founder-member of both the Society of Artists and the Royal Academy, Sandby also collected prints and drawings. He held one sale of prints and drawings during his lifetime, 27 May 1785 (Greenwood), and there were a further six posthumous sales: 2–4 May 1811 (Christie's); 17–19 March 1812 (Christie's); 16–18 April 1817 (Christie's); 26–27 February 1824 (George Jones); 4 March 1824 (George Jones); 11 March 1824 (George Jones).

John, Lord Somers (1651–1716)

Lord Chancellor of England, who became seriously interested in collecting drawings towards the end of his life. He never travelled abroad, but acquired through friends and agents on the Continent. His most important purchase was that of several of the volumes of drawings formerly owned by Padre Sebastiano Resta (*q.v.*) in 1710. Somers had Resta's drawings remounted, transcribing Resta's original notes in a manuscript now in the British Museum and known as Lansdowne 802. A second manuscript, Lansdowne 803, consists of a list of artists in alphabetical order, accompanied by the subject-matter and shelf numbers of drawings by each master represented. This documents the rearrangement of Resta's drawings in Somers's collection, which was carried out by Jonathan Richardson Senior (*q.v.*). The names of the artists written beneath the drawings are in Richardson's handwriting, as are the shelf numbers on the backs of the mounts that correspond to the numbers in the Lansdowne 803 catalogue. Lansdowne 803, which contains 2070 entries, was not a catalogue of Somers's complete collection, which amounted to 3692 drawings at his death. Each volume of drawings was arranged in reverse chronological order, beginning with the most recent, in a clearly didactic arrangement which demonstrated 'the Progress of the Art'. Somers's collection seems to be the earliest example of an art-historical arrangement in Britain , although we know that Jonathan Richardson Senior's collection was also organized chronologically. The sale of Somers's prints and drawings took place on 6 May 1717 (Motteux's), and significant buyers at the sale included Pierre Crozat (*q.v.*), General Guise, the Duke of Devonshire and Jonathan Richardson Senior.

George John, 2nd Earl Spencer (1758–1834)

 (L1630)

Lord of the Admiralty from 1794 to 1801 and Home Secretary during Fox's administration, 1806–07, also President of the Royal Institution, a Trustee of the British Museum for forty years, and in 1812 one of the founders and first President of the Roxburghe Club. A bibliophile, Spencer divided his time between politics and collecting and in his retirement reorganized and enriched the family library at Althorp. An account of the library, the house and its works of art was published by Thomas Frognall Dibdin under the titles of *Bibliotheca Spenceriana* (1814-15), *Ædes Althorpianae* (1822), and *Book of Rarities in Lord Spencer's Library* (1811). The collection was bought in 1892 by Mrs Rylands and became the John Rylands Library in Manchester. His collection of drawings, which Lugt believes to have been formed by his father, 1st Earl Spencer, was sold anonymously during his lifetime, 10–17 June 1811 (T. Philipe) in 899 lots, as the "Superb cabinet of drawings, the entire collection of a nobleman, formed with refined taste and judgement about the middle of the last century". A large number of drawings at Roscoe's sale had Spencer provenances.

Edward, Lord Stanley, later 13th Earl of Derby (1775–1851)

Whig politician and naturalist; styled Lord Stanley until 1832, he became 13th Earl of Derby in 1834. He founded the famous Zoological Collection and Scientific Library at Knowsley Hall, near Liverpool, and was a prominent figure in the science of zoological classification, particularly the taxonomy of birds. He bequeathed his vertebrate collections to the city of Liverpool, where they provided the foundation of the Liverpool Museum. It is possible that Stanley knew William Roscoe through the Linnean Society, but more likely it was through Roscoe's friendship with his father, 12th Earl of Derby, although the three men evidently shared mutual political interests. Very little is known of Lord Stanley's collection of drawings, although he purchased at least 40 lots at Roscoe's sale. They seem to have been sold off gradually over the years, although there is evidence that Stanley sold on some Roscoe drawings to Charles Blundell.

John Talman (1677–1726)

 (L2462)

Son of William Talman the architect, Talman made two extended tours of Europe from about 1698, partly to study but also to make purchases for his father's famous collection of architectural drawings (see exh. cat. 27), prints and books. He spent almost twenty years in Italy, and apart from making acquisitions he also commissioned draughtsmen to make studies of architectural details, ecclesiastical ornaments and regalia, which were of considerable antiquarian interest. He occasionally acted as an amateur dealer and was instrumental in the purchase by Lord Somers (*q.v.*) of the collection of Old Master drawings formed by Padre Resta (*q.v.*). The survival of Talman's copybook of letters written from Italy between 1708 and 1712 clarifies the nature of the negotiations of the Resta purchase. By the time of his death Talman's own collection (comprising that of his father's) was vast, consisting of some 26,000 prints and 7000 drawings. They were divided into categories of architecture; sculpture; vases; jewellery; coronation regalia and royal and ecclesiastical vestments. Talman drawings can be identified not only from his well known triple T mark, but also, where original mounts have survived, by numbers which he wrote in the top right corner or by annotations in his handwriting. Two sales have been traced: the first, 19–26 April 1727 (Cock's), included most of the antiquarian drawings; the second, 5–10 April 1728, was largely of books but included batches of loose prints and drawings as well as Talman's own pen-and-ink sketches. There may have been other sales, whether privately or by auction.

Robert Udney (1722-1802?)

 (L2248)

London-based merchant trading with the West Indies, who built up an impressive collection of paintings and drawings. He regarded his collection as the potential nucleus of a national collection of Old Master paintings and, according to his will, the Royal Academy was to be offered the opportunity to purchase the collection before it was placed on the open market. The offer was declined and the paintings, which included works by Flemish and Dutch artists, were sold at auction, 18-19 May 1804 (Christie's). The large drawings collection, mainly by 17th- and 18th-century Italian artists, included a series of works by Guercino (exh. cat. 32) and also the famous Leonardo cartoon, *The Virgin and Child with St Anne and St John the Baptist* (National Gallery, London). It was sold in 680 lots, 4–10 May 1803 (Philipe and Scott).

Joseph van Aken (ca. 1699-1749)

VH (L2516)

Flemish portrait and genre painter, active in London from *ca.* 1720, and in the 1730s and 1740s employed as a drapery painter for other artists, including Joseph Highmore, Thomas Hudson (*q.v.*), George Knapton, Henry Winstanley, Arthur Pond (*q.v.*) and Allan Ramsay. He was especially known for his fine poses and costumes inspired by Van Dyck and Rubens. In 1748 he travelled to Paris with Hogarth and Hayman, and then by himself to the Netherlands. Allan Ramsay and Thomas Hudson were joint executors of Van Aken's will. His collection of drawings was probably inspired by Thomas Hudson's own collection, although, as stated in John Barnard's catalogue of 1787, "He had nothing very capital". The prints and drawings were sold in 300 lots, 17–20 January 1758 (Langford's).

The 'Reliable Venetian Collector'

This is the name given by A.E. Popham to the author of characteristic annotations in the same hand giving with invariable accuracy a draughtsman's name and place of birth on certain Venetian drawings of the 17th and 18th centuries. The collector who inscribed these drawings was probably Venetian, as the majority of sheets inscribed are Venetian in origin. This unidentified collector, who seems to have been an amateur of considerable taste and knowledge, has also been called the 'Reliable Venetian Hand' or 'Reliable Italic Hand'. He was at one time thought to be the notable collector and scholar Anton Maria Zanetti Senior, but this has been disproved. The collection was probably formed between 1770 and 1780 and dispersed soon afterwards. The majority of drawings which have been traced were in English collections; one drawing, by Gaetano Zompini, bears the mark of John Barnard (*q.v.*), who died in 1784. Finished drawings are rare; the majority are studies for figure paintings of religious or historical subjects. An exhibition at the Fondazione Giorgio Cini in 1966 reunited 183 drawings from the collection (*Disegni di una collezione veneziana del Settecento*, catalogue by Alessandro Brettagno).

The Viti-Antaldi Collection

·R·V· (L.2246)

This collection of drawings by Raphael had been formed by Raphael's older contemporary, fellow-artist and fellow-citizen of Urbino, Timoteo Viti (1469/70–1523), then passed to Viti's descendants, the Antaldi family of Pesaro. In 1714, Pierre Crozat (*q.v.*) managed to purchase a number of drawings from the collection; others may already have found their way into the collection of Sir Thomas Lawrence via J.B.J. Wicar and William Young Ottley (*q.v.*) who were both active buyers in Italy during the Napoleonic period. What remained was purchased by the dealer Samuel Woodburn in 1823. A manuscript catalogue of the collection, drawn up about the middle of the 17th century and obtained by Woodburn in 1824, itemized 48 Raphael drawings altogether: Seven were noted as "not found", and 26 were inscribed "*venduto*" (sold), and the remaining 15 are probably those which passed to Woodburn. It was published in full by Sir J. C. Robinson in his *Critical Account of the drawings by Michel Angelo and Raffaello in the University Galleries at Oxford*, 1870, pp. 340–51. Woodburn eventually sold the drawings to Sir Thomas Lawrence. The Viti-Antaldi drawings are usually inscribed in pen and brown ink with the initials R.V. (for 'Raffaello da Urbino'), probably added to the drawings in the 17th century by a member of the Antaldi family. Unfortunately the initials are not an infallible guarantee of authenticity, as they were applied rather liberally on a number of drawings by pupils, copyists and imitators of Raphael such as Timoteo Viti himself. Those from the Lawrence collection bear the small blind-stamped initials TL in the lower left-hand corner.

Benjamin West (1738–1820)

B · W (L419) dry stamp

American painter and draughtsman, active in England. He studied in Italy from 1760 to 1763; arriving in England in 1763 he immediately became a great success and was soon made Royal History Painter by George III. In 1768 he was one of the founding members of the Royal Academy, succeeding Joshua Reynolds (*q.v.*) as President in 1792. As well as forming his own collection, West was a discreet dealer, buying for the King at auctions and also giving his advice on attributions and prices of paintings. He owned two of the volumes of Fra Bartolommeo drawings which had been discovered by Niccolò Gabburri (*q.v.*) in the convent of Santa Caterina in Florence (now Boymans van Beuningen Museum, Rotterdam); after West's death in 1820, Lawrence purchased the volumes from his family for £2000. West also collected prints and had an important collection of Dutch, Flemish and Italian Old Master paintings (which produced about £15,000 when sold in June 1820). The prints and drawings were sold 9–13 June and 1–5 July 1820 (Christie's) and 11 May 1836 (Sotheby's). His collector's mark was applied to the drawings by the executors of his will.

Jan Pietersz Zoomer or Zomer (1641–1724)

 (L1511)

By 1690 one of Amsterdam's leading dealers in paintings, drawings and prints, with a clientele both Dutch and foreign: in 1711 he claimed to have a stock of 30,000 prints for sale. From about 1660 he had started to form his own collection of drawings, prints and books. His drawings were mostly by Dutch artists, including no less than seven volumes of Rembrandt drawings. He appears to have applied his mark to drawings that passed through his hands as well as into his own collection. He often inscribed the name of the artist on his sheets, although at times he was deliberately optimistic with his attributions, especially with drawings said to be by Italian artists. Zoomer often bought prints and drawings already assembled in albums which he then broke up and reconstituted into new 'series'. In about 1720 he compiled a catalogue of his collection, offering it for sale by private treaty *en bloc*; it included 139 albums of drawings, 100 portfolios of prints, 14 separate portfolios of historical engravings and two volumes of his own drawings. Zoomer's important collection of Rembrandt etchings was bought in London in 1720 by Anton Maria Zanetti the Elder.

Catalogue of
Drawings Exhibited

NOTES ON THE CATALOGUE

The catalogue is arranged geographically, Italian School followed by Northern drawings. Within these sections the drawings have been arranged alphabetically and chronologically. The illustrated Appendix of the rest of the drawings from the Weld-Blundell collection is ordered alphabetically by artist or by school. Measurements are given height before width.

1 ANONYMOUS

Italian school, late 16th or early 17th century

Study of an angler fish

168 × 190 mm, bodycolour and white lead
Watermark on mount D & Co Blauw
Inscribed on mount in pencil *LIGOZZI* (?)
(Hille. C)
PROVENANCE Benjamin West (L419);
C.R. Blundell
WAG1995.278

This study of an angler fish (*Lophius piscatorius* Linn.), commonly found in the waters of the Mediterranean, is typical of the detailed and colourful studies of plants and animals often produced at the courts and universities of Italy in the second half of the sixteenth century as a result of the growth of interest in the scientific study of the natural world.[1] In the university town of Bologna the naturalist Ulisse Aldrovandi (1522–1605) amassed over 2500 natural history drawings, which remain Italy's most important collection of scientific illustrations.[2] In Florence the Uffizi has several large albums of such studies, including one entirely devoted to fish. Another group of animal studies, also including fish, was commissioned by Cassiano dal Pozzo (1588–1657) during the early seventeenth century for his celebrated Paper Museum and is now in the Royal Collection.[3] The Uffizi studies were produced between 1580 and 1600 by a group of young artists attracted to Florence by commissions from Grand Duke Francesco I and scientists and intellectuals attached to his court.[4] Most of the artists remain anonymous. They were expected to produce objective illustrations of the specimens and so had little opportunity to express a personal style with which to differentiate themselves from others. But one amongst them, Jacopo Ligozzi (1547–1627), to whom this drawing was formerly attributed, became celebrated for his abilities as a miniaturist and was employed by the Grand Duke between 1577 and 1591 as a scientific draughtsman, amongst other court commissions. The Liverpool drawing differs significantly from Ligozzi's studies in the Uffizi, which show

an interest in the fishes' scaly sheen and a distinctive use of gold highlights.[5] The more dappled, 'impressionistic' effect of the Liverpool watercolour is if anything closer to the modulated tones applied in broken patches of wash by Vicenzo Leonardi (*fl.* 1621–*ca.* 1646) to his studies for Cassiano dal Pozzo.[6] The angler fish's life-like character, created not only by the shadow under its body and the subtle touches of white highlighting the fins, but also by the drama introduced by the whipping, curling tail and the gaping mouth showing viciously pointed teeth, is not found in Ligozzi's drawings or amongst the studies by the other anonymous draughtsmen of the Uffizi albums. Almost all the Uffizi fish, including two angler fish, one by Ligozzi, are depicted in the same way, all in profile and identified by their Latin and Italian names and none with the lively use of light and shadow and the vivid three-dimensional articulation of the body which distinguishes the Liverpool drawing.[7] The image emerges as more of a 'portrait' of a fish, presented as if swimming out from the page towards the viewer, rather than as a neutral, 'scientific' depiction of a dead natural history specimen. Perhaps it was this portrait-like character and the drama of the image that attracted the American painter Benjamin West to acquire it for his collection of Old Master drawings, or possibly it was his knowledge of the Royal Collection's studies. It must have cut an odd, but amusing, figure alongside the more traditional draped figures and highly finished compositional studies which were typical of West's collection and more useful for the production of his own large-scale paintings of scenes from modern and ancient history.

2 PIETRO PAOLO BALDINI

Rome 1605–1650 Rome

The Adoration of the Magi

397 × 270 mm, pen and brown ink over black chalk and brown wash heightened with white hatching and with touches of blue-grey wash on buff-grey paper within an inscribed arch
Inscribed in ink on mount *Benedetto Luti*; on back in pencil 57
PROVENANCE Unknown collector's mark in brown ink – a crowned shield with a saltire cross within, unrecorded in Lugt; Henry Constantine Jennings (L2771); Benjamin West (L419); C.R. Blundell
EXHIBITION Edinburgh 1972, no. 95, as Giovanni Francesco Romanelli
LITERATURE U.V. Fischer Pace, 'Drawings by Pietro Paolo Baldini', *Master Drawings*, XXIV, 1991, p. 20, pl. 16; Jörg Martin Merz, *Pietro da Cortona: Der Aufstieg zum führenden Maler im barocken Rom*, Tübingen 1991, Anhang V, p. 331, cat. 1b
WAG1995.322

The distinctive use of white hatching, which seems almost chiselled on to drapery, skin and horseflesh to represent the fall of light, confirms that the drawing is by Pietro Paolo Baldini, as Ursula Fischer first pointed out in 1991. A similar use of white highlights with an opaque blue-grey wash and sketchy background figures in a landscape can also be found on Baldini drawings in the British Museum and the Royal Collection.[1] This appears to be a finished study, in reverse and with some changes, for an altarpiece in Sant'Eligio degli Orefici in Rome which was painted in 1639–40 by Baldini's contemporary and colleague Giovanni Francesco Romanelli (*ca.* 1610–1662; fig. 8).[2] The number of alterations to the second king's right hand would suggest that the drawing is an original by Baldini and not a copy with variants by him from an unknown print after Romanelli's painting.[3] Between 1639 and 1646 Baldini was working alongside Romanelli in the Roman church of Santi Domenico e Sisto (see exh. cat. 49) – at the same time as Romanelli was painting the *Adoration of the Magi*.

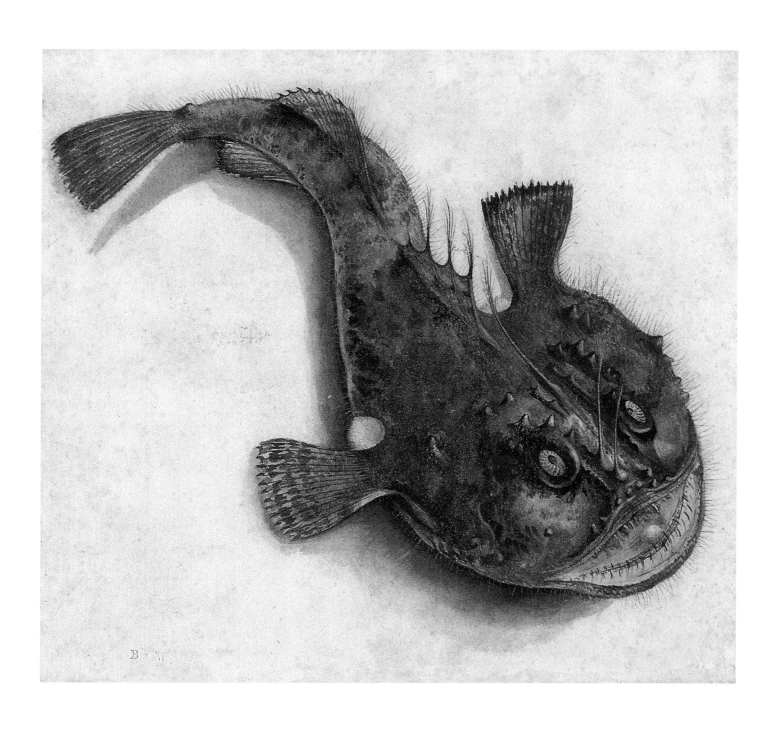

Fig. 8 Giovanni Francesco Romanelli, *The Adoration of the Magi*, altarpiece, Sant'Eligio degli Orefici, Rome

Fig. 9 The Belvedere *Torso*, 1st century BC, Vatican Museums

Their paintings often came to resemble each other's and many of Baldini's highly finished studies are at first glance similar to Romanelli's compositional studies. Presumably the Sant'Eligio altarpiece was originally commissioned from Baldini and taken over by Romanelli later.[4] The paper appears to have faded from its original blue, and the grey-blue wash silhouetting the mid- and background figures would, when first applied, have toned in more subtly, increasing the effect of shadowed recession amongst the royal retinue crowding round the Virgin and her Child.

3 BACCIO BANDINELLI
(Bartolomeo di Michelangelo)
Florence 1493–1560 Florence
Hercules seated on a grassy bank

288 × 208 mm, red chalk
Inscribed in ink on drawing lower left corner *50* (?); on back in ink, lower right corner *19*. The corners have been cut to fit the mount and made up with decorative floral arabesques in ink
PROVENANCE William Roscoe, Liverpool, Winstanley sale, 23–28 September 1816, lot 83, bt. William Ford 10*s*. 6*d*.; C.R. Blundell, as Michelangelo, *Hercules an Academy Figure*, valued at 8*s*. in 1841
EXHIBITIONS Edinburgh 1969, no. 5; *Baccio Bandinelli*, by R. Ward, Cambridge, Fitzwilliam Museum, 1988, no. 8
LITERATURE R. Ward, 'Bandinelli as a Draughtsman', Ph.D., London, Courtauld Institute, 1982, cat. 230, fig. 19
WAG1995.330

Hercules's strangely truncated torso is modelled on the antique sculpture traditionally considered a fragment of a *Hercules* and referred to as the 'Belvedere Torso' ever since its removal to the courtyard of the Villa Belvedere in the Vatican by Pope Julius II in 1509 [fig. 9].[1] The pope's private antiquarium of sculptures in the Belvedere was opened as a 'school' for contemporary sculptors to compete with the classical masters.[2] When the young sculptor Bandinelli first visited Rome in the spring of 1514, as a protégé of the Medici, he came armed with letters of introduction from his patron Lorenzo de' Medici, requesting access to papal and other private collections in Rome.[3] His rendition of the torso is not an exact copy but an interpretation, characteristically made up by adding a Herculean head. Throughout his career as a graphic artist, Bandinelli favoured the pen, particularly a thick-nibbed one (see exh. cat. 4), and it was for his finished drawings in this technique that he garnered the praise of contemporaries. Facility with the gentler medium of red chalk came less easily to an artist who was primarily a sculptor, as is suggested by some of the awkwardnesses of the Liverpool drawing. The hard contours and tight musculature seem to show his effort to find a way of describing a complicated and twisted sculpted pose in a medium that he did not yet handle so well as pen and ink. A similar awkwardness is found in a reclining Adam-like figure in red chalk derived from Michelangelo's Sistine Chapel.[4] It would suggest that the drawing was made early on in his career, perhaps shortly after he had first seen the torso. On his return to Florence in 1515 he was commissioned to produce several temporary constructions in honour of the visit in November of the Medici Pope Leo X, including a colossal wood and clay Hercules placed in the Loggia dei Lanzi fronting the Piazza della Signoria.[5] It is possible that at this time, with Hercules in mind, he attached a bearded head to the suitably herculean, bulbous body of the Belvedere torso he had studied recently.[6] Over time Bandinelli was to become equally fascinated with the *Apollo* Belvedere (see cat. 4), and would often recall their essential forms on the same sheet, contrasting the lithe grace of the *Apollo* with the muscle-bound stolidity of the torso.

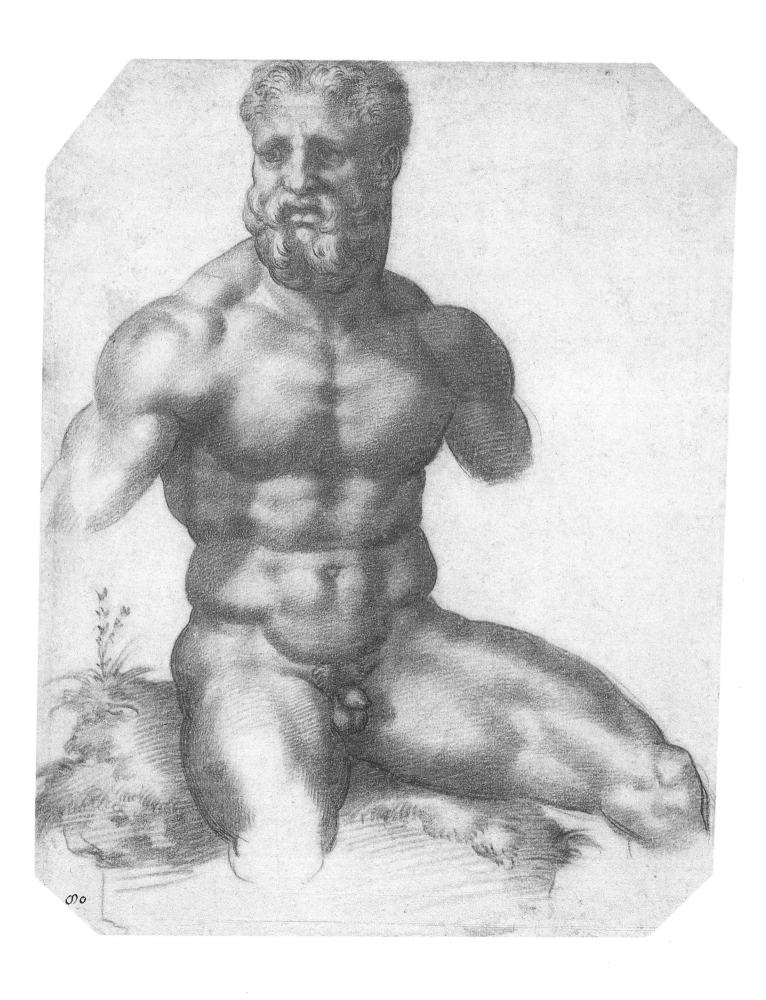

Fig. 10 *Apollo* Belvedere, Roman copy in marble of a Hellenistic bronze, Vatican Museums

Bandinelli habitually sketched the same subject in series, adopting slightly variant stances on separate sheets of paper. They could then be placed side by side for comparison and so help him formulate ideas for his sculpted projects. The Liverpool sheet of sketches is one of several outlining in pen and ink the same central and right-hand figures as seen from different angles.[2] The central nude corresponds to a fairly early stage of the artist's working and probably dates to some time between 1515 and the early 1520s.[3] The other related studies modify and firm up the pose with increased use of finer hatched pen-strokes, until Bandinelli was able to use it in an adapted form for his successful sculpture of *Orpheus* in about 1519, and an unexecuted statue of *Andrea Doria as Neptune* in 1529.[4] Bandinelli's repeated use of the central pose shows his obsession with two sculptural prototypes, one from the antique world and one by his contemporary and rival Michelangelo. The central nude figure relates to the *Apollo* Belvedere [fig. 10], the Roman copy of a Greek original transported to the Vatican by Pope Julius II in 1509 and moved to the Belvedere courtyard in 1511. Until 1532–33, when a bow was added, the statue lacked its left arm below the elbow and a right hand. Bandinelli would have seen it in this condition in 1514 when he

4 BACCIO BANDINELLI
Three nude men flanked by the heads of two older men

340 × 247 mm, pen and ink
Inscribed in ink in lower right corner of drawing *93*, and in lower left corner with illegible numbers
PROVENANCE Pierre Crozat (?), sold Paris, 1741, lot 40;[1] P.-J. Mariette, sold Paris, Basan, 1775, lot 1403? (L1852; inscribed within a cartouche on a blue 'Mariette' mount *Baccio Bandinelli*); Abbé Charles-Philippe Campion de Tersan

(1736–1819; inscribed on back in ink by West (?) *Bt. of Abbé Tersant Paris April 28 1791 for 150 Louis*); Benjamin West (no collector's mark; inscribed in pencil on second mount *West Florentine/ genuine/ a good specimen*); C.R. Blundell (inscribed in ink, lower right corner of mount *m: 1497. m. 1559*)
LITERATURE Ward 1982, cat. 229; A. Forlani Tempesti, 'Il David di Michelangelo nella tradizione grafica Bandinelliana', *Antichità Viva*, XXVIII, 1989, p. 21, n. 11
WAG1995.305

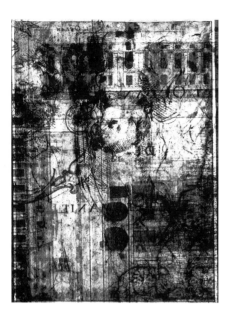

Fig. 11 Bandinelli, exh. cat. 4, photograph taken under transmitted light

first visited Rome. More surprising than Bandinelli's homage to antique sculpture is the hidden acknowledgement of Michelangelo's *David*. The figure's sharply turned head, its pronounced musculature, and above all its rapidly sketched and crossed-out right arm bent upwards as if modelled on David's catapult-holding left hand all relate to Michelangelo's masterpiece. The memory of this work haunted much of Bandinelli's work from 1515 through to the 1530s. Between 1516 to the mid 1520s the two sculptors were in close contact. Michelangelo tried to support the younger Bandinelli by giving him work on the church of San Lorenzo.[5] Bandinelli's repeated, but always carefully masked, use of Michelangelo's *David* in his own drawings suggests that for all their artistic and political disagreements – Bandinelli was a firm supporter of Medici power, Michelangelo of the Florentine Republic – he could not resist in his own work measuring himself against Michelangelo and in so doing expressing his admiration for his rival.

Unusually for Bandinelli the reverse side of the drawing appears to have another ink study (visible under transmitted light) of the same central standing figure [fig. 11]. The architectural elevations, ornamental festoons and ink lettering (which reads *L'OCEAN*[?] *DU GERMANIE*) are on the two sheets of paper used to line Bandinelli's drawing before it was attached to its blue Mariette mount.

5 FEDERICO BAROCCI
Urbino 1535–1612 Urbino
The martyrdom of St Vitalis

440 × 330 mm, pen and brown ink and wash over black chalk, squared in red and black chalks and pen and brown ink, with figures indented with a stylus, pricked and pounced on light-beige paper with losses, tears, abrasions and waterstains and numerous repairs and restored losses, especially along the sides
Inscribed in ink on mount *F Barroccio*; on reverse in pencil, lower left corner *No. 5*
PROVENANCE Unidentified armorial collector's blind stamp (centre lower edge), perhaps Cardinal Leopoldo de' Medici (1617–1675); Benjamin West (L419); inscribed in pencil on mount *West Roman School*; C.R. Blundell

EXHIBITION *The Graphic Art of Federico Barocci: Selected Drawings and Prints*, edd. E. Pillsbury and Louise Richards, Cleveland Art Museum and Yale University Art Gallery, 1978, cat. 45
LITERATURE A. Emiliani, *Federico Barocci: Urbino 1535–1612*, Bologna 1985, p. 170, fig. 339
WAG1995.311

The much battered and worn condition of the drawing shows that it was a 'working' compositional *modello* for Barocci's painting showing the stoning to death of the third-century saint Vitalis and originally commissioned in 1580 for the high altar of the church of the Olivetan Order, San Vitale at Ravenna [fig. 12].[1] The finished picture is a masterpiece of dynamic poses, gestures and glances all revolving around the sprawled body of the saint. Barocci signed the contract with San Vitale's abbot on 20 June 1580, and by April 1583 the Archbishop of Urbino confirmed that the almost four-metre-high painting was finished and ready to send to Ravenna (with the help of three horses, two mules and six men), where it was probably placed on the altar by 28 April, the festival of the church's patron saint.[2] As was customary, Barocci produced a compositional sketch for the church's approval before embarking on such a large-scale project. Although most of the monks approved the overall design one wanted more, and larger, figures, and so Barocci produced a second compositional study to accommodate the demands.[3] A rough inventory of Barocci's studio also mentions a cartoon for the painting with larger-than-life nude and dressed figures drawn in chiaroscuro with white heightening on white paper.[4] The continuous pricking around key figures such as the executioner with his back to us, and evidence of stylus indentations around groups of other figures, show that the Liverpool drawing was used in the process of transferring the design to another sheet, whilst its squared grid suggests the composition was enlarged in transfer, perhaps to the cartoon. There is another, smaller, preliminary *modello* for the altarpiece in the Louvre, but it shows substantial differences from the finished painting, especially in the poses of the foreground figures of a breastfeeding woman and executioner.[5] As the Louvre figures are on a smaller scale it would seem likely that it is the original rejected *modello*,

Fig. 12 Barocci, *The martyrdom of St Vitalis*, oil on canvas, Milan, Brera

whilst the Liverpool drawing, although it also varies from the finished painting, is the second revised and intermediate design from which Barocci then made a large group of detailed figure studies to elaborate the poses. On Barocci's death the San Vitale cartoon, along with other working studio designs, was still in his studio, of which the contents, including two "*cartoncini*" for the San Vitale altarpiece, were offered for sale in 1658 by relatives of his nephew Ambrogio to the keen collector Cardinal Leopoldo de' Medici.[6]

6 FRA BARTOLOMMEO

(Baccio della Porta)

Florence 1473–1517 Florence[1]

Three figures disputing

130 × 132 mm, pen and brown ink
Watermark on backing: fragmented IV
Inscribed in ink on back of paper mount, lower right corner *Franc.º Francia*; in pencil lower left corner: *7/13n*
PROVENANCE Jonathan Richardson Junior (L2170); Benjamin West (no collector's stamp; inscribed in pencil on mount *Fra Bartolommeo di S. Marco/ West Florentine/ genuine and fine*); C.R. Blundell
EXHIBITIONS Edinburgh 1969, no. 8, pl. 1; NACF 1997
LITERATURE C. Fischer, *Fra Bartolommeo et son atelier: Dessins et peintures des collections françaises*, exhib. cat., Paris, Musée du Louvre, 1994, p. 57
WAG1995.360

Fra Bartolommeo's drawings were almost always related to painted projects. This small sketch of a trio of figures caught in amazed discussion or disputation may have been intended for use in a crowd scene in more than one painting, as Fra Bartolommeo's studio practice was carefully to keep drawings for recycling whenever necessary. After taking vows in 1500, Fra Bartolommeo had renounced the practice of painting. On his return to painting in autumn 1504, at the wish of the newly appointed prior Sante Pagnini, his studio in the Dominican convent of San Marco in Florence was geared towards producing collaborative works in which his studio assistants did much of the painting, freeing the artist to work on their design.[2] The figures' odd headgear, probably intended to represent turbans, is similar to that found in Fra Bartolommeo's work from the opening years of the sixteenth century, when he was particularly influenced by the work of the Umbrian artist Perugino, who visited Florence from the mid 1490s onwards. We know from evidence of other drawings, where figures for different paintings are found on the same piece of paper, that during the period 1505–08 Fra Bartolommeo was working on at least four documented altarpieces and several unrecorded works at the same time. The trio in this drawing might have featured in two paintings on which Fra Bartolommeo worked over this period, one a scene from the life of St John the Baptist of 1504–05, the other an unexecuted *Coronation of the Virgin*, which was at a later stage turned into an *Assumption of the Virgin* (minus crowd), of 1507–08, executed for the Compagnia de' Contemplanti in Florence who paid for it in November 1508.[3] The figures are similarly dressed and stylistically related to men shown in the crowd witnessing St John the Baptist's preaching and baptism of Christ in a double-sided pen-and-ink drawing in the British Museum, and in another ink drawing of spectators reacting in amazement to the assumption or coronation of the Virgin.[4] The *Assumption* was his first monumental altarpiece, the area in which Fra Bartolommeo made the most important contribution to the developing High Renaissance style. The altarpiece's large size (over three metres high) and Fra Bartolommeo's extensive use of assistants apparently ensured that, rather than experiment anew, he opted for a conventional composition, perhaps reusing existing drawings.

The drawing once belonged to Benjamin West, the American artist appointed history painter to George III in 1772, who owned at least two large portfolios (some five hundred drawings) by Fra Bartolommeo. According to the art dealer Samuel Woodburn, West made such a great use of his collection of Old Master drawings in the composing of his own paintings that he feared to sell them in public.[5]

7 GIROLAMO MAZZOLA BEDOLI

Viadana 1500–1569 Parma

The Virgin and Child with St Bruno in a doorway

Verso: *Cherub*

145 × 135 mm, red chalk heightened with white lead, partly oxidized

Inscribed in ink on drawing *Parmense*

PROVENANCE Jonathan Richardson Senior (L2183); his attribution in red ink on the mount *Parmeggiano*, and shelfmark on back in ink *L[orZ]c.23/ L[orZ].n.26./ L[orZ].13/ D. 21/ n*; Benjamin West (no collector's stamp; inscribed in pencil on mount *West Lombard/ genuine*; C.R. Blundell

LITERATURE M. di Giampaolo, 'Girolamo Bedoli: ancora due disegni per la *Madonna col bambino e San Bruno* di Monaco', in *Per Maria Cionini Visoni,*

scritti di amici, Turin 1977, pp. 93–95; A.R. Milstein, 'The Paintings of Girolamo Mazzola Bedoli', Ph.D., New York and London 1978, pp. 35, 141, fig. 5; D. Ekserdjian, entry on Bedoli in *The Dictionary of Art*, London 1996, p. 487; noted in M. di Giampaolo, *Girolamo Bedoli*, Florence 1997, no. 7, p. 118

WAG1995.238

Like many of Bedoli's works the drawing was once thought to be by Parmigianino, Bedoli's great mentor and relative by marriage, from whom he took his middle name, and whose style and compositions he closely imitated, as this tender red-chalk study shows.[1] It is in fact related to Bedoli's small-scale painting of a *Madonna and Child with St Bruno* in the Alte Pinakothek in Munich, an early work of about 1534–35 [fig. 13].[2] The finished picture is in reverse and the Virgin no longer turns to the saint

Fig. 13 Bedoli, *The Virgin and Child with St Bruno*, oil on canvas, Munich, Alte Pinakothek

Fig. 14 Verso of exh. cat 7

in an ambiguous confrontation, with her clinging child looking downwards, but has her back to him and instead displays the Christ Child to the devout observer. Both drawing and painting have an obvious devotional intent, but the extremely rare inclusion of St Bruno, the founder of the Carthusian order, who was beatified only in 1514, suggests that the painting must have been intended for a Carthusian monastery.[3] David Ekserdjian has suggested that Bedoli's painting is the one mentioned by Vasari and attributed to Parmigianino in the Carthusian abbot's own cell in the Certosa at Pavia.[4] Faintly discernible in the mass of red-chalk marks that form St Bruno's hands is a sprig of olive, one of his attributes, alluding to the verse in Psalm 52 which was applied to him: "I am like a spreading olive-tree in God's house." Bedoli particularly favoured the attractive medium of red chalk, employed in the Liverpool drawing with a light feathery stroke, which deftly increases the subject's mysterious air. An outline sketch of a baby at its mother's breast in red chalk was discovered on the back of the drawing during conservation work [fig. 14].

Bedoli's entire career was interwoven with that of Parmigianino. From the death of his father in 1505, Bedoli lived with the Mazzola family in Parma and nearby Viadana, training alongside Parmigianino in the workshop of Parmigianino's uncles, which he inherited, along with many of his patrons, on Parmigianino's death. By

adopting Parmigianino's painted and graphic style, Bedoli deliberately associated himself with his more famous cousin-in-law, ensuring that he became Parmigianino's successor. He remained the most popular artist in mid sixteenth-century Parma, not only because he was versatile and industrious, but because he was also reliable and prompt – unlike the volatile Parmigianino.

8 LUCA CAMBIASO
Moneglia 1527–1585 Madrid
Moses seated on clouds

351 × 249 mm, pen and brown ink
Inscribed in ink on drawing *h.51*; in ink on mount, lower right corner *208*; and on reverse in ink, top left corner *24.–4–vfi*; in pencil, top left corner *91–4–oC*
PROVENANCE Padre Sebastiano Resta (*h.51*); Lord John Somers; J. Richardson Junior (L2170; his inscription (?) in ink on mount *L. Cangiassi* and shelfmark on reverse in ink *O.35*); Roscoe sale, 1816, lot 141, "*Moses reclining his head on the Tables of the Law* a most spirited pen sketch", bt. Slater 9*s*. 6*d*.; C.R. Blundell
WAG1995.258

The colossal figure seated on clouds can be identified as the Prophet Moses by the two 'horned' rays of light shooting from his head.[1] With its vigorous calligraphic style of penmanship and its large size, the drawing compares particularly well with

five other pen-and-ink studies by Cambiaso of single-figure saints, allegorical figures and sibyls seated on clouds, three of which are in Princeton Art Museum, one in the Art Institute of Chicago and one in Stockholm.[2] These drawings have been dated on a stylistical basis mainly to between the 1550s and the late 1560s.[3] It was during this period that Cambiaso established himself as the leading artist in Genoa and undertook the grandiose schemes for churches and palaces on which the foundations of the port's tradition in fresco decoration rest. Moses's muscular physique and his pose, seated on clouds holding the tablets of the law, show the influence of Michelangelo, whose work had impressed Cambiaso on his visit to Rome some time between 1547 and 1550. The dynamic line which Cambiaso wields in the Liverpool drawing to outline swirling clouds and slightly geometricized limbs, hands and eyelids, whilst with a few quick flicks of the pen indicating knees, muscles and tendons, all suggest a date for the drawing to some time in the early part of his career, perhaps between 1555 and 1565. Much of the bold hatching and many of the exuberant curving strokes are there to provide decorative interest. Like the Liverpool drawing, none of the stylistically related figure studies in Princeton, Chicago and Stockholm can be definitely related to any of Cambiaso's decorative projects. Although the bold foreshortening is typical of several of his earlier drawings, it also suggests that Moses was meant to be viewed from below, as if on a ceiling or vault. Some saints have been linked to the figures frescoed on the vault in the left-hand crossing of the nave in San Matteo, Genoa, executed before 30 June 1559, but Mary Newcome, though accepting the attribution, does not feel that the Liverpool study corresponds with the San Matteo project.[4]

43

9 LUCA CAMBIASO
Christ led out of Pilate's house

254 × 355 mm, pen and brown ink and brown wash
PROVENANCE John Barnard (L1419; inscribed on back in ink *J:B N°:889/14 by 10*); Roscoe sale, 1816, lot 146, bt. Slater 1 gn.;[1] C.R. Blundell, valued at 16s. in 1841
EXHIBITION Edinburgh 1969, pl. 29, no. 17
WAG1995.362

In the mid 1560s Cambiaso, possibly influenced by Dürer's published studies of human proportions and other German illustrated theoretical treatises, began to use simplified cubic shapes as a shorthand for his bravura draughtsmanship. Realising later that the stylized geometricization of figures into triangles, cones and cubes made them easier to copy, he may have used the style as a training aid for his studio assistants. From 1570 onwards he also refined the subject-matter of his paintings, concentrating on religious themes and particularly scenes drawn from the last few days of Christ's Passion. Most notable are a series of nocturnal scenes produced in his 'cubic' style between 1570 and 1575 and now in the Uffizi.[2] The Uffizi and other variant sheets are unusual in that they do not deal with traditional scenes such as the Way to Calvary, but with the night journey of Christ from the Mount of Olives to the judgement hall of the High Priest Caiaphas. The Liverpool drawing, of which there are no other known versions or copies, probably also dates from the late period and may have been intended for an unknown fresco series.[3] Mary Newcome has pointed out that although the composition is similar to those by Luca Cambiaso, the style of the two children and the elongated two figures on the left seem to have something in common with a pen-and-ink drawing for a fresco of the late 1560s ascribed to his son Orazio.[4] Luca Cambiaso was a prolific draughtsman, who may also have made replicas of those of his drawings most in demand, but also his son Orazio and other pupils and contemporaries copied his drawings and their graphic style, making attributions on the basis of style and handling difficult. The numbers of these sometimes mechanistic drawings increased as Cambiaso's talent came to be more widely admired by collectors across Europe in the seventeenth century. The esteem in which he was held, and some of the reasons for his popularity, can be gauged from William Roscoe's sale catalogue: he owned twenty-eight drawings attributed to Cambiaso, four of which were in the 'cubic' manner. The entry for lot 146,

Christ led from before Pilate, reads, "a striking example of the talents of the artist, who could express all varieties of character without making the features of the face, further than by cubes and angles ... it may justly be said, that in grandeur of conception, truth of drawing and freedom of hand, he has never been excelled."

10 SIMONE CANTARINI

Oropezza 1612–1648 Verona

The Holy Family with infant St John the Baptist

145 × 118 mm, red chalk
Watermark on drawing: three hills with a bird (?) on top within a roundel, similar to Briquet 12.250 (Rome 1572)[1]
Inscribed on mount card a large *S/...ARY* (cut off at left side)
PROVENANCE Benjamin West (L419), possibly sold Christie's, 1 July 1820, lot 43, bt. Du Rouveray 19s.; C.R. Blundell
EXHIBITION Edinburgh 1972, no. 14[2]
WAG1995.75

The gentle, tender mood of this composition, typical of many of Cantarini's drawings of similar devotional themes, belies the character of the supposedly argumentative, volatile artist described by the Bolognese art commentator Malvasia.[3] His proud temperament ensured that his stay in Guido Reni's studio, which he had entered in 1635 and where he learnt to etch, was brief. As one of the most gifted students of Reni, the elder statesman of Bolognese art, he resented his subordinate position in the studio and the use of his skill with the etching needle to spread the fame of Reni's works. Reni's influence is still evident in this composition even though it probably dates from a period after he had polemically broken from Reni's tutelage and established himself as a rival.[4] In 1639 he left Bologna, having disagreed with other Reni followers and important Bolognese patrons, moving first to Pesaro, south of Rimini, and then Rome to seek patronage only returning to Bologna on Reni's death in 1642.[5] The calm, delicate and harmonious Liverpool drawing probably dates from this turbulent period in Cantarini's career. He created two etchings and a painting of the same theme immediately before and just after his arrival in Rome in 1640, although none reproduces the composition exactly.[6] Although some of Cantarini's numerous drawings were created for their own sake, others were produced with paintings or etchings in mind. Malvasia describes how he would often draw several preparatory studies before etching the definitive one. As is evident in the charming Liverpool study, despite such a painstaking process, Cantarini's red-chalk drawings were always characterized by a feathery handling and light sweetness of touch and mood that was greatly admired by his contemporaries. Even Malvasia put aside his role as propagandist for Reni to praise Cantarini's drawings, for he believed, "There has been no more graceful and delightful a draughtsman since the days of Parmigianino."[7] Cantarini's style anticipated eighteenth-century taste to a remarkable degree and the Weld-Blundell collection has a further three drawings attributed to him, all acquired by William Roscoe.

11 DOMENICO MARIA CANUTI
Bologna 1625–1684 Bologna

The Assumption of the Immaculate Virgin with St John the Evangelist and angels

285 × 412 mm, pen and brown ink and brown wash over black chalk within an inscribed arch
Inscribed on paper in pencil, top right corner *Maria Canuti/ 1660*; and in pencil, bottom right corner *canuti 28*
Inscribed on reverse of mount in ink at top *T/ NP 27*; in ink bottom right corner *Domenico Cannuti Born 1623*; in pencil a description of a former mount as *Creme & pink line*
PROVENANCE George John, 2nd Earl Spencer (L8019); Roscoe sale, 1816, lot 427, bt. Slater 14*s*.; C.R. Blundell, valued at 12*s*. in 1841
WAG1995.199

Having first trained in Bologna under Reni and Guercino, Canuti proceeded to make a significant contribution to ceiling painting in Italy, devoting most of his career to the fresco decoration of Bolognese and Roman palaces and churches. His studies in Rome in 1651–55 and his work in Bologna in the 1660s and 1670s were supported by the patronage of the Pepoli, a Bolognese noble family, and especially the distinguished scholar Abbot Taddeo Pepoli. He tirelessly procured commissions for Canuti in the foundations of the Olivetan order, of which he was abbot general, including the Bolognese monastery of San Michele in Bosco where Canuti devoted his final years to two separate fresco campaigns. In 1677–80 he worked on the three vaults of the monastery library and then, despite poor health, he capped his career by frescoing first the apse in 1680–81 and then the main cupola of the monastery church in 1682–84.[1] This finished wash drawing is a *modello* for the apse of the church showing St John the Evangelist, quill pen in hand, composing the description of his vision of the Virgin who appeared "robed with the sun, beneath her feet the moon, and on her head a crown of twelve stars" [fig. 15].[2] St John's description of the Woman of the Apocalypse provided the iconography for the image of the Immaculate Virgin triumphing over Original Sin, which had only been officially recognised by the Roman Catholic Church

in 1671. Canuti's seated Immaculate Virgin rests her feet on the crescent moon and glides swiftly heavenward as she gazes up towards the main cupola where, in his final work, Canuti painted Religion being protected by an Archangel from the seven-headed Beast of the Apocalypse. In another version of the drawing, making it closer to the finished fresco on the apse, Canuti, using less wash, gave the Virgin a halo of stars rather than the illusionistic halo composed of wash and blank paper of the Liverpool image.[3] As usual with Canuti, the preparatory drawing diverges slightly from the finished image on the apse vault, and the painted St John is much older, bearded and flanked by his attribute the eagle. In his drawing Canuti translates what would be the golden light and colours of his fresco to the sensitively applied pale areas of wash which were so admired by eighteenth-century connoisseurs. Roscoe owned a further three wash drawings attributed to Canuti, two with distinguished eighteenth-century provenances, and one probably by his pupil Giuseppe Rolli.[4]

Fig. 15 Canuti, *The Assumption of the Immaculate Virgin and St John the Evangelist*, interior view of San Michele in Bosco

47

Fig. 16 Annibale Carracci, *The Adoration of the Shepherds*, Orléans, Musée des Beaux-Arts

ANNIBALE CARRACCI (?)
Bologna 1560–1609 Rome
1 2 *Studies of angels playing the lute and flute; a study of a hand on a flute*

169 × 214 mm, black chalk on laid, off-white paper
Watermark on mount card D & C BLAUW
Inscribed in pencil on wash border mount
Simon Cantarini
PROVENANCE Benjamin West (L419 on restored part of drawing); C.R. Blundell
EXHIBITIONS *Drawings by the Carracci from British Collections*, by C. Robertson

and C. Whistler, Oxford, Ashmolean Museum, 1996, p. 142, cats. 91, 92
WAG1995.193

1 3 *Studies of angels playing a viol and recorder* (?)

165 × 197 mm, black chalk
Watermark on mount card: Double Z within an escutcheon[1]
PROVENANCE Benjamin West (L419, stamp on restored bottom right corner of paper); C.R. Blundell
WAG1995.194

These two sketches are working drawings for four of the concert of angels seated in glory above a scene of the *Adoration of the Shepherds* painted by Annibale Carracci in Rome and presently dated to around 1597–98 [fig. 16].[2] The painting was possibly commissioned by one of the Ludovisi family, as it appears in a 1633 inventory of that family's collection in Rome. Both drawings develop the figures outlined, very schematically, in a large pen-and-ink sketch for the whole composition in the Fitzwilliam Museum, Cambridge, though they show the figures not as finally painted but in an intermediate stage in their definition, as many changes were made between the execution of the Fitzwilliam drawing and the final painting.[3] Both drawings and painting, with its host of fair angels, represent Annibale's revived interest during the second half of the 1590s in the work of Correggio.[4] The combination of fairly finished parts of the drawing, such as the lute- and viol-playing angels, with the schematically drawn heads of other figures, such as the flute-playing angel, is common in late drawings by Annibale, as is the practice of detailing one part of the composition, such as the right-hand fingering of the flute-player on the same sheet. However, as Clare Robertson has pointed out, the "meticulous chalk strokes of both drawings are not altogether typical of Annibale's late style, and it is possible that the drawing was executed by an assistant".[5] The depressive illness which dominated the last years of Annibale's life, after 1600, exacerbated by the scandalous treatment he received from his patron Cardinal Odoardo Farnese, who refused to reward him properly for his work on the Farnese Gallery, made it more difficult for him to paint and he increasingly entrusted the execution of his designs to pupils. The *Adoration of the Shepherds* is not securely dated, and it is possible that the Liverpool drawings date to a period after 1600. They are unlikely to have been made as copies either from the altarpiece itself, which was in France from 1672, or from engraved prints made after the painting, as they include drapery and parts of musical instruments, such as the lower part of the lute, not visible in the finished painting because hidden by an additional angel's head.[6] A painted copy of the picture, formerly in the Northwick Park collection, seems to have been made before 1695.[7]

The wash border design with which Benjamin West framed the Liverpool drawings, with inner framing lines of black followed by a pale-cream wash border and an outer line in pale grey, is also found around drawings in the Royal Collection, which suggests that West, George III's history painter from 1772, modelled the mounting of his own collection on that of the Royal Collection.

14 ATTRIBUTED TO ANNIBALE CARRACCI
The Lamentation over Christ's body

125 × 196 mm, pen and grey ink
Inscribed on back in ink *G. Fagell's Sale*; in pencil on reverse of mount *contemporary of Rafaelle/ and whom he worked ...*(?); in pencil on backing card in unidentified hand *Agostino Carracci* (?); *probably genuine/ very good*
PROVENANCE Francois Griffier Fagel (?), sold Philipe, 20–25 May 1799; Roscoe sale, 1816, part of lot 362, as Ludovico Carracci, "*Dead Christ with several figures. Pen sketch./ 5h. 7½w*", bt. Slater 10s. 6d. (along with WAG1995.319, see Appendix, Battista Franco); C.R. Blundell, valued at 8s. in 1841
WAG1995.232

At different times in its history this brisk, scratchy, sketch has been attributed to all three main members of the Carracci family. In certain respects it is difficult to see such a rough drawing as Annibale's and the broadly hatched face and heavily outlined eyes of the Virgin are in some ways close to Agostino.[1] Yet Annibale's late pen drawings were often executed in a similarly harsh, even ugly manner.[2] The slashing, spidery strokes which denote the barely formed hands of the Virgin and her dead son and the stylized way of representing the drapery folds radiating from her knee are found in his late graphic style.[3] The drawing is also typical of Annibale's working method in his later years as he repeatedly and schematically tried out different positions, for example for the Virgin's hand and the head of the dead Christ. As a composition it seems to have been sketched very early in the creative process and to relate to a whole series of paintings and a print in which Annibale, between *ca.* 1597 and 1606, at the end of his life, became preoccupied with the theme of the Virgin's lamentation and mourning. In particular the drawing is close to the *Christ* of Caprarola, Annibale's most famous print, dated 1597 and etched whilst on a visit to the Farnese Palace at Caprarola fifty miles north of Rome.[4] In 1598 he repeated the composition in reverse on a silver plaque engraved for Cardinal Antonio Maria Salviati and in the same year his brother Agostino engraved a copy of it.[5] Naturally the Caprarola etching is reversed from the Liverpool drawing; unlike the sketch it shows the Virgin seated behind her son, supporting his back against her lap and helped in her grief by St John the Evangelist and Mary Magdalene amongst others. However, it shares with the Liverpool sketch the semi-upright pose of Christ's torso and, more significantly,

the drooping position of the Virgin's hands and the awkward raised shoulder of Christ, which, though confusingly they do not make visual sense in the drawing, are in the etching poignantly placed respectively to cradle Christ's head and hang lifeless over the Virgin's knee. The rough sketch would therefore seem to be the artist's first attempt to work through separately, but on the same sheet, the possible poses for the Virgin and Christ in the Caprarola print.

15 ATTRIBUTED
TO ANNIBALE OR
FRANCESCO CARRACCI
Nude male figure lying on the ground,
seen from above

213 × 265 mm, red chalk
PROVENANCE   Jonathan Richardson
Senior (L2183); inscribed in ink on
Richardson's mount *Parmeggiano*, and on
reverse in ink *P.60/ Z.14/ L.53/ F.44/*
Zn.32/ K; probably Roscoe sale, 1816, part
of lot 335, Parmigianino, "Six, various
subjects./ From Lanckrinck's, Richardson's
and other Collections", bt. Slater £1. 9s.
(along with WAG1995.57, .58, .71, .296;
see Appendix, attrib. Creti, Roman School,
Italo-Flemish School, and after

Parmigianino); C.R. Blundell, all six as
"Parmegiano", valued at £1. 4s. in 1841
WAG1995.252

During the 1580s and 1590s three of the
Carracci family, Annibale, Agostino and
their cousin Ludovico, deliberately
encouraged the view that they worked
together in a uniform style on their joint
decorative projects. As they once
mischievously replied when asked to
identify who had painted what in a fresco,
"We all did it".[1] The difficulty of
distinguishing the work of the Carracci
family increases with their 'academy'
drawings of nude male figures, where they
not only shared the same aims and
technique but often the same medium –
red chalk. In 1582, as a challenge to then

current training methods, the Carracci had set up their own academy, where young pupils such as Domenichino and Reni could learn their craft training their eye to observe and their hand to draw from the live model in contrasting light conditions, whilst more experienced artists, including the Carracci themselves, could sharpen their skills drawing the figure in a variety of increasingly complex poses intended, like the Liverpool study, to set problems of foreshortening. Occasionally the poses reappear in adapted or unadapted form in painted compositions. The pose of the Liverpool drawing, for example, is akin to some of the drowning figures in a painting of *The Flood* in the Louvre by Antonio Carracci (Agostino's illegitimate son).[2] Sometimes the studies by the Carracci and their pupils show the same model seen from different angles and it is possible that a drawing in Vienna might represent the Liverpool model as viewed from his feet.[3] The Liverpool drawing was first attributed to Annibale Carracci by A.E. Popham, and the schematic hand sketched in behind the model's back is reminiscent of some of Annibale's studies in the 1580s. But a comparison of the way the hair has been drawn, with bold, individual strokes, of the reinforced silhouette and of the broad hatching around the body, to indicate the ground, with a red-chalk study of a *Seated male nude seen from behind* in the British Museum, which has an old attribution to Francesco Carracci, suggests that the Liverpool 'academy' drawing might be by this younger member of the extended Carracci family.[4] Francesco, called Francheschino (1595–1622), the son of the youngest Carracci brother Giovanni Antonio, established his own separate academy at the beginning of the seventeenth century as a rival to that of his elderly relative Ludovico, whom he rudely nicknamed 'the ox'.[5] His early death at the age of twenty-seven and his antagonism towards other members of his family, especially Ludovico, ensured that the Bolognese biographer Malvasia, who lauded the Carracci family, provided little information about him. What little we do know shows that he greatly enjoyed drawing from life – as Malvasia puts it: "there was not a day when he did not draw from the model" – and that his nude studies in red chalk were appreciated in Bologna and Rome, although the list of such drawings attributed to him is meagre.[6]

Exh. cat. 16 verso

16 ATTRIBUTED TO LUDOVICO CARRACCI

Bologna 1555–1619 Bologna
A sheet of studies: a seated youth wearing a plumed hat; a bearded man wearing a cap; a hand resting on a book
Verso: *Virgin and Child with St Dominic and St Catherine of Siena* (?)
325 × 275 mm, black chalk with touches of red chalk; verso, black chalk, the figures of the Virgin and Child outlined with a stylus
Inscribed in pencil on old mount *No–2–*
PROVENANCE Jonathan Richardson Senior (L2184, with his inscription on the old mount in ink *Ludovico ò vero di quella Scuola*, and his shelfmark in ink on the reverse *DD44/ Mm.12/ DD.~1./ J(?).20/ 2a*; Benjamin West (no collector's mark; but inscribed on old mount in pencil *West*

Bolognese School); C.R. Blundell
EXHIBITION Edinburgh 1972, no. 27, as Ludovico
WAG1995.353

The sheet of figure studies is typical of the fine studies from life produced by the Carracci between 1585 and 1590 when they avidly drew studio models, Bolognese street scenes and each other as a means of study and for fun. As the family's early biographer Malvasia reported, the two brothers Agostino and Annibale and their cousin Ludovico drew continuously, bread in one hand, chalk or charcoal in the other.[1] The main figure on the recto is a fine example of just such a study from life. The distinctive plumed hat worn by the figure as he studiously reads a book, his finger carefully underlining each word, also appears on the military guard in Annibale's *Butcher's shop*, a genre painting of the

53

1580s now in Christ Church, Oxford. In the same painting the butcher with the weighing-scales was also originally intended to wear a cap similar to the one on the bearded man in the Liverpool study.[2] As with many drawings of this period (see for example the red-chalk *Nude*, exh. cat. 15), when the Carracci collaborated closely there is confusion as to the author of the drawing. Since at least the eighteenth century it has been attributed to Ludovico but, as Babette Bohn has pointed out, there are elements of the studies that fit better with Agostino's graphic style than with Ludovico's.[3] Neither is the combination of black chalk with slight touches of red chalk to heighten the cheeks, lips and earlobes of both young men's faces typical of Ludovico, who favoured working entirely in one chalk colour at a time, but it does appear in portraits attributed to Agostino in the Royal Collection and a possible *Self-*

portrait in the Woodner Collection.[4] Other informal portraits attributed to Agostino in the Royal Collection suggest that he seems to have executed a whole series of black- or red-chalk drawings of young men wearing the same type of hat as worn by the bearded young man in the Liverpool drawing.[5] However, Agostino's portraits all display his characteristic parallel hatched lines to model the face and hair rather than the tonal smudging of chalk especially noticeable on the hair and beard of the Liverpool figures.

Although there was a particular devotion to St Dominic in Bologna, the site of his tomb, no painting by or engraving after Ludovico is known for the devotional composition on the reverse of the sheet of life studies. But the central pose of the clinging Christ Child and the Virgin gently dropping rosary beads into St Dominic's palm appears to have been transferred and

reversed from that in a small devotional painting by Ludovico of *St Dominic receiving the Rosary from the Virgin* in the Bologna Pinacoteca. The heavy stylus indentations visible around the finalized pose of the Virgin and Child suggest that this central image at least was transferred to another sheet for reuse in some form. The Virgin appears squeezed in between the figures of St Dominic and his female companion, drawn in freehand. Also faintly sketched freehand is an alternative position for the Virgin's head, inclining towards St Dominic and to the left of its present placement, and outlined schematically in the top corners are what seem to be cherubs' heads. If this black-chalk study is by Ludovico it should date to after 1590 when he switched from using exclusively red chalk for his altarpiece studies.

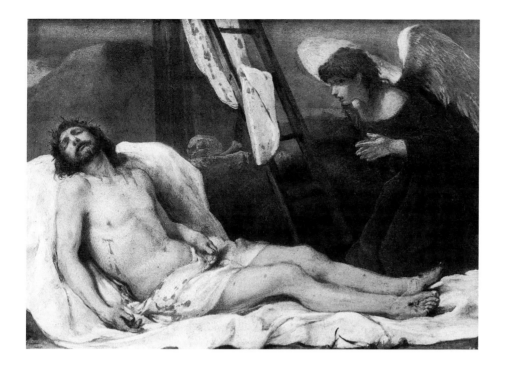

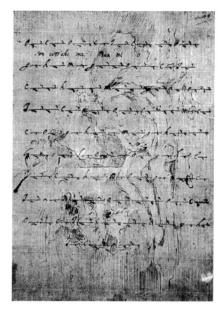

Fig. 18 Verso of cat. 17 showing acrostic poem

Fig. 17 Andrea di Lione, *Angel adoring the dead Christ*, Aix-en-Provence, Musée Granet

17 GIOVANNI BENEDETTO CASTIGLIONE
Genoa 1609–1664 Mantua
A kneeling angel mourning the dead Christ

175 × 245 mm, pen and brown ink
Unidentified watermark on the paper
PROVENANCE Comte de Saint-Morys (?); Roscoe sale, 1816, as part of lot 147, attributed to Valerio Castelli, bt. Slater 14*s.* (along with WAG1995.202 and .198; see Appendix, Merano and attrib. Castiglione); C.R. Blundell, as G.B. Paggi, valued with two others at 12*s.* in 1841
LITERATURE M. Newcome, 'Castiglione in the 1630s', *Nuovi Studi: Rivista di arte antica e moderna*, no. 2, 1997, pp. 59–66, fig. 78
WAG1995.197

The drawing is related to a small painting on copper in the Musée Granet, Aix-en-Provence, which has been attributed to the Neapolitan artist Andrea di Lione (1610–1685) [fig. 17].[2] Lione has removed the tomb behind the angel and replaced it with a ladder leaning against the Cross and draped with a bloodied shroud, but otherwise he has remained relatively faithful both to the composition and to the intense emotional mood of the sketch. The devotional theme of an angel contemplating the death of Christ was particularly Castiglionesque. Although the painting may be by Lione, the spirited sketch shows many traits typical of Castiglione's graphic style of the 1630s, particularly the slashing parallel lines silhouetting the figures, outlined by trembling contours, and defined by small, nervous, dot and dash penstrokes. The style is particularly close to that found on two other drawings by him of the 1630s.[3] The drawing was probably executed during Castiglione's stay in Naples from 1635 to perhaps around 1639, when the two artists are known to have shared compositions and Lione was inspired to paint landscapes in the manner of the Genoese artist.[4] The Aix painting, which is very Castiglionesque in its colouring and technique, is thought to have been painted while Lione was working at the Buen Retiro Palace in Madrid during the 1640s.[5] Castiglione had inherited from his Genoese master Paggi, with whom he spent his formative years, the practice of using both sides of the paper. The reverse of the Liverpool drawing shows ten lines of a coded text in the form of an acrostic puzzle, with the first letter of every word provided, the rest grouped in dots and dashes above and below a line [fig. 18]. The first few words have been translated underneath into Italian: *sono ai me Ben mi o* (I am alas …?). A similar nine-line stanza is found on a 1630s drawing of a *Landscape with sheep by a lake* in the Suida-Manning collection, New York.[6] We know from portraits of poets that Castiglione etched in Rome and Genoa at the end of the 1630s and early in the 1640s that he was associated with literary circles, but whether Castiglione composed poetry is not known.

18 GIUSEPPE CESARI
(Il Cavaliere d'Arpino)
Rome 1568–1640 Rome
Nude striding male figure seen from behind

245 × 140 mm, red chalk, upper corners cut
Inscribed in ink on drawing *Josephino*, and
on mount *Gioseppe d'Arpino*
PROVENANCE Benjamin West (L419);
C.R. Blundell, valued at 12*s*. in 1841
WAG1995.270

Although this handsome red-chalk study
has been drawn from life to show a young
man striding away from the viewer, it may
have been used to compose the frescoed
female figure of the goddess *Venus as the
personification of sunset*, painted on one of
the spandrels of the Loggia Orsini in the
Palazzo Sodalizio Piceni in via di Parione,
Rome, which Cesari was commissioned to
decorate in 1593.[1] The stance adopted by
the male model is close to that in a black-
chalk preparatory drawing of *Venus* made
for the fresco and now in Stockholm
[fig. 19].[2] In the strict moral climate of
Counter-Reformation Rome it would not
have been considered decent for a male
painter to study a naked female model,
particularly a painter like Cesari who was
Pope Clement VIII's favoured artist in the
mid 1590s. It would appear, therefore, that
Cesari drew the male model in a specific
pose, holding what looks like a ribbon,
which he then transferred to the female
figure holding a swirling length of drapery.
The theme of the Loggia Orsini ceiling
decorations was the harmony of nature and
its mythological representations under the
sign of love. It had originally been intended
to celebrate the marriage of Virgilio Orsini
and Flavia Peretti in 1589, but was not
completed until 1594–95. Its central scene
was the crowning of Love by the goddesses
Venus and Juno whilst in the triangular
spandrels between the loggia's arches were
painted four goddesses of light, including a
full frontal view of Juno as dawn and a
back view of Venus as sunset.[3]

The drawing's soft, sensuous shading of
the male torso's muscles and the sketchy
hatching around his silhouette have much
in common with another red-chalk study
(of almost exactly the same width,
142 mm) of another standing male nude
seen from behind, now in the Uffizi,
Florence.[4] The Uffizi drawing is a study for
one of the figures framing one of the

Fig. 19 Cesari, *Rear view of a female nude*, Stockholm, Nationalmuseum

frescos, datable to early 1596, in the Salone of the Palazzo dei Conservatori on the Capitol in Rome. The man's pose in the Liverpool drawing, with his arms outstretched in front of him and his left leg striding out, is also seen reversed, with right leg in front of left, in the half-naked soldier striding over a dead horse's head to attack a horseman with a sword in the foreground of another fresco in the large Sala degli Orazi e Curiazi, *The Battle of Tullus Hostilius against the Veienti and Fidenati*, commissioned in 1595–96.[5] It is possible, therefore, that the Liverpool drawing, having been used as the basis for a female figure frescoed in 1594–95, could have been reused in an adapted form for a man in Cesari's next project. The faint outline of an adjusted, upright, left leg visible on the paper suggests that the study could have been used for more than one pose.

19 GIUSEPPE CESARI
A Prophet and an angel

415 × 275 mm, black and red chalk
Inscribed in ink twice on a blue (Mariette?) mount lower left corner and in centre *J d'Arpino*; with an old semi-obliterated pencil attribution to *Pellegrino Tibaldi*
PROVENANCE Roscoe sale, 1816, possibly lot 349, as Tibaldi, "One, St John the Evangelist; a different design [from lot 348, also Tibaldi]. In black and red chalk; highly finished./ 16½h. 11½w.", bt. W. Ford; C.R. Blundell, as Tibaldi, valued at £1. 4s. in 1841
EXHIBITIONS Edinburgh 1972, no. 37, as *St Matthew*; Il Cavaliere d'Arpino, by H. Röttgen, Rome, Palazzo Venezia, 1973, no. 137
WAG1995.378

This impressive drawing is a rejected study for one of the four Prophets in the pendentives under the dome of the Cappella Paolina in Santa Maria Maggiore, Rome, which was decorated between 1610 and 1612 under Cesari's direction [fig. 20]. Cesari himself painted the dome, pendentives and altar lunette. In the completed fresco the Prophet, like his three other companions, holds a swirling scroll in place of the inscribed stone tablet to which he points in the Liverpool drawing.[1] It is a fine example of Cesari's transitional style of around 1610, combining as it does a controlled use of parallel and cross-hatched lines to give form and three-dimensionality to the Prophet's face and arms with the loose undulating line of his later manner for the angel. The drawing's size and style emphasize the subject's mood of calm dignity and monumentality. The iconography of the chapel, devised by Pope Paul V himself, was militantly Counter-Reformation in tone. The Prophets chosen were those who illustrated the triumph of the Christian faith over that of the East through the intervention of the Virgin Mary.[2]

The important papal commission to decorate the Cappella Paolina in Santa Maria Maggiore, the immense burial chapel for Clement VIII (1592–1605) and Paul V (1605–21), came only three years after the nadir of Cesari's career as papal artist. Any artist closely associated with one pope, as Cesari was with Clement VIII, was at risk when the pope's death led to a change of regime. Cesari's career came to a more dramatic halt than most when in 1607 the nephew of the new Pope Paul V, Cardinal Scipione Borghese, used the pretext of finding a collection of guns in Cesari's house to seize the artist's collection of over one hundred paintings (which still hang in the Cardinal's villa, the Borghese Gallery) and throw him in prison.[3] He resurrected his career by accepting the Borghese's command to superintend the decoration of the funerary chapel in Santa Maria Maggiore.

Fig. 20 Cesari, dome of Cappella Paolina, Santa Maria Maggiore, Rome

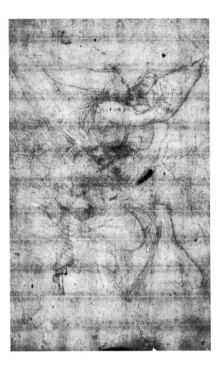

Fig. 21 Verso of exh. cat. 20, photograph taken under transmitted light

20 GIUSEPPE CESARI

An allegorical figure: a young woman blowing a trumpet

325 × 203 mm, red chalk
Watermark on mount card: fleur-de-lys within coat of arms and initials LVG below, countermarked Villandry, close to Heawood 1829 (Holland, 1743)[1]
Inscribed in pencil on drawing *C. d.Arpino*, and in ink on mount *Arpino*
PROVENANCE Benjamin West (L419); C.R. Blundell, valued at 12s. in 1841
WAG1995.310

The plump-cheeked female figure and the long, flowing, continuous line of this drawing are stylistically similar to a couple of Cesari's late red-chalk drawings datable to about 1630, intended, but not used, for *The Rape of the Sabine women* in the Salone of the Palazzo dei Conservatori on the Capitol in Rome.[2] Professor Röttgen has suggested that the sketch might have been an idea for one of the allegorical figures, perhaps Fame blowing her trumpet, who people the simulated 'frames' painted around the frescos in the Palazzo.[3] The suggestion is made even more plausible by the faintly sketched outlines of other figures and motifs: a shadowed, upturned face of what might be a satyr or bearded man

behind Fame, and the odd anchor-like or half-moon shape upon which her foot rests at the bottom of the composition. Cesari obviously changed his mind as to the positioning of the figure and a number of these *pentimenti* can be seen under the rapidly sketched shading. Fame's drapery originally floated in front of her, the position of the trumpet was lower or a second musician may have been intended, whose curved back can be made out behind Fame's. Her elegant, sinuous pose shows Cesari's admiration for the work of Raphael, whilst the female figure on the reverse of the sheet (seen in a photograph taken under transmitted light; fig. 21), whose head is turned sharply to the left, is modelled more on Michelangelo's *Sibyls* from the Sistine Chapel. The Palazzo dei Conservatori, Rome's city hall, was one of Cesari's most important commissions, given to him when he was at the height of his popularity in the late 1590s. By the time he came to finish the series of multiple scenes from Rome's history in the 1630s, his graceful, somewhat mannered style of flowing line but statuesque form, so attractively shown in this drawing, had fallen out of fashion with fellow artists and papal patrons alike, in favour of the Baroque dynamism of painters such as Pietro da Cortona.

(Antonio Allegri)

Correggio 1489?–1534 Correggio

St John the Baptist

190 × 156 mm, red chalk on pink prepared
paper squared up in red chalk
Possibly inscribed in ink on the verso
Inscribed in ink on corner of mount in
monogram *.A.*; in centre of mount
Correggio; in pencil on mount lower right
corner *genuine Waag* (?); on reverse of
mount in ink *J.D.* (or *S.O.?*) *L.74*; on
reverse in pencil, lower right corner
£2.2.0/3; and on opposite side *A. Correggio*;
inscribed on reverse in centre in pencil *A
study for the figure of St John/in the fresco of
the Incoronation of the Virgin formerly/in the
apse of S. Giovanni Evangelista/at Parma,
painted 1522/23/ (destroyed 1586)*
PROVENANCE Benjamin West (without
collector's stamp; inscribed in pencil on
mount *West Lombard*), possibly one of "six
studies in red chalk by Correggio",
Christie's, 9 June 1820, lot 57;
C.R. Blundell
EXHIBITIONS Edinburgh 1969, no. 29;
NACF 1997
LITERATURE A.E. Popham, *Correggio's
Drawings*, London 1957, p. 46, cat. 27;
M. Di Giampaolo and A. Muzzio,
Correggio: I disegni, Turin 1988, cat. 36
WAG1995.325

This is the only known study by Correggio
for the figure of St John the Baptist in the
fresco which formerly decorated the apse
of the Benedictine abbey of San Giovanni
Evangelista in Parma.[1] The apse was part
of a major decorative campaign undertaken
by Correggio from 1520 onwards in the
church and cloisters of one of Parma's
newest and finest Renaissance buildings.
By 1525 he had completed frescos in the
dome, apse, choir and nave vaults,
probably working on the apse between
1522 and 1524. The original apse fresco
represented *The Coronation of the Virgin*,
flanked on the left by St John the
Evangelist and St Benedict and on the right
by the Benedictine monk St Maurus and St
John the Baptist.[2] The theme had a
particular significance in Parma, of which
the principal patron saint was the Virgin,
whose coronation adorned the town seal.
The Baptist's emphatic pointing gesture
highlights the saint's role as both witness to
the mystical event and intercessor for the
abbey's congregation, at whom he gazes.

22 DOMENICHINO
(Domenico Zampieri)
Bologna 1581–1641 Naples
Head of a young woman inclined to the left
Verso: *Head of a woman looking up to the right*

263 × 190 mm, recto: black chalk heightened with white on blue paper; verso: black chalk
Inscribed on old mount in ink *Domenichino*; and in pencil in Waagen's handwriting *genuine Waagen*
PROVENANCE John Barnard, no. 225 (L1419); inscribed on wash border on both sides *J:B*, and on back of mount in ink *J:B: Nº 225/10½ by 7½* B. West (L419); possibly one of "Five studies of heads in black chalk by Domenichino", Christie's, 9 June 1820, lot 54; C.R. Blundell
EXHIBITIONS Edinburgh 1972, no. 41
LITERATURE R.E. Spear, *Domenichino*, New Haven and London 1982, I, cats. 59, 66, p. 75, fig. 233
WAG1995.340

The superbly limpid chalk outlines of female faces on this double-sided drawing are studies for two paintings executed by Domenichino between 1617 and 1621. On the recto is the only known study for his *Madonna della Rosa* [fig. 22], painted in 1618–19 for Guido Nolfi, a leading citizen of Fano who hired Domenichino for a lucrative commission to fresco his family chapel, dedicated to the Virgin Mary, in Fano Cathedral during the artist's stay in this Adriatic town south of Rimini.[1] According to Domenichino's biographer, Giambattista Passeri, Nolfi treated the artist with so much courtesy, lodging him in his own house, that he "always said he had been in paradise the entire time he stayed at Fano", and that his treatment showed in the quality of his work.[2] The altarpiece in the Nolfi family chapel housed an old, venerated image of the Virgin, which may have inspired Domenichino to paint his iconic devotional picture of the Virgin and Child – offering roses in reference to Christ's future crown of thorns, with the painted Latin inscription below, 'You o happy Christ lavish pleasant roses on man, ungrateful man, alas, will give back to you thorns'. The finished picture was obviously close to Nolfi's heart for it was specifically mentioned in his will

and its sale forbidden. In about 1630 Domenichino began painting a variant copy for the Carmelite Church of Santa Maria Vittoria in Rome, which was finished off by an assistant.[3]

The verso of the sheet has what appears to be a study for the Magdalene's head in a later altarpiece by Domenichino, the *Mary Magdalene in glory* of about 1620, although the drawing differs from the painting. In the drawing her hair does not stream behind her as she rises heavenwards but is tied up in a curled plait, nor does the drapery study on the paper's edge relate to

the low-cut bodice of the Magdalene's brocaded dress.[4] It does, however, seem to relate to the shoulder of a dress of the same brocaded fabric worn by one of the girls seen embracing in the centre of the lower half of the *Madonna del Rosario*, which Domenichino painted for the Ratta family chapel in San Giovanni in Monte in Bologna over an extensive period between 1617 and 1622/25.[5] The girl on the left also shares the Magdalene's slightly plump features, open mouth and ecstatic, upturned eyes. Presumably Domenichino was working on both paintings at the same

Fig. 22 Domenichino, *The Madonna della Rosa*, Poznán, Museum Narodowe

time, using the same studio accessory as dress fabric and the same sheet of paper to resolve figure and drapery problems. According to the biographer Malvasia, the two embracing girls were modelled on Domenichino's beautiful sister-in-law.[6] Perhaps that is why the study on the verso of the Liverpool sheet seems to have a stronger sense of flesh-and-blood naturalism, as if it has been drawn from life, compared to the abstract geometric purity of the beautiful but emotionally cool face of the *Madonna della Rosa* on the other side.

Exh. cat. 22 verso

23 DOMENICHINO
Portrait of a young girl

217 × 160 mm, black chalk heightened with white on grey-buff laid paper damaged by water-staining
Inscribed on old mount below frame of double red lines *Domenichino Pittore*; in pencil on verso *Z*
PROVENANCE William Young Ottley (his mount); Roscoe sale, 1816, part of lot 386, "Two, of Heads on one sheet, one of them a Child; black chalk on brown paper. From the same collection [Ottley's]", bt. Slater 9*s*. 6*d*.; C.R. Blundell, valued at 8*s*. in 1841
EXHIBITION Edinburgh 1972, no. 45
WAG1995.77

The rough, grey-brown paper on which this attractive and tender portrait has been drawn is typical of the paper Domenichino used in the 1630s.[1] It was characteristic of Domenichino to use different coloured chalks and papers at different times in his career and for different types of studies: black chalk heightened with white on smooth blue paper for narrative compositions in his youth (see exh. cat. 22) and later black chalk on a grey-buff paper for what would appear to be informal portraits or sketches of servants. In the Liverpool portrait the fibrous paper retains the grainy chalk, helping Domenichino to build up the delicate structure of the girl's face through soft parallel strokes of evenly applied medium. Many of the more than four hundred drawings at Windsor Castle which Domenichino produced for his work in Naples during the 1630s are on sheets of a similar grey tone and of varying degrees of coarseness.[2] Domenichino had moved to Naples in 1631 to decorate the Treasury Chapel of San Gennaro, the Cathedral, but in the summer of 1634 he fled the city to escape both the pressures of the extensive commission for six altarpieces and a major fresco scheme and the aggressive harassment of local artists. According to his close friend and biographer Passeri, it was during the three months he stayed at Frascati, north of Rome, on the estate of his patron Cardinal Ippolito Aldobrandini that he took to sketching portraits and caricatures (see exh. cat. 24) of friends and family as a form of physical and mental relaxation.[3] His only daughter and heir Maria Camilla, on whom he doted, even more so after the death of his two sons

aged four and five in the 1620s, was probably too old in 1634 to have been the child portrayed, as she was born *ca.* 1623 and was of marriageable age in 1641[4] – although we know from another biographer, Malvasia, that he was so captivated by his child's features that he incorporated them into a number of his works.[5] This touching portrait might, however, be the child of another relative or friend or it could relate to another event described by Passeri. During his summer at Frascati, Domenichino was visited by his patrons and supporters the Aldobrandini family, the Cardinal, his princely brothers and their families, who issued an informal commission for a group portrait of themselves to include two little children. Domenichino began the painting but had to leave it unfinished when one of the princes fell ill and the family returned to Rome.[6] It is tempting to suggest that this delightful yet reticent portrait of a pensive young girl might be one of the portrait drawings Domenichino executed to fulfil his patron's informal commission.

24 ATTRIBUTED TO DOMENICHINO
A caricature study of a face

206 × 165 mm, black chalk heightened with
white on very coarse buff woven paper
Watermark on original tissue-paper cover
Watt & Co Patent Copying
Inscribed anonymously on mount in pencil
not genuine; on reverse in hard pencil *Z*
PROVENANCE William Young Ottley
(formerly on his mount inscribed in ink
below a double red line *Il Domenichino Pitt.
Bolognese*); Roscoe sale, 1816, part of lot
386, "Two, of Heads on one sheet, one of
them a Child, black chalk on brown paper.
From the same collection [Ottley's]", on
same mount as Domenichino's *Portrait of a
young girl* (cat. 23), bt. Slater 9s. 6d.;
C.R. Blundell, valued at 8s. in 1841
WAG1995.298

Although the Carracci family, with whom
Domenichino trained, delighted in
sketching caricatures, there are very few
such drawings known by Domenichino and
none in black chalk. But as Richard Spear
has pointed out, the Liverpool caricature is
not unlike, though probably later than, the
portrait drawing that Domenichino
executed in black chalk of the
Aldobrandini's dwarf as a preparatory
study for his frescoed image painted as a
practical joke in 1616–18 on the walls of
their villa at Frascati.[1] We know that during
a later stay at Frascati in July–September
1634, when he was recovering from his
troubled period in Naples, Domenichino
drew several caricatures of friends and
Aldobrandini servants in order to cheer
himself up. One such was the pen-and-ink
sketch of the *Theologian of the Aldobrandini
household*, now at Chatsworth, Derbyshire.[2]
Passeri, who was one of the friends staying
with Domenichino in the villa Belvedere on
the Aldobrandini estate, described how the
artist would sometimes retire to his room
after dinner and secretly draw caricatures
of all those staying at the villa, his resultant
laughter at his efforts so loud that it would
bring neighbouring guests running to his
room. As well as sketching a caricature of
Passeri with guitar in hand, Domenichino
also drew two of the servants, one who was
crippled by gout, and his assistant who,
according to Passeri, "was a ridiculous
fellow".[3] The distorted and swollen face of
the Liverpool drawing might possibly
represent the former servant. The

conditions under which he drew these
ephemeral sketches might account for the
very coarse, creased paper on which the
Liverpool caricature has been sketched.
According to Passeri the caricatures were
collected by Giovan Pietro Bellori. The
caricatured face was mounted underneath
another drawing – the *Portrait of a young
girl* (exh. cat. 23; possibly also drawn at
Frascati), by the connoisseur–collector
William Young Ottley, who attributed both
drawings to Domenichino.

25 PAOLO FARINATI
Verona 1524–1606 Verona
*Study for a decorated spandrel:
Agriculture*

273 × 350 mm, pen and brown ink over
black chalk with brown wash heightened
with white (slightly oxidized) on blue
paper, with a faint black-chalk outline
sketch of torso on lower right
Inscribed in ink on drawing *Paul Farinati*
PROVENANCE W.Y. Ottley, sold 16
June 1814, lot 521;[1] Roscoe sale, 1816, lot
279, attributed to Paolo Farinato (*sic*)
"Ceres with implements of Agriculture.
Ditto [bistre on blue paper]/ CAPITAL/
11h 14w", bt. William Ford 9s. 6d.;[2]
C.R. Blundell, valued at 5s. in 1841

EXHIBITION Venice 1980, no. 37, as
Ceres
LITERATURE Hélène Sueur, 'Dessins
préparatoires aux fresques de la région de
Vérone dans la collection du Louvre', *La
Revue du Louvre*, I, 1989, p. 36, as *Peace*
WAG1995.302

Agriculture is a typically bold, wash *modello*
for the figure frescoed on a spandrel of the
arcaded ground-floor loggia of the former
Palazzo Murari (now the Istituto d'Arte,
'N. Nani') in via San Nazaro, Verona.[3]
Farinati's biographer, Ridolfi, described an
all-round artist, a sculptor, engraver and
military architect as well as a fresco-painter
and prolific draughtsman, and the Murari
palace was just one of the many projects
executed by Farinati, Verona's leading
artist once his more celebrated friend and

compatriot Paolo Veronese had left for
Venice in 1553.[4] The Murari loggia's
frescos, open to the atmosphere, have all
but faded away, although a photograph
taken in 1968 showed the remains of
Agriculture were still just visible.[5] But the
loggia scheme can be reconstructed and the
place of *Agriculture* located within it with
the help of an early nineteenth-century
description and detailed drawings made in
1854 before the frescos disappeared
[fig. 23].[6] On the spandrels between the
loggia's five arches, the frescos depicted
sixteen satyrs and satyresses, who
accompanied scenes from the love of
Venus and Adonis at either end of the
loggia, and above whom were painted four
allegorical figures in monochrome
representing *Agriculture*, *Navigation*, *Peace*
and *War*. Although there are other *modelli*

for the commission in Paris, Weimar and
Chicago, the Liverpool study is the only
one known for any of the allegorical
figures.[7] The scheme was commissioned by
Count Giovanni Murari when Farinati was
at the height of his popularity and
showered with projects, but with the help
of his two sons, Orazio and Giambattista,
who would have executed the drawn
modelli and cartoons provided by their
father, he had finished the loggia by April
1588.[8] With intense vivacious wash and
emphatic highlights on coloured paper the
Liverpool study displays Farinati's
characteristic *chiaroscuro* style, and
demonstrates his gifts as a draughtsman in
wash.

Fig. 23 Luciano Mozzetto and Luigi Marai, *Farinati's Palazzo Murari mural*, including *Agriculture*, Verona, Castelvecchio

Fig. 25 Verso of exh cat. 26

Fig. 24 Raphael, *Sibyls*, Chigi Chapel, Santa Maria della Pace, Rome

Fig. 26 Figino, *Studies for the Agony in the Garden*, pen and ink, Royal Collections (RL 6968)

26 GIOVAN AMBROGIO FIGINO
Milan 1548–1608 Milan

A sibyl and two winged putti

276 × 210 mm, fine black chalk over leadpoint heightened with white on blue paper

Watermark on paper: small fleur-de-lys (partially visible)

Inscribed in ink on drawing twice *figino*, and on mount *(Ambrogio Figino)*; in pencil on mount *After one of the Sibyls of Raphael*; on back in pencil (?), lower left corner, *63; 29/8*

PROVENANCE   C.R. Blundell, valued at 16*s.* in 1841

LITERATURE   A. Perissa Torrini, *Galleria dell'Accademia di Venezia: disegni del Figino*, Milan 1987 (*Catalogo dei disegni antichi* IV), Appendix, p. 18, fig. 55, as from the 'Cultworth' collection WAG1995.294

This is a typically accomplished copy by Figino after Raphael's *Sibyl of the Resurrection*, frescoed *ca.* 1513–14 on the left side of the Chigi Chapel in Santa Maria della Pace, Rome [fig. 24]. The subtlety of the fine surface detail would suggest that it was not drawn from a print but from the fresco itself during Figino's stay in Rome, which is thought to have occurred *ca.* 1576–77, when he diligently made copies after antique and contemporary sculpture and the sculpturally inspired painting of Michelangelo's Sistine Chapel.[1] Figino was one of Milan's most important artists during the second half of the sixteenth century but he is celebrated more as a prolific draughtsman, producing some 430 sheets of drawings, of which 118 are in the Royal Library at Windsor. They fall into two different types: first, large figure studies often copied from paintings or sculpture, usually on blue paper in black chalk, sometimes heightened with white; secondly, sheets, possibly from a notebook, covered on both sides with masses of extremely lively miniature sketches of figures, animals and compositions, usually in pen and ink, sometimes over red chalk. An example of one such thumbnail sketch, but in black chalk, of a draped woman seen from behind, was discovered on the back of the *Sibyl* during conservation [fig. 25].[2] It might simply be thought that the Liverpool Sibyl is only an extremely skilful and beautiful example of a copy-drawing, part

of Figino's artistic education in which he learned to understand form through the eyes of a more celebrated artist, were it not for the fact that the only other occasion that the Sibyl reappears in Figino's mass of graphic work is on two sheets, both in the Royal Collection, crowded with preparatory sketches documenting the creation of two of the paintings Figino produced for Milanese churches. One of the sheets has an ink sketch of the Sibyl on the left edge of the recto surrounded by different trial runs for the *Agony in the Garden*, painted by Figino *ca.* 1586 for the church of Santa Maria Passione in Milan [fig. 26].[3] Its verso is covered with studies

for the *St Matthew and the angel*, itself inspired by the figure of one of Raphael's *Prophets* in the Chigi Chapel, and also painted *ca.* 1586 for San Raffaele, Milan.[4] It is noticeable that Figino has reproduced the Sibyl's commanding gesture, her arm raised heavenwards, on the figure of the advancing angel in the right-hand corner of the same sheet. Having originally drawn the Sibyl as a model to be studied and examined in depth, Figino has, almost a decade later, used it to spark his imagination and launch himself into a series of experimental variations on a theme, resulting in a finished painting.

27 ATTRIBUTED TO THE WORKSHOP OF DOMENICO FONTANA

Lugano 1543–1607 Naples
Design for a papal tomb

476 × 367 mm, pen and brown ink and brown wash with stylus indentations along all the columns and two horizontal creases as if once folded into a smaller album Watermark on tissue paper of old 'Roscoe' mount J Watts & Co Patent Copying Paper Inscribed in ink on back *in Coranatione*; in pencil *Temporary facade of the Church of S. Maria del Fiori/at Florence, designed and executed by Jacopo/Sansovino …? Andrea del sarto, on the arrival/of Leo X in Florence in 1515. Life of Leo X vol.3 p.74/8° Edn*; on old mount *Sansovino Flor*
PROVENANCE John Talman (L2462); Roscoe sale, 1816, part of lot 95, as Sansovino, "a Superb Design for the temporary Facade of a Public Building with statues, bas reliefs, and historical designs, &c.; on occasion of a public rejoicing at Florence. Pen and bistre. Very fine.", bt. W. Ford £1. (along with WAG1995.271, see Appendix, attrib. Marco Marchetti da Faenza); C.R. Blundell, as Sansovino, valued with .271 at 16s. in 1841
WAG1995.272

It was A.E. Popham who first pointed out the resemblance of this impressive design to a Roman monument, the papal tombs in the Sistine and Pauline Chapels of the church of Santa Maria Maggiore, rather than the Florentine Cathedral and the entry into Florence of the Medici Pope Leo X in 1515 with which William Roscoe had wishfully associated it.[1] The monumental elevation seems most closely related to the Sistine Chapel in Santa Maria Maggiore, where a series of steps at the altar end leads up to a central blind arch under which there is an inscribed tablet, and a further set of steps surrounds the entrance to the crypt below. The Sistine Chapel was designed for Pope Sixtus V (1585–90) by his architect Domenico Fontana in order to house the tombs of himself and his papal predecessor Pius V (1566–72), and work had begun on it by 1585.[2] Changes were made at every stage in its construction and tombs were not introduced into the plans until July 1586. The tombs faced each other across the chapel; their design was influenced by the triumphal arches of

ancient Rome and other more temporary structures erected on the elections of popes, but they were executed in a novel way, in a riot of multi-coloured marbles which set off the central white-marble papal figures and the low-relief narrative panels illustrating key events in the popes' careers, with Pius V's tomb representing the papacy at war and Sixtus V's the papacy in peacetime, granting justice and charity.[3] However, the Liverpool design does not reproduce the finished tombs of either Sixtus or Pius. It is instead a variant on them, its panels illustrating different events and the structure embellished with many more free-standing sculpted figures at all levels of the elevation than the caryatids found only on the upper storey of the executed monuments. The increase in sculpture might help identify the anonymous author of the design. In the Sistine Chapel Fontana followed his usual practice of providing the structural design and contracting out the production of the sculpture, as shown by the discovery of a transport bill for the marble statues and panels.[4] Pius V's statue, located in the central niche, was carved by the elderly and relatively unknown Leonardo Sormani (*fl.* Rome 1551–*ca.* 1589) to crown a long career as a restorer of antiquities; as a sculptor he was primarily influenced by Jacopo Sansovino. In the Victoria and Albert Museum there is another ambitious unexecuted design for a papal tomb, probably that of Pius IV (died 1565), tentatively attributed to Leonardo Sormani on the basis of a nineteenth-century inscription, which shows the same distinctive use of 'quotation marks' to indicate the papal inscription and a similar handling of wash on spindly figures as is found on the Liverpool drawing.[5] Sormani based his Pius IV scheme on an aborted project by Guglielmo della Porta for Pope Paul III's tomb.[6] It is indeed possible that the grand Liverpool elevation was produced by Sormani, perhaps as an ambitious trial design for Pius V's tomb which remained unexecuted when Fontana's was preferred by Sixtus V.

28 GIOVANNI BATTISTA FRANCO

Venice *ca.* 1510–1561 Venice
Sheet of figure studies

188 × 267 mm, pen and brown ink
Inscribed in pencil along mount *Battista Franco; M116/Wz 316*
PROVENANCE Sir Joshua Reynolds (L2364); Roscoe sale, 1816, part of lot 283, as Battista Franco, bt. Slater 9s. (with Franco's *Apollo and the Muses*, cat. 29); C.R. Blundell, valued together at 6s. in 1841
WAG1995.249

This sheet of sketches shows much of the "spirit, fire, freedom and delicacy" for which Jonathan Richardson, the painter, art commentator and collector, commended Franco in his *An Essay on the Theory of Painting.*[1] It is probably an early attempt by Franco to work out the poses of soldiers, some still slumped asleep, others reacting in amazement to the Resurrection of Christ. The most fully conceived figure is the helmeted guard sprawled full length on his shield; all the other bodies are only summarily realised in a variety of contorted postures noted with Franco's customary scrolling penwork. Franco worked on the subject from the mid 1540s to his death in Venice in 1561, when he left unfinished a commission from Patriarch Giovanni Grimani for his chapel in San Francesco della Vigna which included a *Resurrection.*[2] However, the drawing probably does not relate to the Grimani fresco, which shows no helmeted soldiers, and its graphic style suggests that it probably dates to *ca.* 1545–51 when Franco was in Urbino and Rome.[3] During this period Franco treated the theme at least four times in painted and printed forms. Whilst working on the vast scheme to fresco the choir at Urbino Cathedral (destroyed with the church's collapse in 1789) he executed an etching of the subject, for which there is an exact study in reverse in Edinburgh, and he produced another etching based on a small painting in his series on the *Life of Christ* commissioned for Osimo Cathedral in 1547.[4] In 1549–50 Franco moved to Rome, where he painted the subject in the Chapel of St Peter Martyr in Santa Maria sopra Minerva, for which there is a study in the Louvre (inv. 4963). A year later, Guidobaldo II della Rovere, Duke of Urbino, commissioned a *Resurrection* as

part of a set of five paintings for the
sacristy of Urbino Cathedral (now in the
Urbino Diocesan Museum). None of the
soldiers on the Liverpool sheet corresponds
exactly with the figures in any of these
compositions, although they adopt similar
crouching and twisted poses. The main
helmeted figure in the drawing appears in
the Urbino altarpiece as if swivelled
through 45° to the left. The Liverpool
figures can best be seen as a group of
inventive doodles worked around the theme
of the soldiers' reactions to Christ's sudden
resurrection.

    Franco made his name as a
draughtsman. He came late to painting,
pressed into service to produce temporary
decorations for the triumphal entry to
Rome by Charles V in April 1536, and
never felt at ease with it, especially on a
large scale, as was acknowledged by his
main patron, Guidobaldo II della Rovere,
and by his friend Giorgio Vasari.[5]
Nevertheless his great talent for drawing
and flair for decorative design are evident
in this typically spirited sheet of delicate
sketches. It was probably his swirling
calligraphic lines and almost abstract
patterning which attracted the eye of the
artist Sir Joshua Reynolds, who once
owned the Liverpool sheet.

29 GIOVANNI BATTISTA FRANCO

Apollo and the Muses on Parnassus with two river-gods

111 × 107 mm (circle 110 × 106 mm), pen and brown ink and wash over black chalk within an inscribed circle clipped at one side

Inscribed in ink on mount *Battista Franco*; on back in ink *B/N.20/ Battista Franco, called il Semolei/was a Venetian, & studied Michelangelo/ lived in Florence, Rome & France, died 1561*; '*Battista Franco*' in two different hands; collector's stamp in black ink *HN*; in chalk lower left corner *N Hickman* or *V Huikman* (?; unidentified in Lugt)

PROVENANCE Nicola Francesco Haym (L1971)?; George John, 2nd Earl Spencer, sold London, Philipe, 10–17 June 1811, lot 313, bt. P[hilipe] 3*s*.; Roscoe sale, 1816, part of lot 283, as Franco, "beautifully designed", bt. Slater 9*s*. (along with cat. 28);[1] C.R. Blundell both valued at 6*s*. in 1841

EXHIBITION Venice 1980, no. 23, as *Orpheus amongst the women of Thrace* (with an identification of *HN* mark for NH of N.F. Haym)

WAG1995.320

The drawing depicts the god Apollo surrounded by his companions the Muses, the nine goddesses of creative inspiration in the arts, eight of whom are shown in pen and ink and the ninth outlined schematically in black chalk on the upper left edge of the group. Several of the Muses are shown pointing towards their favourite, the winged horse Pegasus, whilst in the foreground recline two river-gods representing the springs and fountains over which the Muses presided on Mount Parnassus and from which poured forth artistic inspiration. Another pen-and-ink drawing of the subject (without the addition of wash) places the ninth Muse peering out from the crowded background on the right, but is otherwise a slightly larger exact copy by Franco of the Liverpool composition [fig. 27].[2] Franco's typically lively and light touch of the pen allowed him to make changes up to the last minute before finalizing the result. The circular design has led people to suppose that the drawing must have been one of Franco's designs for a maiolica plate produced between 1545 and 1551, when he was working for Guidobaldo II della Rovere, Duke of Urbino, at the ceramic works of Castel Durante. However, the format and style of the composition are untypical of maiolica designs, being allegorical rather than narrative and lacking the usual arrangement of "figures stretched across the foreground in a frieze-like composition" and a brim around which a separate design is worked.[3] Although the subject of Apollo and the Muses occasionally appears on decorated ceramics it would not seem to be connected with either of the two series on which Franco is known to have worked at Urbino, relating respectively the stories of Troy and of Hercules.[4] In addition, the delicate handling of the light-brown wash applied to the figures, which increases the scene's sense of depth, suggests instead that the drawing may have been intended as a design for a painted roundel, to be seen from below in a decorative scheme for a ceiling. During the last few years of his life Franco worked on several such projects in Venetian palaces and libraries. From 1556 to 1557 he painted three of the ceiling tondi of the Libreria Marciana with circular representations of allegorical figures. None of these depicted Apollo,[5] but as the theme of Apollo and the Muses is so appropriate for a library, it is possible that the design was intended for the Libreria Vecchia, where Franco worked in 1559–60, painting on the lower flight of the staircase eleven panels of gods and allegorical figures and in its antechamber an "Apollo playing the Lyre surrounded by Mercury, Amore, Neptune and Falsehood", none of which have survived the alterations made by Giovanni Grimani in 1577 and the dispersal of works in the following centuries.[6]

Fig. 27 Giovanni Battista Franco, *Apollo and the Muses*, drawing, Snite Museum of Art, University of Notre Dame, Indiana

30 WORKSHOP OF DOMENICO GHIRLANDAIO

Florence 1448/49–1494 Florence

A young man standing profile to the left, draped in cloak and cap

195 × 75 mm, silverpoint heightened with white on pink prepared paper
Inscription: on mount, semi-obliterated, possibly originally reading *Filippino Lippi*; inscribed on back, lower right corner in red ink *Lot 13[0/6?]/4*; and in brown ink *76*
PROVENANCE   Sir Joshua Reynolds (L2364); John Campbell, Duke of Argyll (his coat of arms on mount), sold by T. Philipe, 21–23 May 1798; Roscoe sale, 1816, part of lot 15, as Masaccio, bt. Slater 16s. (along with Appendix, Florentine School, late 15th century, WAG1995.268); C.R. Blundell, valued at 12s. in 1841 WAG1995.82

Metalpoint studies drawn on to paper prepared with a coloured ground and heightened with opaque white bodycolour were common in Florence in the last years of the fifteenth century. They were usually treated as preliminary studies for more detailed drawings for which the artist used the more flexible medium of quill pen and ink – with these he could alter the width and vary the strength of the line by changing the pressure on the nib and the speed with which it moved across the paper.[1] The figure is probably a drapery study from a pattern-book in use in one of the most prolific workshops in late fifteenth-century Florence. The old eighteenth-century (?) attribution on the mount gave the drawing to Filippino Lippi (1457/58–1504), but Bernard Berenson preferred to give it to Davide Ghirlandaio (1452–1525) and it is now attributed to Davide's brother Domenico, in whose workshop Davide was an assistant.[2] Filippino Lippi's interest in the massing of draperies had been inspired by his work in the Brancacci Chapel of the Carmine Church in Florence in the mid 1480s and

his contact there with the celebrated frescos of Masaccio, to whom this drawing was attributed by Roscoe. The focus and rationale of the Liverpool drawing is to study the massing and fall of drapery over a body. Such a drawing could have been copied from by a workshop apprentice, or it might have provided a 'pattern' for a drapery detail in a finished painting or fresco, although the motif would not have been transferred directly but altered or varied when reused. As Ames-Lewis has pointed out, the essence of a drapery 'pattern' study was that it provided a stock design that could be passed down through generations, ensuring that the workshop product was uniform with the master's style and up to standard, whoever of the studio assistants or apprentices used it.[3] The practice also means that it is difficult, if not rather irrelevant, to attribute individual drawings to particular artists. However, there are some distinct differences in the way the two artists, Lippi and Ghirlandaio, handled both the metalpoint and the white heightening, and the poses their figures adopt also allow one to suggest that the Liverpool drawing is more likely to have come from Ghirlandaio's workshop. Lippi's style is characterized by a more forceful metalpoint stroke and a heavier, more vigorous, application of white highlights, especially evident if one compares the Liverpool drawing's fine, light parallel strokes on the drapery and sparing use of white on the face with studies by or attributed to Lippi in Berlin, Chantilly, Paris and Oxford.[4] The Liverpool study seems to be on the same pink prepared paper and show a similar delicate shading as a drawing attributed to Domenico Ghirlandaio of the *Head of an elderly man in profile to right wearing a cap* in the British Museum.[5] In addition the profile pose of the Liverpool figure shows a preoccupation, like other drawings from Ghirlandaio's workshop, with finding a solution to the problem of closing the edges of multi-figured scenes.[6] By the end of the fifteenth century Domenico Ghirlandaio's workshop was the most influential in Florence and through it passed many other artists, including Michelangelo, who was to renounce metalpoint in favour of black chalk.

73

31 LUCA GIORDANO

Naples 1634–1705 Naples

Study of St Mark seated on a cloud from Sant'Andrea della Valle, Rome

569 × 401 mm, red chalk on paper rubbed with red chalk, its corners cut[1]
Inscribed in ink on drawing, lower right corner, *Giordano*; and in top right corner *13*; on back of drawing *d*; and in pencil *2/–*. On old mount Pouncey attribution *after Domenichino* and H. Macandrew (Oct. 74) appended that the Giordano attribution should be taken seriously
PROVENANCE Benjamin West (no collector's stamp; inscribed on mount in pencil *West Neapolitan*); C.R. Blundell (removed from Album for 1984 exhibition)
EXHIBITION *Civiltà del Seicento a Napoli*, Naples, Museo e Gallerie Nazionali di Capodimonte, 1984, II, p. 92, no. 3.37
LITERATURE O. Ferrara and G. Scavizzi, *Luca Giordano*, 2nd edn., Naples 1992, *Disegni* D8
WAG1995.370

This is a copy by Giordano of the figure of *St Mark* which Domenichino had frescoed *ca.* 1625 on to one of the four pendentives under the dome of the church of Sant'Andrea della Valle in Rome [fig. 28]. The impressive study, drawn over a double sheet of a large sketchbook of which the central spine-fold is still visible, is one of a group of copies Giordano produced on his first visit to Rome between 1650 and 1655, when he was still a teenager.[2] He has not copied the fresco completely, leaving out the banner-carrying floating angel and the drapery billowing out behind St Mark's back and inserting a long trailing lion's tail which exists neither in the finished painting nor in the only known drawing by Domenichino for the whole composition, now in Madrid.[3] Giordano arrived in Rome as a follower of the Naples-based Spanish artist Ribera, and yet to be impressed by the works of Pietro da Cortona. As the Liverpool figures show elements of Riberesque types, especially in the children's features, it was probably drawn early in his stay in Rome, before he left for a short visit to Florence in 1652–53. While in Rome Giordano taught himself by assiduously copying figures and details from major works of those 'old masters' who particularly interested him, such as Raphael's Stanza di Eliodoro in the Vatican and Polidoro's Milesi Palace frieze, and of

Fig. 28 Domenichino, *St Mark*, Sant'Andrea della Valle, Rome

leading contemporaries such as Cortona or the recently deceased Domenichino. These often large drawings were produced not only as learning aids for the young artist. All the copied studies display a distinctive technique described by Giordano's Neapolitan biographer Bernardo De Dominici.[4] They were drawn in dark red chalk with deeper shadows reinforced with a red-ink wash on a subtly toned orangey-red background created by rubbing the paper with red-chalk powder. Highlights were created by wiping away the soft ground to reveal the white paper below. The red-chalk background provided a very effective half-tone upon which only a few darker strokes were needed to conjure up a figure. Giordano had devised the technique so that "in a few hours" he could produce handsome and highly marketable finished drawings of major art works for sale to foreign visitors. It was with drawings such as the Liverpool *St Mark* that Giordano gained his nickname from his father's urging that he should speed up his lucrative work, "*Luca, fa presto*".

32 GUERCINO

(Giovanni Francesco Barbieri)

Cento 1591–1666 Bologna

Bathsheba at the bath with two attendants

229 × 320 mm, pen and brown ink and wash
Watermark on mount: partially visible fleur-de-lys with initials I.VG (?) close to Heawood 1835
Inscribed illegibly in ink on reverse of drawing, top right corner; inscribed in ink on mount *Guercino*; and in pencil on mount in Waagen's handwriting (?) *genuine v good W ... n*
PROVENANCE Robert Udny (L2248), sold 4 May 1803, lot 228, "Bathsheba, masterly pen", bt. Ottley (?) £1. 5s. 0d; Roscoe sale, 1816, lot 397, bt. Slater 1 gn.; C.R. Blundell, as Domenichino, valued at 16s. in 1841
EXHIBITION Edinburgh 1972, no. 69
LITERATURE Noted in D. Mahon and N. Turner, *The Drawings by Guercino in the Collection of Her Majesty the Queen at Windsor Castle*, Cambridge 1989, p. 143, under cat. 430
WAG1995.356

This is a preparatory compositional study for the large painting commissioned from Guercino in 1640 by the Bolognese nobleman Count Astorre Hercolani. Although the painting is now lost, it is recorded both in Guercino's account book covering the years 1629 until his death in 1666 (from which we know that on 23 August 1640 he was paid 375 *scudi*, which is what he usually charged for three life-size figures in a large painting) and in an 1816 guidebook to Bologna.[1] As Mahon and Turner point out, the painting may also have been recorded in a smaller painted format known only from an old photograph and in the pen-and-wash school drawing they discuss in their catalogue of the drawings by Guercino at Windsor.[2] They believe the Liverpool study to be "an autograph pen drawing of the subject, likely to be preparatory for the ... commission at an earlier stage" and consider that the school drawing, which is in poor condition and feebly reworked by a later hand, might reflect another autograph compositional study. The Liverpool study shows a number of differences from both the Windsor drawing and the painted copy

and it is obvious from the visible *pentimenti* that Guercino was continuously changing his mind in attempting to visualize the story of King David's adultery with Bathsheba.[3] Originally Bathsheba's head was turned round, deliberately catching the eye of the king, but Guercino fiercely scrubbed this idea out, hiding it under a bushy tree, perhaps because the assertive action does not coincide with Bathsheba's essentially passive role in the story. Instead he shows her looking intently down at what the larger Windsor study reveals to be a jet of water spurting into her bath, but which in the Liverpool drawing is so sketchily defined that it could almost be a mirror into which she peers to catch sight of David. Guercino's eventual solution was to move David on his balcony from right to left, so ensuring that the king got a view of her seductive breasts rather than that of her spine offered by his isolated position in the earlier composition, and to turn

Bathsheba's head towards her maids, who carry towels and one of whom looks out meaningfully at the viewer. His changes transformed the introspective Liverpool scene to one that strenghtened the underlying narrative. His superb graphic skills with pen and ink were admired even early in his career and were never affected by the eye defect which led a Bolognese art patron and admirer, the Marquese Enzo Bentivoglio, to coin his nickname, "*guercino*" or squinter.[4]

33 AFTER GUERCINO, ATTRIBUTED TO SIR JOSHUA REYNOLDS
Plympton 1723–1792 London
An angel sheathing the flaming sword with St Roch and St Sebastian in a landscape

225 × 170 mm, pen and brown and black ink over black chalk
Inscribed on back in ink upper left *e*
PROVENANCE Thomas Hudson (L2432); Roscoe sale, 1816, lot 396, as Guercino, "a saint bound to a tree and comforted by a pilgrim, who shews him an angel descending; fine pen/9h 7w/From Mr. Hudson's Collection", bt. Slater, 11*s.* 6*d.*; C.R. Blundell, mistakenly as Domenichino, valued at 8*s.* in 1841
LITERATURE Noted in *Guercino Master Draughtsman: Works from North American Collections*, exhib. cat. by D.M. Stone,

Fig. 29 Guercino, *Angel sheathing sword with Sts Roch and Sebastian*, Snite Museum of Art, University of Notre Dame, Indiana

Harvard University Art Museum, Cambridge MA, 1991, cat. 30, pp. xxvii, xxx, nn. 52–60; *Drawings by Guercino from British Collections*, exhib. cat. by N. Turner and C. Plazzotta, London, British Museum, 1991, p. 30, n. 65.; S.B. Spiro and M.F. Coffman, *Drawings from the Reilly Collection*, University of Notre Dame, Indiana, 1993, cat. 7 WAG1995.233

The Liverpool drawing is a copy of a compositional study in pen and ink by Guercino for the now lost altarpiece painted between 1632 and 1634 for the church of Nonantola, which lay between his home town of Cento and Modena [fig. 29].[1] The presence of the kneeling St Roch and the partly naked St Sebastian, both saints who were thought to protect against the plague, and of an angel sheathing its sword, a popular symbol of the ending of disease, confirm that the altarpiece was commissioned in gratitude after the plague that had stricken the area in 1630 had receded, to be placed in the oratory that had been built in the hope of protecting the town from further suffering. The completed altarpiece, known only from a poor painted copy, replaced the angel with a Madonna and Child and reversed the composition. David Stone's

originally speculative suggestion (endorsed by Sir Denis Mahon) that the copy is by Joshua Reynolds is given added credibility by the collector's mark of the portrait painter Thomas Hudson (1701–1779), Reynolds's master.[2] It could have been executed by Reynolds when he was in Hudson's studio *ca.* 1742–43; at that time the original may already have been in England, having been bought *ca.* 1741–42, along with many other Guercino drawings, by John Bouverie (*ca.* 1722–1750), the cousin of Sir Jacob Bouverie, the first President of the Society of the Arts.[3] Hudson certainly had contacts with the Bouverie family in 1749, when he was commissioned by Sir Jacob to paint a series

of ten portraits, and he may also have acted as the family's art advisor.[4] The early dating of the Liverpool copy is further confirmed by the inscription on the back of another Reynolds copy after Guercino, which states, "This drawing is by Sir Joshua Reynolds while Pupil to M. Hudson".[5] As Reynolds's teacher Hudson had encouraged the gifted young artist to copy from the works of Old Masters and specifically recommended Guercino's drawings as suitable models. These copies by Reynolds were particularly praised by his pupil James Northcote for the skill they displayed, which was such that many were later "considered as originals".[6] In the Liverpool drawing

Reynolds paid tribute to the Bolognese artist by producing a copy which faithfully emulated Guercino's typically scratchy, looping lines describing swirling drapery. In size the copied image and the original coincide almost exactly – the difference in paper size being accounted for by a bare border of between 14 and 16 mm along the top and left side of the copy. Reynolds became the most forthright supporter of seventeenth-century Bolognese painting. As an artist, lecturer, first President of the Royal Academy and collector (notably of an album of Guercino's caricatures now at Princeton Art Museum), Reynolds did more than any of his colleagues in England to fuel admiration for Guercino's drawings. Although when the drawing was in William Roscoe's collection it was attributed to Guercino, Roscoe owned two other drawings described as copies by Reynolds after Guercino, which he had bought from one of the sales of Hudson's studio on 25 February 1785.[7]

34 AFTER GUERCINO, ATTRIBUTED TO SIR BENJAMIN WEST

Springfield PA 1738–1820 London
A Prophet (?) with his left arm raised

296 × 208 mm (image size 294 × 203 mm), pen and brown ink
Watermark: two on the mount card, one with a fleur-de-lys, another with a crown[1]
Inscribed on mount in ink, lower right corner, *Guercino*. An attribution to a previous drawing in the mount written on the wash border and below has been erased; inscribed on reverse of mount in ink *K.77/K.a.4*
PROVENANCE Benjamin West (no collector's mark; inscribed in pencil on mount *West Bolognese/genuine*);
C.R. Blundell
LITERATURE Noted in D. Mahon and N. Turner, *The Drawings of Guercino in the Collection of Her Majesty the Queen at Windsor Castle*, Cambridge 1989, under no. 190
WAG1995.287

This spirited study has been drawn on used mount card within a wash border previously designed around another drawing which was detached before the sketch was made.[2] It is described by Denis Mahon and Nicholas Turner as a freely based copy (showing for example a clearly defined right hand) after a pen-and-wash drawing by Guercino in the Royal Collection at Windsor.[3] The Windsor sheet was one of hundreds of Guercino drawings which Richard Dalton (1715?–1791), Librarian to George III, bought in Bologna

ca. 1759–64 from Carlo Gennari (1712–1790), grandson of one of Guercino's nephews and heirs, Cesare Gennari (1637–1688). Its original title in the royal inventory was *St Paul preaching*, but Mahon and Turner thought it more likely depicted an Old Testament Prophet. They also tentatively suggested that Benjamin West might be its copyist after his appointment as George III's history painter in 1772. Compared to the Windsor drawing, the copy not only lacks grey wash but displays a greater emphasis on a

stylized linearity in the loops and swirls of
the sleeves and its insistent, repetitive use
of tight loops and hooks to define the mass
of hair and beard, whereas in the original
the hair was differentiated by looser wavy
curls. The copy's shadowed face has been
drawn with a hatched line-and-stipple
technique rather like that used by
engravers. In 1764 Dalton had invited the
celebrated Florentine engraver Francesco
Bartolozzi over to Windsor to produce a
series of engravings after the royal
collection, having been impressed by his
"matchless Imitations of Drawings of
Guercino" whilst in Bologna *ca.* 1763–64.[4]
Sometimes Bartolozzi made a drawn copy
first, before making an engraved
reproduction, but no engraved copy by
him of the Windsor *Prophet* is known and
the manner of his own copies after
Guercino do not show the stylistic quirks
of the 'West' drawing.[5] The possibility that
the mount on which West drew his copy
might have once supported the Windsor
Guercino (which is smaller by about
20 mm all round than the copy's image
size) has been dismissed because no
George III mounts are known to have had
an inner gold strip as part of their border
design, as this has.[6] Like Reynolds, his
predecessor as President of the Royal
Academy, West obviously had an interest
in Guercino's graphic art and owned three
copies after Guercino attributed to
Reynolds.[7] Some of his own pen-and-ink
drawings show a Guercinesque style and
the dramatic gesturing figure of the *Prophet*
seems to be reflected in at least one of his
works, *The Return of the Prodigal Son* of *ca.*
1771.[8] That both Benjamin West and
Reynolds copied original drawings by
Guercino (see exh. cat. 33) demonstrates
the avid interest in the Bolognese artist's
graphic work in eighteenth-century
England, where large numbers of his
drawings were collected, and attests to the
admiration the country's artists had for the
virtuoso draughtsman.

35 ALESSANDRO MAGNASCO
Genoa 1667–1749 Genoa
A seated old beggar in cloak and hat

191 × 130 mm, brush and brown oil
pigment with traces of red chalk with white
bodycolour applied later on oiled or waxed
(?) slightly torn paper applied to board
Inscribed in ink on verso *AIBX/3/8*
PROVENANCE Benjamin West (L419);
C.R. Blundell
WAG1995.246

This is a typically fluid brush drawing by
Magnasco of an isolated figure slumped
over his stick holding out his begging mug.
Magnasco began his career as a *figurista*,
providing the small figures which enlivened
the large landscapes and architectural
scenes of his collaborator Antonio
Francesco Peruzzini. It was not until the
1720s that he began to paint his own
landscapes teeming with monks, friars, the
lame or wounded, beggars, thieves and
other social outcasts. Consequently there

are very few compositional studies by Magnasco. Most of his drawings, many of which are in the Uffizi, show single figures or small groups isolated against summarily sketched woods and footpaths, which he inserted into painted settings. Such figures were capable of being adapted and reused. A slumped beggar similar to the Liverpool figure can be found in two of Magnasco's collaborative landscapes: seated beside the roadside in the background to the left of the *Journey of the monks* painted in Florence between 1703 and 1709 for someone attached to the court of Grand Prince Ferdinand de' Medici; and in the shadowy left foreground of the large *Landscape with travelling Capuchin friars* painted between 1719 and the early 1720s as part of a set of four probably for a Milanese or noble Lombard family.[1] Both men may represent poor wayside pilgrims begging alms and both show the same shadowed, introspective, almost pathetic characterization of the Liverpool beggar. Magnasco was much influenced by the Dutch and Flemish 'low-life' paintings he found in the Medici collections in Florence and by the Spanish and Italian picaresque literature, full of the adventures of beggars, vagabonds and gypsies, which was popular at the cultured Medici court. In Milan, where he returned in 1709, he found a further source of inspiration for his low-life and monastic figures in the protests against monastic corruption and social prejudice led by the progressive noble families for whom he worked.[2] The Liverpool sketch shows his characteristic technique: always preferring brush to pen, he created his figures from layers of warm muted colours of wash and rapid, nervous brushstrokes which suggested the nocturnal shadows and form-dissolving, flickering light of his paintings. The Liverpool beggar may have been touched up later, as under ultra-violet light two different types of opaque white bodycolour seem to have been applied to the cloak, face and hands of the figure, and the drawing's shadows have a sheen as if they have been 'oiled'.[3] It is perhaps significant that Benjamin West, a fellow artist, should have owned the drawing, as Magnasco's works, having been extremely popular in the eighteenth century, fell out of favour with collectors in the nineteenth century and his reputaion was not revived until the 1920s.

36 ANDREA MANTEGNA
Isola di Carturo 1430/31–1506 Mantua
Three studies for a figure of St John the Baptist

174 × 185 mm, pen and brown ink on paper prepared with red chalk
Inscribed in ink on drawing *g.128*; on back in ink *F/Nº4* followed by an inscription *Giorgione da castelfranco, Venitian, born 1477 died 1511/ Scholar to Gio: Bellini, imitated Leonardo da Vinci/painted History & Portraits*; in light, faint-brown ink *L* (or) *Z. 63*; in dark-black blurred ink *NH*;[1] in red chalk, lower left corner *36*; in pencil, lower right corner *6/230* (or?) *L38*
PROVENANCE Padre Sebastiano Resta (*g. 128*) with an attribution to Giorgione;[2] Lord John Somers; Nicola Francesco Haym (L1970); and Haym's mark (as rarely found), accompanied by a cross (L2908); George John, 2nd Earl Spencer (L8019; with his attribution to Giorgione on the mount), sold 10 June 1811, lot 353, as Giorgione, "a historical or saint-subject of four figures", bt. P[hilipe] for 8*s.*; Roscoe sale, 1816, part of lot 238, as Giorgione, bt. Ford for 19*s.* with Appendix, after Titian, WAG1995.248; C.R. Blundell, as Giorgione, valued with WAG1995.248 at 12*s.* in 1841
EXHIBITIONS *Italian Art and Britain*, London, Royal Academy, 1960, no. 516, as Giovanni Bellini;[3] Venice 1980, no. 5, as Mantegna, dated to 1450–55; NACF 1997
LITERATURE H.D. Gronau, 'Ercole Roberti's *Saint Jerome*', *Burlington Magazine*, XCI, 1949, p. 244, fig. 5, as Giovanni Bellini and datable to 1470; G. Fiocco, 'I disegni di Giambellino' *Arte Veneta*, 1949, p. 45, fig. 51, as G. Bellini; F. Heinemann, *Giovanni Bellini e i Belliniani*, Venice 1959, no. 345, fig. 151; G. Robertson, *Giovanni Bellini*, Oxford, 1968, p. 26, pl. Xa, as "more probably Mantegna"; noted in B. Degenhart and A. Schmidt, *Corpus der Italienischen Zeichnungen*, Berlin 1968, Part I, ii, p. 363, n. 13 for pp. 345–46; noted in D. Ekserdjian, *Andrea Mantegna*, exhib. cat., London, Royal Academy, 1992, p. 173, cat. 23, fig. 81, also cat. 24, dating it to early 1460s; G. Agosti, 'Su Mantegna, 2. (All'ingresso della "maniera moderna")', *Prospettiva*, October 1993, pp. 66ff., fig. 14, dating it to 1499; noted in *Five Centuries of European Drawings: the Former Collection of Franz Koenigs*, Moscow,

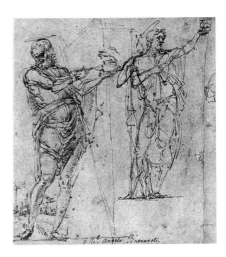

Fig. 30 Mantegna, *Two studies of St John the Baptist* (detail), Moscow, Pushkin Museum

Pushkin State Museum of Fine Arts, 1995, cat. 89, p. 167; WAG1995.324

The three freely sketched figures of St John the Baptist show the artist searching for a suitable pose for the saint, whether seated or standing, holding his attributes as the prophet of Christ's coming – a long cross and a lamb (Agnus Dei) lying on a book. The red-chalk dust of the prepared paper has been unevenly applied across the sheet, suggesting that it might have been a remnant and adding to the impression that the sketch was drawn very early in the planning stages for a fresco or painting. Until recently no Mantegna work had been identified in which St John the Baptist featured alone nor looking down on the figure of a praying donor or donor couple. Consequently the drawing has been dated on stylistic grounds and linked to a group of early drawings, in particular three sheets identified by their common technique – a scratchy, sketchy pen-and-ink style on a prepared pink paper.[4] Partly because so few of Mantegna's earliest drawings have survived, and the ones that have display such a generic, sketchy manner, they have posed difficult problems of connoisseurship and have in the past been attributed to Giovanni Bellini, Mantegna's brother-in-law. The three sheets of drawings which share the same technique as the Liverpool drawing have all been associated with Mantegna's first major altarpiece, in San Zeno, Verona, painted in 1456–59, after which he moved to Mantua to take up the post of court painter to the Gonzaga family

and for them he produced some of the finest work of the classically inspired fifteenth-century Renaissance. The Koenigs figures are thought to be preliminary studies for the bearded St John the Baptist who stands on the edge of the raised platform on the right wing of the San Zeno triptych. The Liverpool sheet has been closely linked to the Koenigs drawing as it appears to share the same faded pink paper and to be almost the same height, as though both sets of figures might once have been on the same sheet of paper [fig. 36].[5] However, the two sheets display differences of drawing style and figure type. The Koenigs figures are

standing and bearded with distinctive fringes of hair made up of repeated small circles; they are more monumental in build and their hatched shadows are drawn in an angular, geometric manner, whereas the Liverpool saint is younger, clean-shaven and appears drawn in a looser, more fluid manner. Recently Giovanni Agosti has suggested that the Liverpool drawing might be a preliminary sketch related to a commission of 1499 from Cardinal Georges d'Amboise, Archbishop of Rouen and first minister to the French king Louis XII, for a painting intended for his chapel in the Archbishop's Palace in Rouen.[6] The cardinal was particularly devoted to St John

the Baptist, whose image appeared on his personal seal, on his tomb and on a relief originally in his castle at Gaillon and now in the Louvre.[7] He specifically requested from Mantegna, the greatest painter in the world ("*primo pictore del mondo*"), a rectangular painting of St John being adored by the cardinal with the saint being shown larger than the donor, and in 1500 the cardinal visited Italy, making a grand ceremonial entrance to Milan on Easter Day.[8] The artistic practice of placing donors at prayer in an 'abyss' below the saint who was sometimes raised on a 'stage' became common in the Verona area between 1470 and 1530.[9] It enabled the artist to distinguish the holy space from that of the sinful human donor, portraying him or her as less significant than the saintly figure yet allowing the donor a life-size scale. In the Liverpool drawing Mantegna would have chosen the modern solution to the compositional problem rather than the medieval miniaturization requested by the cardinal. Previously the Liverpool sheet has been supposed to have been produced early in Mantegna's career as it was believed that he did not produce such sketchy pen drawings after about 1464 (certainly none seem to have survived from after that period), and switched instead to drawing highly elaborate, exactingly finished compositions, some of which were intended as presentation drawings.[10] The latter *modelli* were more attractive to artists and collectors and so were more likely to survive than the rough preparatory sketches, which in some cases may not have been identified as by Mantegna at all. Whether the drawing relates to Georges d'Amboise's request for a devotional image in 1499 or to an unidentified 1460s' commission the result is a swift, vibrant and rather beautiful example of the artist's inventive mind 'thinking out loud' in pen and ink.[11]

37 GIROLAMO MUZIANO
Brescia 1532–1592 Rome
The Descent of the Holy Spirit

296 × 228 mm, red chalk squared with red chalk
Inscribed in ink on drawing *Del Muziano*; on back of mount in ink at top *M/ nº12*
PROVENANCE George John, 2nd Earl Spencer (L1530), sold 10–17 June 1811, lot 500, as by Mutiano, bt. P[hilipe] 1s. 6d.; Roscoe sale, 1816, lot 280, as Girolamo Mutiano, bt. Slater 10s. 6d.; C.R. Blundell, valued at 8s. in 1841 inventory.
EXHIBITION Edinburgh 1969, no. 47
WAG1995.361

Muziano was one of the leading religious artists in late sixteenth-century Rome, continuously active painting altarpieces, supervising fresco schemes and designing mosaics. The drawing illustrates the events of Pentecost, marking the foundation of the Christian Church, when the Holy Spirit descended on the Virgin Mary and the Apostles, who began to talk in many tongues (Acts 2:1–4). Muziano is known to have painted this theme twice, once on the vault of Santa Maria sopra Minerva and also for the Vatican's Stanza dei Paramenti, where he worked in the late 1570s and 1580s.[1] Although the latter painting bears some compositional resemblance to the drawing there are a number of changes which suggest that the squared drawing was not the basis for the Vatican painting. The drawing is a much more confined, almost claustrophobic, composition whilst the painting was expanded sideways to give the Virgin greater 'breathing space' and more prominence, as was her due as the embodiment of the Church and the spiritual mother of the Apostles. As Rosamund Mack was first to indicate (in the Edinburgh catalogue) and Taco Dibbits has confirmed, Muziano appears to have reused some of the Apostles and adapted them to another (now lost) Marian composition of the *Assumption of the Virgin*, painted for San Luigi dei Francesi (and later moved to San Paolo fuori le Mura) and known only through a print by Jacques Callot.[2] Such repetition of figures is unusual in Muziano's work and, as Dibbits has suggested, "it is not inconceivable that the subject changed over time" from a *Pentecost* to an *Assumption*, as it took Muziano over six years to finish the project, which he had begun before 1584,

and there was disagreement between Muziano and the patron Matteo Contarelli. A compositional drawing for the *Assumption*, previously attributed to Federico Zuccaro by John Gere, but with the same handling of red chalk and distinctive figures with coal-lump eyes as the Liverpool study, has recently been identified in the Louvre by Taco Dibbits.[3] The Liverpool drawing would seem to be the only known study for the earlier commission and is typical of Muziano's 1580s' style with its red-chalk figures in a tight dense mass of regular strokes, weighed down by rich drapery, with stumped shadows, showing the influence of Michelangelo's frescos in the Cappella Paolina in the Vatican.

38 JACOPO PALMA
IL GIOVANE
Venice *ca.* 1548–1628 Venice
Study for an Annunciation

390 × 270 mm, pen and brown ink and wash over black chalk heightened with white (oxidized) on brown, irregularly edged paper, with the lower half squared in black chalk and numbering up the right side
Watermark on paper: anchor within a circle with three balls above, close to Briquet 568 (Verona, datable to 1591–93); on mount: partial fleur-de-lys within a crowned cartouche and a countermark V
Inscribed in ink on mount *Bonesi*[1]
PROVENANCE Roscoe sale, 1816, lot 434, as a "Capital drawing by Gio. Girolamo Bonesi", bt. Slater 16s.; C.R. Blundell, as Bonesi of the Bolognese School, valued at 13s. in 1841
EXHIBITION Venice 1980, cat. 47
WAG1995.205

It has previously been suggested that this drawing might relate to the painting in San Nicolò da Tolentino, Venice, dated to *ca.* 1615, although major compositional differences were noted, especially in the background.[2] In fact the compositional study has a much closer resemblance to the altarpiece for the cathedral at Salò, both in its architectural background and in its portrayal of the adult angels, as well as cherubs, swooping down from the sky.[3] The archway of the finished altarpiece can be seen faintly drawn in above the street scene in the drawing. Although the painting is signed in capital letters and dated 1628, the last year of Palma Giovane's life, the altarpiece was originally commissioned from him by the cathedral authorities in January 1609, with a request for one or two *modelli* of the design for their approval.[4] On 11 February 1609 the artist sent what was described as a very beautiful drawing, after which no further documentation for the commission is known, until Palma's death, when the finished altarpiece was found in his studio, possibly having been completed by a pupil. The partial squaring of the drawing suggests that it may well be one of the original 1609 *modelli* from which the completed altarpiece was adapted. The way that thick highlights have been applied on weighty 'sculptural' forms is closer to

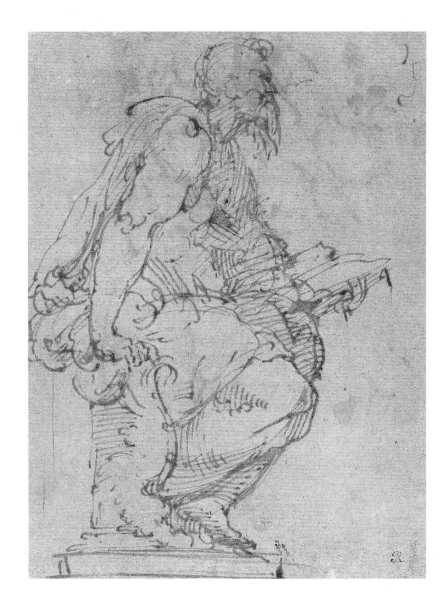

Palma's early drawing style than that found in the 1620s and shows the influence of his friend Jacopo Tintoretto, on whose death in 1594 Palma had assumed the mantle of Venice's foremost artist. Whoever finished off the painting, by adding a figure of God the Father above the dove of the Holy Spirit, also changed the unusual pose of a demure Archangel Gabriel, eyes lowered and arms crossed over the chest (a pose more usually associated with the Virgin), to the more conventional figure holding a lily and blessing Mary.[5]

39 PARMIGIANINO
(Girolamo Francesco Maria Mazzola)
Parma 1503–1540 Casalmaggiore
A seated man holding a book[1]

143 × 109 mm, pen and brown ink on pink washed paper
Inscribed on the back in ink at top *CC 32/AA 43/2r 31/d*; also on mount (see next)
PROVENANCE Richard Houlditch; Jonathan Richardson Senior (L2184, with his attribution to "Pordenoni" on the mount and his inscription on the back *in exchange from Mr. Houlditch/for a small Bernini*, below which in pencil the comment *true/A. Pond*); Roscoe sale, 1816, lot 257, attributed to "Gio. Ant. Licini called Pordenone An Apostle sitting in Meditation, a book open in his left hand",

bt. Slater 9s.; C.R. Blundell, valued at 8s. in
1841
EXHIBITION Edinburgh 1969, no. 53,
pl. 39
LITERATURE A.E. Popham, *Catalogue of
the Drawings of Parmigianino*, New Haven
1971, no. 781, pl. 77
WAG1995.358

Popham considered that the drawing was
early, sketched before Parmigianino's
journey to Rome in 1524 and apparently
for a figure in a *Christ disputing with the
Doctors*. Popham was probably comparing
it with another pre-Roman pen-and-ink
drawing, which was larger and not on pink
paper, of a *Large group of seated men with
books inside a building*, believed to be a
compositional study for a left side of a
Christ disputing.[2] In the early 1520s
Parmigianino was still in the studio of his
uncles Pier Ilario and Michele Mazzola,
with the example of Correggio's work as
the major stimulus to his early
development. Between 1522 and 1524 he
worked on the frescoed decoration of
several chapels on the left side of San
Giovanni Evangelista in Parma, at a time
when Correggio was also busy on the apse
and dome.[3] Mario di Giampaolo has
floated the possibility that the Liverpool
sketch could have been related to a figure
in the chapels (only three of which retain
Parmigianino's decoration), perhaps the
seated profile figure of St Nicholas of Bari
painted on the underside of the entrance
arch to the fourth chapel.[4] There is a
drawing for the figure of St Vitalis in the
Galleria Estense di Modena once attributed
to Parmigianino's contemporary Giovanni
Antonio Pordenone.[5] William Roscoe,
although the drawing was attributed to
Pordenone when he owned it, particularly
prized the work of Parmigianino, notably
his etchings and woodcuts, as his accounts,
sale catalogue and letters to the dealer and
auctioneer Thomas Philipe testify.[6]

Fig. 31 Verso of exh. cat. 40, photograph taken under transmitted light

40 PARMIGIANINO
Shepherds in adoration

118 × 135 mm, pen and brown ink and
brown wash, patched along the top with a
thin strip of paper on to which the tops of
heads and arms have been drawn and also
along the right side
Inscribed in ink on mount *Parmoggiano*; on
the reverse in ink Barnard's inventory
number *724*, also in top left corner *3 W 16*;
lower right corner, an obliterated number;
in pencil, lower left corner *Nᵒ – 34*
PROVENANCE Peter Lely (L2094); John
Barnard (L1419; no. 724); V (or W) R;[1]
Benjamin West (L419); C.R. Blundell
Reproduced in reverse by C.M. Metz in
*Imitation of Ancient & Modern Drawings
from the Restoration of the Arts in Italy to the
Present Time ...*, 1798, as "in the collection
of B West Esq. President of the Royal
Academy"[2]
LITERATURE Popham 1971, no. 782,
pl. 152
WAG1995.359

Popham dated the drawing to Parmigianino's 1524–27 stay in Rome, where the artist had immediately attracted the attention of Pope Clement VII and obtained patronage at the papal court thanks to his ingenious painted *Self-portrait in a convex mirror* (now Vienna, Kunsthistorisches Museum). Rome was crucial to his development as a graphic artist. There he began to make prints, employing Jacopo Caraglio to produce engravings after his designs and later etching his own – becoming the first artist in Italy to make independent etchings.[3] The drawing is related to the alternative schemes Parmigianino produced in about 1526 for two prints of the *Adoration of the Shepherds*, in which the Virgin bathes or dries off the Christ Child, one a vertical and the other a horizontal composition, engraved by Caraglio.[4] There are a number of other preparatory drawings in pen and wash and black chalk for both these prints in Florence, London, New York, Paris, Weimar and Windsor. Some, like those in Florence, New York and Weimar, are more

elaborate than others, but none focusses solely, as does the Liverpool sketch, on the crowd of excitable shepherds rushing on to the scene, and only the chalk drawing at Windsor has any indication of the figure at the back of the crowd drawing the viewer into the event by looking out of the picture.[5] The Liverpool shepherds are closer to the Uffizi's crowd, eagerly jostling each other as they approach to present their gifts, adding movement and emotion to the intimate, dignified main event which Parmigianino placed in the background. It perhaps also resembles the horizontal composition, which has a group of five shepherds, the first three bowing their heads low in acknowledgement of the Christ Child and one offering a sacrificial lamb, but neither print – both of them more restrained compositions – has the dramatic gestures of arms thrust forward and upward in celebration.

Another drawing is visible on the verso. Transmitted light photography shows a tousled head of a young man at a 90° angle to the recto and other hatching and the

suggestion of a lamb slung across the shepherd's shoulders [fig. 31]. The drawing was already in an English collection by the late seventeenth century, when it was owned by Sir Peter Lely (1618–1680); he might have acquired it through his court connections as both Earl Arundel and Charles I had owned Parmigianino albums or sketchbooks earlier.[6]

41 PARMIGIANINO

An antique sacrifice of a goat

67 × 100 mm, pen and brown ink with
brown wash heightened with white
(oxidized) on pink tinted paper
Inscribed in ink on drawing, lower right
corner *70*
PROVENANCE 'Pseudo-Crozat' (L474);
comte de Saint-Morys (1743–1795) as by
Raphael; Henry Blundell (?)
WAG1995.171

This small compositional sketch did not
feature in Popham's catalogue of
Parmigianino's drawings, published
posthumously in 1971, although the
annotation on the album page shows he
knew it and considered it to be a late work.[1]
Mario di Giampaolo has confirmed the
attribution and dating to the period after
Parmigiano's return to his native Parma,
having fled the sack of Rome by Charles
V's troops.[2] The pink-tinted paper is
commonly associated with his Parma
periods, particularly the second.[3] Certainly
Parmigianino worked on the theme of a
sacrifice or libation to a flaming altar, for a
chiaroscuro woodcut and a preparatory
drawing for it are known.[4] The subject of
an animal sacrifice before an altar, whether
of a bull or goat, was popular amongst
several of Raphael's followers and appears
on many gems and medals engraved by the
papal goldsmith Valerio Belli
(*ca.* 1468–1546), who, like Parmigianino,
worked for Pope Clement VII.[5] It is
possible that the theme was suggested to
him by antique Roman cameos and that

their intricate carving inspired him to
produce this small drawing. Along with
most of the other examples in the second
Blundell album, the drawing was once
owned by the anonymous collector referred
to by Frits Lugt as 'Pseudo-Crozat', who
may in fact be identified as the wealthy
French aristocrat the Comte de Caylus
(1692–1765).[6] His antiquarian interests
would no doubt have attracted him to this
rather curious scene. Later it was
apparently owned by Charles Etienne
Bourgevin Vialart, comte de Saint Morys,
who, having fled the French Revolution,
etched it, inscribing his monogram, the
date "12 Sept 1793 London" and the
attribution "Rafaello Sancio d'urbino".
The print was subsequently pasted into the
Weld-Blundell album beside the drawing.[7]

42 BALDASSARE PERUZZI
Ancaiano 1481–1536 Rome
Design for a papal medal: Pope Clement VII and a young emperor with Vulcan

135 × 142 mm, pen and brown ink and
pale grey-brown wash
Inscribed in ink on drawing *mano de
Baldesar da Siena*; with an inscription
around the edge of the 'medal' *ANNO
IUBILEI IAM DIU EXPETITO SUB
CLEMENTE VII PONTIFICE MAXIMO
OPTIMO*
PROVENANCE W.Y. Ottley, sold 6 June
1814, lot 939; Roscoe sale, 1816, part of lot
93, as Peruzzi, "Design for a Medallion of
Clement VII/... From Mr. Ottley's
Collection", on the same "Leaf" as "a
Female Figure in Meditation. Free pen"
(Appendix WAG1995.244, Peruzzi) and
"Apollo and the Muses on Mount
Parnassus" (Appendix WAG1995.97,
Italian School), bt. Slater 17*s*.; C.R.
Blundell, valued at 13*s*. in 1841
EXHIBITION Edinburgh 1969, no. 65,
pl. 15
LITERATURE C.L. Frommel, *Baldassare
Peruzzi als Maler und Zeichner*, Beiheft zum
Römischen Jahrbuch für Kunstgeschichte, XI,
1967, p. 132, no. 94, fig. LXXa
WAG1995.245

This design for the reverse of a papal
medal to be struck to celebrate the Jubilee
Year of 1525 is one example of the many
tasks that the painter/designer/architect
Peruzzi performed for the papacy during
the reign of Giulio de' Medici, Pope
Clement VII (1523–34). There was a
tradition of producing papal medals to
commemorate Holy Years when, every
twenty-five years, the pope would forgive
all repentant sinners visiting Rome. But
Peruzzi's design is particularly intriguing as
it seems to allude to political and military
events in Italy in 1525 and especially to the
aftermath of the Battle of Pavia in
February. On the right is a pope, shown
with Clement VII's features, gesturing
towards an army commander wearing
ancient Roman armour and probably
representing the Holy Roman Emperor
Charles V (1519–1556), whose support had
helped Giulio de' Medici to the papal
throne but whose troops were to be
victorious over those of the papal-backed
French at Pavia. In the background,

watched over by God, a nude man
identifiable as the ancient Roman god
Vulcan hammers out weapons to defend
the city (Rome?) behind. The Battle of
Pavia increased Charles V's control over
Italy and seriously damaged papal power,
provoking a conflict between secular and
religious authorities which was not resolved
until the plundering of Rome in May 1527
by Charles V's troops (who imprisoned
Peruzzi for a short time). This politically
sensitive design was rejected or never used.
Instead the medal that was struck showed
the Pope opening the Holy Door of
St Peter's Basilica – a purely ceremonial
and apolitical event which only occurred in
Holy Years. The drawing's close link to
one of the foremost Medici popes,
Clement VII, who completed the Sistine
Chapel by commissioning *The Last
Judgment* from Michelangelo, must have
attracted William Roscoe, who idolized the
Medici, to purchase it from Ottley's

collection in 1814. Another Peruzzi sketch
bought from Ottley by Roscoe may have
on its reverse a very schematic first idea for
the entrance vestibule of the Palazzo
Massimo alle Colonne, a major
architectural project and Peruzzi's final
work.[1] It shows Peruzzi's versatility as a
designer that he could move easily from
minting medals to building palaces. On his
death he was honoured by burial in the
Pantheon alongside Raphael, with whom
he had worked in the Vatican and the Villa
Farnesina.

Fig. 32 Primaticcio, *Ulysses winning the archery contest*, preparatory drawing (?), Stockholm, Nationalmuseum

43 FRANCESCO PRIMATICCIO

Bologna 1504–1570 Paris

Ulysses winning the archery contest in the presence of Penelope's suitors

243 × 324 mm, red chalk heightened with partly oxidized white on light red prepared paper

Inscribed in ink on mount *Primaticio*; on verso *The history of Ulysses, painted at Fontainebleau*

PROVENANCE Sir Joshua Reynolds (L2364); Roscoe sale, 1816, lot 346, bt. Slater for £1. 14s.;[1] C.R. Blundell, valued at £1. 4s. in 1841; sold Christie's, London, 11 December 1990, lot 62, bt. NMGM with the help of the NACF in 1991 after an export stop.

The composition was engraved by Theodor van Thulden in 1633[2]

EXHIBITIONS Edinburgh 1969, no. 69, pl. 48; NACF 1997

LITERATURE S. Béguin, J. Guillaume, A. Roy, *Primatice: La Galerie d'Ulysse à Fontainebleau*, Paris 1985, pp. 284–86, fig. 299; D. Ekserdjian, 'Francesco Primaticcio: An Old Master Drawing

Returns to Merseyside', *NACF Review*, 1992, pp. 10–11

WAG10843

This extremely attractive compositional drawing is a preparatory *modello* for the thirty-ninth fresco relating the story of Ulysses (the Greek hero Odysseus) in the Galérie d'Ulysse, commissioned by the French king Francis I for his palace at Fontainebleau. The 150-metre-long gallery depicted, in fifty-eight scenes, the adventures of Ulysses after leaving Troy and was Primaticcio's largest single project at the château, executed between 1537 and 1570. By 1560 Primaticcio had been made director of all palatial construction and had handed over the painting of the frescos to his studio, headed by his Italian assistant Niccolò d'Abbate, who had arrived in 1552. The Gallery was demolished in Louis XIV's remodelling of 1738–39 and so the only visual record of this important decorative scheme are the drawings, of which the dating is disputed, Sylvie Béguin proposing a hypothetical date of 1550–55 and Per Bjurström one between 1541 and 1547.[3] In Stockholm there is another slightly larger preparatory (?) drawing for

the same fresco, also in red chalk with white highlights but displaying a looser handling of the chalk and slightly varied details, including a lightly sketched bow, missing from the Liverpool *modello* [fig. 32].[4] The drawing illustrates the scene from Homer's *Odyssey* (XXI. 30–434) in which Ulysses, having arrived home in disguise after his long absence of twenty years at the Trojan War, wins the archery contest set by his wife, Penelope, to prove that he is the best suitor for her hand in marriage. He is shown skilfully shooting his arrow through a row of rings without leaving his seat, watched by his son Telemachus on the extreme right, rival suitors and his divine guardian the goddess Athene (standing behind him with a shield), whilst in the background Penelope climbs up to her private rooms to await the successful suitor. French translations of the story were confused as to whether the competition consisted of shooting through the rings on the end of axe-handles or through the rings of the weights used to stretch the woven tapestry. Primaticcio chose to show the latter, thus making an allusion to the patience and fidelity of Penelope who, whilst waiting for her husband to return, had put off other suitors by insisting she would make her decision only when she had finished the tapestry she was weaving, which she unpicked every night. Homer's account of Ulysses's adventures proved popular at the French court, where the Greek hero was associated with military prowess and prudence, amongst other virtues suitable for a monarch.[5] As the *Odyssey* had rarely been illustrated it provided many new scenes for Primaticcio to test his inventive skills in creating novel compositions. As his painted work was collaborative, his own style is most beautifully revealed in his finished drawings, populated by athletically built yet graceful figures. He had been greatly influenced by the elongated and gracious figures of Parma artists, and his red-chalk drawings on paper tinted to match, with drapery and flesh picked out in fine white hatching, show him combining the soft painterly qualities of Correggio with Parmigianino's stylized forms to create his own polished style.

Fig. 33 Raffaellino da Reggio, drawing, Munich, Staatliche Graphische Sammlung

44 RAFFAELLINO DA REGGIO

(Raffaello Motta)

Codimondo 1550–1578 Rome

Design for the façade of the house of Francesco da Volterra

200 × 256 mm, pen and brown ink and wash over red and black chalk
Inscribed in ink on edge of drawing *EVEXIT AD AETHERA VIRTUS*;[1] in ink on a separate piece of paper removed from its original mount *Rafaelino da Reggio/Primo pensiero della facciata della Casa del Volterra Architetto, posto vicino a Casali in Campo Marzo*
Watermark on paper: unidentifiable fragment of a fleur-de-lys (?) in a circle
PROVENANCE Roscoe sale, 1816, part of lot 200, all as Raffaello Motta, bt. Slater 12s. (with Appendix WAG1995.54 and .55, attributed Casolani); C.R. Blundell, valued at 12s. in 1841
EXHIBITION Edinburgh 1969, no. 73, pl. 16
LITERATURE C.P. Ridolfini, *Le case romane con facciate graffite e dipinte*, Rome, Palazzo Braschi, 1960, pp. 32–33, pl. VI; noted in J.A. Gere, *Mostra di disegni degli Zuccari*, Florence, Uffizi, 1966, no. 88, p. 55; noted in *Italienische Zeichnungen 15.–18. Jahrhundert*, exhib. cat., Munich, Staatliche Graphische Sammlung, 1967, cat. 64; noted in J.A. Gere and P. Pouncey, *Italian Drawings in the British Museum: Artists Working in Rome c.1550–c.1640*, London 1983, cat. 236
WAG1995.323

This is a complete design for the now lost decoration executed in fresco by Raffaellino on the exterior of the house of the architect Francesco da Volterra in the via di Campo Marzio, Rome, which he rented from 8 April 1573.[2] The main scene on the façade was described in 1642 by the biographer Baglione as representing Virtue leading Hercules by the hand and going together with Genius towards the Temple of Eternity, Hercules being identified by the club he carries.[3] While the other preparatory drawings in Florence, Lille, London and Munich provide alternative designs for the main scene, none shows the whole façade, including the colourful little putti clambering above the window frames, nor do they include the Latin motto, probably also painted on the façade, which translates roughly as 'Virtue (or excellence) has borne [its practitioners] to the heavens'.[4] Raffaellino came from a poor country family, whom he supported by painting façades in Reggio Emilia and other nearby towns. In about 1572–73 he was taken to Rome by the leading Roman architect Francesco da Volterra, who had been impressed by his skills when both had worked for Prince Cesare I Gonzaga on his palace at Guastalla. Volterra continued to support his protégé during Raffaellino's stay in Rome, cut short by his early death in 1578, and his wife Diana executed prints reproducing Raffaellino's work.[5] In Rome Raffaellino established himself and became Federico Zuccaro's assistant, adopting the Zuccaro style, as this soft, smoky wash drawing shows. Raffaellino may have been inspired to create this design for an artist's house for Volterra, his friend and sponsor, by Federico Zuccaro, who some twenty years later painted an illustrated life of his brother Taddeo which included a scene of Taddeo entering Rome accompanied by Wit and Design.[6] The idea of an artist's uphill battle to gain achievement was common in the second half of the sixteenth century and was usually expressed by showing the hero accompanied by allegorical figures who ensured his success.[7] That this might have been the source for Raffaellino's composition is suggested by the alternative Munich design, in which a man is led towards the temple by Mercury and a helmeted Minerva, representing Commerce and Wisdom respectively, whilst the naked figures of Venus, Cupid and Bacchus, representing the earthly desires of sex and drink, are left behind in the background [fig. 33].[8]

EXERIT AD AETHERA VIRTVS

45 GUIDO RENI

Bologna 1575–1642 Bologna

Head and shoulders of a youth looking up to the left

290 × 235 mm, black and white chalk on buff-grey paper

Watermark on mount card: fleur-de-lys within crowned escutcheon and below G R; and across the fleur-de-lys LA...R, similar to Heawood 1849 (undated).[1]

Inscribed in ink on mount *Dominichino*; on reverse *2* in blue pencil

PROVENANCE Benjamin West (L419; inscribed in pencil *West Bolognese/ genuine v good*); C.R. Blundell

LITERATURE Noted in R.E. Spear, *The 'Divine' Guido: Religion, Sex, Money and Art in the World of Guido Reni*, New Haven 1997, p. 371, n. 31[2]

WAG1995.64

This is a study for the head of the Archangel Gabriel, seated to the left of the Archangel Michael, in Guido Reni's fresco *Allegory of the Triumph of Christ* painted in about 1614–15 on the cupola of the Chapel of the Holy Sacrament in Ravenna Cathedral [fig. 34].[3] When Reni received the commission from the Archbishop of Ravenna, Cardinal Pietro Aldobrandini, nephew of the former Pope Clement VIII, he had just returned to settle for the rest of his life in his native town of Bologna after a successful thirteen-year stay in Rome. Reni and his team of three assistants were paid for their work in Ravenna Cathedral, which also included painting other cupolas and an altarpiece, between August 1614 and May 1616. The cupola was painted quickly, the rapidity of its production perhaps encouraged by the unpleasantness of a lengthy stay in the declining city of Ravenna, described by a friend and contemporary as hot and disease-ridden, and notorious for its awful wine and infamous water.[4] As Reni did not enjoy the tedium of working in fresco on a large scale he left the actual execution of the *Allegory* to his assistants, concentrating instead on producing the cartoons for the whole composition and on a range of figure studies and details in black chalk and pen and ink.[5] He thus followed the practice of the Carracci studio in which he had been trained, using pen and ink for preliminary compositional sketches, then black chalk for detailed studies of drapery, heads,

Fig. 34 Guido Reni, *Allegory of the Triumph of Christ*, cupola of the Chapel of the Holy Sacrament, Ravenna Cathedral

hands and feet, made from the live studio model. Although the study of the young man's head was no doubt drawn from a live model Reni has imbued it with an air of elegant refinement appropriate to the heavenly figure of Archangel Gabriel. The fresco is no longer in a good condition, having been restored twice in the last two centuries, and a study such as this one remains the best way to enjoy the graceful beauty of Reni's original concept, which won the praise of contemporaries, and admire the refined naturalism that characterized Reni's early art. As Cavaliere d'Arpino is reported to have said of him, whilst "we paint like mere mortals, he paints like an angel".[6]

46 GUIDO RENI
The Holy Family

153 × 196 mm, pen and brown ink
Inscribed in ink on drawing *Guido bolognese*
.f.; in ink on the back of drawing
Pianove (?); on the back of the old mount
in pencil *N°4* (?)*B*
PROVENANCE Sir Peter Lely (L2092 or
L2094); Sir Joshua Reynolds (stamp on
back of old mount, L2364); Paul Sandby
(L2112); Roscoe sale, 1816, part of lot 408,
as Reni, bt. Slater for 12s. 6d. (with cat. 47,
Assumption of the Virgin, on the same
Roscoe 'tissue-paper' mount);
C.R. Blundell, valued at 8s. (with cat. 47)
in 1841
LITERATURE C. Johnston, review of
V. Birke, *Guido Reni Zeichnungen*, in
Master Drawings, XX, 1982, p. 42, fig. 1;
A. Sutherland Harris, forthcoming article,
Master Drawings
WAG1995.293

The flourish with which Guido Reni has
signed the drawing suggests that he
considered it to be a finished composition.
Like another pen and brown ink drawing of
the Holy Family in the Getty Museum,
similar in style and size, it has usually been
thought that he meant to reproduce it as an
etching.[1] Reni very rarely engaged in
printmaking and when he did so he usually
produced small devotional images such as
this one of the Holy Family, in which the
Virgin Mary cradles a lively baby whilst
Joseph gazes on solemnly. None of the
several etched variants known on this
theme relate exactly to the Liverpool
drawing, although some do show the
Family, sometimes joined by an infant
St John the Baptist, seated around a draped
table similar to the one covered by a
fringed cloth roughly sketched in here by
Reni.[2] His production of prints has also
been linked to his early training with the
prolific printmaker Agostino Carracci,
whose vigorous hatching style seems to
have inspired Reni's. Both Catherine
Johnston and Stephen Pepper have dated
the Weld-Blundell drawing to between the
mid and late 1590s on the assumption that
Reni would only show characteristics of
Agostino's style early in his career.[3]
However, in a recent article on Reni's pen-
and-ink drawings Ann Sutherland Harris
has proposed that its "looser, less focussed

Fig. 35 Guido Reni, *The Assumption of the Virgin*, Lyons, Musée des Beaux-Arts

manner" is more reminiscent of Reni's late, 'shaggy' chalk studies.[4] She has suggested that rather than being an early preparatory drawing for an etching it could well be a late, signed, gift for a student or friend, or even done for a quick sale to raise money to pay off the gambling debts which plagued him late in his life.[5]

47 ATTRIBUTED TO GUIDO RENI
The Assumption of the Virgin

115 × 80 mm, pen and brown ink on very thin paper, with an illegible inscription on verso

PROVENANCE Unknown Bolognese (?) collector, his inscription in ink on mount *del Signor Guido Rheni*;[1] Roscoe sale, 1816, part of lot 408, attributed to Reni (with *The Holy Family*, cat. 46), bt. Slater 12s. 6d.; C.R. Blundell, valued at 8s. (with cat. 46) in 1841
WAG1995.303

This is an example of the small, schematic sketches with which Reni would first try to work out a compositional problem. For Reni drawings, particularly those in pen and ink, were primarily functional – to be used as aids or studies towards a finished painting, fresco or print. Reni returned repeatedly to the devotional subject of the Virgin's ecstatic assumption into heaven

throughout his career, producing images of many sizes and in a variety of media. As '*primi pensieri*' are liable to be substantially different from the finished work it is difficult to relate such a small sketch precisely to a painting, particularly one of such a common theme. Pepper has suggested that stylistically it might be dated to *ca.* 1612, towards the end of Reni's period in Rome.[2] However, the combination of a standing Virgin with two child angels supporting her feet and the way the drapery falls over her left knee, outlined by two cursory strokes of Reni's pen, seem to appear only in Reni's large painting of the subject now in Lyons, Musée des Beaux-Arts [fig. 35].[3] The painting was bought from Reni in 1637 by Cardinal Luigi Capponi, the papal legate in Bologna, for the Oratorians in Perugia, who wanted a work by the artist, whom they considered the painter without equal in the land, to grace appropriately their Chapel of the Assumption.[4] The Lyons *Assumption* represents the last and most graceful phase of Reni's meditation on the theme of glorious images of the Virgin in ecstasy surrounded by heavenly clouds. As we know from Reni's principal biographer, the proudly Bolognese Count Carlo Cesare Malvasia, by this late stage in his career, into his sixties, a physically weak Reni was overworking himself in order to keep out of debt.[5]

48 GIOVANNI FRANCESCO ROMANELLI
Viterbo *ca.* 1610–1662 Viterbo
Laocoön attacked by the serpent

240 × 376 mm, pen and brown ink and brown wash heightend with white on orangey-brown washed paper
PROVENANCE King George III (?), as Pietro da Cortona; Benjamin West (no collector's mark; inscribed in pencil on mount *Mr West's Colln Romanelli – Roman School*), possibly among the "eight historical drawings by P. da Cortona" sold Christie's, 13 June 1820, lot 95; C.R. Blundell
Printed in reverse in F. Bartolozzi, *Seventy-three Prints engraved by Bartolozzi & C. from the original Pictures & Drawings of Michelangelo, Domenichino ... P. Da Cortona ... in the Collection of His Majesty &c.*, 1765, no. 9, as Pietro da Cortona
LITERATURE Noted in B. Jatta, *Francesco Bartolozzi Incisore delle Grazie*, Istituto Nazionale per la Grafica, Villa Farnesina, Rome, 1995, cat. 28d
WAG1995.315

This dramatic scene of the Trojan priest Laocoön and his two sons being attacked and crushed to death by a sea-serpent, having warned the Trojans against accepting the Greeks' gift of a wooden horse, was formerly attributed to Pietro da Cortona. Romanelli is first recorded in 1631 in Cortona's studio, working, as part of the artistic household of Cardinal Francesco Barberini, on the Palazzo Barberini, as he continued to do throughout most of the decade. During this period he also worked on schemes in the Vatican for the Barberini pope Urban VIII (1623–44), including frescos and tapestries depicting mythological scenes. The drawing probably dates from the early 1630s as it is stylistically close, particularly in the handling of drapery, to other early compositional studies by Romanelli.[1] There are close parallels with the drawing on similar brown-washed paper of *Moses and the Israelites* once in the Roberto Ferretti collection – and with a drawing at Windsor both in the patchy application of white heightening and in the facial features of Moses and Laocoön.[2] The drawing shows Romanelli's characteristically strong contrast of light and dark with brilliant flashes of white lead illuminating the bare backs of the fleeing Trojans against the sinister gloom of the wash background. In 1765 Romanelli's drawing was reproduced as a Pietro da Cortona by Francesco Bartolozzi amongst a group of seventy-three engravings, most of which were then in the collection of King George III.[3] The possibility that the drawing was once in the Royal Collection is strengthened by the design of its mount, which has the distinctive inner black strip immediately adjoining the drawing and other black border lines found on many drawings in the Collection mounted in the 1770s and 1780s.[4] However, the *Laocoön* is not listed among the three volumes of drawings by Pietro da Cortona and his circle in Inventory A of the Royal Collection, compiled shortly after 1800.[5] Other works of art are known to have been 'separated' from George III's collection at this time and were sold in the 1780s and 1790s from the collections of Sir Joshua Reynolds and of Richard Dalton, the King's Librarian and from 1778 his Surveyor of Pictures.[6] It was Dalton who had commissioned Bartolozzi to engrave the Royal Collection and who whilst on his travels in Italy in the late 1750s and early 1760s bought most of the drawings. He had a reputation as unscrupulous and, though his purchases were ostensibly for his royal master, contemporaries and courtiers noted that he had a rather relaxed attitude to their ownership.[7] It was presumably through this route that Benjamin West acquired the drawing.

Fig. 36 Romanelli, *The Madonna of the Rosary*, Santi Domenico e Sisto, Rome

49 GIOVANNI FRANCESCO ROMANELLI
The Madonna and Child handing rosaries to Sts Dominic and Catherine

294 × 205 mm, pen and brown ink and brown wash with small patches of grey wash over black chalk
Watermark on drawing paper IHS;[1] on mount: fleur-de-lys similar to Heawood 1826 (England, 1741)
Inscribed in brown ink on drawing Houlditch's number *RH3*; and in lower right corner *ad/* (?);[2] in ink on mount *Fran^co Romanelli*; and lower right corner *_i/.*; on reverse in ink Richardson's (?) shelfmark and comment *D.25/1735/ 'Pascoli in his life of Romanelli mentions this picture as painted in the Church of the Monks of St. Dominik in Rome'*; in ink, top left corner *1 W. 14/n3 Nrg 3N*
PROVENANCE J. Richardson Senior (no collector's stamp); Richard Houlditch (L2214), sold by Langford, 12–14 February 1760, no. 3?; Roscoe sale, 1816, lot 211, bt. Ablett (?) 12s.;[3] C.R. Blundell, as Romanelli, *Virgin and Child*, valued at 8s. in 1841
EXHIBITION Edinburgh 1972, no. 61, illus. p. 94, as possibly Giacinto Gimignani[4]
WAG1995.344

This is a very close study for the *Madonna of the Rosary* in the church of Santi Domenico e Sisto in Rome [fig. 36]. The only elements missing from the drawing that appear in the finished altarpiece are the capitals and architraves of the columns behind the Virgin's outstretched arm and the crown around the Dominican nun's habit of St Catherine of Siena. St Domenic was believed to have invented the special sequence of prayers to the Virgin Mary used in saying the rosary and is thus shown receiving from her in a vision the rosary, or string of beads used to recall the prayers, accompanied by Catherine of Siena, a leading saint of the Dominican Order. The church of San Sisto had been given to St Domenic in the thirteenth century for his order of nuns and admitted only members of the nobility. It was at their expense that a newly refounded church was constructed in the late sixteenth century. Romanelli's altarpiece, commissioned by Sisters Ortensia and Caterina Celsi and finished by him in 1652, completed the church's interior

decoration.[5] The *Madonna of the Rosary* was one of the finest altarpieces executed by Romanelli after his return in 1648 from Paris, whither he had gone in search of patronage from Cardinal Mazarin, having fallen from papal favour with the death of Urban VIII in 1644. In Paris he had worked along with Eustache Le Sueur (see exh. cat. 71), on whose style he had an important effect, and he returned to the city to decorate the Queen's appartments in the Louvre in 1655. There are similarities here with a drawing for a tapestry design of the Paris period in Düsseldorf, particularly in the use of dark wash in the drapery shadows and around the eye sockets and in kindred flying cupids or putti.[6]

50 ANDREA SCHIAVONE
Zadar? *ca.* 1510?–1563 Venice
The Three Fates

245 × 250 mm, pen and brown ink with brown wash heightened with white lead (oxidized) on thin brown paper in a mount made up of strips of blue paper[1]
PROVENANCE Unknown; C.R. Blundell, attributed to Parmigianino and valued at £1. 4s. in 1841
EXHIBITION Venice 1980, no. 27, as Schiavone[2]
WAG1995.326

In Greek mythology the Three Fates, daughters of Zeus, were the spinners of human life. The goddess Clotho with her wheel and spindle can be seen spinning the thread of life, Lachesis measures it across her chest and Atropos prepares to snip it with her shears. The present attribution to Schiavone is based on a close facial similarity to two female figures seated on the right of the *Allegorical coronation of Doge Grimani* in the British Museum, a design for an embroidered altar-frontal dated by Richardson to *ca.* 1549–50.[3] The figures have in common certain elements characteristic of Schiavone's style *ca.* 1545–55 although the *Fates* are more boldly drawn and their hairstyle less neat. From his establishment in Venice at the end of the 1530s Schiavone focussed on developing his etching skills, which became technically increasingly elaborate and inventive, and throughout the 1540s his

drawings showed a great debt to another painter/etcher, Parmigianino.[4] The debt is particularly shown in the female figure types of this pen-and-brush drawing, though the lank forelocked hair is distinctively Schiavone's own. Few of Schiavone's drawings have been related to his prints, and even fewer to his paintings. He seems to have enjoyed exploring different effects for their own sake and experimenting with a variety of ink-and-wash techniques in pen and brush on different coloured papers. His use of dark wash-coloured papers may have been influenced by the chiaroscuro woodcuts popular in North Italy, and the Liverpool drawing might have been meant as a preparatory study for just such a print. But the all-enveloping dark wash also has an expressive pictorial effect, merging the Fates into the dense surrounding atmosphere and obscuring their faces, so that their separate identities fuse into an ominous and forbidding group controlling human destiny.

51 ELISABETTA SIRANI
Bologna 1638–1665 Bologna
The Virgin crowned by the Christ Child with roses

210 × 162 mm, grey-brown wash over red chalk
Inscribed in ink on drawing, quarter way down on left *fata*; a long inscription in ink on former backing card *A first sketch for her picture on this subj./painted for the Pope's brother./In her list of her own pictures it is thus/enumerated* and a quotation from Malvasia
PROVENANCE John McGouan (his mark, L1496, partially erased on reverse), sold 1 February 1804, lot 646, as Sirani, *The Madonna and Child*, red chalk and Indian ink; Roscoe sale, 1816, lot 415, bt. Slater 10s.; C.R. Blundell, valued at 8s. in 1841
WAG1995.76

This is an exact study for the painting described by Sirani's biographer, mentor and admirer Carlo Cesare Malvasia as "a Blessed Virgin half figure with the Child, which is in the act of placing a crown of roses on her head, she holding him seated on a cushion on her lap for Don Mario

brother of the Pope".[1] The picture, painted for Don Mario Borghese, was signed and dated 1663 and is now in the National Museum of Women in the Arts, Washington [fig. 37].[2] Malvasia's reference comes from Sirani's *Note delle pitture*, a dated list of her paintings which she compiled as proof against contemporary forgeries. It is possible that the word *fata* (done) was scribbled on the drawing by Sirani as a means of reckoning the prodigious output in her brief but celebrated career, cut short by her death aged twenty-seven. During the ten years that she worked as the main breadwinner for her sisters and father, whose painting career had been crippled by arthritis in the

hands, she reportedly painted around 190 works, many for private patrons.[3] Malvasia recounts various stories of her rapid working procedures. In 1664, during a visit to her studio by Prince Cosimo de' Medici, she executed so quickly a Madonna he had ordered that it was dry and could be taken home immediately.[4] Her drawings are also distinguished by their fluid, bravura brushwork – used in the Liverpool study to outline swiftly in wash the Virgin's bodice, sleeves and turban and to reinforce the facial expressions captured in red chalk. Although she also worked on a large scale Sirani made her greatest mark with her small devotional paintings of the Holy Family, the infant Jesus and St John and

Fig. 37 Elisabetta Sirani, *The Madonna with the Christ Child crowning her with roses*, Washington, National Museum of Women in the Arts

Sirani; an eminent painter of Bologna – all of whom/ painted but Elisabetta was the most distinguished. Her pictures/ date from the 17th to the 26th year of her age, when she died/ by poison administered by a servant, but at whose instigation/ could never be ascertained. She was buried in the same tomb/with Guido, which gave rise to the following/ Epitaphium/ Sirani Tumulus cineres hic claudit Elisa/ Guidonis Rheni qui quoque justa tegit/ Sic duo picturae, quae non miracula[?] junxit/ Vita, hoc in Tumulo jungere mors potuit/ Her pictures possess great merit. Her style is closely allied/to that of Guido, but is sufficiently characterized by an elegance/ peculiarly her own. Her drawings are executed in different/ modes – with red chalk – with the pen or by washed tints –/ in all these she excelled as she also did in her Etchings/ which are very beautiful & highly esteemed; on reverse top left corner in pencil *P.31*; in red chalk *15*; in ink lower left corner *n⁰* (number cut off)
PROVENANCE F.M. Niccolò Gaburri, sold London *ca.* 1760; Charles Rogers; Roscoe sale, 1816, lot 413, bt. Ford £1.; C.R. Blundell, valued at 16*s.* in 1841
EXHIBITION Edinburgh 1972, no. 103, illus. p. 74
LITERATURE Noted in J. Byam Shaw, *Drawings by Old Masters at Christ Church Oxford*, 1976, I, cat. 1031 and dated to after *ca.* 1660;[1] N. Turner, 'The Gabburi/Rogers Collection of Drawn Self-portraits', *Journal of the History of Collections*, V, no. 2, 1993, p. 213
WAG1995.345

Nicholas Turner suggested that the self-portrait in red chalk may be the one mentioned by the Florentine collector Francesco Maria Niccolò Gabburri (1676–1742) in his *Vite di pittori* as having been used by Sirani for her image in *The Baptism of Christ* which she painted for the Bolognese church of San Girolamo della Certosa in 1658. The Charterhouse *Baptism* was Sirani's first major public commission, a large multi-figure work she painted at the age of twenty, in which she inserted a self-portrait at the back of the crowd on the left, but looking straight out at the viewer rather than in the three-quarters profile of the Liverpool drawing.[2] Her features and loose hair-style seem closer to those on a small self-portrait painted on copper in the Bologna Pinacoteca [fig. 38].[4] The Liverpool self-portrait may have been drawn at the same time as an independent work of art for the

Fig. 38 Elisabetta Sirani, *Self-portrait*, Bologna, Pinacoteca

large collector's market which had already developed for Sirani's image in her own lifetime. Sirani's fertile talent as an artist and her reputed beauty – both evident in the steady gaze, gentle half-smile and soft curls of her Liverpool self-portrait – quickly brought her European fame. Her studio became an attraction where she entertained male and female members of the nobility with conversation, dinner and song along with her two artist sisters Barbara and Anna Maria and her pupils.[4] She produced several other painted and drawn self-portraits, sometimes portraying herself as a lady of rank, sometimes more seductively bare-shouldered, but none with the informal air of the Liverpool drawing.[5] The Liverpool self-portrait is framed by one of the distinctive and elaborately decorated mounts designed for the collection of Niccolò Gabburri, the curator of the Uffizi's collection of painted self-portraits, who also amassed for himself an equivalent graphic collection of artists' portraits as a part of his vast collection of drawings, which was dispersed in London around 1760 and bought by Charles Rogers (1711–1784).[6] Sirani's supposed death by poisoning, of which her rather infatuated biographer friend Malvasia was convinced, added to the frisson of delight in owning her self-portrait for collectors such as Rogers, who wrote the lengthy inscription, based on Malvasia, on the

every possible variant of the Virgin and Child. They were often extremely simple but tender and intimate compositions such as the Liverpool scene in which the child turns playfully to crown his mother with a garland of roses in a naturalistic interpretation of an oft depicted subject that alluded to the rosary. Sirani's work was greatly admired and sought after by contemporaries, partly because of her skill in bringing a fresh approach to old themes such as this.

52 ELISABETTA SIRANI
Self-portrait

218 × 173 mm (mount size 362 × 250 mm), red chalk with some pigment stains, on beige paper, surrounded by an elaborate drawn frame with a grey-blue outer mount Watermark on drawing: encircled fleur-de-lys closest to Briquet 7106–07 (Ferrara 1583 and 1586); on supporting mount: part of a fleur-de-lys within a cartouche. Inscribed on verso of drawing in ink: *Elisabetta* (?); inscribed in ink on mount *Ritratto d'Elisabetta Sirani Bolognese/ Originale de sua mano*; inscribed in ink under Gabburi mount in English by Charles Rogers *Elisabetta Sirani/ Her own Portrait/ born in 1638 one of the three accomplished daughters of Gio./ Andrea*

mount. She is more likely to have died, prosaically, from a bleeding stomach ulcer brought on by overwork. Malvasia's effusive eulogy, "the prodigy of art, the glory of the female sex, the gem of Italy, the sun of Europe Elisabetta Sirani", ensured that her fame lived on centuries after her death.[7] The Bolognese provided her with a magnificent funeral and as a mark of their esteem buried her next to Guido Reni, as both artists had brought renown to their native city.

53 ANTONIO TEMPESTA
Florence 1555–1630 Rome
The defeat of Sennacherib

335 × 460 mm, pen and brown ink and wash over black chalk, with spray of ink dots in top right corner
Popham attribution on mount to Cambiaso. Pouncey disagreed. Attribution initialled *AP* (?): *late 18th/early 19th Italian/ someone like Cades (?)/ and of the Gandolfi followers/ etc*
PROVENANCE Benjamin West (no collector's mark; inscribed on mount in pencil *West*, possibly among the "twenty designs of battles in pen and ink by Tempesta" from West's collection sold Christie's 13 June 1820 lot 64);
C.R. Blundell
WAG 1995.376

King Sennacherib was the Assyrian who in the eighth century BC assembled a large army of 185,000 men against the rebellious Hezechiah, King of Judah, and besieged the holy city of Jerusalem. As divine punishment for this blasphemous conduct God sent his angel to destroy the Assyrian camp.[1] This violent scene, with its confused mass of bodies, dangerously waving battle standards and horses bolting, stumbling and crashing to the ground, is typical in its subject-matter and composition of much of Tempesta's work. The pupil of the northern artist Joannes Stradanus, Tempesta began his career working for Giorgio Vasari on the interior decoration of the Palazzo Vecchio in Florence in 1579–80. On his move to Rome in 1580 he began to decorate palaces, villas and the Vatican, predominantly with landscape, hunting and battle scenes which provided him with unlimited opportunities to display his

ability to portray animals, especially horses. Despite his activity as a painter he is best known today as a printmaker and draughtsman. Between 1589 and 1627 he produced over one thousand prints, which were widely circulated in Europe during his lifetime and were often used as models by other artists. They were mainly series of engravings and book illustrations, including a particularly outstanding series of 220 scenes from the Old Testament in the British Museum. The impressive Liverpool

composition appears similar in certain details, though not in overall composition, to an engraving published as part of a series of biblical battle scenes entitled *Sacra Bella Sanctae Veterum Bibliorum Historiae*[2] [fig. 39]. Whereas the print shows a view of Jerusalem in background and is clearly set in a tented army camp, the drawing merely suggests a tent with a swathe of fabric in the right corner and a sketchy view of its interior. The drawing's vengeance-seeking God, propelled forwards through a break

in the cloud by surrounding cherubs, is
changed in the print to a sword-bearing
angel. The print also made use of the
soldiers on horseback on the right and
centre of the drawing but changed the
foreground and left-hand side of the
composition. Sometimes Tempesta
modelled the powerfully built horses in his
drawings on those he had engraved in his
Horses of different lands, published in 1590,
but none in the Liverpool drawing can be
linked in this way.[3] Both the rearing horse
on the extreme left and the fallen horse
seen rump-on in the centre also appear
reversed in Tempesta's engraving
*Alexander the Great battling with the
Persians*, from a series of twelve prints
published in 1608.[4]

Fig. 39 Tempesta, *The death of Sennacherib*, print in *Sacra Bella Sanctae Veterum Bibliorum
Historiae*, London, British Museum

54 PIETRO TESTA
Lucca *ca.* 1611–1650 Rome
The Martyrdom of St Angelo

380 × 255 mm, pen and ink with brown
and black wash over red and black chalk,
heavily indented with a stylus around most
of the figures and the arched top[1]
Inscribed by the artist in ink on drawing *per
S. Marti' d Monti*; and on the right *piu qua*;
in ink in lower right corner of drawing *2*; in
ink on mount, lower right corner *Pietro
Testa*
PROVENANCE Pierre Crozat, no. 2 (?),
sold as part of lot 271 – eighteen drawings
by Testa of the Martyrdom of St Angelo
the Carmelite, 10 April–13 May 1741,
Paris; Benjamin West (L419), possibly one
of the fourteen drawings by Testa sold
Christie's, 9 June 1820, lots 66, 85, and 13
June, lot 110; C.R. Blundell
Reproduced in reverse while in the Crozat
collection by the comte de Caylus and
Nicolas Le Sueur as an etching and a
chiaroscuro woodcut and published in
*Recueil d'Estampes d'après les plus beaux
tableaux et ... dessins qui sont en France*,
Paris 1729, no. 136
EXHIBITION Edinburgh 1972, no. 111,
illus. p. 87
LITERATURE Noted in E. Cropper,
Pietro Testa: Prints and Drawings, London
1989, p. 196, n. 6.; noted but not illus. in
U. Fischer Pace, 'Un album di disegni a
Santa Maria in Via a Camerino', in *Disegni
marchigiani dal Cinquecento al Settecento*,
edd. M. Di Giampaolo and G. Angelucci,
Florence 1995, pp. 106–07
WAG1995.357

Saint Angelo was a Carmelite friar stabbed
to death whilst preaching in Leocato,
Sicily, by Berengarius, a man whom he had
denounced for incest.[2] In his drawing of
the subject Testa has focussed light and
attention on the falling saint as he clutches
the cross in one hand, continuing to pray
for the people and his murderers, whilst
with the other hand he orders the turbulent
crowd not to avenge his death. The
aggression and anger on the crowd's face is
dramatically conveyed through Testa's use
of ink, wash and bare paper. Although the
drawing would seem to be a finished
modello for one of the side altarpieces
commissioned by Prior Giovanni Antonio
Filippini in 1645 for the Carmelite Church
of San Martino ai Monti in Rome, it was
never actually used by Testa for the

completed painting.[3] Instead Testa painted
*St Angelo's vision of Christ while a hermit on
Mount Carmel*, a finished and squared-up
drawing for which is in Darmstadt.[4] The
fact that Testa was working up ideas for
both a *Vision* and a *Martyrdom* of St
Angelo at the same time is confirmed by a
drawing in an Italian collection which has
studies for both subjects on the same
sheet.[5] The Italian drawing for the

martyrdom has colour notes written on the
clothing by Testa, showing how far he
went towards completion of the subject
before abandoning it. Testa was known for
his unconventional or unusual iconography
or subject-matter. An example can be seen
in the upper half of this drawing, where
God the Father is seen blessing three
angels as they carry up to him on a sheet
three figures kneeling around a box or

casket. The imagery may be related to the movement of the saint's body in a decorated silver casket from the church in which he was martyred to a newly built church in 1623.[6] The star-like flowers floating around the angels may refer to the lilies found growing on his original burial site, which miraculously renewed themselves whenever they were cut.[7] Testa reproduced part of the imagery of angelic figures kneeling around a box from which float flowers in his finished altarpiece of the *Vision of St Angelo*.

The Liverpool drawing once belonged to the great French collector of drawings Pierre Crozat (1665–1740), who owned eighteen Testa drawings relating to the St Angelo project. The large number of studies related to one work confirms the view of one of Testa's biographers, Passeri, who in describing another Testa commission in San Martino, for a fresco in the apse, noted that he took such a long time over the conception of the project, ordered in 1642, that the prior finally revoked it.[8] His rejection profoundly affected the sombre and moody Testa, who was increasingly convinced that as the result of envy and slander he was not receiving due recognition. His final five years were typified by an increasing retreat from commerce and the public until he committed suicide by drowning in the Tiber.[9]

55 ALESSANDRO TIARINI
Bologna 1577–1688 Bologna
Christ being shown to the people

103 × 109 mm, pen and brown ink over black chalk on very thin paper stuck on to card. The paper has been trimmed on the left
PROVENANCE Roscoe sale, 1816, as part of lot 428, Tiarini, "Six historical, &c. on two sheets", bt. Slater 7s. 6d.;
C.R. Blundell
EXHIBITION Edinburgh 1972, no. 113, illus. p. 61
LITERATURE Noted in D. Benati, *Disegni emiliani del Sei-Settecento, come nascono i dipinti*, Milan 1991, under no. 24; E. Negro and M. Pirondini, *La scuola dei Carracci dall'Accademia alla Bottega di Ludovico*, Modena 1994, p. 295, fig. 368
WAG1995.335

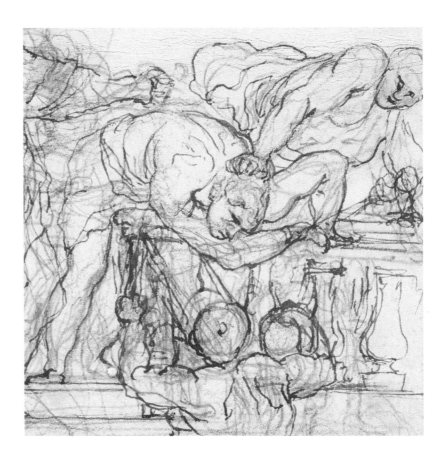

Christ being shown to the people is one of seven drawings in the Weld-Blundell collection by or attributed to the Bolognese artist Tiarini, the greatest number of works by any one artist in the collection and the largest by Tiarini in any collection in Britain. Philip Pouncey first pointed out in the 1972 Edinburgh catalogue that this compositional sketch was a preliminary study for the painting of *Ecce Homo* in the Basilica of the Santa Casa in Loreto.[1] Loreto, near Ancona, is the site of the Holy House in which the Virgin Mary was said to have lived at the time of the Annunciation and which was miraculously transported to Italy by angels in 1295. It was a major centre for pilgrimage and attracted many gifts and donations, one of which was Tiarini's large painting, given to the Basilica by Pietro Raffaelli di Cingoli.[2] Tiarini probably painted *Ecce Homo* shortly after he had returned to Bologna in 1606 from an eight-year stay in Florence, where he had fled after a brawl, acceding to the request of Ludovico Carracci who had pleaded with him to reinforce the artistic ranks in Bologna, by now reduced by deaths and departures for Rome.[3] It is one of several works he painted before 1611 in which he experimented with strong contrasts of deep shadow and bright light. In this case he depicted as a night-scene the event in which Christ is shown to the contemptuous, gesticulating people before being led to his execution. It is a much more aggressive composition, with Christ's face brought forcefully to notice as the soldiers thrust his head over the balustrade towards the crowd below, than the usual representation of Christ in this scene, standing upright, calm, dignified and still, which Tiarini himself used a few years later in another painting of the subject.[4] The violence of the painted image is mirrored by Tiarini's graphic style in which, typically, from a chaotic mass of tangled black-chalk lines figures emerge with a few rapid defining strokes of the pen. Despite its seeming an impetuously sketched first idea, the small drawing is an almost finished study for the painting, to which only a few details remain to be added or changed – the hat of one of the crowd becomes a bonnet-like cap, the figure on the left (cut off by the edge of the drawing) 'shows' Christ to the people with both arms rather than one and, more significantly, Christ receives a distinguishing beard.

56 ALESSANDRO TIARINI
Study for a lunette: the Annunciation with angels

350 × 566 mm, black chalk and brown wash, heightened with white (oxidized) on faded blue-grey semicircular paper
Inscribed in ink on drawing, lower left corner *l carrache*; in lower right corner *15*; in ink on outer mount above lunette *No1*; and on reverse of mount cut out from old mount and reattached *No:2*[1]
PROVENANCE Benjamin West (L419; inscribed in pencil on mount *West Bolognese*); C.R. Blundell
EXHIBITION Edinburgh 1972, no. 112, illus. p. 62, attributed to Tiarini by J. Stock
WAG1995.377

The fluidly drawn composition is closely related to a fresco by Ludovico Carracci for a lunette above the arch in the choir of the Cathedral of San Pietro in Bologna, painted in 1618–19 [fig. 40].[2] It is not, however, just another example of a younger artist, at the beginning of his career, paying homage to an older master such as Ludovico. The drawing may have been meant as a direct critique of Ludovico's fresco, his last finished work, which attracted so much virulent criticism that, according to Malvasia (whose pages are full of such incidents of rivalries between Bologna's artists), Ludovico retired to his bed ill with depression and died.[3] The attacks on the vast wall-painting focussed on the Archangel's supposedly badly placed foot, which Ludovico had positioned without taking into account the perspective of the viewer below. Whether or not an ageing Ludovico, whose eyesight was failing, made such an elementary mistake, we know from a letter to a friend that what especially hurt him was the fact

that the malicious criticisms had come from fellow artists and so marked the loss of his status as the head of Bologna's artistic community.[4] Malvasia noted that one of these artists was Tiarini, who had already worked in the cathedral choir and was a jealous rival for the lunette commission, which he believed would have been awarded him had it not been for the intervention of Ludovico's friend Bartolomeo Dulcini, a canon of the cathedral, and Ludovico's undercutting him on price.[5] It was not the first time that Tiarini had come into conflict with Ludovico, who had refused the young artist training in the Carracci academy.[6] His rivalry was probably stoked by the fact that his own work owed much to Ludovico's style, displaying similarly large, elongated figures, wrapped in complex floating drapery, topped by small heads. Tiarini has done everything he could to make his *Annunciation* different from Ludovico's, reversing the two main figures, altering their poses, so they look up rather than

Fig. 40 Ludovico Carracci, *The Annunciation*, fresco, San Pietro, Bologna

down, and moving the angelic host closer
to earth, yet the composition remains so
close to the fresco in scale, concept and
mood that it could almost be Tiarini's
finished study for the commission he never
received but felt was his due.

57 JACOPO TINTORETTO

(Jacopo Robusti)

Venice 1518–1594 Venice

*Study of the head of Giuliano de'
Medici by Michelangelo*[1]

390 × 255 mm, black and white chalk on
coarse buff paper with the remnants of a
brown-ink framing line

Inscribed in ink on drawing *G Tintoretto*[2]

PROVENANCE Benjamin West (L419;
inscribed in pencil on mount *from Mr
West's Collection Venetian School*), possibly
one of "three heads in black chalk by
Tintoretto" sold Christie's, 10 June 1820,
lot 73; C.R. Blundell

EXHIBITIONS Venice 1980, cat. 19;
NACF 1997; London 1998, no. 86

Watermark on drawing paper: in centre of
paper sunburst (?) with rays or flower with
petals (?); on mount: fleur-de-lys within
crowned escutcheon and looping line
design below

WAG1995.191

This is a typically vigorous study in black
chalk after the head of Giuliano de' Medici
from his tomb sculpted by Michelangelo in
the Medici Chapel in San Lorenzo,
Florence. Jacopo Tintoretto is known to
have owned a plaster cast of the figure,
executed by Daniele da Volterra in 1557.[3]
But it is probable that he had access to
earlier copies either already on the
Venetian market at the beginning of his
career in the 1540s or obtained through his
contact with Pietro Aretino, who
commissioned a work from him in 1545
and owned two drawings of the Medici
tomb figures, sent to him by Vasari in
1535.[4] Many other studies after Giuliano's
head from Tintoretto's studio exist, some
of which have been attributed to Jacopo
and dated to the 1540s and 1550s, others
attributed to his son and daughter
Domenico and Marietta or to other studio
assistants.[5] The Liverpool study, with its
long strokes of hatching in the shadows, its
repeated curls of hair and spare use of
white heightening, has most in common
with one of the studies in Christ Church,
Oxford, attributed by Byam Shaw to
Jacopo, in which the head is seen from
above looking sharply downwards to our
right.[6]

The cast of Giuliano was used, like
other pieces of sculpture owned by Jacopo
(see exh. cat. 58), as a studio prop to help
him learn and teach others in his workshop

G. Tintoretto

111

how to draw from the single figure and, in particular, to draw the face in sharply foreshortened or twisted angles. The frequency with which accidental dark resinous stains can be found on the drawings suggests that they were treated as a workaday part of the studio as does the coarseness of the paper used. The Liverpool drawing is on paper in which bits of old string and gritty granules of chalk can be seen with the naked eye. We know from his biographer Carlo Ridolfi that Jacopo preferred to draw these studies at night, with the sculpture lit by candles, so as to create strong tonal contrasts of light and shade across the three-dimensional surface.[7] His studies were, therefore, not meant as direct copies of the sculpture but as interpretations made for pictorial reasons. The use of sculpture as a workshop training exercise may explain the frequent reuse of drawings, with copies, by Jacopo and others, of the recto image often found on the verso either reversed or upside down. It may also account for the variety of angles from which the bust was drawn. The Liverpool study, for example, is unique and does not replicate any other pose. Although such a closely focussed study of a head was primarily meant to help practise drawing from the figure, studying sculpture from all angles also provided possible poses to be used later in paintings. Curly-haired young men with elegantly but unnaturally twisted necks similar to the Liverpool study can be found in several early works by Jacopo Tintoretto – for example the wreathed male figure seen sharply from below in the octagonal *Rape of Europa* in the Galleria Estense, Modena, painted *ca.* 1541–42.

58 ATTRIBUTED TO JACOPO TINTORETTO
Study of the head of the bust of 'Emperor Vitellius'

383 × 245 mm, black chalk heightened with white on faded blue paper
Inscribed in ink on drawing *G. Tintoretto*; and a large cursive *E*
PROVENANCE Benjamin West (L419 on a restored strip of paper in lower left corner), possibly one of "three heads in black chalk by Tintoretto" sold Christie's, 10 June 1820, lot 73; C.R. Blundell WAG1995.251

The study is of a cast from a marble antique head of the 'Roman Emperor Vitellius' bequeathed to the state of Venice by Cardinal Domenico Grimani in 1523 and now in the Archaeological Museum, Venice, and dated to the first half of the second century AD.[1] Between 1525 and 1593 the marble head was displayed in the Ducal Palace, where favoured artists could study and make plaster casts of it. One such artist must have been Jacopo Tintoretto as a copy of the head was bequeathed by Jacopo's son, Domenico, to one of his own young pupils on 20 October 1630.[2] The cast is probably the same one as appears in the background of a *Portrait of an unknown gentleman* in Birmingham City Art Gallery by an early seventeenth-century follower of Jacopo Tintoretto. Domenico's will, which states, "I bequeath to my brother [Marco] all the casts in the studio. And if Bastian [Sebastiano Cassieri] my boy will still be in my service at the time of my death I bequeath him four of these casts, namely a head of Vitellius, a full-length figure and two torsos of his own choice", demonstrates the significant role that these casts played in Tintoretto's studio in teaching anatomy and practising drawing from the figure. The large number of drawings of the 'Vitellius' head, more than twenty-five sheets in collections around the world, confirms the importance of the Vitellius for studying the face in particular.[3] Of course Jacopo used other means to compose his paintings, placing little figures made from wax or clay and fabric on, or hanging from threads above, small wooden stage-sets lit by candles to help him create his multi-figured compositions.[4] All twenty-five other sheets are in black chalk, all but two heightened with white, on a variety of blue, green, grey and buff papers ranging in size from 430 × 280 mm to 260 × 200 mm, and show the plaster cast from various angles, many of them (unlike the Liverpool study) from below. The Liverpool study appears closest in handling to those identified as by Jacopo in Christ Church, Oxford, and in Erlangen University Library (B1542), although neither shows the distinctive short zig-zag hatching over a layer of smudged chalk under the chin.[5] Nor can it be linked to drawings by other family members of the workshop. The drawing in Milan inscribed as by Jacopo's eldest daughter Marietta (*ca.* 1554–*ca.* 1590) and probably executed in the 1570s depicts the hair more loosely and shows the chin as a jowly, fleshy mass, as if it were a human rather than a sculpted head; perhaps significantly she was primarily a portrait painter.[6] The Liverpool drawing emphasizes the sculptural effect by retaining the head's blank eyes and its 'blocky', bull-necked qualities. Perhaps reflecting an awareness of Vitellius's reputation as a cruel glutton, his face, with its small mouth, heavy jowls and full cheeks, proved a particularly suitable model for plump, well fed officials and guests in banqueting scenes, or for proud Pharisees or the Roman governor Pilate in paintings such as Jacopo's early work of the 1540s, *Christ in the house of the Pharisee* in the Escorial Chapter House, or his *Christ before Pilate* in the Scuola di San Rocco, or *The Last Supper* in San Polo in Venice.[7]

Fig. 41 Francesco Trevisani, *Christ baptizing Saint Peter*, St Peter's, Rome

59 FRANCESCO TREVISANI
Treviso 1656–1746 Rome
A sheet of studies: half-draped male figure; a hand; a self-portrait

232 × 175 mm, black chalk on brown paper
Watermark on mount: large fleur-de-lys within a crowned coat of arms with the initials LVG below, similar to Heawood 1829 (Holland, 1743)[1]
Inscribed in ink on mount *Trevisani il suo ritratto*
PROVENANCE Benjamin West (no stamp; inscribed on mount in pencil *West Venetian*), possibly among the "five historical drawings by Trevisani" sold Christie's, 14 June 1820, lot 74;
C.R. Blundell
WAG1995.316

The small detail of a hand clutching drapery between the first and second finger is a precise study for Christ's left hand in Trevisani's *Christ baptizing St Peter*, the large painted cartoon produced for one of the mosaic lunettes in the vestibule of the Baptismal Chapel in St Peter's, Rome [fig. 41].[2] Although Trevisani's finished design shows a fully clothed, monumental Christ with his right arm raised to pour the water over the saint, it is quite probable that the half-draped figure sketched from the right side with its arm raised was also a first idea for Christ's calm and dignified frontal pose, as the sketch is in essence a drapery study in which Trevisani was more concerned to define the fall of the mantle's folds than the pose of the figure.
Trevisani's commission for the lunettes, dome and pendentives of the Chapel's vestibule, all based on the theme of baptism, had a long gestation period. He actually painted the cartoons for the lunette mosaics between September 1732 and the summer of 1737, but some oil sketches for the lunettes, showing minor compositional changes, were completed as early as 1710, shortly after Trevisani had been awarded the commission on the death of Giovan Battista Gaulli in 1709.[3] Similar half-draped male figures were used by Trevisani in paintings datable between 1710 and 1714, so it may be that this pose was in his mind when he first began to formulate ideas for the baptismal composition.[4] The papal commission for St Peter's was Trevisani's most prestigious and he produced for it his most monumental and admired work, among the last completed paintings of his career. Only one other preparatory drawing, on similar paper, is known for the six lunettes, and that also combines anatomical and drapery details.[5] It was common for Trevisani to draw on the same sheet studies of different parts of the anatomy, gestures and drapery to varied scales. In the Liverpool sheet,

however, the portrait of the artist himself may have been added at a later date, perhaps in the 1720s, for his weary, care-worn face appears to be older than that shown in the self-portrait in a fur hat, representing himself aged about sixty-one, which he painted in 1717 as a gift for his important patron Prince-Bishop Lothar Franz von Schönborn (1693–1729) [fig. 42].[6] This informal portrait of Trevisani in his work clothes, wearing a painter's turban over his bald head, was only ever meant to be seen by the artist's own eyes, so unlike a painted self-portrait (which even when informal always retains an element of public presentation) this is direct and honest.

60 ALESSANDRO TURCHI
Verona 1578–1648/49 Rome
Hercules and Omphale

200 × 266 mm, brown wash over black chalk
Watermark on mount: unidentified lozenge pattern[1]
Inscribed on drawing, lower right corner *Alex.ro*; in ink on mount *Alessandro Veronese*; on reverse in ink *no.4*[2]
PROVENANCE Roscoe sale, 1816, lot 270, bt. Slater 14*s*.; C.R. Blundell, valued at 9*s*. in 1841
EXHIBITIONS Edinburgh 1972, no. 114, illus. p. 88; Venice 1980, no. 51
WAG1995.354

This is a finished design or *modello* for the large painting of *Hercules and Omphale* in Munich, one of Turchi's most famous

works from his early Roman period [fig. 42].[3] It can be dated to about 1620, as Giulio Mancini refers to Turchi's *Hercules in the act of spinning* as already finished in 1621.[4] The Liverpool drawing is an almost exact study for the painting, unlike two other apparently finished drawings of the same subject in Stuttgart and Paris.[5] It is typical of Turchi's drawing technique in being a finished composition and relying for its effective creation of strong contrasts of light and shade on a delicately applied wash over lightly sketched chalk contours – like those on the comparable drawing, of almost exactly the same size, for the pendant picture of *The Fury of Hercules*, also in Munich.[6] Turchi had arrived in Rome *ca.* 1614–15 and first worked with friends from Verona in the artistic team decorating the papal summer palace on the Quirinale. He soon acquired a reputation

Fig. 42 Alessandro Turchi, *Hercules and Omphale*, Munich, Bayerische Staatsgemäldesammlungen

and picked up patronage from the Roman nobility and clergy, including the pope's nephew Cardinal Scipione Borghese, for his easel paintings of biblical and mythological scenes. He prided himself on the polished surface finish evident in the Munich *Hercules and Omphale*. According to Greek myth Omphale was the Lydian queen who enslaved the legendary strong-man Hercules as her lover, making him perform women's work such as spinning thread in women's clothes and scolding him if his clumsy fingers crushed the spindle. Classical writers made his servitude to Omphale an allegory of how easily a strong man can become enslaved by love for a lecherous and ambitious woman.[7] Turchi shows the slumped, dejected Hercules holding the spindle whilst Omphale, wearing Hercules's lion's skin and leaning on his giant club, looks on in amusement with her ladies in waiting and Cupid, the god of love. The number of times that Turchi worked on the theme suggests that the story of Hercules and Omphale, with its excuse for half-naked female flesh accompanied by a warning against dominant women, appealed to those of Turchi's patrons with a taste for a mildly erotic and amusing mythological story-line.

61 GIORGIO VASARI

Arezzo 1511–1574 Florence

Three reclining river- and lakeland gods

247 × 330 mm, pen and brown ink with brown wash heightened with white (partly oxidized) on grey-green paper[1]
Watermark on mount [B]LAUW[2]
Inscribed in ink on drawing *MENCIO BENACO/TESINO PO/F*; and in black chalk very faintly, lower left corner *Vasari*
PROVENANCE Benjamin West (no collector's mark; inscribed in pencil on mount *West Vasari Florentine*, and in a different hand *genuine*); C.R. Blundell
LITERATURE A. Cecchi, 'Qualche contributo al corpus grafico del Vasari e del suo ambiente', in *Il Vasari storiografo e artista: Atti del Congresso internazionale nel IV centenario della morte* (1974), Florence 1976, p. 147; A. Cecchi, 'Nuove acquisizioni per un catalogo dei disegni di Giorgio Vasari', *Antichità Viva*, XVII, no. 1, 1978, p. 55, fig. 4
WAG1995.314

This is a design for one of the four large panels which Vasari painted in monochrome to decorate the auditorium in which Pietro Aretino's comedy *La Talanta* was performed during the Venice Carnival of February 1542.[3] Vasari travelled to Venice in the autumn of 1541 at the request of his friend Aretino to organize the decoration of the ceiling and walls of the temporary theatre in which the Compagnia dei Sempiterni, the gentleman's amateur drama club who had commissioned the play, were to perform, and his studies were probably finished by January.[4] The performance may have been held in one of the unfinished buildings in the Canareggio district of the city, and the decorations removed as soon as the play's run was over. Other studies for the decorative scheme, depicting the gods and goddesses for two more of the main wall panels, are in Paris and Berlin.[5] Vasari's part in the production is described in his letter to Ottaviano de' Medici in Florence and repeated decades later in Vasari's life of his assistant Cristofano Gherardi.[6] The large panels placed around the temporary auditorium represented the gods of the rivers, lakes and islands of Venice and its hinterland. As described by Vasari, the Liverpool gods represent the lake of Benaco (more commonly known as Garda) and the small rivers of Mincio (symbolized by an oar) and Ticino which flow from it as tributaries of the mighty river Po whose estuary fed and fertilized the plain south of Venice and who is shown holding two cornucopiae overflowing with water and fruits. The allegorical figures were not directly related to the play, about the bawdy adventures of a Roman courtesan called Talanta, but were intended to translate its ribald themes and comic mood from a theatrical to a visual art form. Vasari seems to have enjoyed the opportunity provided by this commission for a temporary installation to give free rein to his inventive skills, injecting wit as well as coarse lewdness into his design – with the venerable lake Benaco pouring forth its waters by urinating into an urn held out towards Po by Ticino, shown as a foreshortened young man, because, as Vasari wittily put it, the river only runs for a short length.[7] An interesting comparison can be made between this composition, created for a comedy performed during the licentious period of the Venetian carnival, and Vasari's more typical allegorical

figures, such as one finds in his designs for the apartments of the Palazzo Vecchio, the Medici's administrative centre in Florence (see exh. cat. 62) – sometimes rather cold, aloof figures intended to represent serious intellectual concepts. Amidst the vulgarity Vasari also created one of his most handsome designs, its attractive pictorial effects enhanced by the use of delicately applied wash and finely hatched white lead to model the gods' muscles and bedraggled hair, which impressed Venetian artists and, according to Vasari, received compliments from Titian himself.

62 GIORGIO VASARI
The triumph of the goddess Cybele

268 × 201 mm, pen and brown ink and wash in an oval
Inscribed in ink (in a different hand from Barnard's) *Triumph of Cybele by Vasari*; in pencil on mount *genuine*; and with Popham's agreement to the Vasari attribution
PROVENANCE Anonymous Italian collector whose inscription is on the reverse of the oval drawing;[1] John Barnard (L1419; no. 290; inscribed in ink on mount *J:B*; on reverse in ink *J:B No:290/10¾ by 8/Cybele and her Priests the Corybantes*; Charles Rogers?; Roscoe sale, 1816, lot 98, as Vasari, "The Triumph of Cybele Pen and bistre; an oval 11h 8½w The original from which Mr Rogers has published a facsimile in his Imitations of Drawings 2 vols folio.",

bt. Ford 13*s*.; C.R. Blundell, valued at 10*s*. in 1841
WAG1995.342

This is a study for the central oval panel set into the ceiling of the Sala d'Opi in the Apartment of the Elements in the Palazzo Vecchio, Florence, which Vasari and his assistant Cristofano Gherardi (1508–1556) painted some time between 1556 and 1557.[2] Vasari had begun his career at the court of Cosimo I de' Medici (1519–1574), when in 1555 the duke entrusted him with the transformation of the medieval Palazzo Vecchio into his official and princely residence. Vasari's usual working practice in the Palazzo was to sketch a design himself and delegate much of its execution to a trusted associate such as Gherardi, while retaining overall control of the whole creative enterprise, its style and successful completion.[3] The Apartment of the Elements formed part of the private suite of rooms on the top floor of the Palazzo Vecchio, and included the main terrace with its views across Florence, the river Arno and the countryside beyond. Its overall decorative theme was the heavenly gods and their relationship to nature, with four rooms devoted to each of the elements in turn – Earth, Fire, Air and Water – and one room representing all four. Although it was painted before the Apartment of Leo X, on the floor below, the decorative schemes chosen for each of the rooms were directly related to the themes of those below, which were to be painted with scenes from the lives of the 'earthly gods', the Medici family. The Room of Ops, goddess of plenty and wife of Saturn, god of agriculture, who together ensured the fertility of the earth and the prosperity of the human race, was paired with that of Lorenzo the Magnificent (outstanding in the fields of culture, politics and patronage) in the room immediately below.[4] Friezes around the sides of the room showed allegorical figures representing the four seasons and the twelve months. Ops was also the patron goddess of married couples and their offspring, and her cult spread widely in antiquity under other names, including Cybele. Vasari has shown the goddess, with a crown of turrets, being drawn by lions in triumph on a chariot surrounded by her priests and devotees the Corybantes, who were known for their frenzied dancing and their loud playing of cymbals and drums.

There are slight differences between the finished painting and the drawing, in which Cybele's sceptre slopes forwards rather than backwards and one of the priests in the procession in front of the goddess holds no wand of office in the air as he does in the painting. What would seem to be a poor contemporary copy of the Liverpool drawing, larger and with some variations, is in the Louvre, having formerly been in the collection of Jonathan Richardson Senior, where it was attributed to Perino del Vaga.[5]

63 FEDERICO ZUCCARO
Sant'Angelo in Vado 1540/42–
1609 Ancona
St Paul shaking off the viper

270 × 411 mm; pen and brown ink and brown wash heightened with white lead on faded blue-green paper with a triangular shaped top squared in red chalk
Inscribed in pencil on mount *genuine*
PROVENANCE Jonathan Richardson Senior (L2184; with his attribution to Federico Zuccaro in ink on mount and his shelf mark on the reverse *M 42/Zt 2* (or *zb*), possibly sold 6 February 1746/47 as part of lot 13, "Four drawings P. Farinati, Zuccaro, St Paul in Crete &c." for 10s. 6d.; Benjamin West (no collector's mark; inscribed in pencil on mount *Mr West's Collection Roman School*), sold Christie's, 1 July 1820, lot 178, as Federico Zuccaro, *St Paul shaking off the viper*, bt. Smith £1. 6s.; C.R. Blundell
EXHIBITION Edinburgh 1969, no. 97, plate 27
WAG1995.372

Fig. 43 Federico Zuccaro, *St Paul shaking off the viper*,
Cappella Paolina, Vatican

Fig. 44 Federico Zuccaro, *Taddeo Zuccaro at work on the Palazzo Mattei admired by Michelangelo and Vasari*, Vienna, Albertina

This is the only known study for the fresco in the triangular space above the chancel of the Cappella Paolina in the Vatican which Federico Zuccaro worked on between 1580 and 1584 [fig. 43].[1] The decoration of the narrow Pauline Chapel, sited near the Sistine Chapel and intended for the pope's private ceremonies, had been begun reluctantly by an elderly Michelangelo in 1542; he painted only two of the six frescos on the side walls. In 1580 Federico was given the task of completing the decorative scheme by frescoing the final bay, the vault and the lunettes at either end of the chapel – but in December 1581 he was expelled from Rome by the Bolognese-born Pope Gregory XIII (1572–1585) for exhibiting a painting which satirized the Bolognese art establishment and members of the papal household who had dared to criticize one of Zuccaro's works.[2] After representations by patrons and friends he was eventually pardoned by the pope and returned in December 1583 to finish the work in the chapel.[3] Although awkwardly placed, the fresco was crucially positioned immediately above the worshipper's line of sight to the main altar: it was therefore important that the composition would 'read well' and be clearly understood both visually and intellectually. The incident shown in Zuccaro's drawing occurred after St Paul had been shipwrecked on the island of

Malta as he was on his way for trial in Rome. The islanders lit a fire to warm the cold and wet survivors and as St Paul was adding more wood a viper driven out from the pile by the fire bit his hand. He flung the snake off into the fire but the islanders were so amazed that he had not died from poisoning that they believed him a god.[4] The finished fresco depicts neither fire nor snake but seems to show instead other events which took place on Malta after the saint had cured, by prayer and laying on of hands, the fever and dysentery of the father of his host the chief magistrate, and had attracted many other Maltese for healing.[5] The viper story was much more anecdotal, even ridiculous, and, imputing their conversion to Christianity, as it did, to the credulity of the Maltese, it was almost blasphemous compared to the more conventional subject finally chosen. It is possible that the drawing, squared as if ready to be transferred on a larger scale to the wall, was Federico's first idea for the space, perhaps produced before he was banished from Rome and on his return thought better of; he may have changed it to a more 'theologically correct' subject in tune with the militantly Counter-Reformation papacy of Gregory XIII, who required religious art clearly to demonstrate a saint's piety and faith.

64 TADDEO ZUCCARO
Sant'Angelo in Vado 1529–1566 Rome
Alexander the Great taming Bucephalus

215 × 352 mm, pen and brush with red ink and wash over red chalk in an oval[1]
PROVENANCE Jonathan Richardson Senior (L2184; in an octagonal Richardson mount), sold 3 February 1746/47 as part of lot 19, "Four, Taddeo Zuccaro, Curtius leaping into the lake, Baroccio ... Salembeni, stoning Stephen", for £2. 12s.; Nathaniel Hillier, no. 311 in the manuscript catalogue of his collection, as Taddeo Zuccaro, *Marcus Curtius leaping into the Gulph*, with a lengthy description and valued at £1. 11s. 6d.;[2] 'Pseudo-Crozat' (L474); Henry Blundell (?), originally in a Blundell album (254)
EXHIBITION Edinburgh 1969, no. 100, pl. 26
LITERATURE Noted in J.A. Gere, *Taddeo Zuccaro. His Development Studied in his Drawings*, Chicago 1969, pp. 97 (n. 1), 215, under no. 254, pl. 127b
WAG1995.331

This finished study or *modello* for an oval ceiling fresco in the Palazzo Caetani (formerly the Palazzo Mattei) in the via delle Botteghe Oscure, Rome, which Taddeo painted between March 1559 and October 1560 for Alessandro Mattei,[3] differs from the fresco only in there being three fewer soldiers on the left. Taddeo is known to have decorated three buildings with scenes from the life of Alexander, the celebrated king and military commander and namesake of Alessandro Mattei, the earliest occasion being the six scenes he painted *ca.* 1550 on the façade of a Roman house next to Santa Lucia della Tinta. Then in 1559–60 he undertook, with the assistance of his younger brother Federico, two series of fresco cycles in the Palazzo Caetani and in the Castello Orsini at Bracciano, north of Rome.[4] Another oval study for the Caetani series was once owned by the important French connoisseur Pierre Crozat (1665–1740), a close friend of the comte de Caylus (1692–1765), who may be identified as the anonymous collector (nicknamed 'Pseudo-Crozat' by Frits Lugt) whose black-ink stamp of a large capital *C* is found on the Liverpool study.[5] In 1560 Taddeo was at the height of his short-lived career, brought to an abrupt end by his death after a brief

illness in 1566. His talent as a façade painter and fresco artist was widely recognized in Rome by patrons and artists such as Michelangelo, whose appreciation of Taddeo's work was recorded by his brother Federico in a composition which he drew decades later showing Michelangelo and Vasari admiring Taddeo as he painted the façade of the Palazzo Jacopo Mattei in 1548 [fig. 44].[6] Taddeo's artistic flair was more evident in his drawings, such as this rich pictorial image with its innovative use of brush point and red wash combined with red chalk, which he favoured in the late 1550s, than in the few of his frescos that survive undamaged. Typically he combined passages of naturalism – evident in his repeated attempts to place the back legs of the horse – with stylized decorative elements and figures. In the Liverpool study Alexander is shown seated bareback and without reins on the rearing Bucephalus, whom only he could tame and ride, while each one of his soldiers expresses his admiration with a different and elegant pose.

65 ATTRIBUTED TO TADDEO ZUCCARO
Christ healing the blind man

381 × 410 mm, pen and brown ink over black chalk on blue paper
Inscribed in ink on drawing, lower right *...deo Zucch...dis*; in ink on mount *Federigo Zucchero*
PROVENANCE Benjamin West (L419), sold Christie's, 13 June 1820, lot 88, "two drawings by T Zuccaro *Christ restoring sight* and *The Judgement of Solomon*", for 16s.; C.R. Blundell
EXHIBITION Edinburgh 1969, no. 96, pl. 28, as Federico Zuccaro
LITERATURE *Dessins de Taddeo et Federico Zuccaro*, exhib. cat. by J. Gere, Paris, Musée du Louvre, 1969, noted under Federico Zuccaro, cat. 66[1]
WAG1995.375

Following the old eighteenth-century (?) attribution on the mount the drawing was until now considered to be by Taddeo's younger brother Federico.[2] It was thought to be either an unused or a discarded idea for an altarpiece Federico painted in the Cathedral at Orvieto in 1568, two years after the sudden death of his brother, or derived from that composition and used for an unknown commission.[3] Other drawings by Federico which are much closer to the painted composition are to be found in Oxford, Paris and Poughkeepsie.[4] There are many differences between the finished painting and the drawing in Liverpool – the main one being that the altarpiece is vertical in format, with a giant column in the background to the left with figures clambering up it, by contrast to the oblong 'landscape' composition of the drawing. Apart from the Christ and the blind man and two men in the crowd to the left, none of the other main figures remains the same: the disciple on the right is turned to face the viewer and holds a book whilst the man standing with his back to us half-bends and wears a turban. Although it would appear to be a finished study, the repositioned legs of the man on the right, scribbled in black chalk further down the paper, show that it was a working drawing in which the composition was still in the process of being shaped. The figure of Christ in Federico's drawings in the Ashmolean and the Louvre seems heavier in build with a less mannered face and beard and without the distinctive 'electric-shock' type halo. It has always been difficult, even with documented works, to distinguish between Taddeo's drawings and those by Federico, who learned his brother's style as his chief workshop assistant and never, even after he had developed an independent career in the 1560s, ceased to borrow from him. In addition to the partially obliterated attribution to Taddeo on the drawing, there is some documentary evidence in the archives in Orvieto that before Federico took on the commission Taddeo had been involved in some unresolved way in decorating the church with large paintings of the miracles of Christ for the side chapels.[5] The Liverpool study, with its wiry figures and its white lead highlights applied in a fine parallel hatching, has more in common with Taddeo's than with Federico's manner.[6] It is quite possible, therefore, as supported by James Mundy, that the drawing is by Taddeo, perhaps intended for the Orvieto commission, and that it passed on his death to Federico, who used it as the basis of his own composition.

123

66 ANONYMOUS

Antwerp School, *ca.* 1520

An interior scene with a seated man and woman and two children playing and fighting

253 × 225 mm, pen and ink heightened with white on slate-blue prepared paper within an inscribed arched top
Inscribed in ink on mount *Lucas van Leyden*; on mount in pencil partially obliterated *doubtful but* (?) *very good*
PROVENANCE Roscoe sale, 1816, lot 451, as Lucas van Leyden, "a Gentleman and lady seated at a table, in conversation, children playing before them; black chalk on indigo ground, heightened and highly finished", bt. Slater 10s. (along with a print by Metz of Lucas's drawing of *St Luke painting the Virgin* in the same style as the drawing); C.R. Blundell, valued at 8s. in 1841
WAG1995.329

This beautiful but battered drawing, which has suffered from pigment loss owing to creasing and water damage, was attributed by Popham to the Antwerp-based artist Dirck Jacobsz Vellert (*ca.* 1480/85– *ca.* 1547). Vellert made his name as a designer of stained glass and became internationally renowned when he was chosen to design the monumental windows in King's College Chapel, Cambridge, for Henry VIII. Although Vellert was praised by his contemporaries, including Dürer, in whose honour he held a banquet on the occasion of his visit to Antwerp in 1521, by the seventeenth century his name and abilities had been forgotten.[1] He worked on a smaller as well as a monumental scale, producing painted-glass roundels which were often fitted into the top lights of house windows. The 'arched' top to the Liverpool drawing may in fact be the rim of a circle which has been clipped on all four sides. However, Vellert's designs were usually on cream paper; on only a few does he use white bodycolour as heightening and on none so distinctively as we find it in the Liverpool drawing where, enhanced by the deep blue of the paper, it simulates the shimmering surfaces of reflected light in a darkened interior and the effect of heat from the fire at which the man warms one of his hands behind his back.[2] Moreover, the elaborate costume and fluttering ornate drapery is more typical of the style employed by some Antwerp Mannerists in the 1520s and 1530s, and they often used slate-grey and sometimes blue-grey paper.[3] This was also the most creative and prolific period for the production of stained-glass roundels. Most of Vellert's stained-glass designs were of traditional religious subjects, such as the life of the Virgin Mary or Apocalyptic themes based on Dürer's prints, unlike the obscure, puzzling subject of the Liverpool drawing, which might be drawn from one of the more abstruse incidents in the Old Testament or classical Roman history or could even be secular in meaning. It is unclear whether the man is intending with his gesturing hand, palm down, to ward off the child who is pulling at his clothes or to reject the woman's suggestion as she points to another (bed?)room. A toy cart lies abandoned at the side, the children preferring to fight each other rather than play with it. The children's inclusion suggests that a possible title for the subject might be 'the ill-disciplined household'. Such a moralistic subject would have appealed to certain sections of society, for example the city's *rederijkerskamers*, amateur theatrical groups which were usually made up of merchants, artists and other craftsmen. They wrote their own moralizing stories stressing the virtues of sobriety, thrift and fidelity, such as the cautionary tale of *Sorgheloos* (Carefree), a secular version of the parable of the Prodigal Son which was made into a stained-glass series.[4] They might have welcomed the opportunity to commission such an image as the Liverpool *Interior* from an Antwerp artist.

125

Haarlem 1660–1704 Haarlem

67 *A seated man holding a jug and pipe*

235 × 160 mm, black and red chalk on coarse oatmeal-coloured paper with ink framing lines
Inscribed, in lower left corner in graphite, with monogram *AO*
WAG1995.85

68 *A young man filling his pipe from a tobacco tin*

298 × 110 mm, black and red chalk on oatmeal-coloured paper with ink framing lines
Inscribed, lower right corner, with monogram *AO*; on verso in graphite *Guy* (?), with an *o* above
PROVENANCE C.R. Blundell[1]
WAG1995.254

Dusart was one of the finest Dutch draughtsmen of the last decades of the seventeenth century, whose attractive style is best seen in his single figure studies in chalks of two or three colours. The studies mostly depict roughly dressed peasant types, focussing closely on their gestures, clothing and other trappings but drawn in a refined and technically skilful manner. He painted, etched and drew mainly peasant scenes and in this was strongly influenced by his master and teacher Adriaen van Ostade (1610–1685), the contents of whose studio, including many drawings by Adriaen and his brother Isaack (1621–1649) and by other Haarlem artists, Dusart inherited in 1685. Dusart's own studio was auctioned in Haarlem on 21 August 1708. He made use of the large cache of drawings from Ostade in various ways, copying some, reworking others by 'completing' them with figures, backgrounds and watercolour washes or, as in the case of the Liverpool studies adding to his own figures Adriaen van Ostade's monogram.[2] All these practices made the Ostade drawings and his own more valuable as elegant, finished works of art for sale to connoisseurs. It has been assumed that the extremely careful execution of Dusart's drawings meant that he never intended to use them as motifs to be incorporated into compositions but only as independent works made for the market. It is possible, however, that Dusart's drawings were 'framed up' with ink lines and monograms added to raise their price once they had been used in painted compositions. The pose of the young man filling his pipe, for example, with his distinctive bent-legged stance, is reproduced almost exactly in a painted inn scene dated 1689 in Leipzig but on an older man whose tall felt hat is not stoved in at the top [fig. 45].[3] Although no related painting is known for the other drawing, of a man holding his empty pipe whilst ruefully peering into an apparently empty jug, an equivalent half-length painting of a single man wearing exactly the same type of hat and holding a similar jug and pipe was recently on the market.[4] Both the Liverpool figures hold clay pipes like those produced in the Dutch town of Gouda. Unlike earlier Dutch exponents of the peasant genre tradition, Dusart does not treat his peasant types as unsavoury characters, or mock them or use their image to make coarse satirical points at their expense. On one of his etchings, *The violin-player* of 1685, he added the inscription *The Rustic enjoys sincerely, not darkened by Hypocrisy.*[5] Dusart's figures seem to capture their honest pleasure and experience their spirited and spontaneous reactions without the moralizing gloss seen earlier in the century, when drinking and smoking were associated with sexual overindulgence, the smoker was a well known symbol of idleness and the Dutch term for someone who looked into his empty tankard, *kannekijker*, meant a drunkard.[6]

Fig. 45 Cornelis Dusart, *Inn scene*, Leipzig, Museum der bildenden Kunst

69 FRANS FLORIS I
Antwerp 1519/20–1570 Antwerp
The metamorphosis of Cyane

277 × 190 mm, pen and brown ink with
blue wash heightened with lead white and
another opaque white on a darkened pale
blue paper
Signed in blue wash with a monogram *FF
IV*; inscribed below in ink on drawing
Mutiano; and in a different ink *5*; in pencil
on mount *West the Flemish Raphael*;[1] on the
back in pencil *No–11– Frans Floris*
PROVENANCE Joseph Vanhaecken
(L2516);[2] Benjamin West (L419);
C.R. Blundell
LITERATURE K.G. Boon, *L'Epoque de
Lucas de Leyde et Pierre Bruegel: Dessins des
anciens Pays-Bas, Collection Frits Lugt
Institut Néerlandais*, Paris 1980–81, p. 92;
*The Netherlandish and German Drawings of
the XVth and XVIth Centuries of the Frits
Lugt Collection*, 1992, I, Text, p. 118, as
Mary Magdalene
WAG1995.283

Until recently the drawing had been
identified as showing a penitent Mary
Magdalene, but it in fact depicts the
nymph Cyane, who changes into water, as
described in an episode from the lengthy
Metamorphoses by the celebrated Roman
poet Ovid.[3] Floris's figure was engraved,
although unusually in the same direction as
the drawing, by Cornelis Cort before his
departure for Italy in 1565 and published
by Gerard de Jode in 1566, at the height of
Floris's success, as one of four prints
relating the story of Pluto and Proserpina.[4]
For centuries visual artists had derived an
inspiration from Ovid's *Metamorphoses*,
which lyrically described the strange
transformations of gods and mortals into
various animals and other natural
elements.[5] It would have been available in
Antwerp to Floris, noted for his literary
learning, in a number of Latin and Dutch
versions. The poem relates many of the
most famous tales from ancient mythology,
including the story of Pluto, the god of the
underworld, and his love for his young
niece Proserpina, in which the water-
nymph Cyane features. Driven by his
passion, Pluto kidnapped Proserpina but
the path of his chariot was blocked by
Cyane, who vainly pleaded for Proserpina
with the angry god. Having failed to
prevent the abduction and seen her
fountain destroyed by Pluto she was so

overcome with anguish that, as Ovid relates, "Cyane, grieving for the rape of the goddess and for her fountain's right thus set at naught, nursed an incurable wound in her silent heart, and dissolved all away in tears; and into those very waters was she melted, whose great divinity she had been but now. You might see her limbs softening .... And first of all melt the slenderest parts: her dark hair, her fingers, legs and feet; for it is no great change from slender limbs to cool water .... And finally, in place of living blood, clear water flows through her weakened veins and nothing is left that you can touch."[6] Floris has movingly focussed his pictorial attention and invention on the single figure of Cyane as she metamorphoses, her trailing hair "melting" into the stream's rivulets whilst the anguish of her "silent heart" is visualized through her tear-stained face and her hands knotted in prayer. The overwhelming mood of grief is enhanced by the blue wash which the artist brushed across paper which was originally of a paler, eggshell-blue – darkened by a later application of some sort of varnish (?).[7] The white heightening on the British Museum drawing is much less heavy, and the two sorts of white used on the Liverpool figure confirm the impression that the drawing has been touched up, perhaps by Benjamin West, who had the wash border mount made in colours that harmonized with the original paper.

70 JOSEPH HEINTZ
THE ELDER
Basle 1564–1609 Prague
An allegory of the triumph of Justice

355 × 260 mm, pen and brown ink and wash heightened with white, signed with the artist's monogram and dated 1601, corrected to 1602 by the artist
Inscribed on the back of the mount in ink *2 U. Z (or L?). iy*
PROVENANCE 'Pseudo-Crozat' (L474); Henry Blundell (?), originally in an album
LITERATURE J. Zimmer, *Joseph Heintz der Ältere. Zeichnungen und Dokumente*, Munich 1988, pp. 146–47, A75, fig. 117
WAG1995.93

The full title of the group of allegorical figures is *The triumph of Justice, Truth/Time and Charity over Greed*, with each personification holding his or her identifying attributes, Justice with her sword and weighing-scales, Truth/Time with a radiant sun-disk and hour-glass, Charity her children and Greed his overflowing moneybag. Its date suggests that the drawing was designed by Heintz the Elder to celebrate the ennoblement in 1602 of himself and his brother, Daniel Heintz the Younger, by the Holy Roman Emperor Rudolf II (1576–1612). The rise in status coincided with an event of more personal and familial pride when Daniel was installed as Master of the Works at the Minster in Berne, a post which had once been held by their father Daniel the Elder. Joseph Heintz the Elder was the most celebrated member of a Swiss dynasty of architects and sculptors, who, having spent a number of years in Italy, became painter, architect and artistic adviser to Emperor Rudolf in Prague and Augsburg. He was known as an outstanding draughtsman whose style, displayed handsomely in the Liverpool allegory, was typified by a decorative application of watercolour wash and a use of white heightening to increase the sense of movement and refined modelling of form. The Liverpool drawing appears to have been something of a swansong for Joseph, as shortly after he executed the design and after his ennoblement he seems to have stopped painting, to work for the last seven years of his life primarily as a more socially acceptable architect. But the drawing came to have a greater significance than that of

the mere expression of a family's pride in its artistic achievements. In 1603 Heintz commissioned Lucas Kilian to engrave the allegory, and its publication by Dominicus Custos in Augsburg ensured that it had a widespread visual influence.[1] It has been suggested that the playful liveliness of Charity's children might have influenced the same figure designed by the sculptor and architect Bernini to be placed beside the tomb of Pope Urban VIII in St Peter's, Rome, which he worked on between 1642 and 1647.[2] The drawing's size almost certainly related to its importance to the Heintz family – it is larger than most drawings designed to be engraved. Presumably Heintz's combination of allegorical figures had also been chosen for their personal significance but the universal meaning of the virtues and vices they personified and the triumph of good over evil that they represented lent themselves to a wider application. In 1674 Kilian's engraving was used to preface a thesis in Vienna and so helped develop an important artistic form in southern Germany.[3]

ΦEink.F. 1602

Fig. 46 Le Sueur, *St Paul preaching at Ephesus*, Paris, Musée du Louvre

71 EUSTACHE LE SUEUR

Paris 1617–1655 Paris

Study of a bearded, hunched man carrying books

359 × 254 mm; black chalk heightened with white partially worn away and overdrawn in places with graphite, on grey-brown paper varnished (?) with brown. Two upper corners missing[1]
Watermark on mount: fleur-de-lys within a crowned escutcheon with a knot of lines below
Inscribed on back in pencil *No –7–*
PROVENANCE Possibly from the collection of M. Jean de Jullienne (1686–1766), sold as part of lot 745, "S. Paul & un Homme courbé qui porte des livres: belles Etudes du Tableau qui est à Notre-Dame, où Saint Paul prêche à Ephese & fait bruler aux Gentils leurs livres de magie", Paris, 30 March 1767;[2] Benjamin West (no collector's stamp; inscribed in pencil on mount *West*); C.R. Blundell[3]
LITERATURE A. Merlot, *Eustache Le Sueur*, Paris 1987, p. 239, cat. 85, D.232, fig. 304
WAG1995.347

This is a chalk figure-study for one of the men in Le Sueur's painting of *St Paul preaching at Ephesus*, considered one of his finest works, originally installed in the Chapel of St Genevieve in Notre-Dame

Cathedral in Paris in 1649 [fig. 46].[4] Le Sueur, who had helped found the Académie Royale the previous year, was commissioned by two members of the Parisian goldsmith guild, Phillippe Renault and Gilles Crévon, to produce the 'May', the painting that the guild customarily presented to the Cathedral every 1st May and which since 1630 had traditionally taken its subject from the *Acts of the Apostles*. The scene chosen shows St Paul preaching at Ephesus, indicated in the background by its famous Temple of Diana with a statue of the huntress goddess placed outside it, and persuading the Ephesans through his oratory to burn their pagan and heretical books.[5] It was an ambitious project for the artist, more used to working on a smaller scale, which probably explains the elaborate care he took in planning it, producing two painted *modelli* as well as four preparatory drawings for the whole composition and many studies for individual figures.[6] These show that after submitting the *modelli* to the Guild for approval he made many changes to the composition, for example, as illustrated by two drawings in Frankfurt, replacing the original rather distracting scene of an act of charity in the background to the right by a line of men queuing to burn their books. Le Sueur has carefully differentiated them – young, middle-aged and old, clean-shaven and bearded – and placed at their head the striking figure of the elderly, stooping man for which the Liverpool drawing is a study. Although the Liverpool study was produced late in the planning process Le Sueur still made one more change, for the painted figure is elderly, bald and white-bearded whereas the drawing shows a middle-aged man with a full head of hair and dark beard, whose books and parchment roll are more stable than the precariously toppling pile in the painting.[7]

The figure-study shows Le Sueur's preferred use of black chalk on a dark grey-brown paper, to which he applied white highlights to give the figure greater depth. But it also appears to be on a browner velvety ground, which is so uniform that it might be the result of a brown wash or varnish applied across the paper.[8] It would also appear that another later artist, perhaps Benjamin West, has in graphite pencil gone over some of the black-chalk drapery folds on the figure's arm and the parchment scroll. The strongly

Raphaelesque style of Le Sueur, whose reputation as the 'Raphael of France' was still strong in the nineteenth century, would have attracted Benjamin West, himself an admirer of the Italian artist.

JAN-ERASMUS QUELLINUS

Antwerp 1634–1715 Mechelen

72 *The Martyrs of Gorkum brought before a Calvinist judge*

498 × 411 mm, black chalk, brush and grey ink, grey and turquoise-blue wash heightened with white gouache on very thin light-brown paper laminated on to white paper within a pointed arch
Inscribed and dated on drawing in ink with a monogram *JEQuellinus/A° 1704*; in ink on mount *Geo: Erasmo Quellino*
PROVENANCE Benjamin West (L419), possibly Christie's, June 12 1820, as part of lot 77; C.R. Blundell
WAG1995.368

73 *The capture of the Martyrs of Gorkum by the Calvinist 'sea-beggars'*

520 × 451 mm, black and red chalk, brush and grey ink and wash with white gouache and turquoise-blue wash on thin, light-brown paper within a pointed arch shape
Inscribed in black chalk and partially obliterated in lower right corner *I E.../1704*; in ink on mount *Gio: Erasmo Quellino*
PROVENANCE Benjamin West (L419), possibly Christie's, June 12 1820, as part of lot 77 (with cat. 72); C.R. Blundell
WAG1995.369

These two large-scale drawings were intended as finished *modelli* for the Martyrs of Gorkum series of four large canvases painted for the south aisle of the Abbey of St Michael, Antwerp, which was destroyed during the Belgian struggle for independence in 1830.[1] The martyrs of Gorkum were nineteen Catholic priests and monks who were captured on 26 June 1572 by a group of Calvinist sailors, the 'sea-beggars', during the fight for Dutch independence from Spain, and beatified by Pope Clement X in 1675. Exh. cat. 72 shows them brought before a Calvinist judge and refusing to recant their belief in papal primacy, thus condemning themselves to execution.[2] Having continued to refuse to recant, despite brutal treatment by the 'sea-beggars' of both young and old, they were hanged several weeks later. The sailors' aggression is indicated in exh. cat. 73 by the knives they point at the clergymen. The series of paintings for the Abbey of St Michael was Jan-Erasmus's most notable commission, and the paintings were placed in a prominent didactic position in the church, along the vaulted aisle behind the preacher's pulpit. Unlike these drawings, dated 1704, two paintings in the series were dated to 1676 and have been mistakenly attributed to Jan-Erasmus's father, Erasmus II Quellinus, who died in 1678.[3] In fact Jan-Erasmus received the commission from abbot Macarius Simeono in 1675 and by 1695 had painted two of the series, with two more expected soon. Carl Depauw has suggested that the delay in completing the set was probably due to the abbot's death.[4] The grandeur of the classical architecture and the lively arrangement of the figures on a raised balustraded terrace shows the influence of Veronese, whose work Jan-Erasmus had seen and copied during his stay in Venice in 1660–61. Compared to earlier finished drawings of 1674 by Jan-Erasmus for other commissions in the abbey the two Liverpool compositions also show a greater intensity of colouring.[5] The fact that the artist has signed his name and the date in ink suggests that the drawings may have been intended as *modelli* or presentation pieces to be shown to the abbey's authorities before they gave the artist approval to start painting. Jan-Erasmus Quellinus, the son of one artist and son-in-law to another, David Teniers the Younger, built up a career painting a large number of monumental altarpieces and other religious compositions for various abbey and monastic churches between Antwerp and Brussels, of which the commission for the Abbey of St Michael was the most notable. He was, however, to end his career near blind and bankrupt. He used a laminated paper for both his *modelli*, with a firm white paper underneath providing support for the very thin, soft, tissue-like paper on top – its brown colour acts as a mid-tone for the chalk and colourful wash. Both Liverpool drawings were owned by Benjamin West, who as a painter of large-scale narrative scenes probably admired Quellinus's lively compositional sense and his ability to mass crowds of figures successfully.

74 STUDIO OF REMBRANDT HARMENSZ VAN RIJN

Leiden 1606–1669 Amsterdam

Mercury, Argus and Io

175 × 291 mm, pen and brown iron-gall ink and some brown wash with white chalk used to cover mistakes. The paper has been irregularly cut out around the heads of Argus and his staff, Mercury and the background cattle, and another sheet inserted and partly drawn on in brown ink[1]
PROVENANCE Probably Roscoe sale, 1816, as part of lot 500, "Rembrandt Two historical. Pen.", bt. Slater 9s. (along with Appendix WAG1995.348, Italian School); C.R. Blundell, valued together at 8s. in 1841
LITERATURE O. Benesch, *The Drawings of Rembrandt*, 2nd edn., London 1973, III, p. 168, no. 598, fig. 773
WAG1995.332

The cow which seems to stare so knowingly out at us from the foreground represents princess Io, one of the god Jupiter's many lovers, whom he had

changed into the animal so as to hide her from his wife Juno. But Juno had her guarded by the giant shepherd Argus. Jupiter sent his messenger Mercury to kill Argus, which, after first lulling him to sleep with music, he successfully did.[2] Mercury, usually identified by his winged cap, is here in disguise, wearing a broad-brimmed hat with flaps that may hide his wings, whilst the lyre, which he invented, has been changed to a pipe more suitable for a shepherd and appropriately phallic in shape.

Otto Benesch considered the drawing to be by Rembrandt and dated it to about 1647–48.[3] He compared it in style with a landscape in Berlin also of 1647–48 and in subject with several other Rembrandt sketches of *ca.* 1648–52, of which the one in the Louvre is closest (in the curly-haired features of Argus).[4] However, the white chalk used to cover over and correct 'mistakes' in the positioning of Argus's hand as he examines Mercury's pipe, and the insertion of another sheet of paper with additional landscape features, possibly drawn by another artist to 'complete' the drawing, suggests that the sketch was made

as part of Rembrandt's practice in the late 1640s of setting himself and his studio a theme for all his pupils to work on.[5] Whether the resultant drawings were then corrected with pen and bodycolour by Rembrandt or by the pupils themselves is often very difficult to tell. Peter Schatborn suggests that although the penwork is close to Rembrandt's the figures could be by Willem Drost, one of Rembrandt's pupils in the late 1640s, although Sumowski is cautious and would prefer it to remain an unattributed studio work.[6] The coarsely sketched hatching, the smudged splodges of wash and the idiosyncratic, barely described cattle in the background are all similar to those found in drawings attributed to Willem Drost.[7] Little is known about Drost, other than that his creative period spanned from *ca.* 1650 to 1670 and that his style was based on Rembrandt's work of *ca.* 1650. Drost did, however, paint a picture of this subject *ca.* 1660, showing a bearded Argus asleep whilst Mercury wearing a hat plays his pipe.[8]

75 STUDIO OF REMBRANDT HARMENSZ VAN RIJN
The Good Samaritan paying the innkeeper

162 × 190 mm, pen and brown iron-gall ink with corrections in white bodycolour
PROVENANCE Probably Roscoe sale, 1816, as part of lot 500, bt. Slater 9s.; C.R. Blundell
LITERATURE Benesch 1973, III, p. 175, no. 629a, fig. 760
WAG1995.346

Like the other exhibited drawing from Rembrandt's studio (exh. cat. 74), Otto Benesch attributed this sketch to Rembrandt himself and dated it to *ca.* 1648–50, although he noted no other drawing of this particular subject,[1] nor could he find a painting by Rembrandt of the specific scene in which the Samaritan pays an innkeeper to look after the traveller whom he has rescued from near death after a roadside mugging.[2] Rembrandt's drawings were not necessarily preparatory studies for other work, for he often treated his activity as a draughtsman as distinct from his work as a painter or printmaker. Sumowski, who formerly accepted

Benesch's attribution to Rembrandt, is no longer certain of its correctness because of the overworked and unclear passages in parts of the drawing.[3] White lead has been used to cover up 'mistakes' over the Samaritan's knee and a repair on his head. Schatborn has suggested that the *Good Samaritan*, like exh. cat. 74, could very well be by Willem Drost.[4] As well as the distinctive parallel hatching the drawing also shows Drost's habit, evident in some drawings in the British Museum dating to the 1650s, of reinforcing a silhouette with a heavy pen outline and denoting eyebrows as one thick line.[5] There is also at least one other drawing attributed to Drost and

dated to the mid 1650s illustrating the Samaritan story, a night scene lit by lamp-light, of *The Good Samaritan before the inn*.[6] Whoever drew the sketch, amongst the many pupils in Rembrandt's studio in the late 1640s and the 1650s, he had absorbed Rembrandt's striking ability to stage a scene and to bring to it an acute psychological interpretation. Unusually, the centre of attention is not the injured tra-veller, whose profile is barely visible above the bench in the foreground, and whose presence only makes itself felt through the sorrowful look of pity bestowed on him by the kneeling woman. Instead attention is focussed on the Samaritan as he rummages around in his satchel for the money to pay the innkeeper, who looks on expectantly whilst an older woman stares greedy-eyed in anticipation – all this variety of expression is described with a few bold strokes of the pen.

76 PETER PAUL RUBENS
Siegen 1577–1640 Antwerp
Figures from a satire against the clergy, after Hans Weiditz

125 × 110 mm, pen and brown ink
Inscribed in pencil on mount with an anonymous attribution *Van Dyke by order of Rubens*
PROVENANCE Roscoe sale, 1816, sold as part of lot 455, as Holbein, *Sir Thomas More Going to his Execution*, bt. Slater 16s. (along with Maerten de Vos, *St Sebastian*, cat. 80); C.R. Blundell, both as Maerten de Vos, valued at £1. 4s. in 1841
WAG1995.247

The figures in this small sketch have been copied from the left-hand section of a woodcut by Hans Weiditz (otherwise known as the Petrarch Master) showing clergy and nuns worshipping a satanic animal used to illustrate Chapter XIII of Petrarch's *De Remediis Utriusque Fortunae* (On the remedies of good and bad fortune) which was published in an extremely popular German translation, *Von der Artzney bayder Glück, des guten und widerwertigen*, in 1532 [fig. 47].[1] The book's popularity was due mainly to its lively and witty illustrations, which also provided a rich pictorial source for artists and Rubens could have known one of many editions –

Fig. 47 Hans Weiditz (the Petrarch Master), *Satire against the clergy*, woodcut, London, British Museum

perhaps those published in Frankfurt in 1591 and 1596.[2] Rubens has copied the figures fairly faithfully, apart from adding a woman's profile on the extreme left, perhaps adapted from the face shown immediately behind the central monk, and changing a wimpled nun into a man with a fringe. However, as in other copies from German prints he made during his teenage apprenticeship, Rubens made subtle changes to the composition by concentrating on a group of figures and isolating them from their context. He has particularly focussed on the clergyman and nun in the foreground, enlarging their bulk, simplifying the fall of their drapery and changing the clergyman's expression from downcast eyes to a fixed stare ahead. In addition, by removing the rosary from the hands of the open-mouthed cleric on the right he has subtly changed him from a passively praying figure to one actively beseeching the clergyman next to him, introducing an enlivening narrative to the group of figures. Perhaps it was this motif that led William Roscoe mistakenly to entitle the drawing *Sir Thomas More being led to his execution*.[3] An illustration of such

an important event in England's history would no doubt have appealed to the Liverpool politician and historian. We know from a conversation that Rubens had with the artist and author Joachim Sandrart, whilst they were on a boat-trip between Utrecht and Amsterdam in 1626, that in his youth, before travelling to Italy in 1600, Rubens had admired and made copies of prints by earlier German masters such as Holbein and Tobias Stimmer.[4] He had also made copies in pen, as was his practice when drawing from woodcuts and engravings, of figures from other Weiditz prints illustrating *Von der Artzney*, although stylistically the Liverpool sketch is closer to his copies after Stimmer dating to ca. 1596–97.[5] The fact that Rubens has kept closely to the printed composition and made no more than a few and relatively minor and tentative changes to the figures would suggest that the drawing dates from an early part of his apprenticeship with Otto van Veen, ca. 1594–98 when he was still in his teens. As is evident from other drawings in the Weld-Blundell collection (exh. cats. 77, 79), his practice of copying the work of other artists continued into his

maturity, and well past the stage when he needed to copy to train eye and hand – as if only by redrawing figures could he hope to absorb their forms and stimulate ideas for future adaptation and reuse.

77 PETER PAUL RUBENS
God creating Adam, after Michelangelo

255 × 286 mm, red chalk and wash heightened with gouache and buff oil overpaint. Irregularly cut out and patched in lower left corner
Inscribed in red ink on mount *Rubens*; in pencil, anonymously, doubting the attribution; in pencil Jaffé's comment *Certainly by Rubens – and red wash with the point of brush*; and on the back of mount in ink '*R*'

PROVENANCE Jonathan Richardson Senior (L2184), sold 11 February 1746/47 as part of lot 54, bt. Trevor £3. 11*s.*; Roscoe sale, 1816, lot 476, bt. Slater £1. 2*s.*; C.R. Blundell, valued with two other drawings in 1841 at £2. 8*s.* Drawing engraved in same direction by J.C. Loedel
EXHIBITIONS NACF 1997; London 1998, no. 90
LITERATURE M. Jaffé, 'The Interest of Rubens in Annibale and Agostino Carracci: further notes', *Burlington Magazine*, XCIX, November 1957, p. 376, n. 12, fig. 17; *idem, Rubens in Italy*, Oxford 1977, p. 21, pl. 24; L. Burchard and R.-A. d'Hulst, *Rubens' Drawings*, Brussels 1963, noted on p. 45, cat. 24; J.S. Held, *Rubens: Selected Drawings*, revised edn., Oxford 1986, noted p. 44
WAG1995.83

To a young artist such as Rubens on his first trip abroad to Italy in 1600, copying from the Sistine Chapel, the most celebrated work by his venerated predecessor Michelangelo, meant more than simply practising an established method of artistic instruction. In Rubens's early years in Italy, crucial for the development of his art, his confrontation with the power and vitality of Michelangelo's art helped excite his imagination.[1] When he returned to Antwerp in 1608 he brought back many study drawings after Michelangelo's painted and sculpted works; these formed the core of his large collection of copies, carefully kept in a chest in his studio, that acted as 'art reference material' for himself and his workshop apprentices, pupils and assistants to study and copy.[2] The Liverpool copy faithfully records its model from the central part of the Sistine Chapel ceiling, yet it also enhances and embellishes Michelangelo's qualities and overlays them with Rubens's own – the cherubs become more vigorous, God's face becomes even more intense and his muscular torso ripples more emphatically through the clinging tunic. Rubens's handling shows a mastery of red chalk, though the medium was relatively new to the artist, more used to the pen and ink with which he drew some of his earliest copies from the Sistine.[3] His combination of red chalk with red wash tipped in with fine brushstrokes, to strengthen the drapery shadows, and of buff oil paint to heighten faces and features shows close stylistic similarities with four other Sistine Chapel copies, in the Louvre and in the British Museum.[4] These drawings are thought to have been made on Rubens's first trip to Rome in 1601/02, when his employer Vincenzo Gonzaga, Duke of Mantua, was at war in Croatia and left Rubens to travel freely; their distinctive heightening was applied much later, in his Antwerp studio in the early 1630s.[5] Rubens's copies were not just *aide-memoires*: they were also used to help him solve compositional problems. Jaffé suggested that Rubens adopted the cross-legged pose of God's legs almost directly as a prototype for the crucified Christ in his *Raising of the Cross* of 1602.[6] Later, when he had fully blended Michelangelo's artistic vocabulary into his own, Rubens's translations were not so literal. Echoes of this study are to be found in many airborne assumptions and apotheoses with their curly-haired cherubs clambering around clouds, seemingly mimicking those of Michelangelo's.[7] As Joannides has commented, of all his copyists Rubens was the first powerful enough not to be overwhelmed by Michelangelo's masterpiece and able still to make creative use of his youthful copies into his maturity.[8]

78 PETER PAUL RUBENS
Study for the Circumcision

410 × 322 mm (including a strip along the top, 45 mm deep, which is overlapped by the main sheet by 9 mm), trimmed on all four sides; black and red chalk squared in brown ink with numbers *1–12* below. The squaring on the strip is more distinct and added later to overlap slightly the abraded squaring on the main sheet[1]
Inscribed in ink on front of mount, lower right corner *nº 35*; and on reverse in centre *1756*. Typed label on old mount with attribution to Follower of Rubens with pencilled attributions to Jordaens and Van Dyke
PROVENANCE Richard Houlditch (L2214, initials *R H* in ink in lower right corner); Roscoe sale, 1816, lot 483, for £1. 10s., as a "Capital drawing by Rubens", bt. Slater;[2] C.R. Blundell, as Rubens, valued in 1841 with two other drawings at £2. 8s.
LITERATURE P. Watson, *The Observer*, 26 June 1988, p. 4; M. Jaffé, 'Rubens and Nicolò Pallavicino', *Burlington Magazine*, CXXX July 1988, pp. 525–27, fig. 39, where the relationship with the altarpiece was first discussed
WAG1995.215

This is a preliminary compositional drawing for one of Rubens's earliest large-scale altarpieces, *The Circumcision* commissioned by the Jesuits in 1605 for the Genoese Gesù, now known as Santi Andrea e Ambrogio [fig. 48].[3] Rubens passed through Genoa early in 1604, on his return from the gift-bearing embassy he had led to the Spanish court on behalf of his patron Duke Vincenzo Gonzaga. He reclaimed his expenses for the extended Spanish visit from Niccolò Pallavicini, the Gonzaga's banker in Genoa, who had a role in the Gesù commission.[4] The Jesuit Order placed special emphasis on the Circumcision, as it was the occasion on which Jesus was named saviour and the event also alluded to the spilling of his blood in atonement for mankind. The altarpiece remains in the church whilst Rubens's *modello* for it, painted in oil, is in Vienna [fig. 48].[5] The drawing concentrates entirely on the earthly scene, omitting the golden glory of angels hovering above in the *modello* and the altarpiece, although reference is made to their presence by the two rabbis in the

Fig. 48 Peter Paul Rubens, *The Circumcision*, Gesù, Genoa

background who gaze upwards, one adjusting his spectacles to do so. What makes the Liverpool study important is that it was obviously made early on in Rubens's plans for the composition, when he had yet to resolve various significant features found both in the *modello* and in the finished work. Rubens has not yet finalised the position of the Christ Child nor of the man's hands as he performs the circumcision. The latter are a mass of scribbled red-chalk lines. Nor has he decided on the placing of the hands of the bearded rabbi on the extreme right, whose forefinger acts as a 'bookmark' in the *modello* but not in the drawing. Rubens is shown literally in the process of changing his mind about the female witness seen in profile in the left background of both the Viennese and Genoese paintings. The Liverpool drawing has her as a younger woman with her face both in profile and facing out at the viewer. The architectural setting was also changed, from a colonnade with a view through a round arch to a large square doorway with no intervening colonnade and a view of a clouded sky beyond. A number of figures feature in the

141

drawing but are eliminated from the painting: an elderly woman prominently placed bending over the head of Christ; the second rabbi who peers skywards through his spectacles; a small child also gazing upwards and holding a *tazza*, visible below the priest's elbow; and finally a small dog peeking out from underneath the table and sniffing the drops of blood. The last may have been deleted because of its crude overtones. But the most significant change is in the position of Christ's mother who, in the drawing, holds the cloth away from the Christ Child's body with her right hand whilst averting her eyes from the painful operation. In the painting Rubens placed her right arm up by her cheek and veil, a gesture of virginal modesty he derived from the antique statue of *Venus Pudica*, which he would see in the Vatican during his stays in Rome in 1602–03 and from November 1605.[6] This alteration suggests that the drawing dates from before Rubens's arrival in Rome for his second visit and that it was probably drawn in Mantua in 1605. He presumably started work on the altarpiece for the Genoese Jesuits once he had finished the decoration of the tribune of the Jesuit church at Mantua, commissioned by Vincenzo Gonzaga and completed by 25 May 1605. The finished altarpiece arrived in Genoa at the end of 1605. The square grid numbered along the bottom edge would have been used to transfer the drawn composition, scaled up, to the much larger painted *modello* of 105 × 74 cm, which was presumably shown to the Jesuits for their approval before the commission went ahead. No other compositional drawings for the Gesù altarpiece are known, although Rubens's estate included a sketch on panel of the *Circumcision*, which was given by his heirs to the Antwerp engraver Anthonie Wrancx.[7] A sketch of the composition was also owned by Sir Thomas Lawrence, and sold in 1830.[8]

79 PETER PAUL RUBENS AND FEDERICO ZUCCARO
The Conversion of Mary Magdalene

431 × 508 mm, pen and brown ink and brown wash on pale-blue paper covered with a grey-brown wash, a triangular-shaped portion on the left added by Rubens in black chalk, pen and point of brush with purpley-brown ink and white, pink and buff oil-paint and a *pentimento* of a woman's profile in black chalk
Inscribed on drawing in ink and partially obliterated *By Zucerro*[1]
PROVENANCE Peter Paul Rubens; Prosper Henry Lankrink (L2090);[2] unidentified collector's mark (L2330 or L2331); Benjamin West (L419), possibly sold Christie's, 13 June 1820, lot 88, as "T. Zuccaro, Judgement of Solomon"; C.R Blundell
LITERATURE M. Jaffé, 'Rubens as a Collector of Drawings: Part Two', *Master Drawings*, III, no. 1, 1965, p. 25, pl. 16;[3] J. Byam Shaw, *Drawings by Old Masters at Christ Church, Oxford*, Oxford 1976, noted under cats. 540, 551; M. Jaffé, *Rubens and Italy*, Oxford 1977, pp. 38, 51, pl. 142
WAG1995.371

The drawing is a composite one in which, in a graphic style he adopted in the mid 1630s, Rubens has added figures in a triangular section running from the top left corner to the seated woman holding her child, to complete a composition originally by Federico Zuccaro. The Zuccaro design was a study for the right half of the fresco on the left side-wall of the Grimani Chapel in San Francesco della Vigna, Venice, which he had been commissioned to paint by Cardinal Giovanni Grimani in 1563–64 as one of his first works independent of his brother Taddeo (see exh. cats. 64, 65). It depicted the occasion when Mary Magdalene knelt in recognition before Christ to remonstrate with him over the death of her brother Lazarus whilst her sister Martha acknowledged Christ as the Messiah.[4] By the early eighteenth century the frescoed *Conversion* was already being destroyed by a combination of Venice's pervasive dampness and the addition of another external façade to the wall on which it had been painted. The many figure-studies, *modelli* and copies after part or all of the original fresco are therefore important documents of a lost work.[5] Federico's working method was to make a

number of large-scale studies on different coloured papers of both the whole and parts of a composition, making adjustments to the design as he went along and incorporating them into later *modelli*. In addition, two different large-scale studies were engraved in reverse by Aliprando Caprioli and Cornelis Cort – which may account for the number of copies.[6] The Liverpool study is related not to the design as shown in either the drawing in the Uffizi or the Cort engraving but perhaps instead to the rejected, or later, *modello* in Munich.[7] By the time Rubens acquired the study it must have been torn or damaged and he set about 'completing' the composition and 'improving' the design. Rubens may well have sought out and acquired drawings from Federico Zuccaro when he was in Rome between 1605 and 1608, as Rubens's own master in Antwerp, Otto van Veen, had known Zuccaro as a young man and by Rubens's day he was an established elder statesman of Roman art, whose house Rubens would probably have visited.[8] Throughout his career Rubens collected drawings by older masters and his contemporaries – some for pleasure and others for his own future reference and to teach his pupils. He valued this collection so greatly that in his will he insisted it be kept together until such time as no member of his family was prepared to continue the studio.[9] It was not sold until seventeen years after his death. Despite his regard for the drawings it was a common practice of Rubens to retouch other artists' work. Sometimes, as is partly the case with the *Conversion*, he was renovating and repairing a damaged original or a studio copy.[10] But the fact that Rubens has not just copied Zuccaro's figures but invented three new ones – the sumptuously draped and veiled women seated on the ground to the left – to fill the empty space in Zuccaro's original design suggests that this practice may have served to stimulate his own inventive powers.[11] Neither has he attempted to copy Zuccaro's style, even when reconstructing a figure such as the woman with her child; instead he drew them in with 'painterly' brushstrokes in his own 'shimmering' style of the 1630s, inspired by Veronese. This results in a full-bodied Baroque vitality, in which the chubby-cheeked child and the women's costume, modelled by Rubens in ink and oil paint, contrast with the linear details of Zuccaro's Mannerist graphic manner.

80 MAERTEN DE VOS
Antwerp 1532–1603 Antwerp
The Martyrdom of St Sebastian

99 mm diameter, pen and brown ink and wash over black chalk, indented around all figures except the inscription in ink,
. M . D . VOS
Verso: all the figures and landscape reproduced in reverse in ink
Watermark on mount: part of a small fleur-de-lys above an elaborate shield, Heawood 75 (Amsterdam, 1730)
PROVENANCE Roscoe sale, 1816, lot 455, as de Vos, bt. Slater 16s. (along with cat. 76, then attributed to Holbein); C.R. Blundell, valued with cat. 76 at £1. 4s. in 1841
WAG1995.289
The fact that the silhouettes and internal details of all the figures and landscape have been heavily indented with a stylus and someone has used the indentations to reproduce the design in reverse on the back confirms the idea that the design was meant to be reproduced in some other form, whether as an engraving or a medal in bronze or precious metal. Carl Depauw has suggested that it might have been intended for some sort of commemorative plaquette or medal for a guild or an individual member.[1] Although most of the five hundred known drawings by Maerten de Vos were designs for prints, no engraving is known which directly reproduces the *St Sebastian*; however, the pose of the saint and the general placing of the archers is similar to that found in reverse in a rectangular engraving by Raphael Sadeler I, *ca.* 1584, after Maerten de Vos.[2] It is also similar in style to a set of seven roundels, now in the Ashmolean, Oxford, and the Metropolitan Museum, New York, illustrating military events that took place in Antwerp in August 1577, one of which is dated 1577 and inscribed *MERTEN DE VOS F.*[3] They were made by the Maerten de Vos workshop under his supervision and were meant as working sources for a medal-maker: they were indented for transfer to plaster, where they would have appeared in reverse, and then cast in bronze, so regaining the drawings' original direction. Depauw knows of another drawing in a private Dutch collection, executed by Maerten de Vos himself, which was also a preliminary study for a medal.[4] As well as being a painter of altarpieces Maerten de Vos was the most prolific print designer of his generation; about 1600 prints are known after his designs, and his busy, large workshop translated these into many media – furniture and household furnishings such as embroideries as well as medals and book illustrations, which were widely reproduced and distributed across Europe. He also influenced the work of his own pupils, such as Hendrick de Clerck (1570–1629), who painted an altarpiece for the Church of St Martin in Asse with a central panel of *The Martyrdom of St Sebastian* basing the pose of the saint in his preparatory drawing on this by de Vos.[5] St Sebastian was a Roman soldier who suffered martyrdom for his Christian faith in the late third century under the Emperor Diocletian, who ordered him shot to death with arrows; but Sebastian survived to confront the emperor again and was finally killed by being beaten to death with clubs. As well as being the patron saint of archers and soldiers he was believed to be able to protect against the plague (see exh. cat. 36), for it was thought that his courage in facing the arrows enabled him to immunize his devotees against the disease. Presumably whichever guild might have commissioned the *St Sebastian* from Maerten de Vos had a particular connection with the saint – perhaps it was the Guild of Old Crossbowmen for whom he painted an altarpiece in 1590.[6]

ACKNOWLEDGEMENTS

The research for this catalogue and exhibition would not have been possible without a grant from the J. Paul Getty Foundation which funded my research and my replacement at the Walker Art Gallery for eighteen months. I would particularly like to thank Miranda Stacey for stepping into my shoes so ably and enthusiastically, for her work on collectors' biographies for the catalogue and for her assistance in the organization of the exhibition. As someone relatively new to the world of drawings I have relied more than most on scholars and curators in Europe and America and in particular on my colleagues in the Prints and Drawings Department in the British Museum. I am particularly grateful for all the help, advice and facilities they offered me during my period of research there. The comments of many other scholars who have been generous in sharing their knowledge with me are acknowledged in the respective catalogue entries. I would particularly like to thank Anna Petrioli Tofani at the Uffizi for giving up her time to discuss the attributions of a number of the Italian drawings; Giovanni Agosti for his helpful suggestions and the use of his invaluable address book; and Charles Dumas at the RKD in The Hague for his advice on the Northern European drawings. I am also grateful to Derald H. Ruttenberg for contributing towards the costs of the catalogue and thus enabling it to be more richly illustrated and thereby more informative than it would otherwise have been.

All of the drawings on display have been restored for the exhibition and in some cases new discoveries have been made. I am extremely grateful for the sensitive work of the paper conservation department. Examination and discussion of the drawings with them has always proved revealing and informative. My thanks also go to Colin Jackson for the colour photography and to David Flower and his staff for the photography of the rest of the collection.

Xanthe Brooke

BIBLIOGRAPHY

Other references appearing in shortened form in the following notes are given in full either in immediately preceding notes to the same catalogue entry (sometimes the preceding one if involving the same artist) or in Exhibitions or Literature in the catalogue entry itself (or preceding one if same artist).

Account of the Statues, Busts, Bass-relieves, Cinerary Urns and Other Ancient Marbles and Paintings at Ince, Liverpool 1803

C.M. Briquet, *Les Filigranes: Dictionnaire historique des Marques du Papier*, Paris 1907

G. Chandler, *William Roscoe of Liverpool*, London 1953

W.A. Churchill, *Watermarks in Paper in Holland, England and France in the XVII and XVIII Centuries*, Nieuwkoop 1985

M. Edgeworth, *Letters from England 1813–1844*, ed. C. Colvin, Oxford 1971

Edinburgh 1969: *Italian Sixteenth-Century Drawings from British Private Collections*, exhib. cat., Edinburgh, Scottish Arts Council for the Edinburgh Festival, 1969

Edinburgh 1972: *Italian Seventeenth-Century Drawings from British Private Collections*, exhib. cat., Edinburgh, Scottish Arts Council for the Edinburgh Festival, 1972

J. Gere, 'William Young Ottley as a Collector of Drawings', *British Museum Quarterly*, XVIII, June 1953, pp. 44–53

E. Heawood, *Watermarks mainly of the 17th and 18th Centuries* [1950], edn. Hilversum 1986

J.A. Hilton, *Catholic Lancashire from Reformation to Renewal 1559–1991*, Chichester 1994

Luigi Lanzi, *History of Painting in Italy*, trans. T. Roscoe, Liverpool 1828

London 1998: *Art Treasures of England: The Regional Collections*, exhib. cat. by G. Waterfield *et al.*, London, Royal Academy, 1998

F. Lugt, *Les Marques des collections de dessins et d'estampes*, Amsterdam 1921; *Supplément*, The Hague 1952

NACF 1997: *Treasures for Everyone: Saved by the National Art Collections Fund*, exhib. cat., London, Christie's, 1997

Henry Roscoe, *Life of William Roscoe*, Liverpool 1833

G. Vaughan, 'Henry Blundell's Sculpture Collection at Ince Hall', in *Patronage & Practice: Sculpture on Merseyside*, ed. P. Curtis, Liverpool (NMGM) 1991

Venice 1980: *Disegni veneti di collezioni inglesi*, exhib. cat. by J. Stock, Venice, Fondazione Giorgio Cini, 1980

NOTES:
INTRODUCTION

1. The sale of drawings was held 23–28 September 1816 at T. Winstanley, Liverpool. Some of Roscoe's books and paintings were bought back by his friends and are now in the Liverpool Athenaeum, which he had helped found, and the Walker Art Gallery, where his early Italian and Netherlandish works form the core of its Old Master collections.
2. *The Diary of Joseph Farington R.A.*, ed. K. Cave, New Haven and London, XIV, 1984, p. 4877, entry for 22 July 1816 "His [Roscoe's] debt to the former [Charles Blundell], who possesses abt. £6,000 per annum is £8,000; He behaved brutally. The other creditors towards 400 in number, acted most liberally." The amounts given are doubtful: Liverpool Record Office Roscoe Papers 2525, Roscoe's letter to John McCreery, 18 June 1816, complains that Blundell had behaved badly, changing his mind after all the creditors had agreed to Roscoe's proposals and that he "has ever since done all in his power to injure us". Martin Hopkinson has suggested (in an unpublished draft article on Roscoe as a print collector in the Walker's archives) that Blundell objected to what he saw as collusion between Roscoe and his debtors to prevent the use of their money to pay off the creditors.
3. W. Irving, *The Sketchbook of Geoffrey Crayon*, London and New York (Everyman) 1963 first published 1820, p. 12.
4. *Ibid.* "… where literature and the elegant arts must grow up side by side with the coarse plants of daily necessity, and must depend for their culture, not on the exclusive devotion of time or wealth, but on hours and seasons snatched from the pursuits of worldly interests, by intelligent and public-spirited individuals"; see also the speech made by G.C. Verplanck on the opening of a New York Institution for the Encouragement of Literature and Science, quoted in Henry Roscoe, *Life of William Roscoe*, Liverpool 1833, II, Appendix III, pp. 489–90.
5. *Sketchbook* (*cit.* note 3), pp. 11–12.
6. Roscoe 1833, I, p. 60.
7. Note to Roscoe sale (see note 1), lot 592, which claims that the drawing was bought at the sale of 56 drawings from the Hudson collection held at Twickenham, 25 February 1785.
8. Roscoe 1833, p. 149.
9. *The Diary of Joseph Farington*, edd. K. Garlick and A. Macintyre, New Haven and London 1978, II, p. 628, entry for 2 August 1796.
10. F. Haskell, *History and its Images: Art and the Interpretation of the Past*, New Haven and London 1993, p. 210.
11. The red-chalk drawing, now attributed to Naldini (Appendix: WAG1995.230), was attributed to Andrea del Sarto by Roscoe, who may

also have annotated its tissue-paper mount with the observation that its subject was an allusion to the return of Cosimo de' Medici from exile.
12. *Diary of Joseph Farington*, II, p. 628, entry for 2 August 1796.
13. *Copenhagen* [1807], reprinted in G. Chandler, *William Roscoe of Liverpool*, London 1953, pp. 115, 269–70: this criticized Nelson's refusal to acknowledge Denmark's neutrality and his launching an attack on the city.
14. Sotheby's, London, 13 July 1972, lot 12; Roscoe 1833, II, pp. 348 54.
15. *Ibid.*, II, pp. 71–72, 407.
16. Appendix: WAG1995.352; Fuseli, *Four men fighting snakes*, Nationalmuseum, Stockholm Z73/1954.
17. Lady Eastlake, *Life of John Gibson RA Sculptor*, 1870, p. 31; T. Matthews, *The Biography of John Gibson*, 1911, p. 12.
18. M. Edgeworth, *Letters from England 1813–1844*, ed. C. Colvin, Oxford 1971, pp. 12–13. One of the Fuselis was his *Death of Lorenzo de' Medici*, which was designed specially for the chimney-piece of the dining-room, see H. Macandrew, 'Henry Fuseli and William Roscoe', *The Liverpool Bulletin*, VIII, 1959, p. 37 no. 13. The description of *The dream of Michelangelo* in Roscoe's sale catalogue, lot 78 ("A figure [marked Gio. Scultore] representing his own portrait, is seen issuing, in great wrath from an Arcade: and five naked figures, pursued by Serpents are making their escape by different ways. At the bottom is written in his own hand, '"Sogno fatto adi 16 di Aprile 1560, la notte della domenica seconda dopo pasqua'") does not coincide with the drawing in the Courtauld Institute entitled *The dream of human life* (Princes Gate 424).
19. Roscoe 1833, II, p. 454.
20. WAG1995.352; Liverpool Record Office and Library, *Leo X*, ch. XXII, p. 242 and Luigi Lanzi, *History of Painting in Italy*, trans. T. Roscoe, 1828, II, opposite p. 72. The Lanzi print is annotated by Roscoe with the comment: "Copy of drawing found amongst the other drawings of Raffaelle in the Volume in Mr. Coke's Library at Holkham and copied from the Cieling [*sic*] of Michelagnolo's in the Sistine Chapel: which may be considered as a proof that Raffaello enlarged and improved the style on seeing the works of Michelagnolo." The *Leo X* is inscribed similarly but without mention of the so called 'Raphael Sketchbook' in Holkham Library. The prints loosely reproduce all but the right-hand quarter of the composition.
21. Liverpool Public Library, Roscoe Papers 2961, Philipe letters to WR, 14 January 1795; RP 2965, 26 June 1811; RP 2971, 3 August 1812.
22. F. Lugt, *Les Marques des collections de dessins et d'estampes*, Amsterdam

1921, L1496; 26 January–4 February 1804, lot 646.

23. Liverpool, Roscoe Papers 2964, 2965.

24. Roscoe 1833, I, p. 254.

25. J. Gere, 'William Young Ottley as a Collector of Drawings', *British Museum Quarterly*, XVIII, June 1953, pp. 44–53; *Dictionary of British and Irish Travellers in Italy 1701–1800*, compiled J. Ingamells, New Haven and London 1997, pp. 728–29.

26. For other Ottley/Roscoe drawings in the Weld-Blundell collection see Cantarini's *Studies for a Madonna and Child and a St Sebastian*, WAG1995.284, and an attributed Cantarini WAG1995.290; Peruzzi, exh. cat. 42 and WAG1995.244; and the Italo-Flemish?, *Street scene*, WAG1995.71.

27. Roscoe 1833, I, p. 462.

28. Gere 1953, pp. 48–49.

29. There are at least 32 in the Weld-Blundell collection of which 14 were Roscoe's.

30. From Houlditch Roscoe derived, via Richardson, a Parmigianino, exh. cat. 39; a Romanelli, exh. cat. 49; and Rubens's *The Circumcision*, exh. cat. 78; from Hillier a Taddeo Zuccaro, exh. cat. 64; and from Barnard, a Cambiaso, exh. cat. 9; Vasari, exh. cat. 62; a *Landscape* attributed to Domenichino, WAG1995.217; a Florentine School drawing, WAG1995.255; a copy after Michelangelo, WAG1995.307; and another after Parmigianino, WAG1995.296. The Weld-Blundell collection has a further four drawings: a Domenichino, exh. cat. 23; a Parmigianino, exh. cat. 40; a Bolognese School *Head of an elderly man*, WAG1995.301; and a Florentine School *The Lamentation*, WAG1995.374, as well as some prints from Barnard's collection.

31. Attributed to Francesco Salviati, WAG1995.59.

32. Attributed to Annibale Carracci, exh. cats. 14, 15; Domenichino, exh. cats. 22, 24; Guercino, exh. cats. 32, 33; Reni, exh. cats. 46, 47; Canuti, exh. cat. 11; Sirani, exh. cats. 51, 52; Tiarini, WAG1995.211, WAG1995.3 333–337 and possibly WAG1995.78.

33. For Cambiaso see exh. cats. 8, 9 and WAG1995.257, .259 and .279; Cavaliere d'Arpino, exh. cat. 19; Vasari, exh. cat. 62; Zuccaro brothers, exh. cat. 79, WAG1995.56; Perino del Vaga, WAG1995.207 and WAG1995.209; Polidoro da Caravaggio, WAG1995.313.

34. Italian School, WAG1995.267; *Life of Lorenzo*, 8th edn., London [n.d.], revised T. Roscoe, p. 186, note 55.

35. Edgeworth 1971, pp. 10, 14.

36. *Ibid.*, p. 10, in which she contrasts the gentility of nearby Chester with Liverpool, a fine and grand commercial town which "would make a glorious figure in a table of exports and imports" but where the smell of ship even pervaded her bedroom and

the crowds full of "money making faces, every creature full drive after their own interest, elbowing, jostling, headlong after money! money! money!".

37. Roscoe 1833, II, p. 114.

38. *Ibid.*, pp. 53, 55–56.

39. The tissue paper sometimes has a John Hayes watermark of 1814.

40. Roscoe 1833, II, p. 88. According to Roscoe, Jones had perfected a method of erasing creases by stretching the page on a frame and covering the affected area with a solution of vellum.

41. A.E. Popham and C. Lloyd, *Old Master Drawings at Holkham Hall*, New York 1986, p. 8, note 12, p. 87, exh. cat. 194.

42. *Diary of Joseph Farington*, XIV, p. 4770, entry for 28 January 1816.

43. Correggio's *Group of angels*, Victoria and Albert Museum, Dyce 270; Dürer's *Nude self-portrait*, Kunsthalle, Bremen. Thirty-seven drawings from his collection were bought by the British Museum in 1905.

44. Identified by Fr Francis Edwards SJ in letter 4 October 1976, referring to Dom H.M. Birt OSB, *Obituary Book of the English Benedictines from 1600–1912*, Edinburgh 1913, p. 139.

45. Henry Blundell's sculpture collection is now owned by National Museums and Galleries on Merseyside and its display split between the Walker and the Liverpool Museum.

46. J.A. Hilton, *Catholic Lancashire from Reformation to Renewal 1559–1991*, Chichester 1994, pp. 78–79; letters H. Blundell to S. Tempest, 17 February 1789 and 26 May 1789, Tempest family archives, XV/33.

47. Letter H. Blundell to C. Townley, 10 February 1799, British Museum Townley Papers.

48. *Account of the Statues, Busts, Bass-relieves, Cinerary Urns and Other Ancient Marbles and Paintings at Ince*, Liverpool 1803, p. 250, CXLI, CXLII.

49. Krannert Art Museum, Urbana-Champaign, Illinois, inv. 67-1-1 to inv. 67-1-5; Gerard Vaughan, '*Vincenzo Brenna Romanus: Architectus et Pictor*, Drawing from the Antique in late eighteenth-century Rome', *Apollo*, October 1996, p. 40, figs. 4, 6.

50. Letter H. Blundell to C. Townley, 10 February 1799, British Museum Townley Papers.

51. Liverpool Museum, Ince no. 523, illustrated in *The Ince Blundell Collection of Classical Sculpture*: I, Part I: *The Female Portraits*, edd. J. Fejfer and E. Southworth, London (HMSO) 1991, p. 14, fig. 3.

52. *Account* 1803, pp. 179–80, Appendix p. 310.

53. Henry Blundell, 'A Letter Intended for a Friend' (autobiographical notes), Tempest Family Archives, Box XV, bundle 33B, p. 6: "… & when I was in England sent me

drawings of such things as were on sale and which he thought worth my attention".

54. Lugt 1921 and *Supplément*, The Hague 1956, L474.

55. The British Museum Prints and Drawings Department has 43 such drawings amongst its French and Italian collections.

56. Sienese school, 16th century, *The Coronation of Virgin with monk below*, WAG1995.74, L2781 (three fleurs-de-lys and a spread eagle with coronet?); Lanfranco circle, *Sts Peter and Paul seated on clouds*, WAG1995.210. Four other Roscoe drawings not bought by Charles Blundell also have sale entries referring to Caylus (lots 112, 225, 282, 501). A later collector, Sir John Charles Robinson, Superintendent of the Victoria and Albert Museum, also identified the stamp as that of Caylus when cataloguing Bandinelli, *Andre Doria in the guise of Neptune*, BM 1895-9-15-553.

57. *Correspondance inédite du Comte de Caylus, avec le P. Paciaudi, Theatin (1757–1765), L'Abbé Barthelemy et P. Mariette*, Paris (Charles Nisard) 1877, II, p. 117, 14 April 1765; L2919.

58. Haskell 1993, p. 180.

59. *Correspondance* (*cit.* note 57), p. 347.

60. G. Vaughan, 'Henry Blundell's Sculpture Collection at Ince Hall', in *Patronage & Practice: Sculpture on Merseyside*, ed. P. Curtis, Liverpool (NMGM) 1991, p. 14. Furthermore, according to Gerard Vaughan (in conversation, 16 January 1998) Townley acquired antique sculpture from Caylus's collection after his death, although Henry Blundell did not.

61. 7 June 1732; *Conférences de L'Académie Royale de Peinture et de Sculpture … sur les artistes écrivains*, ed. M. Henry Jouin, Paris 1883, pp. 369–77.

62. Later he commented that he believed that grandeur of a design would be communicated even by the feeblest of copies, 2 June 1760, *Correspondance* (*cit.* note 57), p. 194.

63. *Biographie Universelle*, Paris, pp. 1523–24.

64. *Comte de Caylus: Voyage d'Italie 1714–15*, ed. Amilda-A. Pons, Paris 1914, Introduction, p. IV, quoting Mariette writing to Paciaudi one year after his death: "Vous ne pouvez croire à quel point il est oublié."

65. Joullain, 11 December 1784. None of the 17 lots appears to tally with Weld-Blundell drawings.

66. *Disegni originali d'eccelenti pittori incisi ed imitati nella loro grandezza parte 1*, undated (1796?) copy in the Victoria and Albert Museum Department of Prints, Drawings and Paintings, inv. 15865.79.

67. Italian School, WAG1995.138; manner of Bernini, WAG1995.154; attributed Pieter van Laer, WAG1995.143; after Anton Domenico Gabbiani (?),

WAG1995.157; School of Raphael, WAG1995.151; Sienese School, early 16th century, WAG1995.134.

68. F. Arquié-Bruley, J. Labbé and L. Bicart-Sée, *La Collection Saint-Morys au Cabinet des Dessins du Musée du Louvre*, Paris (RMN) 1978.

69. William Richardson sale, London, 24 February 1814. Saint-Morys may well have known Townley, who kept open court to French exiles in his London town house (information from Gerard Vaughan, in conversation 16 January 1998).

70. WAG1995.186; Caylus etchings after the *Cabinet du roy*, no. 67.

71. There are eight drawings after or attributed to the Carracci; seven to Raphael and school; five to Rubens and school; four or five to Parmigianino; three to Guercino; and one each to Michelangelo, Titian, Tintoretto and Veronese. F. Villot, *Catalogue des planches gravées … au Musée National du Louvre*, Paris 1881, nos. 100–322. Caylus also etched a collection of Leonardo caricatures owned by Crozat and the king, *Recueil de testes de caractère et de charges dessinées par Leonard de Vinci Florentin et gravées par M. le C. de C.*, Paris 1730. Many of these prints carried Caylus's mark, a plain capital C sometimes followed by a full stop or a small star.

72. *Account* 1803, XXVIII, an Andrea del Sarto bought in Paris in 1772. He also owned a Le Nain possibly bought in France, XCVIII, and a Biltius bought from Arras College, Louvain, in 1770, I.

73. Letter H. Blundell to Townley, 10 February 1799, British Museum, Townley Papers: "The rambling life he has led for many years, living mostly at Inns, not visiting families, without any employ, pursuit or taste for social amusements, usual at this time of life, renders him I think, not so happy as I could wish him. His chief employ here is reading the newspapers and magazines, walking, visiting his horses and going out now and then with his gun. Had he a wife and family, his time wd be better filled up and he might become a different character in life"; H. Blundell to Eliza Tempest, 19 October 1803, "I never saw one who has so little turn for society", Tempest Family Archives XV/33A and others in family archive.

74. Ed. M.R.D. Foot, *The Gladstone Diaries*, Oxford 1968, II, p. 564, entry for 15 January 1839. The £78,000 presumably came via Charles's bequests to the Right Revd Dr Branston of London (died 1836) and the Right Revd Dr Thomas Walsh of Wolverhampton. The former was a Catholic convert and the latter might have been related to the Walsh boys who were educated alongside Charles Blundell at the English Academy in Liège between 1775 and 1781. Prime Minister Gladstone was the son of the Liverpool corn merchant John

Gladstone, Charles Blundell's friend, business adviser and executor, to whom he bequeathed two paintings by Richard Wilson.

75. Blundell *v.* Stonor 1842, PRO Chancery Records, C13 Div. III, Kipling & Gawler 2047(13).

76. PRO Chancery Records, C13 Div. III, as above; Lancashire Record Office DDIn/55-187 8, September 1810. In addition servants were prohibited from taking money to show the collection to visitors.

77. Another inventory known to have been drawn up before Henry Blundell's death by the sculptor and furniture-designer George Bullock unfortunately does not seem to have survived amongst other legal documents either at the Public Record Office or in the uncalendared Blundell family material at the Lancashire Record Office.

78. *Correspondance* (*cit.* note 57), II, p. 349, letter Mariette to Paciaudi, 9 August 1767; *Biographie Universelle*, XLI, pp. 181–82.

79. *Diary of Joseph Farington*, ed. K. Cave, XVI, New Haven and London 1984, pp. 5535–36, entry for 9 July 1820.

80. Christie's, Newman Street, London 9–14 June and 1–4 July 1820; Sotheby's, 11 May 1836.

81. 13 June, lot 88, Taddeo Zuccaro, *Christ restoring sight to a blind man*, see exh. cat. 65, sold along with a *"Judgement of Solomon"*, possibly the Federico Zuccaro and Rubens, *Conversion of the Magdalen*, see exh. cat. 79; 1 July, lot 43, Cantarini, *Holy Family*, see exh. cat. 75; and lot 178, Federico Zuccaro, *St Paul shaking off the viper*, exh. cat. 78, with no stamp.

82. H. von Erffa and A. Staley, *Benjamin West: The Paintings*, New Haven 1986, p. 150; Sotheby's, 11 May 1836.

83. Letter Woodburn to the Prince of Orange's agent, 3 September 1840, The Hague, Archives of the Royal House, Ms A 40 VIII-128 quoted by Chris Fischer, *Fra Bartolommeo, Master Draughtsman of the High Renaissance*, exhib. cat., Rotterdam, Museum Boymans-Van Beuningen, 1990, p. 15.

84. Von Erffa and Staley 1986, p. 20.

85. Gustav Waagen, *Art Treasures of Great Britain*, London 1854, III, Letter XXVI, p. 260.

86. Follower of Grimaldi, prov. West, WAG1995.250; attributed Parmigianino, prov. Roscoe, WAG1995.253; after Tintoretto, prov. Roscoe, WAG1995.260; Cantarini, prov. West, exh. cat. 10; Domenichino, prov. West, exh. cat. 22; Guercino, prov. Roscoe, exh. cat. 32; Rubens after Michelangelo, prov. Roscoe, exh. cat. 77.

NOTES:
ITALIAN DRAWINGS

1 ANONYMOUS
1. Identification of fish provided by Dr Alwyn Wheeler, formerly of the Natural History Museum, London.
2. L. Tongiorgi Tommasi, 'Bologna, Biblioteca Universitaria, Museo Aldrovandiano', in *Drawing: Public Collections in Italy*, edd. A. Petrioli Tofani, S. Prosperi Valenti Rodinò, G.C. Sciolla, Turin 1993, I, pp. 212–13; G. Olmi and L. Tongiorgi Tomasi, *De Piscibus. La bottega artistica di Ulisse Aldrovandi e l'immagine naturalistica*, Rome 1993.
3. *The Paper Museum of Cassiano dal Pozzo*, exhib. cat., London, British Museum, 1993.
4. L. Tongiorgi Tomasi, 'L'immagine naturalistica nelle antiche collezioni degli Uffizi', *Fonti e documenti. Gli Uffizi: quattro secoli di una galleria*, Florence 1982, p. 17.
5. According to L. Tongiorgi Tomasi (see 'Museo Aldrovandiano' above), the Ligozzi study in Bologna may be by Jacopo's cousin Francesco di Mercurio Ligozzi, who worked for the Medici in Florence in 1590–91.
6. London 1993, pp. 36–37.
7. R.P. Ciardi and L. Tongiorgi Tomasi, *Immagini anatomiche e naturalistiche nei disegni degli Uffizi Secc. XVI e XVII*, Florence 1984, cats. 66–71, 74–79; Florence, Uffizi, Gabinetto de Disegni, *Tavole di Pesce*, 2043 Orn., under Jacopo Ligozzi, 2014 Orn.

2 PIETRO PAOLO BALDINI
1. *Horatio about to stab his sister*, London, British Museum, 1847–3–6–9; *Martyrdom of St Paul*, inv. 4503 and *Conversion of St Paul*, inv. 4510, Windsor Castle.
2. The link to Romanelli's Sant'Eligio altarpiece was first noted by Philip Pouncey, but the architectural surround also seems modelled on that in Giacinto Gimignani's *Adoration* for the chapel of the Palazzo di Propaganda Fide in Rome, dated 1634.
3. Baldini is known to have produced copy-drawings after paintings, see for example the Windsor and Frankfurt drawings in Fischer 1991, p. 20. As Fischer also observed, Baldini often adopted the practice of conflating elements from two paintings to create his own version.
4. Suggested to the author in conversation with Ursula Fischer, June 1997.

3 BACCIO BANDINELLI
1. Ruth Rubinstein at the Warburg Institute was the first to point out this relationship. The attribution to Bandinelli was first made by A.E. Popham. See F. Papafava, *Vatican*, Vatican City 1993, p. 149. For the confusion as to whether the torso was owned by the Colonna family in 1514, see P. Bober and R. Rubinstein, *Renaissance Artists and Antique Sculpture: A Handbook of Sources*, Oxford 1986, pp. 167–68.
2. F. Haskell and N. Penny, *Taste and the Antique*, New Haven 1982, pp. 148–51.
3. Ward 1982, p. 25.
4. London, British Museum, inv. Pp. 1–61. Other early red-chalk drawings after antique sculptures include two studies in Milan, Biblioteca Ambrosiana, Cod.F.269inf. and one in Paris, Louvre, inv. 53.
5. Ward 1982, pp. 25, 119, citing Vasari. He also worked with the theme between 1526 and 1534 for the much criticized *Hercules and Cacus*, the 'pair' to Michelangelo's *David*.
6. The head is facially similar to Sansovino's painted terracotta *Head of the Etruscan King Porsenna*, ca. 1515–20; see *L'Officina della maniera*, exhib. cat., Florence, Uffizi, 1996, cat. 46.

4 BACCIO BANDINELLI
1. Possibly one of the 'Figures d'Academie' which Mariette purchased from the Crozat sale for his own collection of fifteen sheets by Bandinelli, as suggested by Ward 1982, p. 60.
2. Malibu, Getty Museum, inv. 85.GB.227; New York, Janos Scholz Collection, Pierpont Morgan Library, inv. 1986.83; Oxford, Christ Church, inv. 0082; Stockholm, National Museum, inv. 133, and Ward 1982, cat. 387r; Vienna, Albertina, inv. 238. For a related study in red chalk, see *Two men – one nude and one draped*, Berlin, KdZ15451.
3. For the dating see Ward 1982, cat. 385, and Forlani Tempesti 1989, p. 20.
4. The study for which is in the British Museum, 1895.9.15.553.
5. P. Joannides, *Michelangelo and his Influence: Drawings from Windsor Castle*, London 1996, p. 110, cat. 31.

5 FEDERICO BAROCCI
1. Milan, Pinacoteca di Brera, 392 × 269 cm. Rubens made a copy of the altarpiece in coloured washes; M. Jaffé, 'Rubens as a Collector of Drawings. Part Two', *Master Drawings*, III, 1965, p. 28, pl. 22.
2. Emiliani 1985, p. 169, citing documents in the Arch. Notarile, Ravenna, vol. 652, Bernardino Mengoli, a. 1580, c. 48 r.; and H. Olsen, *Federico Barocci: A Critical Study in Italian Cinquecento Painting*, Copenhagen 1955, cat. 33, pp. 134–36.
3. *"pluribus figuris augere et accrescere"*; documents published by S. Muratori in *Felix Ravenna*, fasc. 6, April 1912, pp. 244–59; and C. Ricci, *Felix Ravenna*, fasc. 11, July 1913, pp. 479–80.
4. *"figure maggiori del naturale, vi sono nudi e vestiti, e bon numero di figure; fatto in carta bianca di chiaroscuro alumata con biacca"*; Emiliani 1985, p. 170, citing Calzini in *In studi e notizie su F. B.*, Florence 1913, p. 77.
5. Paris, Louvre, pen, brown ink and wash heightened with white on tinted paper, 337 x 224 mm, Collection Jabach, inv. 2858; repr. H. Olsen, *Federico Barocci*, Copenhagen 1962, figs. 46–47. There are also studies for individual figures in Amsterdam, Berlin, Chatsworth, Edinburgh, Florence, Urbino and Vienna.
6. Emiliani 1985, p. 169.

6 FRA BARTOLOMMEO
1. Date of birth revised to 21 August 1473 in *Fra Bartolommeo*, exhib. cat., Florence, Palazzo Pitti, 1996, as quoted by C. Ellis in an exhibition review, *Burlington Magazine*, CXXXVIII, September 1996, p. 629.
2. *Fra Bartolommeo: Master Draughtsman of the High Renaissance*, exhib. cat. by Chris Fischer, Rotterdam Museum Boymans-Van Beuningen, 1990, p. 106.
3. Formerly Berlin, Kaiser Friedrich Museum destroyed in 1945; illus. Rotterdam 1990, p. 144, fig. 74. Both the Coronation and the Assumption of the Virgin are celebrated on the same feast day of 15 August. The suggested dating of the figures to between 1500 and 1504 was proposed by Fischer 1994, pp. 56–57, and in a letter 16 July 1996.
4. London, British Museum, inv. Pp. 1–53 recto; Paris, Fondation Custodia, Collection F. Lugt, inv. 7193 recto.; Rotterdam 1990, pp. 109, 144–47; see also Uffizi, 457E verso in *Fra Bartolommeo*, exhib. cat. by Chris Fischer, Florence, Uffizi, 1986, cat. 31.
5. Rotterdam 1990, p. 15, citing Samuel Woodburn's letter of 3 September 1840 to the Prince of Orange's agent, The Hague, Archives of the Royal House, Ms A 40 VIII–120, which states that West: "took so much from the draperies into his pictures that he decided they should never be sold publicly". For a similar trio of figures in discussion in a painting by West, see *Caesar reading the history of Alexander's exploits*, Richmond, Virginia Museum of Fine Arts, illus. H. von Erffa and A. Staley, *The Paintings of Benjamin West*, New Haven 1986, cat. 26.

7 GIROLAMO MAZZOLA BEDOLI
1. A.E. Popham originally thought it was by or after Parmigianino and then reattributed it to Bedoli, an attribution confirmed by P. Pouncey and M. di Giampaolo.
2. Inv. 5289. The identification was first published by Giampaolo 1977; Milstein 1978 related it to another painting. Other compositional studies are in Bergamo, Accademia Carrara, pen and ink, 100 × 75 mm, inv. 531 (with the Virgin with her back to the saint behind her to the right); and Chatsworth, a

badly damaged *Holy Family*, red chalk, rose and white bodycolours, oxidized, 246 × 179 mm, in M. Jaffé, *The Devonshire Collection of Drawings: Bolognese and Emilian Schools*, London 1994, p. 215, no. 644/803, which assumes that the background figure is St Joseph. Jaffé believed it to be a copy whereas M. di Giampaolo, *Disegni emiliani di Rinascimento*, exhib. cat., Modena 1989, no. 41, regarded it and the Weld-Blundell drawing as original.
3. L. Réau, *Iconographie de l'Art Chrétien*, Paris 1955–58, I, p. 249. St Bruno's cult was only authorized by the Carthusian order at the end of the fifteenth century and all early sixteenth-century images of the saint in Italy are in Carthusian monasteries.
4. D. Ekserdjian in conversation, 28 October 1996. G. Vasari, *Le vite de' più eccellenti pittori, scultori ed architettori* [1568], ed. G. Milanesi, Florence 1878–85, V, p. 237.

8 LUCA CAMBIASO
1. The medieval and Renaissance tradition of depicting Moses as 'horned' derived from a mistranslation of the Latin for shining, haloed or flashing with rays of light in the Vulgate Bible.
2. Princeton Art Museum, *Fortitude?*, 400 × 226 mm, inv. 48–640; *St Jerome reading*, 291 × 217 mm, inv. 48–629; *Sibyl attended by a genius seated on a cloud*, 401 × 282 mm, inv. 48–654; Chicago Institute of Art, *Standing male nude with book (Saint Jerome?)*, 407 × 285 mm, inv. 1922.3281; Stockholm, National Museum, *Sibyl*, 362 × 250 mm, inv. NM1590/1863.
3. F. Gibbons, *Italian Drawings in the Art Museum in Princeton University*, Princeton 1977, I, pp. 35–36, no. 89; *Fortitude*, early 1550s; Gibbons I, p. 38, no. 95; *Sibyl*, ca. 1557; Gibbons I, p. 34, no. 87; *St Jerome*, late 1560s; S.F. McCullogh and L.M. Giles, *Italian Drawings before 1600 in the Chicago Institute of Arts*, Chicago 1997, cat. 57, dated to the 1550s; P. Bjurström, *Drawings in Swedish Public Collections: Volume Three. Italian Drawings*, Stockholm 1979, no. 301, dated to latter half of 1540s.
4. Letter, 23 May 1996.

9 LUCA CAMBIASO
1. According to the copy of William Ford's annotated Roscoe sale catalogue in the British Museum, the lot was bought by Esdaile.
2. Florence, Uffizi, *Christ on the Mount of Olives*, inv. 13733, pen and ink with no wash; *Captive Christ being led over a bridge*, inv. 848E, 245 × 350 mm; *Captive Christ led through a wood*, inv. 847E; 13681F, *Christ led by neck past trees*. The last is considered by Newcome (M. Newcome, *Disegri genovesi dal XVI al XVII secolo*, Florence 1989, no. 7) to be by another artist making drawings 'alla Cambiaso'. Other cuboid scenes from Christ's

Passion dated to *ca.* 1570–75 include a variant of the Uffizi, inv. 848E, *Christ led away by soldiers*, New York, Janos Scholz Collection, 250 × 353 mm (the closest in size to the Liverpool drawing); British Museum, *Christ crossing a bridge*, inv. 1946–7–13–286; Oxford, Ashmolean, *Betrayal of Christ*, Parker 133; *Taking of Christ*, Virginia, Williamsburg, College of William and Mary, Muscarelle Museum of Art.
3. W. Suida and B.S. Manning, *Luca Cambiaso, la vita e le opere*, Milan 1958, fig. 401, *Ecce Homo*. The Spanish art historian Céan Bermúdez, *Diccionario histórico de los más ilustres profesores de las bellas artes en España*, 1800, described a canvas of *Pilate presenting Christ to the people* above the door of the prior's cell in the large cloister of the Escorial where Cambiaso worked his final years with his son between 1583 and 1585, but the *Ecce Homo* painting is not related to the Liverpool composition.
4. Christie's, London, 4 July 1995, lot 41; M. Newcome, letter, 23 May 1996.

10 SIMONE CANTARINI
1. Also found on a Ludovico Carracci (?) drawing dated *ca.* 1585, *Virgin and Christ Child in a landscape*, Amsterdam, Historisch Museum, inv. A–18082.
2. According to the Edinburgh catalogue entry the old mount was inscribed in ink *Elisabetta Sirani* and in pencil in Waagen's hand *probably not of her, more of the Venetian School*. The attribution to Cantarini was due to John Gere.
3. C.C. Malvasia, *Felsina pittrice*, [1678], edn. Bologna 1841, II, pp. 373–83.
4. Compare the compositional similarities with the Reni etching in V. Birke, *The Illustrated Bartsch*, XL, New York 1982, B.7 (283).
5. P. Bellini, *Simone Cantarini: Disegni, incisione e opere di riproduzione*, San Severino 1987, pp. 19–20.
6. The painting from the early 1640s is in the Galleria Borghese, Rome. For the etchings see P. Bellini, *L'opera incisa di Simone Cantarini*, Milan 1980, cats. 31, 34, pp. 128–30. A larger and more sketchy red-chalk drawing of the subject is in the Accademia, Venice, see M. di Giampaolo, *Disegni emiliani dell'Accademia di Venezia*, Milan 1993, no. 8, with other variant drawings particularly in Brera, Milan, inv. 48, 59, 99, 501.
7. Malvasia 1841, II, p. 382.

11 DOMENICO MARIA CANUTI
1. Simonetta Stagni, *Domenico Maria Canuti pittore*, Rimini 1988, cat. 49, p. 201, quoting C.C. Malvasia, who was a friend of the artist; *Le pitture di Bologna* [1686], ed. A. Emiliani, Bologna 1969, pp. 329–30.
2. Rev. 12: 1–2.
3. Stuttgart, Staatsgalerie, Schloss Fachsenfeld Collection, inv. III 372.

4. Roscoe sale, 1816, lots 424, 425, and Appendix WAG1995.99.

12, 13 ANNIBALE CARRACCI (?)
1. Both watermarks are those of the D & C Blauw paper-making company whose card was used to mount drawings in the Royal Collection in the late eighteenth century, according to information from Alan Donnithorne.
2. Orléans, Musée des Beaux-Arts, 103 × 85 cm, inv. 1129. D. Posner, *Annibale Carracci*, London 1971, II, cat. 102a, pp. 44–45.
3. Cambridge, Fitzwilliam Museum, 514 × 378 mm, inv. 2911. Oxford 1996, no. 90, p. 141.
4. Posner 1971, I, pp. 83–85.
5. Oxford 1996, no. 91.
6. For the painting's history in French collections, including that of Louis XIV, see Posner 1971, pp. 44–45. Engravings are known by Pietro Santi Bartoli and C. Normand.
7. Christie's, London, 29 October 1965, lot 38, and Leger Galleries advertisement in *Apollo*, Jan. 1966, attributed to Agostino Carracci, 98 × 76 cm.

14 ATTRIBUTED TO ANNIBALE CARRACCI
1. *Virgin and Child*, pen and ink, Royal Collection, Windsor, RL 2315.
2. *Apollo receiving the lyre from Mercury*, ca. 1603–04, and *Self-portrait on an easel*, ca. 1604, Royal Collection, Windsor, illus. in Oxford 1996, cats. 97, 98.
3. For example, compare the fingers with the splayed stubby feet of *Mercury and Apollo*, illus. Oxford 1996, p. 148, cat. 97.
4. Babette Bohn, *The Illustrated Bartsch*, XXXIX, New York 1996, Commentary part 2, no. 3906.017, pp. 220–35.
5. Silver plaque, Naples, Museo Nazionale, illus. in O. Kurz, 'Engravings on Silver by Annibale', *Burlington Magazine*, XCVII, September 1955, pp. 282–87, figs. 23, 24.

15 ATTRIBUTED TO ANNIBALE OR FRANCESCO CARRACCI
1. A. Sutherland Harris, 'Ludovico, Agostino, Annibale ... l'abbiamo fatta tutti noi', *Accademia Clementina Atti e Memorie*, XXXIII–IV, 1994, pp. 69–84.
2. Illus. in E. Negro and M. Pirondini, *La scuola dei Carracci dall'Accademia alla bottega di Ludovico*, Modena 1994, cat. 199, p. 157.
3. Vienna, Albertina, Annibale Carracci, inv. 2176; recto *Academy nude lying on ground*, red chalk heightened with white, 280 × 420 mm. A Carracci school drawing in Düsseldorf (Staatliche Kunstakademie, inv. FP329) illustrates the Academy's practice of drawing whilst seated in a semicircle around the model.

4. British Museum, 1972–6–17–5, illus. in Negro and Pirondini 1994, p. 93, fig. 94. The attribution was also suggested to the author by Babette Bohn, letter 12 August 1997.
5. F. Lollini in Negro and Pirondini 1994, pp. 91–93.
6. C.C. Malvasia, *Felsina pittrice* [1678], edn. Bologna 1841, I, pp. 373–74.

16 ATTRIBUTED TO LUDOVICO CARRACCI
1. C.C. Malvasia, *Felsina pittrice* [1678], edn. Bologna 1841, I, p. 334.
2. Recto of a drawing in the Royal Collection, RL 2017, illus. in Oxford 1996, cat. 51, pp. 96–97.
3. Letter, 12 August 1997, commenting (from a photograph) particularly on the "carefully modelled, specific delineation of drapery folds", different from Ludovico's usual style for the period *ca.* 1588–90, to which she had tentatively attributed the drawing. See also the drawings discussed in Bohn's article on 'Chalk Drawings of Lodovico Carracci', *Master Drawings*, XXII, no. 4, 1984, no. 4, pp. 423–25.
4. Two portraits of women, R. Wittkower, *The Drawings of the Carracci at Windsor Castle*, London 1952, no. 170, fig. 21, thought to be related to a portrait of 1598 and no. 171, pl. 42; Woodner Collection, New York, Schab Gallery, 1971, no. 41.
5. Wittkower 1952, no. 167, pl. 27, inv. 2116 dated 1590 and no.168, pl. 28, inv. 2276, recto and verso.

17 GIOVANNI BENEDETTO CASTIGLIONE
1. The drawing, then attributed to Pietro Testa, was etched with an inscription *London 14 June 1793*, and published by the comte de St-Morys in his *Disegni Originali d'Eccelenti Pittori*, no. 63, a copy of which is in the Victoria and Albert Museum, inv. 15865.34.
2. Musée Granet, inv. 860.1.17. The connection between the two was first indicated to the author by Mary Newcome in conversation, 12 July 1996. Newcome 1997, p. 63, suggests that the painting in Aix might possibly be an early Castiglione work.
3. Newcome 1997, fig. 72, *Sacrifice of Abraham*, inscribed *Gio. Benedetto Castiglione*, ca. 240 × 160 mm, private collection; fig. 75, *David holding the head of Goliath*, Windsor, Royal Collection, RL 4000.
4. For another example of Lione using a Castiglione image as a model for a painting, see J. Byam-Shaw, *Frits Lugt Provenance: Italian Drawings*, Paris 1983, cat. 428, pl. 486.
5. *Escales du Baroque*, exhib. cat. by F. Viatte, Marseille 1988, no. 46, pp. 164–65.
6. Newcome 1997, p. 63, figs. 77, 82.

18 GIUSEPPE CESARI
1. A suggestion made by Professor Dr Herwarth Röttgen in a letter, 27 August 1997.
2. Stockholm, Nationalmuseum, inv. 382; see also *Il Cavaliere d'Arpino*, exhib. cat. by H. Röttgen, Rome, Palazzo Venezia, 1973, cats. 98, 16.
3. H. Röttgen, 'Giuseppe Cesaris Fresken in der Loggia Orsini', *Storia dell'arte*, III, 1969, pp. 279–95.
4. Uffizi, Horne, inv. 5581; Rome 1973, cat. 107.
5. Rome 1973, cat. 17; *Gli affreschi del Cavalier d'Arpino in Campidoglio*, exhib. cat., Rome, Palazzo dei Conservatori, July–September 1980.

19 GIUSEPPE CESARI
1. For a preparatory study for another pendentive see the *Prophet* in Parma's Archivio di Stato, illustrated in *Drawing: Public Collections in Italy*, edd. A. Petrioli Tofani, S.P. Valenti Rodinò, G.C. Sciolla, Turin 1994, part I, p. 216, fig. 265.
2. Rome 1973, pp. 42–43.
3. *Ibid.*, pp. 45–46, quoting G.P. Bellori *Le vite de' pittori, scultore e architetti*, 1672.

20 GIUSEPPE CESARI
1. There is a similar watermark on a Thomas Sandby drawing in the Royal Collection, *Master Drawings in the Royal Collection*, exhib. cat. by J. Roberts, London, Queen's Gallery, 1986, pp. 189, 191, cat. 120.
2. Zurich, Kunsthaus, N 56/I; Rome 1973, cats. 143, 144.
3. Letter, 27 August 1997. Much earlier in his career Cesari had painted another airborne figure of Fame blowing a trumpet, the drawing for which is in New York, Metropolitan Museum 1986.318.

21 ANTONIO CORREGGIO
1. There is a copy of the Liverpool drawing, perhaps from Vasari's own collection, in the Louvre, red chalk, 200 × 150 mm, inv. 6019.
2. The *Dictionary of Art* entry by David Ekserdjian identifies 'St Maurus' as John, the first abbot of the monastery.
3. Studies for the central section of Christ crowning the Virgin are in Budapest, Szépművészeti Múzeum, inv. 2100, 2101; London, Courtauld Galleries, Seilern Collection 352; Oxford, Ashmolean Parker no. 204; Paris, Louvre, invs. 5916, 5918, 5943; Poitiers, Musée Sainte-Croix, inv. 822–I.187; Rotterdam, Boymans-van Beuningen, inv. I.381. The study for *St Benedict gesturing to his left* is in the Chicago Art Institute, inv. 1996.337.
4. Both the Courtauld and the Poitiers studies for *Christ crowning* are squared in red ink or chalk, as is the early drawing for the Virgin in the Louvre, inv. 5916.
5. The red-chalk ground also appears on the Chicago drawing.

22 DOMENICHINO
1. Spear 1982 does not exclude the possibility that it could be a study for a lost *Holy Family* (cat. 61, fig. 226) of the same period, which is known through stylistically close studies at Windsor, J. Pope-Hennessy, *Drawings of Domenichino ... at Windsor Castle*, London 1948, nos. 1192–94.
2. G. Passeri, *Vite de' pittori, scultori et architetti che anno lavorato in Roma morti dal 1641 fino al 1673* [1677], ed. J. Hess, Leipzig and Vienna 1934, pp. 37–38.
3. Now at Chatsworth House, Derbyshire. Spear 1982, no. 107, fig. 351.
4. St Petersburg, Hermitage Museum, illus. Spear 1982, no. 66, fig. 232. A possible later study for the Magdalene's head with loose hair may be found on the verso of a black-chalk drawing heightened with white at Windsor, RL 050, Pope-Hennessy 1948, no. 1135.
5. Pinacoteca Nazionale, Bologna, illus. Spear 1982, no. 62, fig. 228, pl. 4.
6. C.C. Malvasia, *Felsina pittrice* [1678], edn. Bologna 1841, II, p. 241. Domenichino had just married in 1619, aged thirty-eight, Marsibilia Barbetti of Bologna, described by Passeri (1934, p. 43) as a "singularly beautiful" woman.

23 DOMENICHINO
1. Spear 1982, p. 77.
2. See in particular Pope-Hennessy 1948, nos. 517 (dated to spring 1635), 967 (1628–32), 1136 (*ca.* 1635), 1262 (*ca.* 1630), 1393 (1635–40).
3. G. Passeri, *Vite de' pittori, scultori et architetti che anno lavorato in Roma morti dal 1641 fino al 1673* [1677], ed. J. Hess, Leipzig and Vienna 1934, pp. 62–63.
4. Ibid., pp. 56, 65, n. 1, for the bizarre story of his sons' death through undernourishment by their mother. Spear 1982, pp. 14, 22.
5. *Felsina pittrice* [1678], edn. Bologna 1841, II, p. 231.
6. Passeri 1934, pp. 63–64, n. 4: "*facesse li ritratti delle figlioline, una del Principe e di Da Olimpia; e le altre due del fratello del Principe; e del cardinale; e di Da. Carlotta Savelli; e determinarone forle tutte insieme in una tela*".

24 DOMENICHINO
1. Letter, 15 April 1996; Spear 1982, no. 55 iii, pl. 183; Pope-Hennessy 1948, no. 1124.
2. Chatsworth, Derbyshire (inv. 512), illus. *Old Master Drawings from Chatsworth*, exhib. cat., Los Angeles County Museum, 1987, p. 65, no. 29.
3. G. Passeri, *Vite de' pittori, scultori et architetti che anno lavorato in Roma morti dal 1641 fino al 1673* [1677], ed. J. Hess, Leipzig and Vienna 1934, p. 63.

25 PAOLO FARINATI
1. The Ottley sale also included three other Farinati drawings on blue paper in the "same manner": *Charity*, and figures for a pediment, which was also bought by Roscoe; *Perseus and Andromeda* and *Season of autumn*, a man surrounded by fruits and children.
2. One of five drawings by Farinati owned by Roscoe; others had come from Lely's collection, *Pan with his pipe and goat at feet*, and another from Ottley's collection, *Charity*. But none of the Farinati drawings described in the 1816 catalogue coincides with the one now in New York's Metropolitan Museum (Rogers Fund, 1962 62.119.9), *Project for the decoration of a spandrel: winged female figure holding a tablet and a crown*, which is supposed to be from Roscoe's collection.
3. As was first identified in the Venice 1980 exhibition by Terence Mullaly.
4. C. Ridolfi, *Le maraviglie dell'arte ovvero le vite degli illustri pittori Veneti e dello Stato* [1648], ed. D.F. von Hadeln, Berlin 1924, II, pp. 129, 133.
5. *Paolo Farinati Giornale (1573–1606)*, ed. L. Puppi, Florence 1968, fig. 31.
6. S. dalla Rosa, *Catastico delle pitture ... esistenti nelle chiese e luoghi pubblici ... in Verona ... e aggiunta delle pitture a fresco che si vedono nelle facciate ... di tutta la città*, 1804, Ms. 1803–04, p. 248, in the Biblioteca Communale, Verona, cited by Sueur 1989 at n. 41; the drawings by Luciano Mozzetto and Luigi Marai in Verona's Museo di Castelvecchio, inv. 22320 2–1303, mistake *Agriculture*'s corn sheaf for a scythe.
7. The Louvre has studies for two of the four Venus and Adonis panels, *Death of Adonis*, and *Venus trying to dissuade Adonis from the hunt*, invs. 4862, 4854; studies for the groups of male and female satyrs and putti are in the Goethe Collection of Weimar Nationalen Forschungs- und Gedenkstätten and Chicago, Art Institute inv. 1922.766.
8. *Giornale* 1968, pp. 88–90, 121.

26 GIOVAN AMBROGIO FIGINO
1. A. Perissa Torrini, 'Figino' entry in *The Dictionary of Art*, London 1997. Others such as R.P. Ciardi, *Giovan Ambrogio Figino*, Florence 1968, have placed the Roman trip later, to *ca.* 1577–1581/83.
2. The woman holds some of her drapery in her right hand and appears to be running away, glancing sharply to the left. Along the lower edge of the sheet there is a faint outline of another woman's head and torso on a larger scale.
3. Windsor, RL 6968; A.E. Popham and J. Wilde, *Italian Drawings at Windsor*, London 1949, cat. 100, fig. 70. On the other sheet, RL 6971 verso, Popham and Wilde 1949, cat. 103, the Sibyl in ink over red chalk is surrounded by figures of horses,

soldiers and executioners, illus. in Ciardi 1968, p. 317, fig. 213, cat. 296.
4. See Windsor, RL 6969, Popham and Wilde 1949, cat. 101.

27 ATTRIBUTED TO THE WORKSHOP OF DOMENICO FONTANA
1. Philip Pouncey attributed it to Francesco Salviati and Julien Stock to Vincenzo Borghini.
2. R.U. Montini, *Le Tombe dei Papi*, Rome 1957, p. 332, no. 226; p. 341, no. 228.
3. Alexandra Herz, 'The Sistine and Pauline Tombs', *Storia dell'arte*, XLIII, 1981, pp. 242–45.
4. Enzo Borsellino, 'Il Monumento di Pio V in S Maria Maggiore', in *Sisto V: Roma e il Lazio*, edd. M. Fagilo and M.L. Madonna, Rome 1992, I, p. 841, citing Archivio di Stato, Rome, Camerale I v. Giustificazioni di Tesoreria, b. 7, fasc. 8, cc. 1–12.
5. Inv. 2261, 387 × 212 mm, P. Ward-Jackson, *Italian Drawings*, London 1979–80, I, cat. 320. W. Gramberg attributed another drawing with 'quotation marks' in the Victoria and Albert Museum, inv. 8941, to Sormani, see 'Guglielmo della Portas Grabmal fur Pope Paul III Farnese in S Pietro Vaticano', *Römisches Jahrbuch für Kunstgeschichte*, XXI, 1974, p. 280, fig. 17, cat. 3.Z.7.
6. Sormani is not known to have worked for Guglielmo della Porta but he did work between 1585 and 1587 with another member of the large sculptural workshop, Tomaso della Porta, a dealer in antique sculpture; see Borsellino 1992, p. 843.

28 GIOVANNI BATTISTA FRANCO
1. J. Richardson, 2nd edn., London 1725, p. 152.
2. The decoration was completed by Federico Zuccaro, see exh. cat. 79.
3. W.R. Rearick, 'Battista Franco and the Grimani Chapel', *Saggi e memorie di storia dell'arte*, II, 1958–59, p. 127, fig. 12.
4. *The Illustrated Bartsch: Italian Artists of the Sixteenth Century*, XXXII, ed. H. Zerner, p. 174, 18 (125), National Gallery of Scotland, D634; Chatsworth, inv. 294, a pen-and-ink model for Bartsch XVI, p.158, no.13; see M. Jaffé, *The Devonshire Collection of Italian Drawings: Venetian and Northern Schools*, London 1994, cat. 793.
5. G. Vasari, *Le vite ...*, ed. G. Milanesi, Florence 1878–85, VI, p. 581.

29 GIOVANNI BATTISTA FRANCO
1. Another circular drawing by Franco with a Spencer-Roscoe provenance, *The Virgin and Child with two saints*, is in the Cleveland Museum of Art, inv. 65.16.
2. On loan to the Snite Museum of Art, University of Notre Dame,

Indiana, L94.18.2, diameter 122 mm. The author would like to thank Anne Lauder for revealing its present location and for her comments on the Liverpool drawing.
3. Letter, John Mallett, 4 September 1996.
4. T. Clifford and J. Mallett, 'Battista Franco as a Designer for Maiolica', *Burlington Magazine*, CXVIII, June 1976, pp. 387–410.
5. They showed *Work*, *Agriculture* and *Hunting*; J. Schulz, *Venetian Painted Ceilings of the Renaissance*, Berkeley and Los Angeles 1968, pp. 93–95. Despite the circular format of the canvases, the known drawings in the Louvre are octagonal, making it unlikely that the Liverpool drawing is a rejected design for the Marciana.
6. W.R. Rearick, 'Battista Franco and the Grimani Chapel', *Saggi e memorie di storia dell'arte*, II, 1958–59, pp. 120–21, quoting M. Boschini and A. M. Zanetti, *Descrizione di tutte le pubbliche pitture*, edn. 1733, p. 89, and a 1797 guidebook, *Della pittura veneziana*.

30 WORKSHOP OF DOMENICO GHIRLANDAIO
1. C. Fischer, 'Ghirlandaio and the Origins of Cross-hatching', in *Florentine Drawing at the Time of Lorenzo the Magnificent*, ed. E. Cropper, Bologna 1994, p. 245.
2. Letter from Bernard Berenson, 24 August 1955, stuck to old backing board, attributes it to David Ghirlandaio.
3. F. Ames-Lewis, 'Drapery "Pattern" – Drawings in Ghirlandaio's Workshop and Ghirlandaio's Early Apprenticeship', *Art Bulletin*, LXIII, 1981, pp. 49–62.
4. Berlin, Kupferstichkabinett, KdZ474, KdZ5043 and KdZ5150 recto, all dated to *ca.* 1480–85; Musée Condé, Chantilly, inv. 10(8); Paris, Louvre, inv. 1253; Oxford, Christ Church, no. 0021.
5. Inv. Pp–01–3. See also Florence, Uffizi, inv. 160E, ochre paper, 190 × 70 mm, a draped and capped young man standing in profile to right, of a similar size and in a pose about the reverse of that in the Liverpool study, attributed to either Domenico or Davide Ghirlandaio.
6. Ames-Lewis 1981, p. 53.

31 LUCA GIORDANO
1. The figures have been stained later with some sort of darkened fixative. The chamfered corners were probably cut in the eighteenth century when it became a common collector's practice on mounting or pasting drawings in albums.
2. Other such drawings include: the British Museum's *Jacob's Dream*, after Raphael Ff.4–32, and *Standing man seen from rear*, after Polidoro da Caravaggio, 1920–4–20–8; the Uffizi's detail from the Palazzo Barberini *Allegory of Justice*, after Pietro da

Cortona, 15141F, also over a double sheet 423 × 641 mm; and in Naples, Museo San Martino, inv. 20556, another copy after Polidoro from the Palazzo Ricci façade.
3. Real Academia de Bellas Artes de San Fernando, no. 254, red chalk, 475 × 553 mm, illus. in A.E. Pérez Sánchez, *Catálogo de los Dibujos*, Madrid 1967, pp. 83–84, pl. 16.
4. B. De Dominici, *Vite dei Pittori, Scultori et Architetti Napoletani*, Naples 1742–45, pp. 396–97.

32 GUERCINO
1. *Libro dei conti*, in J.A. Calvi, *Notizie della vita e delle opere del Cavaliere Giovan Francesco Barbieri detto il Guercino da Cento*, Bologna 1808, p. 93; 1841, p. 320; C. Giardini, *La collezione Hercolani nella Pinacoteca Civica di Pesaro*, Bologna 1992, p. 125, Appendix 2, quoting from *Guida agli amatori delle belle arti ... per la città di Bologna ... del sacerdote Petronio Bassani*, 1816, I, pt. 1, "Q.[uadro] grandissimo Bersabea nel Bagno, ed alcune Damigelle f.i. del Guercino".
2. Windsor, RL 2673, 249 × 388 mm; painting photographed when it was in the Perticari collection in Pesaro, reproduced in N. Grimaldi, *Il Guercino, Gian Francesco Barbieri 1591–1666*, Bologna 1957, pl. 105; 1968, pl. 185.
3. II Samuel 11: 2–5.
4. G. Passeri, *Vite de' pittori, scultori et architetti che anno lavorato in Roma mocti dal 1641 fino al 1673* [1677], ed. J. Hers, Leipzig and Vienna 1934, pp. 346–47, 350.

33 AFTER GUERCINO, ATTRIBUTED TO SIR JOSHUA REYNOLDS
1. Snite Museum of Art, University of Notre Dame, Indiana, gift of Mr John D. Reilly, class of 1963, inv. 94.49.6, 218 × 152 mm.
2. Stone 1991, p. xxvi, and Sir Denis Mahon, orally, 30 November 1995.
3. The correct acquisition date of the Bouverie collection (previously thought to be 1768) was identified and extensively discussed by Nicholas Turner in his 'Introduction' in Turner and Plazzotta 1991, pp. 22, 29–30, nn. 53–61.
4. Reynolds also had access to the Bouverie collection when it was owned by Sir Jacob's son the Hon. Edward Bouverie (1738–1810), whose wife he portrayed twice between 1768 and 1770.
5. *Head of a monk in profile*, 250 × 200 mm, referred to in Turner and Plazzotta 1991, cat. 126. For other Guercino copies thought to be by Reynolds see Turner and Plazzotta 1991, cat. 127, *Bearded old man gesturing to the right*, private collection, Massachusetts, and Appendix nos. 46, 48, *Head of an old man*, Museum of Fine Arts, Budapest, inv. 2480, 165 × 194 mm, formerly in Hudson's

collection, and a *Seated St Gregory*; three copies in the Fondation Custodia, Institut Néerlandais, Paris, inv. 545, 1043, 1981–T30, all formerly owned by Benjamin West; two drawings, one red chalk, one in pen and wash, formerly in the Mahon collection, *Guercino Drawings from the Collections of Denis Mahon and the Ashmolean Museum*, 1986, nos. 49–50; and one owned by John Nicholas Brown, Providence, RI.
6. J. Northcote, *The Life of Reynolds*, 1813, I, p. 13.
7. Roscoe sale, 1816, lot 592, "Two drawings by Sir Joshua Reynolds one An old Man's head after Guercino, probably copied by Sir Joshua whilst he was a pupil with Hudson, having been bought at his sale, 25th Feb. 1785", bt. Heber. This may be the drawing in the Museum of Fine Arts, Budapest, inv. 2480.

34 AFTER GUERCINO, ATTRIBUTED TO SIR BENJAMIN WEST
1. The crowned fleur-de-lys (Strasbourg Lily) was a common watermark in the eighteenth century and it also featured repeatedly on card used to mount drawings in the Royal Collection, *ca.* 1765–75, and on the mounts of West's own collection; see exh. cats. 20, 45, 58, 71.
2. The remains of the glue which originally attached this missing drawing are visible along the left-hand edge of the drawing. The shelfmark inscribed on the back of the mount suggests that the original drawing had been in Jonathan Richardson's collection.
3. RL 2637, pen and greyish wash on light-buff paper, 272 × 187 mm.
4. Turner and Plazzotta 1991, p. 21.
5. Vienna, Albertina, inv. 2381, thought to be by or after Bartolozzi.
6. Letter, Martin Clayton, 26 August 1997. Gold slips do feature on the mount designs of some drawings owned by Jonathan Richardson, so confirming the likely provenance of the mount as from his collection.
7. Paris, Fondation Custodia, Institut Néerlandais, inv. 545, 1043, 1981–T30, see J. Byam Shaw, *Italian Drawings from the Frits Lugt Collection*, Paris 1983, cats. 355–57. They were part of lot 45 from Christie's sale of West's collection, 9–14 June 1820, "Four heads in pen & ink by Sir J. Reynolds after Guercino".
8. *Three seated women*, pen and wash, Edinburgh, National Gallery of Scotland, D2408, and *Standing man*, pen and ink, Sidney, Art Gallery of New South Wales, inv. 7388. H. von Erffa and A. Staley, *The Paintings of Benjamin West*, New Haven 1986, no. 321.

35 ALESSANDRO MAGNASCO
1. *Journey of the monks*, Turin, Galleria Sabauda, inv. 555 in L. Muti and D. de Sarno Prignano, *Alessandro Magnasco*, ed. E. Martini, Ravenna

1994, cat. 330; *Landscape with travelling Capuchin friars*, Milan, Brera, inv. 4964, formerly in the monastic choir of Santa Maria delle Grazie, Gravedona, in Muti and de Sarno 1994, cat. 174, p. 81, figs. 83, 262, and in the exhibition catalogue *Alessandro Magnasco*, Milan, Palazzo Reale, 1996, cat. 44, p. 189.
2. Muti and de Sarno 1994, pp. 63–64; Fausta Franchini Guelfi, 'Alessandro Magnasco', entry in *The Dictionary of Art*, London 1996.
3. The 'oiled' paper is unusual for Magnasco as was pointed out by Mary Newcome, orally, May 1996. Two different types of white and a darkened 'fixative' were also found on the brush study by Frans Floris (exh. cat. 69), also owned by Benjamin West.

36 ANDREA MANTEGNA
1. Alongside it a black mark which is possibly inadvertent but might be the lower half of a crude cross as sometimes found beside Haym's initials, though probably not that of Giovanni Matteo Marchetti, Bishop of Arezzo (L2911), as suggested in the Venice 1980 exhibition catalogue.
2. The manuscript catalogue of Resta's collection in the British Museum Prints and Drawings Department, Lansdowne Ms 802, Lib.G.128: "Lo stimano di Giorgione, io dubito che sia di Gio. Bellini. 1419. 1509". Album g. was the first volume in a chronological series of albums put together by Resta in the 1690s, according to G. Warwick, 'The Formation and Early Provenance of Padre Sebastiano Resta's Drawing Collection', *Master Drawings*, XXXIV, 1996, pp. 242, 243.
3. In his catalogue entry Popham first proposed that there were good reasons to suggest Mantegna as the artist.
4. J. Wilde, *Catalogue of the Seilern Provenance: Italian Paintings and Drawings, Addenda*, London 1969, pp. 37–41 and *Corrigenda and Addenda*, London 1971, p. 45; British Museum, *Standing saint reading*, inv. 1895–9–15–780; *Three standing saints*, Thaw collection, Pierpont Morgan Library, New York; *Two studies of St John the Baptist and four standing saints*, formerly in the Koenigs collection, Boymans-van-Beuningen Museum, Rotterdam, inv. I.487, now in the Pushkin Museum, Moscow.
5. The Koenigs drawing is made up of two sheets of figure-studies glued together later, those of St John on the left are attributed to Mantegna and measure 172 × 152 mm, whereas the four saints on the right sheet are thought by Ekserdjian to be copies after the artist, although this was queried by G. Goldner in his review of the Royal Academy exhibition in *Master Drawings*, XXXI, 1993, pp. 272–73 under no. 23. Giles Robertson also observed that the pose of the

standing St John in the Liverpool drawing recalls that of the soldier beside the Crucifixion in the predella of the San Zeno altarpiece (now in Louvre).
6. Agosti 1993, p. 67ff: discussing letters from Gemetto de Nesson and Jacopo d'Atri to the Marchese Francesco Gonzaga on 26 October, 4 November and 13 November 1499, in the Mantua archives, b. 1633; b. 2908, *libro 162*, cc. 46r–v.
7. For the seal and tomb see *La Renaissance à Rouen*, exhib. cat. by J. Delaporte, Musée des Antiquités, Rouen, 1980, p. 17, n. 5, Musée des Antiquités, inv. 1724/17; for the relief, Louvre inv. A.F. no. 1265.
8. Rouen 1980, p. 18, cat. 6a.
9. A. Chastel, 'Le Donateur in abisso dans les pale' [1977], in *Fables, formes, figures*, Paris 1978, II, pp. 130, 135, 139.
10. R. Lightbown, *Mantegna with a Complete Catalogue of the Paintings, Drawings and Prints*, Oxford 1986, pp. 228–29.
11. The sketches could for example relate to Mantegna's stay from May or June 1466 in Florence, where the patron saint was St John the Baptist.

37 GIROLAMO MUZIANO
1. F. Titi, *Studio di pittura, scoltura et architettura nelle chiese di Roma* [1674], ed. H. Honour, Florence 1987, I, p. 228; illus. in Venturi, *Storia dell'arte italiano*, IX, pt. 7, Milan 1934, p. 459, fig. 258. Muziano also painted the same subject in one compartment of the vault of Cappella Gabrielli in S Maria sopra Minerva, but this bears only a slight relationship to the Liverpool drawing.
2. R. Borghini, *Il Riposo*, Florence 1584, pp. 575–76; J. Lieure, *Jacques Callot*, Paris 1924, III, no. 42. I am extremely grateful to Taco Dibbits, who is working who is working on a catalogue raisonné of Muziano, for sharing with me his information on the drawing.
3. T. Dibbits, letter 4 April 1998. In Paris, Louvre, inv. 10.202, the figures are in red chalk and the clouds and architecture in black chalk. A detailed study of the figures on the right side of the *Assumption* is in Rome, Gabinetto Nazionale, inv. FC. 127667; see S. Prosperi Valenti Rodinò, *Three centuries of Roman Drawings from the Villa Farnesina, Rome*, Rome 1993, no. 8.

38 JACOPO PALMA IL GIOVANE
1. A.E. Popham was the first to attribute the drawing to Palma Giovane.
2. Venice 1980, quoting S. Mason Rinaldi.
3. S. Mason Rinaldi, *Palma il Giovane: L'opera completa*, Milan 1984, cat. 267, pp. 108–9, fig. 797.
4. A.M. Mucchi, *Il Duomo di Salò*, Bologna 1932, pp. 257–59; Mason Rinaldi 1984, p. 69.

5. A preparatory study in black chalk for the Virgin is in the Fogg Art Museum, Cambridge MA, inv. 1898.19.

39 PARMIGIANINO
1. Another ink drawing on the reverse is also visible.
2. Oxford, Ashmolean Museum, Parker 436; Popham 1971, no. 331, pl. 77.
3. See exh. cat. 21.
4. M. di Giampaolo, in conversation, 31 October 1997; see B. Adorni, *L'abbazia benedettina di S. Giovanni Evangelista*, Parma 1979, pp. 137–41, p. 132, where the 'pendant' fresco of Sant'Ilario is illustrated.
5. Inv. 1169, V. Romani in *Disegni della Galleria Estense di Modena*, Modena 1990, pp. 66–69, 72–77.
6. Liverpool Public Library, Roscoe Papers, 2966, 2968, 2970–2971, letters between Roscoe and Philipe in October 1811 and August 1812.

40 PARMIGIANINO
1. See also Appendix, WAG1995.349, Florentine School, *Pietà*. This anonymous collector's mark was not used by William Roscoe on the drawings in the Weld-Blundell collection, as suggested in Lugt, L2645.
2. West had a large collection of Parmigianino drawings, several of which were illustrated by Metz in 1798.
3. Popham 1971, p. 17.
4. Parmigianino's etching, *The Illustrated Bartsch: Italian Artists of the Sixteenth Century School of Fontainebleau*, ed. H. Zerner, XXXII, p. 10, 3(7); Caraglio's engraving Bartsch XV, p. 684, illus. in Popham 1971, fig. 18.
5. Florence, Uffizi, inv. 747E; London, British Museum, 1853–10–8–3 and 1856–6–14–2 verso; New York Metropolitan Museum, inv. 46.80.3; Paris, Ecole des Beaux-Arts, inv. 37143 and Louvre, inv. 6385; Weimar, Graphische Sammlung, KK.7393, a finished compositional *modello* for the Caraglio engraving; Windsor, RL 0535, and two drawings that attempt to fix a pose for the shepherd with his arm raised aloft in Oxford, Christ Church, and an unknown collection; see Popham 1971, nos. 350 and 805, pls. 144–152.
6. J. Roberts, *Italian Master Drawings, Leonardo to Canaletto, from the British Royal Collection*, London 1987, p. 72, no. 27.

41 PARMIGIANINO
1. Its omission from the catalogue may have been due to its being kept in the album, where it was attributed to Raphael, and not loose in a portfolio as were the other two Weld-Blundell drawings by Parmigianino.
2. Orally, 31 October 1997.
3. Popham 1971, no. 640.
4. Bartsch XII, 152.21; formerly Anthony Blunt collection, cat. 2a–b.

5. *Autour de Raphael. Dessins et peintures du Musée du Louvre*, exhib. cat., Paris, Louvre, 1984, cat. 100; E. Maclagan, *Catalogue of Italian Plaquettes*, London, Victoria and Albert Museum, 1924, p. 64; see also Marco da Ravenna's engraving of a ram awaiting sacrifice, Bartsch XIV, 181.220.
6. Lugt and *Supplément*. The reasons for this identification are explained in the Introduction.
7. Unlike others owned by Saint-Morys it was not published in his *Disegni originali d'eccelenti pittori incisi ed imitati nella loro grandezza col. parte 1*.

42 BALDASSARE PERUZZI
1. See Appendix WAG1995.244, Peruzzi's *Penelope mourning* on recto. Suggestion made by Christoph Frommel, orally, Rome, June 1997.

43 FRANCESCO PRIMATICCIO
1. The Slater details are from William Ford's annotated sale catalogue in the British Museum. The Liverpool annotated catalogue states the buyer as Lord Stanley. Roscoe had acquired the drawing through Thomas Philipe along with a presently unlocated *Ulysses taking leave of Alcinous* which was not bought by Blundell.
2. Van Thulden's black-chalk drawing is in Vienna, Albertina, inv. 8971, and his engraving formed the basis for the illustration of John Ogilby's *Homer his Odysseus*, published in London 1665. Van Thulden executed a complete set of engravings after the wall frescos.
3. S. Béguin *et al.* 1985, pp. 88–92; P. Bjurström, *Swedish Public Collections: French Drawings*, Stockholm 1976, nos. 29–47. David Ekserdjian suggested a date of 1555–59.
4. Nationalmuseum, inv. 831/1863, 265 × 365 mm. One of nineteen drawings in Stockholm for the Ulysses Gallery mainly in red chalk on red tinted paper but smaller than inv. 831, Bjurström 1976, and Béguin *et al.* 1985, fig. 298. It was previously believed that the Liverpool drawing might be a good studio replica of the Stockholm one. There are two drawn copies in London, British Museum, Palange album, no. 38, and Paris, Louvre, album J. Belly, and a painted copy in store at Fontainebleau, see Béguin *et al.* 1985, figs. 301–03.
5. Primaticcio illustrated scenes in the Cabinet and Chambre du Roi at Fontainebleau, Béguin *et al.* 1975, p. 103. For further reasons for the popularity of Ulysses see Ekserdjian 1992.

44 RAFFAELLINO DA REGGIO
1. The first word is cut through the middle by the paper's edge and so could read *FLEXIT*.
2. Gere and Pouncey 1983, citing *Il Vasari*, VIII (1936–37), p. 111.
3. G. Baglione, *Le vite de' pittori, scultori e architeti ... nel 1642*, ed. V Mariani, Rome 1935, pp. 25–26:

"*diversi puttini molto ben coloriti, e assai gratiosi, e alcune historiette di chiaro e scuro, e nel mezzo evvi la Virtù, che tien per mano Hercole, e 'l Genio, e vanno verso il Tempio dell'Eternità*".
4. Or 'turns towards' the heavens if 'flexit' is the preferred reading. Lille, Musée des Beaux-Arts, Collection Wicar, as by Cavaliere d'Arpino, Gernsheim photo 17995; an almost exact copy of the Lille figures but not squared in Florence, Uffizi, inv. 3885⁵, 382 × 260 mm; London, British Museum, inv. Ff 2–104, where the figures are identified as *Hercules, Minerva and Mars*, 382 × 238 mm; Munich, Staatliche Graphische Sammlung, inv. 2611, 249 × 171 mm.
5. M. Pirondini and E. Monducci, *La pittura del Cinquecento a Reggio Emilia*, Milan 1985, pp. 166–67, 169–70.
6. D. Heikamp, 'Vicende di Federigo Zuccari', *Rivista d'arte*, XXXII (Series III, vol. 7), 1957, p. 209, no. 16, fig. 18, Uffizi, inv. 11018, one of a series of twenty-four illustrations (twenty in the Uffizi).
7. K. Hermann-Fiore, 'Die Fresken Federico Zuccaris in seinem Römischen Kunstlerhaus', *Römisches Jahrbuch für Kunstgeschichte*, XVIII, 1979, pp. 36–112.
8. Gere and Pouncey 1983 note a Federico Zuccaro drawing of essentially the same scene in an oval cartouche in the border of a drawing at Hamburg (Gernsheim photo 16999) which is for a *Calumny of Apelles* dated 1572.

45 GUIDO RENI
1. Also found on a Giuseppe Manocchi (1731–1782) drawing in the Royal Collection, J. Roberts, *Master Drawings in the Royal Collection*, London 1986, cat. 118, pp. 149, 188, 191.
2. With an attribution to Reni suggested by Aidan Weston-Lewis.
3. D. Stephen Pepper, *Guido Reni*, Oxford 1984, cat. 45, pp. 230–31, pls. 72, 98.
4. G. Rivani, 'Guido Reni a Ravenna', *Il Comune di Bologna*, XVIII, April 1931, p. 26, quoting from a letter of G.B. Marino's published in Venice in 1673. Spear 1997, p. 227, suggests that Reni would have liked to have refused the commission.
5. One such full-length figure-study for Gabriel's seated counterpart, the Archangel Raphael, is at Windsor Castle, RL 3357; see also the pen-and-ink *Study for Archangels*, Bologna, Pinacoteca, as discussed by C. Johnston in *L'Œil*, 1969, p. 26, no. 66, or C. Johnston, *The Drawings of Guido Reni*, Ph.D. Courtauld Institute of Art, London 1974, no. 89 or Pepper 1984, no. 45.
6. C.C. Malvasia, *Felsina pittrice* [1678], edn. Bologna 1841, II, p. 19.

46 GUIDO RENI
1. *Holy Family with an angel*, 142 × 200 mm, Malibu, John Paul

Getty Museum, 83.GA.267; see also another larger but stylistically close drawing in the British Museum, *Holy Family with the infant St John*, inv. 1895.9.15–699, 166 × 191 mm, where the downward strokes of the fringed cloth reflect those in the Weld-Blundell drawing.
2. Ed. V. Birke, *Illustrated Bartsch: Italian Masters of the Sixteenth and Seventeenth Centuries*, XL, New York 1982, pp. 155–58, nos. 8(283), 9(284), 10(285).
3. G.R. Goldner, *European Drawings, I: Catalogue of the Collections*, Malibu 1988, no. 41.
4. Ann Sutherland Harris kindly allowed the author to see a draft of her article and discussed the Liverpool drawing with her.
5. C.C. Malvasia, *Felsina pittrice* [1678], edn. Bologna 1841, II, pp. 32–33, describes Reni's debilitating overwork as the result of his frequent gambling losses.

47 ATTRIBUTED TO GUIDO RENI
1. The inscription is similar to that found on some other Bolognese drawings in the Weld-Blundell collection, Appendix, Tiarini, WAG1995.333, and attr. Tiarini, WAG1995.337.
2. In conversation, 22 July 1996.
3. Lyons, Musée des Beaux-Arts, oil on canvas, 242 × 161 mm, inv. A 123. There is a fully finished compositional drawing in red chalk on light-brown paper after Reni (?) in the Amsterdam Historisch Museum, coll. Fodor, 450 × 310 mm, inv. A–11012. Another similar painted treatment of the theme dated 1626–27 in the parish church of Castelfranco Emilia is more static compared to the swirling drapery of the Liverpool sketch.
4. M. Feuillet, 'Contributo alla storia dell'*Assunta* dei Filippini di Perugia di Guido Reni: il ritorno alla luce di un capolavoro del Musée des Beaux Arts in Lione', *Atti e memorie di Accademia Clementina*, XXV, 1990, p. 131, quoting from F. Angelini, *Libro delle Memorie*, before 1697, f. 34.
5. C.C. Malvasia, *Felsina pittrice* [1678], edn. Bologna 1841, pp. 32–33; and see cat. 46 above.

48 GIOVANNI FRANCESCO ROMANELLI
1. J.M. Merz, letter 28 February 1997. There is a copy of the Liverpool drawing of almost exactly the same size in Vienna, Albertina, inv. 91394, 239 × 375 mm.
2. Royal Collection, *The Story of Caeculus*, RL 6802. J.M. Merz, *Pietro da Cortona*, Tübingen 1991, p. 335, Cortona School, cat. 2e, figs. 328, 350. The bearded Jephta in Romanelli's *Jephta meeting his daughter*, British Museum, inv. Pp. I–133, also seems to be based on the same model.

3. As above. Thirty-one of the prints were by Bartolozzi the rest by others including Richard Dalton. Those drawings not from the Royal Collection seem to be explicitly identified as such.
4. Conversation with Alan Donnithorne, October 1996. The design might also be accounted for by West's using the Royal Collection as a model for mounting his own, see cats. 1, 12, 13, 57.
5. Martin Clayton of the Royal Collection, letter 26 August 1997.
6. *A King's Purchase: King George III and the Collection of Consul Smith*, exhib. cat., London, Queen's Gallery, 1993, p. 18. Dalton's sale took place in London on 11 May 1791.
7. D. Mahon and N. Turner, *The Drawings of Guercino in the Collection of Her Majesty the Queen at Windsor Castle*, Cambridge 1989, p. xxxii, n. 56, quoting a letter of 1772 from Lord Nuneham to Lord Harcourt as well as other comments from Horace Mann and Mrs Delaney.

49 GIOVANNI FRANCESCO ROMANELLI
1. Only partially visible, possibly close to Heawood 2975 (Rome 1646).
2. There is possibly an abraded inscription or signature in ink along the lower edge of the drawing.
3. Identified in E.K. Waterhouse's copy of the sale catalogue as Ablet Esq. of Lanbidda Hall (*i.e.* Llanbedr Hall near Llanbedr Dyffryn Clwyd, Denbighshire). In William Ford's copy of sale catalogue in the British Museum, lot 211 is annotated with name of Slater.
4. Attributed by Pouncey as possibly Gimignani and titled *The Virgin and Child dropping the rosary to St Thomas*.
5. J.J. Berthier, *Chroniques du Monastère de S Sisto et de S Domenico*, 1920, II, p. 202.
6. J.M. Merz, letter 28 February 1997; Düsseldorf Kunstmuseum, *Aeneas leaving Dido*, inv. IP740. See also the same facial type as the Virgin on a woman in an unidentified *Scene from antiquity* in the British Museum, Ff. 3–196, illus. in N. Turner, *Italian Baroque Drawings*, London 1980, cat. 21, no. 2, in Houlditch's collection.

50 ANDREA SCHIAVONE
1. A narrow strip of thin paper has been added along the top of the paper and the design carried over on to it. Marks along the side edges suggest that the drawing was previously stuck into an album.
2. Popham had changed the traditional attribution of Parmigianino to Giuseppe Porta, called Salviati.
3. London, British Museum, 1938–12–10–2. F.L. Richardson, *Andrea Schiavone*, Oxford 1980, p. 125, cat. 175, fig. 140.
4. The Weld-Blundell collection also has three Schiavone prints, WAG1995.103–105: *The finding of*

Moses, Richardson 1980, cat. 2; *Christ and the women on the staircase*, on yellow paper, Richardson 1980, cat. 14; *The Holy Family with saints*, Richardson 1980, cat. 63, fig. 143, probably all with a Roscoe provenance. Roscoe was particularly keen on Schiavone as a printmaker and suggested that the dealer Philipe consider buying his work as an alternative to Parmigianino; letter, 3 August 1812, Liverpool Public Library, Roscoe Papers, 2971.

51 ELISABETTA SIRANI
1. Count C.C. Malvasia, *Felsina pittrice vite de' pittori bolognesi* [1678], edn. Bologna 1841, II, p. 398.
2. Washington, National Museum of Women in the Arts, Holladay Collection.
3. F. Frisoni in *Scuola di Guido Reni*, edd. E. Negro and M. Pirondini, Modena 1991, pp. 343–45.
4. Malvasia 1841, p. 389.

52 ELISABETTA SIRANI
1. Mistakenly referring to the Roscoe drawing as a painting.
2. Illus. in Frisoni 1991, pp. 354–55, figs. 336–38.
3. Bologna, Pinacoteca, oil on copper, 155 × 125 mm, inv. 368, cat. 503 which was first drawn to the author's attention by Babette Bohn, letter 12 August 1997.
4. Frisoni 1991, pp. 343–45.
5. Oxford, Ashmolean, brush and ink, 231 × 171 mm, showing her full length walking up a staircase with a page holding her train, and also with a Gabburri/Rogers provenance; see K.T. Parker, *Catalogue of the Collection of Drawings in the Ashmolean Museum*, 1972, II, no. 953, fig. 328; Oxford, Christ Church, black and red and some white chalk on grey paper, 386 × 270 mm, dated by Byam Shaw to *ca.* 1660; circular painted portrait of a bare-shouldered woman painter, attributed to Sirani, 152 mm diameter, sale catalogue Heim Gallery, London, autumn 1968, no. 21.
6. The discovery whilst in the conservation studio of four rusted 'pinholes' in the corners of the drawing and differential acidification across the supporting backing card, probably caused by the drawing paper protecting the back from the damaging effects of light, suggests that it was displayed for lengthy periods rather than kept in a protective album or portfolio.
7. C.C. Malvasia, *Felsina pittrice* [1678], edn. Bologna 1841, pp. 386–87.

53 ANTONIO TEMPESTA
1. Old Testament, Kings II 18:13, 19:35.
2. *Clades Senacherib*, no. 21, British Museum Prints and Drawings, shelfmark 157*a38. *The Illustrated Bartsch*, XXXV, 1984, p. 82, 256(131).

3. Uffizi, *The Conversion of St Paul*, 312 × 409 mm, inv. 10052S, illus. *Sixteenth-century Tuscan Drawings in the Uffizi*, exhib. cat. by A. Petrioli Tofani and G. Smith, Detroit Institute of Arts, 1988, no. 62; *The Illustrated Bartsch*, XXXVI, 1983, nos. 941–68.
4. New York, Metropolitan Museum, Bartsch XXXV, nos. 545–56, illus. in C. Höper's entry on Tempesta in *The Dictionary of Art*, London 1996, p. 429.

54 PIETRO TESTA
1. The indentations were probably made when prints of the drawing were produced by the comte de Caylus and N. Le Sueur.
2. *Butler's Lives of the Saints*, edn. revised and supplemented by H. Thurston SJ and D. Attwater, London 1956, pp. 81–82, 5 May.
3. A. Sutherland Harris, 'The Decoration of Martino ai Monti', *Burlington Magazine*, CVI, 1964, pp. 58–69. The prior had published a book on the life and miracles of St Angelo in 1641, *La vita e molti miracoli di S Angelo Vergine, e Martire Gerosolimitano*.
4. Darmstadt, Hessisches Landesmuseum, AE1447. Other drawings for the *Vision* are in Haarlem, Teylers Museum, B86, and in Genoa, Palazzo Rosso.
5. Camerino, Museo Diocesano, 423 × 276 mm, illus. Fischer Pace 1995, pl. 10.
6. *Dictionnaire d'histoire et de géographie ecclésiastiques*, ed. A Baudrillart, Paris 1924, pp. 5–9.
7. *Acta Sanctorum*, ed. J. Carnandet, Paris 1863–75, May, II, p. 57.
8. G.B. Passeri, *Vite de' pittori, scultori e architetti*, ed. J. Hess, Vienna 1934, p. 187.
9. *The Illustrated Bartsch*, edd. P. Bellini and R.W. Wallace, XLV, New York 1990, pp. 134–35.

55 ALESSANDRO TIARINI
1. Illus. in Modena 1994, fig. 369.
2. *Inventario degli oggetti d'arte d'Italia, VIII: Provincie di Ancona e Ascoli Piceno*, 1936, pp. 137–38. The painting measures 205 × 250 cm.
3. C.C. Malvasia, *Felsina pittrice* [1678], edn. Bologna 1841, II, p. 123.
4. Bologna, Pinacoteca Nazionale, illus. Modena 1994, fig. 374.

56 ALESSANDRO TIARINI
1. The present mount is made from one mount stuck on to another. The design of the inner mount frames the drawing sheet with an inner thick black line, a gold slip and a strip of deep-blue card similar to the colour of the mounts of Mariette who had a large group of drawings by Tiarini.
2. Hence a previous French collector's (Mariette?) identification to "l. carrache" on the drawing.
3. C.C. Malvasia, *Felsina pittrice*, [1678], Bologna 1841, I, p. 322. The possibility of its being a deliberate response to the San Pietro fresco was

discussed with me by Babette Bohn, letter, 12 August 1997. See also B. Bohn, 'Ludovico's Last Decade', *Master Drawings*, XXV, no. 3, 1987, p. 231.
4. G. Feigenbaum, 'Lodovico Carracci: A Study of his Later Career and a Catalogue of his Paintings', Ph.D., Princeton, published Michigan 1984, p. 476, citing Bottari-Ticozzi, 1822, I, Let. XCVIII; Malvasia 1841, I, p. 322.
5. *Ibid.*, II, p. 138; Feigenbaum 1984, pp. 474, 478–79, in general on the *Annunciation* pp. 473–80.
6. Malvasia 1841, II, p. 131.

57 JACOPO TINTORETTO
1. Another head of Giuliano can be seen upside down on the verso under transmitted light with the eye positioned to the left of the mouth on the recto image.
2. The inscription *G Tintoretto* is in the same eighteenth-century hand as appears on all eleven Tintoretto drawings with a Reynolds provenance in the Victoria and Albert Museum, P. Ward-Jackson, *Italian Drawings*, London 1979–80, I, p. 156, cats. 328–38.
3. C. Ridolfi, *Le maraviglie dell'arte ovvero le vite degli illustri pittori veneti e dello stato* [1648], ed. D. von Hadeln, Berlin 1924, II, p. 14.
4. P. Rossi, *I disegni di Jacopo Tintoretto* (*Corpus Graphicum* I), Florence 1975, pp. 4–5.
5. Other comparable studies include notably: Berlin, Kupferstichkabinett, inv. 5376, Jacopo or Domenico; British Museum 1907-7-17-30, on the verso of a Domenico oil sketch; Edinburgh, National Gallery of Scotland, inv. 1853, 1855, School of Tintoretto; Florence, Uffizi, inv. 1840F, 1841F, School of Tintoretto; Horne Collection inv. 5665 (on deposit with Uffizi); Frankfurt, Städelsches Kunstinstitut, inv. 564, 15701 recto and verso; Milan, Rasini Collection, inscribed as by Marietta; Oxford, Christ Church, inv. 0357, and the later 0358.
6. Oxford, Christ Church, inv. 0357, 357 × 238 mm. J. Byam Shaw, *Drawings by Old Masters at Christ Church, Oxford*, Oxford 1976, cat. 758, pl. 429.
7. Ridolfi, *cit.* note 3. Ridolfi believed that this was part of Tintoretto's attempt to combine the drawing of Michelangelo with the colour of Titian and so resolve the sixteenth-century aesthetic debate as to which of these should have primacy.

58 ATTRIBUTED TO JACOPO TINTORETTO
1. Inv. 20. Currently thought to be an unknown official from the time of Emperor Hadrian, AD 117–138. Vitellius ruled only from 2 January to 22 December AD 69, before being assassinated. M. Perry, 'Cardinal Domenico Grimani's Legacy of

Ancient Art to Venice', *Journal of the Warburg and Courtauld Institutes*, 1978, p. 234. But see S. Bailey, 'Metamorphoses of the Grimani "Vitellius"', *J. Paul Getty Museum Journal*, V, 1977, p. 105, n. 1, who believes the bust dates from the first quarter of the sixteenth century when it was supposedly dug up in Rome.
2. H. Tietze and E. Tietze-Conrat, *The Drawings of the Venetian Painters in the 15th and 16th Centuries*, New York 1944, p. 258.
3. For a full listing and a discussion of their often disputed attributions see Rossi 1975, pp. 46–47, 51 and Bailey 1977, pp. 105–122.
4. Ridolfi, edn. 1924, p. 15.
5. Oxford, Christ Church, inv. 0363 393 × 263 mm., illus. in J. Byam Shaw, *Drawings by Old Masters at Christ Church, Oxford*, Oxford 1976, cat. 766, pls. 440–41, see also inv. 0362, cat. 765, pls. 438–39.
6. A. Morassi, *Disegni antichi della collezione Rasini in Milano*, Milan 1937, p. 33, inscribed *"Questa testa si (di?) é de man de madona Marietta"*. Nor is the Liverpool study like those attributed to Domenico Tintoretto (1560–1635) in the British Museum, inv. 1907-7-17-42, 43, 53.
7. Suetonius, *Twelve Caesars*, trans. by R. Graves, Harmondsworth 1979, ch. IX, pp. 273–74.

59 FRANCESCO TREVISANI
1. The watermark is also found on a Thomas Sandby watercolour in the Royal Collection, illus. in J. Roberts, *Master Drawings in the Royal Collection*, London 1986, cat. 120, pp. 189, 191.
2. The painting, 350 × 275 cm, now hangs beside the throne in the Benediction Loggia of St Peter's.
3. The oil sketch for another lunette, *St Sylvester baptizing Constantine*, was executed about 1710 and the joined canvases which form the *modello* for the dome mosaics also date from about 1710, although the cartoons were not painted until 1738–45. F.R. DiFederico, *Francesco Trevisani, Eighteenth-Century Painter in Rome*, Washington DC, 1977, cat. 102, pp. 27, 66–69, pl. 87.
4. A *Noli Me Tangere*, Burghley House, England, DiFederico 1977, cat. 34, pl. 28, and one of the brothers in *Joseph being sold by his brothers*, National Gallery of Victoria, Melbourne, acc. 3209/4, DiFederico 1977, cat. 70, pl. 57.
5. For the *St Sylvester baptizing Constantine*, Florence, Uffizi, *Drapery and three heads*, inv. 14151F, DiFederico 1977, fig. 40, and DiFederico, 'A Group of Trevisani Drawings in the Uffizi', *Master Drawings*, X, 1972, p. 10, pl. 6, where the drawing is dated to 1710–20.
6. Pommersfelden (near Bamberg), Schloss Weissenstein, Collection Graf von Schönborn, DiFederico 1977, cat. P7, pl. 101, p. 21. See also the Uffizi

self-portrait of 1682, in *Gli Uffizi: Catalogo generale*, Florence 1979, p. 1024.

60 ALESSANDRO TURCHI
1. The good-quality paper has a number of tears around the edges which have been well patched probably in the eighteenth century.
2. Turchi was sometimes referred to as Alessandro Veronese after his birth place Verona, hence the identifying name on the eighteenth-century mount. He was also nicknamed l'Orbetto, the little blind boy, as his father, whom he always accompanied as a child, was a blind beggar.
3. Munich, Alte Pinakothek, no. 496.
4. G. Mancini, *Considerazioni sulla pittura* [1617–ca.1625], edd. A. Marucchi and L. Salerno, Rome 1956, I, p. 255. Mancini does not mention its Munich pair *The Fury of Hercules*, suggesting that it was not yet painted.
5. Stuttgart, Staatsgalerie, Schloss Fachsenfeld collection III 1547, brown wash over black chalk, 251 × 348 mm, probably an earlier idea for the Munich painting with eight figures instead of seven; Paris, Louvre, inv. 11707, brown wash over pen and brown ink, 407 × 542 mm, a *modello* for another lost painting known only through a contemporary copy. E. Schleier, 'Drawings by Alessandro Turchi', *Master Drawings*, 1971, p. 143, no. 4, pl. 20 and no. 8, fig. 9, pl. 23a. A grisaille sketch of the subject attributed to Turchi by Pouncey was sold at Sotheby's, New York, 13/14 January 1989, lot 100. As Schleier's article predated the Edinburgh exhibition in 1972 he did not mention the Weld-Blundell drawing.
6. *The Fury of Hercules*, brown wash over red chalk, 200 × 265 mm (formerly in the 'Pseudo-Crozat' collection), in the Prague collection of B. Lenz in 1937, illus. in Schleier 1971, no. 5, pl. 21. Few single figure studies by Turchi are known. For another finished design by Turchi in the Weld-Blundell collection see Appendix WAG1995.175 (also with a 'Pseudo-Crozat' provenance).
7. Apollodorus, *Bibliotheke*, 2.6:3, cited in J. Hall, *Dictionary of Subjects and Symbols in Art*, London 1974, p. 151; R. Graves, *The Greek Myths*, Harmondsworth 1960, II, p. 165h.

61 GIORGIO VASARI
1. The paper has been repaired, patched and strengthened probably sometime in the eighteenth century with ink retouchings around the edges.
2. The watermark of D & C Blauw, the Dutch paper company (1733–1827) that made much of the mount card for the Royal Collection in the late eighteenth and early nineteenth centuries, information from Alan Donnithorne.
3. J. Schulz, 'Vasari at Venice', *Burlington Magazine*, CIII, December 1961, pp. 500–06.

4. C. Monbeig–Goguel, *Inventaire général des dessins italiens: Vasari et son temps*, Paris 1972, cat. 216.
5. Paris, Louvre, *Five water-gods*, pen and brown ink and brown wash with white heightening over black chalk on blue paper, 250 × 340 mm, illus. in Monbeig-Goguel 1972; Berlin, KdZ15260, *Two water-gods*, brown ink and wash with white heightening, 251 × 324 mm, illus. Schulz 1961, fig. 14. See also the copy after Vasari in Florence, Uffizi, inv. 92184F, of *River and mountain gods: Arno, Appennines and Tiber*, illus. Cecchi 1978, fig. 3; and Düsseldorf, Kunstmuseum, FP6422, an allegorical figure of the *Fourth Hour of the Day*, possibly for the ceiling.
6. Letter of 22 February 1542, K. Frey, *Der Literarische Nachlass G. Vasaris*, Munich 1923–30, I, pp. 111–16; Vasari, *Vita del Cristofano Gherardi* [1568], ed. G. Milanesi, Florence 1878–85, VI, p. 224.
7. "*Benaco, lago di Garda ... faceva di se stesso un' lago et pisciando, per la natura si convertiva nun fiume, il quale era il Tesino, giovane et in scorcio, perché dura poco; porgendo verso Benaco un urna, riteneva tutto quello che versava Benaco per farne presente al Po.*" For the full extract from the letter, see Frey 1923–30, p. 116, and Cecchi 1978.

62 GIORGIO VASARI
1. The inscription read on a photograph taken with transmitted light, *qualle Libro stampato me discorre il Principe/ di fiorenza _ _[?]/ Giorgio vasari fa mentione della sua/ opera di questo disegno fatta in fiorenza/ per Gli sii.[?] Medici/ qu.[?] nomina la retrotincta Dea/ Con Gli noe. [nomine] Sacerdoti Coribanti/ _[?] Libro mi fa prestato della bon.[?] mem. dell si.[?] Bernardo M/ et poco volumine p.[er] quella mi posse recordare*; at the bottom of the paper in the same ink *p iii C ss*[?]. I should like to thank Dr C.P. Lewis for help in transcribing the inscription.
2. The original terracotta tiled floor in the room is dated 1556 and the terrace was decorated during the summer of 1557: A. Cecchi in *Palazzo Vecchio. Guide to the Building, the Apartments and the Collections*, Florence 1989, pp. 84–85 and illus. P. Rubin, *Giorgio Vasari: Art and History*, New Haven and London 1995, p. 14, pl. 9.
3. Rubin 1995, p. 27.
4. Cecchi 1989, pp. 80–90. The complicated symbolism was explained at length in Vasari's *Ragionamenti*, ed. G. Milanesi, Florence 1878–85, VIII.
5. Paris, Louvre, pen and brown ink and wash, 273 × 208 mm, oval, inv. 2158, C. Monbeig-Goguel, *Inventaire général des dessins italiens: Vasari et son temps*, Paris 1972, cat. 343, pp. 217–18. The draughtsman appears to have misunderstood the cymbals played by the foreground priest for a vase.

63 FEDERICO ZUCCARO

1. F. Baumgart and B. Biagetti, *Gli affreschi ... nella Cappella Paolina in Vaticano*, Vatican City 1934, pp. 61–62, pl. III. Other known studies include *The liberation of St Peter from prison*, Baltimore, Walters Art Museum, pen, ink and brown wash, inv. 1932.73.23, for the lunette at the other end of the chapel; *St Paul healing a demoniac*, Florence, Uffizi, inv. 11004F, pen and brown wash heightened with white and squared in red chalk on faded blue-green paper; for a tondo, illus. in *Mostra di disegni degli Zuccari*, exhib. cat. by J. Gere, Florence, Uffizi, 1966, cat. 66, fig. 48.
2. *Renaissance into Baroque: Italian Master Drawings by the Zuccari*, exhib. cat. by E.J. Mundy, New York, National Academy of Design, 1990; *Porta Virtutis: Minerva triumphant over Ignorance and Calumny*, cat. 85, p. 242.
3. D. Heikamp, 'Vicende di Federigo Zuccari', *Rivista d'Arte*, XXXII (Series III, vol. 7), 1957, p. 195.
4. Acts 28:2–7.
5. Acts 28:7–9.

64 TADDEO ZUCCARO

1. What appear to be wood 'burns' on the back of the mount suggests that at one time the drawing was framed rather than kept in an album. The secondary support has the remains of a paper tax stamp in red with a *GR* and crown surrounded by lettering which probably reads *DUTY CUSTOMS PAPER STAINED*, of a type stamped on the wrappers of imported wallpaper in the eighteenth and early nineteenth centuries. I would like to thank Mr Harry Dagnall for this information.
2. British Museum, Prints and Drawings Department. See Collector's Marks and Biographies under Haym (L1974). It is not possible to identify definitely the drawing in either of the Hillier sales at Christie and Ansell, 6–20 February and 15–22 March 1784.
3. Illus. in Gere 1969, pl. 127a. The frescos have been removed from the ceiling and now hang in a different room. An old, smaller, red-wash copy of the Liverpool study is amongst the anonymous Italian drawings at Windsor Castle, RL 5201, Gere 1969, no. 254.
4. In the Palazzo Caetani they painted ten scenes from Alexander's life in two small rooms, Gere 1969, pp. 94–97. For drawings related to the four other frescos in the same room as the *Bucephalus* see also Munich, Herbert List Collection, Gere 1969, nos. 135, 136; Vienna, Albertina, inv. 449; Gere 1969, no. 236. None of these is in red chalk and wash as Taddeo has typically varied his drawing technique with each study.
5. Vienna, Albertina, *Alexander and Timocles*, inv. 449, black chalk, pen and ink and brown wash heightened with white on light blue paper in

elongated oval, *ca.* 230 × 365 mm (paper size 244 × 378 mm), illus. V. Birke, *Die Italienischen Zeichnungen der Albertina*, Vienna 1992, I; see Lugt and *Supplément*, L474, and Introduction, above, pp. 17–18, for the identification of 'Pseudo-Crozat' as the comte de Caylus.
6. Vienna, Albertina, inv. 575. Federico Zuccaro's drawing shows Michelangelo on horseback and Vasari standing with his back to us on the right with Taddeo on the platform surrounded by the three figures of Grace, Wit and Pride; D. Heikamp, 'Vicende di Federigo Zuccari', *Rivista d'Arte*, XXXII (Series III, vol. 7) 1957, p. 211, no. 20.

65 ATTRIBUTED TO TADDEO ZUCCARO

1. Although Gere eventually favoured an attribution to Federico over Taddeo he noted that the Weld-Blundell drawing had some qualities that were unusual in Federico's work.
2. However, the 1820 sale catalogue of Benjamin West's collection suggests that he attributed it to Taddeo. Unfortunately the 'West' drawings are not separately identified in the Weld-Blundell inventory of 1841.
3. The altarpiece was commissioned on 14 November 1568 for the fifth chapel on the left and is now in the Museo dell'Opera del Duomo, see L. Fumi, *Il Duomo di Orvieto e suoi restauri*, Rome 1891, p. 416, doc. cxviii.
4. Oxford, Ashmolean, Parker 750, pen and brown wash, heightened with body-colour on faded bluish-grey paper, 403 × 278 mm; Paris, Louvre, inv. 4417, pen and brown ink with brown wash with white highlights on tan paper, 415 × 282 mm; and an identical study but on faded orange prepared paper is presently on deposit at Vassar College (Frances Lehman Loeb Art Center), Poughkeepsie, from the Suida Manning collection, Forest Hills, 396 × 275 mm. A study which is even closer to the altarpiece is known only through two copies, in the Louvre, inv. 4526, and in Frankfurt, Städelsches Kunstinstitut inv. 4475.
5. A. Garzelli, *Museo di Orvieto: Museo dell'Opera del Duomo*, 1972, pp. 21–22, 34. Taddeo had also been commissioned in 1559 to paint frescos in Orvieto cathedral. Federico incorporated into the second painting, commissioned from him in November 1568, *The resurrection of the son of the widow of Nain*, a portrait of his deceased brother.
6. An observation supported by James Mundy, letter 19 August 1997. I should also like to thank James Mundy for discussing the Zuccaro drawings with me and allowing me to see copies of his data sheets on the Suida Manning and Louvre studies for *Christ healing the blind man*, which will form part of his forthcoming catalogue raisonné of Federico Zuccaro's drawings.

NOTES: NORTHERN DRAWINGS

66 ANONYMOUS

1. *Dürer: Schriftlicher Nachlass*, ed. H. Rupprich, Berlin 1956, I, p. 169; E. Konowitz, entry in *The Luminous Image: Painted Glass Roundels in the Lowlands 1480–1560*, exhib. cat. by T.B. Husband, New York, Metropolitan Museum, 1995, chapter 9, pp. 142ff.
2. Vellert's *Presentation in the Temple*, roundel heightened with white, in the British Museum, 1952.1.21.85, is on a grey-green prepared paper. Other drawings attributed to Vellert, such as Paris, Fondation Custodia, Collection F. Lugt, *Judith and Holophernes* (?), 275 mm diameter, inv. 1978–T.4, show much finer pen hatching in the shadows.
3. Antwerp Mannerists were divided into four anonymous groups by M. Friedlander, 'Die Antwerpner Manieristen von 1520', *Jahrbuch der königlichen preuszischen Kunst-sammlungen*, XXXXVI, 1915, pp. 65–91. The British Museum, *St Luke painting the Virgin*, on grey prepared paper, *ca.* 1520–25, and Weimar, Staatliche Kunstsammlungen, *Dance of Salome*, on grey-blue paper have been associated tentatively with Jan de Beer, *ca.* 1475–1528?.
4. New York 1995, p. 88.

67 CORNELIS DUSART

1. There is evidence that both were hinged down the left and in an album and that WAG1995.85 was previously stuck on to a blue support or mount. There are no Dusart of this description in the Roscoe sale.
2. B. Schnackenberg, *Adriaen van Ostade, Isaak van Ostade: Zeichnungen und Aquarelle*, Hamburg 1981, pp. 60–63.
3. The foreground figure on the right of a crowded *Inn scene* with carousing men and women drinking and smoking in Leipzig, Museum der bildenden Kunst, inv. 576.
4. New York, Christie's, 31 May 1991, lot 64a.
5. *Dutch Prints of Daily Life*, exhib. cat., Lawrence, Spencer Museum of Art, University of Kansas, 1983, p. 153, cat. 40.
6. *Adriaen van Ostade: Etchings of Peasant Life in Holland's Golden Age*, exhib. cat., Athens GA, Georgia Museum of Art, 1994, p. 91, cat. 38, citing A. Heppner, 'The Popular Theatre of the Rederijkers in the Work of Jan Steen and his Contemporaries', *Journal of the Warburg and Courtauld Institutes*, III, 1939–40, p. 26.

69 FRANS FLORIS I

1. Frans Floris's nickname in the eighteenth century.
2. Not mentioned under either Floris or Mutiano in Vanhaecken sale, London, Langford, 11–27 Feb. 1750/51.

3. I should like to thank Carl Depauw (letter 18 March 1997) for first drawing my attention to the subject.
4. *De Geschiedenis van Pluto en Prosperina*; see Carl van de Velde, *Frans Floris. Leven en Werken*, Brussels 1975, cat. P73, pl. 226 and p. 313, cat. S176; *Cornelis Cort*, exhib. cat. by M. Sellink, Rotterdam, Boymans van Beuningen Museum, 1994, cat. 35, neither of which mentions the Liverpool drawing.
5. N. Llewellyn, 'Illustrating Ovid', in *Ovid Renewed: Ovidian Influences on Literature and Art from the Middle Ages to the Twentieth Century*, ed. C. Martindale, Cambridge 1988, pp. 151–66.
6. Publius Ovidius Naso, *Metamorphoses*, Book VII, 425–436, quoted from Loeb Classical Library XLII–XLIIII, compiled and translated into English by F.J. Miller, London, 2nd revised edn. 1984, I, p. 277.
7. A similar blue wash has been used to outline the figures in a study for the *Rape of Proserpine*, which was not engraved for the Cort series. British Museum 1922–6–27–1.

70 JOSEPH HEINTZ THE ELDER

1. Hollstein's German Engravings, Etchings and Woodcuts, XVII, Amsterdam 1967, p. 147, no. 541; J. Zimmer, *Heintz der Ältere als Maler*, Weissenhorn 1971, B15, pl. 111.
2. L.O. Larsson, 'Gianlorenzo Bernini and Joseph Heintz', *Kunsthistorisk Tidskrift*, XLII, 1973, p. 144 and XLIV, 1975, pp. 23–26.
3. Anette Michels, 'Philosophie und Herrscherlob als Bild: Anfänge und Entwicklung der süddeutschen Thesenblattes im Werk des Augsburger Kupferstechers Wolfgang Kilian (1581–1663)', *Kunstgeschichte. Form und Interesse*, X, 1987, p. 352f., no. 33, pl. 81.

71 EUSTACHE LE SUEUR

1. The missing corners suggest that it may previously have been attached to an album page.
2. As suggested by Alain Merlot, possibly sold along with another drawing, Paris, Louvre, inv. 30.646 (Merlot 1987, cat. D.221), a *Study of St Paul*.
3. Formerly attributed to Benjamin West. I should to thank Hugo Chapman for first pointing out to me the connection with Eustache Le Sueur.
4. Now Paris, Louvre, inv. 8020; F. Félibien, *Entretiens sur les vies et sur les ouvrages des plus excellens peintres*, 1688, V, p. 37.; Merlot 1987, cats. 83–85, pp. 236–41.
5. Acts 19:19.
6. Painted *modelli*: Algeria National Museum of Fine Arts, inv. 2370, and London, National Gallery, inv. 6299; composition drawings: Madrid, Biblioteca Nacional, inv. 8927; Frankfurt, Städelsches Kunstinstitut,

inv. 1003–04; Paris, Louvre, inv. MI909; figure studies: six in the Louvre, and one each in Paris, Ecole des Beaux Arts, inv. 1192; Chantilly, Musée Condé, inv. 282; St Petersburg, Hermitage, inv. 14.331; Vienna, Albertina, inv. 11.665; London, British Museum, inv. 1911–9–26–1, and Liverpool, WAG1995.347.

7. It must have been made after the second Frankfurt drawing and as the preferred alternative to the man carrying books in the Louvre, inv. 30.675, and Ecole des Beaux-Arts, inv. 1192.

8. See the exhibited drawings by Frans Floris and Magnasco for two other drawings owned by Benjamin West which have had a similar-looking darkened 'varnish' applied to them.

72 JAN-ERASMUS QUELLINUS
1. Three paintings from the series are on permanent loan to the Abbey church of Tongerlo, thirty kilometres east of Antwerp, from the Royal Museum of Fine Arts, Antwerp, invs. 284–286, 525 × 455 cm.
2. *New Catholic Encyclopedia*, New York 1967.
3. Jacobus de Wit, *Maatschappij der Antwerpsche Bibliophilen. Uitgrave Nr. 25. De Kerken van Antwerpen*, Antwerp 1910, p. 155; M.-L. Hairs, *Dans le sillage de Rubens: Les peintres d'histoire anversois au XVIIe siècle*, Liège 1977, pp. 286–87.
4. C. Depauw, letter 18 March 1997, citing Papebrochius in his *Acta Sanctorum* of 1695.
5. London, Victoria and Albert Museum, inv. 4588–90, E220–1949, E221–1949.

74 STUDIO OF REMBRANDT
1. Scientific analysis of the ink has shown that faint traces of dark iron-gall ink has been mixed in with a lot of chalk (calcium carbonate) throughout the drawing which is probably why the acidic ink has not 'eaten' through the paper and which may account for the differences in ink tone across the drawing.
2. Ovid, *Metamorphoses*, I, 668–721, especially 718–720.
3. Benesch probably made his attribution from a photograph. A.E. Popham, who alerted Benesch to the drawing, also considered it "a very fine original Rembrandt drawing".
4. Benesch 1973, no. 752, fig. 899, *Village street with three cows and a rider*, pen and bistre and wash, 195 × 265 mm, Berlin, heirs to Rathenau; no. 884, fig. 1094, Paris, Louvre, RF.4693, dated *ca.* 1650–52, pen with a few touches of brush in bistre and a correction in white on the right hand of Argus, 178 × 146 mm, without Io and Argus asleep; no. 627, fig. 763, Warsaw University Library (Stanislaus Polocki Collection), T.1155 N.12, *ca.* 1648–50; and no. 567a, fig. 701, London, Leo Franklyn Collection,

ca. 1645, pen and brush and bistre, 200 × 165 mm, with Argus awake, both much more summary in the treatment of animals.
5. M. Royalton-Kisch, *Drawings by Rembrandt and his Circle in the British Museum*, London 1992, p. 16, cats. 87–89. The second (?) artist has sketched a summarily outlined landscape of a cottage (?) and trees in the background on the right and above Argus's shoulder and an alternative position for Argus's staff.
6. P. Schatborn, letter 17 September, 1997; W. Sumowski, letter 14 March 1996 both having seen black-and-white photographs of the drawing.
7. Bremen, Kunsthalle, *Ruth and Naomi*, inv. 54/437, pen and brown ink and white bodycolour, 187 × 235 mm, *ca.* 1651; Paris, Louvre, *Penitent St Jerome*, inv. 22.998, pen and ink and wash, 178 × 146 mm, early 1650s, attributed to Drost by W. Sumowski, *Drawings of the Rembrandt School*, ed. W.L. Strauss, New York 1980, III, nos. 546, 550x; P. Schatborn, *Bulletin van het Rijksmuseum*, II, 1985, pp. 100–01.
8. Dresden, Gemäldegalerie, inv. 1608, W. Sumowski, *Gemälde der Rembrandt Schüler*, London 1983, I, p. 623, no. 314.

75 STUDIO OF REMBRANDT
1. Popham also considered it "a very fine original by Rembrandt", but Christopher White in an annotation on the mount doubted the attribution. For other scenes from the story see Benesch 1973, no. 615, fig. 744, *The Good Samaritan lifting the wounded man from the mule*, Weimar, Staatliche Kunstsammlungen, formerly attributed to Govaert Flinck, 197 × 205 mm, and no. 621, fig. 752, *The Good Samaritan attending the wounded man*, Rotterdam, F. Koenigs Collection, inv. R.34, 126 × 123 mm, both dated to *ca.* 1648–49. See also F. Bol's *Samaritan before the inn*, Berlin, Kupferstichkabinett, inv. 5214, from the second half of the 1640s, which, though a different composition, shows the innkeeper being paid off illus. W. Sumowski, *Drawings of the Rembrandt School*, New York 1980, I, p. 500, no. 238x.
2. Luke 10:34.
3. W. Sumowski, letter 14 March 1996.
4. P. Schatborn, letter 17 September 1997.
5. London, British Museum, *Judith triumphant*, inv. 1900–12–21–2, early 1650s; *Young man asleep with a hat*, 1900–4–11–4, mid 1650s, Sumowski 1980, III, nos. 548x, 559x. Also compare the kneeling woman in the Liverpool drawing with the geometrically simplified figure of Hagar in Sumowski 1980, no. 551x, *Hagar and Ishmael in the desert*, Berlin, Kupferstichkabinett, inv. 1120, early 1650s.
6. Sumowski 1980, no. 569xx, pen and brush and brown ink with much dark

heavy hatching, 195 × 265 mm, Frankfurt, Städelsches Kunstinstitut, inv. 15321. See also a painting in the Louvre and its preparatory drawing in the Chicago Art Institute of *The Good Samaritan arriving at the inn*, attributed to Drost by M. Royalton Kisch in his review of Rembrandt publications in *Burlington Magazine*, CXXXII, 1990, pp. 131–32.

76 PETER PAUL RUBENS
1. It was also known as the *Glücksbuch* (Fortunebook) or the *Trotspiegel* (Fool's Mirror). British Museum, 1876–10–14–158, Campbell Dodgson, *Catalogue of Early German and Flemish Woodcuts in the British Museum*, London 1980, II, p. 175, cat. 80; W. Scheidig, *Die Holzschnitte des Petrarca-Meisters: Zu Petrarcas Werk, Von der Artzney bayder Glück*, Berlin 1955, p. 57. First identified by Popham as after the Petrarch Master and possibly by Rubens and confirmed in an annotation on its old mount by Jaffé as a very early copy by Rubens.
2. T. Musper, *Die Holzschnitte des Petrarkameisters: Ein kritische Verzeichnis*, Munich 1927, p. 33.
3. Two different Weiditz prints were used to illustrate a copy of *Ein glaubwirdige anzangundes tods Hern. Thome. Mori ...* (A trustworthy account of the death of Sir Thomas More ...), 1536.
4. *Joachim von Sandrarts Teutsche Academie* [1675], ed. A.R. Peltzer, Munich 1925, p. 106.
5. Rotterdam, Boymans-van Beuningen Museum, *Studies of soldiers*, nos. V.100–101, L. Burchard and R.-A. d'Hulst, *Rubens Drawings*, Brussels 1963, pp. 17–18, cats. 5–6; Paris, Louvre, illus. F. Lugt, *Inventaire général des dessins des Ecoles du Nord: Ecole Flamand*, Paris 1949, II, no. 1116; for other copies after Stimmer in the Pierpont Morgan Library, New York, and a private collection in the Netherlands, Hilversum, see J.S. Held, *Rubens: Selected Drawings*, revised edn., Oxford 1986, cats. 5, 6.

77 PETER PAUL RUBENS
1. For a more detailed description of Michelangelo's impact on Rubens see Jaffé 1977, especially pp. 19–22.
2. *Rubens Cantoor*, exhib. cat., Antwerp, Rubenshuis, 1993.
3. Illus. Jaffé 1977, p. 19, pls. 11–13.
4. It is particularly close to Paris, Louvre, *Creation of Eve*, inv. 20.257, F. Lugt, *Inventaire général des dessins des Ecoles du Nord: Ecole Flamand*, II, 1949, no. 1035, pl. XXXII, and *Hezekiah*, inv. 20.270, Lugt 1949, no. 1048, pl. XXXIV; British Museum, *Ignudo*, 1870–8–13–882, with no buff heightening, and its greatly reworked heightened counterproof, 1870–8–13–883.
5. J. Müller Hofstede, 'Some Early Drawings by Rubens', *Master Drawings*, 1964, pp. 13–14, disputes, however, the later dating of the white

heightening and Jaffé's caption to the British Museum's *Ignudo*, 1870–8–13–882; he dates it to Rubens second visit to Rome *ca.* 1606. The Liverpool study was probably made after the eight larger copies in red and black chalk in the Louvre, *Six prophets and two sibyls*, nos. 20.226–20.233, Lugt 1949, nos. 1040–47, which appear less fluent and supple in Rubens's handling of the chalk.
6. Commissioned by Archduke Albert, governor of Flanders, known only in a seventeenth-century painted copy in Grasse Cathedral, illus. Jaffé 1977, pl. 187.
7. See for example the Royal Collection's *modello* of *The Assumption of the Virgin* of *ca.* 1611–15.
8. P. Joannides, *Michelangelo and his Influence. Drawings from Windsor Castle*, exhib. cat., Washington DC, National Gallery of Art, 1996, pp. 28, 31.

78 PETER PAUL RUBENS
1. The old mount had attached tissue paper with a watermark of John Hayes, 1814. This mount is of a sort which William Roscoe had specially made for his drawings, possibly to protect them from damage during viewing for the sale.
2. According to William Ford's copy of the sale catalogue (in the British Museum Prints and Drawings department) it was bought by Slater. According to annotated catalogues in Liverpool and in a private collection (thought to be Charles Blundell's copy) it was sold to Brooke, an unidentified buyer.
3. *Rubens e Genova*, exhib. cat., Genoa, Palazzo Ducale, 1977–78, cat. 5, pp. 221–29.
4. Jaffé 1977, pp. 11, 87 and Jaffé 1988.
5. Vienna, Akademie der Bildenden Künste.
6. Jaffé 1977, p. 81. There is a study from life showing the Liverpool pose of the Madonna in the Victoria and Albert Museum, D.967–1900 (Lawrence Collection), black and red chalk with white heightening, illus. Jaffé 1988, fig. 40. See also Jaffé 1977, p. 32 for the influence of Correggio on the Gesù altarpiece.
7. Genoa 1977–78, p. 229, quoting P. Genard, 'La succession de Rubens, *Bulletin des Archives d'Anvers*, II, 1870, p. 95. Almost certainly, according to Jaffé 1988, p. 525 n. 11, the Vienna *modello*.
8. M. Rooses, *L'Œuvre de P.P. Rubens*, Antwerp 1886, I, pp. 202–03. Jaffé 1988 did not believe this was the Weld-Blundell drawing.

79 PETER PAUL RUBENS AND FEDERICO ZUCCARO
1. There is also evidence that the drawing was in a previous mount with a gold slip as flakes of gold were found along the left side. The flecks of dark ink spattered on the centre of the drawing are similar to those found on

the drawing by Tempesta (exh. cat. 53), also owned by Benjamin West, and were presumably accidentally caused by the person drawing the ink-and-wash border on the new mount.
2. Lankrink was a major collector of drawings by Rubens (the artist whom he desired to emulate), particularly copies after or retouched works by other artists which he probably bought at or immediately after the sale of Rubens's studio in 1657 in Antwerp, where Lankrink had been brought up.
3. Identified by Jaffé as a Rubens addition after a visit to the Weld-Blundell collection at Ince-Blundell in 1955, confirming an attribution by Popham.
4. In the Grimani Chapel, as in the Bible, the scene was paired with *The Raising of Lazarus*, John 11:1–44.
5. For a full account of the fresco and most of the related drawings and copies see W.R. Rearick, 'Battista Franco and the Grimani Chapel', *Saggi e memorie di storia dell'arte*, II, 1958–59, II, pp. 132ff.; J. Mundy, *Renaissance into Baroque: Italian Master Drawings by the Zuccari, 1550–1600*, exh. cat., New York, National Academy of Design, 1989, cat. 52.
6. For a drawing perhaps for the Aliprando print see Munich, Kupfer-stichkabinett, pen and wash on tan paper, Herbert List Collection, no. 88, Rearick 1958–59, p. 135; Cort illus. in Jaffé 1965, fig. 4, and 1977, pl. 141.
7. In the Liverpool study the seated woman in the centre, whose face has been entirely drawn by Zuccaro, looks at the Magdalene rather than Christ as she does in the Uffizi *modello* for the whole composition, inv. 11036F, 418m × 702 mm, pen and brown ink heightened with white with traces of black chalk on greeny-grey paper and squared in black chalk, illus. *Mostra di disegni degli Zuccari*, exhib. cat. by J. Gere, Florence, Uffizi, 1966, no. 47, fig. 34. The index finger and thumb of Christ may also be Zuccaro's work (only partially overdrawn by Rubens) and point upwards, not to his right as in the Uffizi drawing. There are also a number of differences in the background crowd.
8. Jaffé 1965, p. 21; Jaffé 1977, p. 16. Rubens retouched at least two other drawings by Federico Zuccaro in his collection: Paris, Louvre, *Marriage of the Virgin*, no. 4521; Oxford, Christ Church, *Last Supper*, no. 1384.
9. Jaffé 1977, p. 12.
10. If, as has been suggested by James Mundy (letter, 19 August 1997), it could be a Zuccaro studio copy, that might have encouraged Rubens to 'fix it up'. Both Jaffé and Popham believed it to be by Federico himself.
11. "Pour échauffer son génie" in the words of R. de Piles's *Conversations sur la conaissance de la peinture*, Paris 1677, as quoted by J.S. Held, *Rubens: Selected Drawings*, revised edn. New York 1986, p. 43, n. 7. There is no evidence of Zuccaro's penmanship under the women on the left, nor under the child and part of his mother, nor in Christ's right arm, which Rubens repositioned three or four times before 'attaching' it to the fingers drawn by Zuccaro.

80 MAERTEN DE VOS
1. C. Depauw, letter 7 February 1997.
2. *Hollstein's Dutch and Flemish Etchings, Engravings and Woodcuts 1450–1700*, ed. D. De Hoop Scheffer, Rotterdam 1996, XLIV, no. 1134.
3. Four of the drawings were recently acquired by the Ashmolean, pen and brown ink and wash, 155 mm diameter (the same dimensions as the respective plaquettes). See U. Mayr-Harting in *NACF Review*, 1997.
4. C. Depauw letter, *cit.* note 1.
5. Illus. in *Kleur en Raffinement: Tekeningen uit de Unicorno collectie*, exhib. cat. by C. Dumas and R.J. te Rijdt, Amsterdam, Rembrandthuis, 1994, cat. 3, pp. 35–36. I should like to thank Dr Charles Dumas of the Rijksbureau voor Kunsthistorische Documentatie for first bringing the drawing to my attention.
6. To *The Triumphant Christ* in Antwerp, Royal Museum of Fine Arts, there is reference in Christiaan Schuckman's entry on Marten de Vos in the *The Dictionary of Art*, London 1996.

Appendix: Checklist of Drawings not Exhibited

WAG 1995.90

GIUSEPPE AGELLIO
Sorrento *ca.* 1570–
ca. 1650? Sorrento
God the Father in glory
387 × 265 mm, red and black chalk
within an oval
In 'Roscoe' tissue-paper mount
watermarked *John Hayes/ 1814*
Inscribed on back in pencil *Ros.80;*
in ink *Sk 10* (?); in pencil an
attribution to *Allori*
Provenance: J. Pzn. Zoomer
(L1511); Roscoe, part of lot 603,
"six in four sheets by various Italian
masters", bt. Slater 16*s.*;
C.R. Blundell
WAG1995.90

Formerly attributed by Pouncey to
Cristoforo Roncalli, called Il
Pomerancio.

ATTR. ANTWERP SCHOOL
16th century
*Design for a large altarpiece with
scenes from the Life of the Virgin*
280 × 222 mm, pen and brown ink
and brown wash
Provenance: 'Pseudo-Crozat'
(L474); Henry Blundell (?), no. 25,
as Diepenbeck
WAG1995.141

Formerly attributed to South
German School, 16th century.

ATTR. AMICO ASPERTINI
Bologna 1474/75–1552 Bologna
*Artemis with the revived Hippolytus
and Aesculapius with Cupid and other
figures*
255 × 195 mm, pen and brown ink
and wash
Provenance: 'Pseudo-Crozat'

WAG 1995.141

WAG 1995.135

157

(L474); T. Hudson (L2432); Henry
Blundell (?), no. 9, attr. to
J. Halse
WAG1995.135 (in album)

Attribution by Popham to Biagio
Pupini (?). Figures and composition
comparable but in reverse to those
found on two Roman sarcophagi
showing the story of Hippolytus
and his stepmother Phaedra in the
Uffizi and the Campo Santo, Pisa
(C. Robert, *Die Antiken
Sarkophagreliefs*, Berlin 1890, III,
no. 164).

PIETRO SANTE BARTOLI
(after Raphael and workshop)
Perugia 1615–1700 Rome
*Copy after the Vatican Loggie fresco:
God shows Noah the Rainbow of the
Covenant*
75 × 225 mm, pen and brown ink
and wash heightened with white
Initials inscribed in ink on drawing,
lower left corner *R.V.*
Provenance: Viti-Antaldi collection
(L2246); Roscoe sale, 1816, part of
lot 179, as by P. San Bartoli after
Raffaelle, "Eight pieces of History
of the Old Testament", bt. Ford
£2.; C.R. Blundell, valued at
£1. 12*s.* in 1841
WAG1995.220

A copy after the monochrome
basamento fresco on the third bay of
the Vatican Loggie. The drawing is
in the same direction as Pietro
Sante Bartoli's precise engraving of
the now barely visible original
(N. Dacos, *Le loggie di Raffaello*,
Rome 1977, pp. 294–302,
pl. CXXXVIIa).

PIETRO SANTE BARTOLI
after Raphael and workshop
*Copy after the Vatican Loggie fresco:
Cain and Abel*
75 × 230 mm, pen and brown ink
and wash heightened with white
Initials inscribed in ink on drawing
lower left corner *R.V.*
Provenance: Viti-Antaldi collection;
Roscoe sale, 1816, part of lot 179,
as above
WAG1995.221

A copy after the monochrome
basamento fresco on the second bay
of the Vatican Loggie. The drawing
is in the same direction as Pietro
Sante Bartoli's precise engraving of

the now barely visible original
(Dacos 1977, pp. 294–302,
pl. CXXXVIc).

PIETRO SANTE BARTOLI
after Raphael and workshop
*Copy after the Vatican Loggie fresco:
Jacob fighting the angel*
70 × 230 mm, pen and brown ink
and wash heightened with white
Inscribed in ink on drawing, lower
left corner *R.V.*
Provenance: Viti-Antaldi collection;
Roscoe sale, 1816, part of lot 179,
as above
WAG1995.222

A copy after the monochrome
basamento fresco on the sixth bay of
the Vatican Loggie. The drawing is
in the same direction as Pietro
Sante Bartoli's precise engraving of
the now barely visible original
(Dacos 1977, pp. 294–302,
pl. CXXXIb).

PIETRO SANTE BARTOLI
after Raphael and workshop
*Copy after the Vatican Loggie fresco:
King David promises Bathsheba that
Solomon will rule*
73 × 230 mm, pen and brown ink
and wash heightened with white,
oxidized
Initials inscribed in ink on drawing,
lower left corner *R.V.*
Provenance: Viti-Antaldi collection;
Roscoe sale, 1816, part of lot 179,
as above
WAG1995.223

A copy after the monochrome
basamento fresco on the eleventh
bay of the Vatican Loggie. The
drawing is in the same direction as
Pietro Sante Bartoli's precise
engraving of the now barely visible
original (Dacos 1977, pp. 294–302,
pl. CXLIIIa).

PIETRO SANTE BARTOLI
after Raphael and workshop
*Copy after the Vatican Loggie fresco:
Scene from the Life of Solomon*
70 × 230 mm, pen and brown ink
and wash heightened with white
Initials inscribed in ink on drawing
in centre *R.V.*
Provenance: Viti-Antaldi collection;
Roscoe sale, 1816, part of lot 179,
as above
WAG1995.224

WAG 1995.220

WAG 1995.221

WAG 1995.222

WAG 1995.223

WAG 1995.224

A copy after the monochrome
basamento fresco on the twelfth bay
of the Vatican Loggie. The drawing
is in the same direction as Pietro
Sante Bartoli's precise engraving of
the now barely visible original
(Dacos 1977, pp. 294–302,
pl. CXLIVa).

PIETRO SANTE BARTOLI
after Raphael and workshop
*Copy after the Vatican Loggie fresco:
Joseph reconciled with his brothers*
70 × 235 mm, pen and brown ink

and wash heightened with white
Initials inscribed in ink on drawing
in centre twice *R.V.*
Provenance: Viti-Antaldi collection;
Roscoe sale, 1816, part of lot 179,
as above
WAG1995.225

A copy after the monochrome
basamento fresco on the seventh bay
of the Vatican Loggie. The drawing
is in the same direction as Pietro
Sante Bartoli's engraving of the
now barely visible original (Dacos
1977, pp. 294–302, pl. CXLa).

WAG 1995.225

WAG 1995.226

WAG 1995.227

WAG 1995.92

PIETRO SANTE BARTOLI
after Raphael and workshop
*Copy after the Vatican Loggie fresco:
Joshua talking to the people of Israel*
70 × 230 mm, pen and brown ink
and wash heightened with white
Provenance: Viti-Antaldi collection;
Roscoe sale, 1816, part of lot 179,
as above
WAG1995.226

A copy after the monochrome
basamento fresco on the tenth bay of
the Vatican Loggie. The drawing is
in the same direction as Pietro
Sante Bartoli's engraving of the
now barely visible original (Dacos
1977, pp. 294–302, pl. CXLIIb).

PIETRO SANTE BARTOLI
after Raphael and workshop
*Copy after the Vatican Loggie fresco:
Abraham sacrificing Isaac*
75 × 233 mm, pen and brown ink
and wash heightened with white,
oxidized
Initials inscribed in ink on drawing,
lower left corner *R.V.*
Provenance: Viti-Antaldi collection;
Roscoe sale, 1816, part of lot 179,
as above
WAG1995.227

A copy after the monochrome
basamento fresco on the fourth bay
of the Vatican Loggie. The drawing
is in the same direction as Pietro
Sante Bartoli's precise engraving of
the now barely visible original
(Dacos 1977, pp. 294–302,
pl. CXXXVIIIa).

AFTER FRA BARTOLOMMEO
*Study of a cloaked bearded man
standing with profile to left*
122 × 62 mm, pen and brown ink
Provenance: George John, 2nd Earl
Spencer (L1530), sold T. Philipe,
10–17 June 1811, possibly as lot 30,
Fra Bartolommeo, "A prophet or
apostle, standing – free pen", bt.
Coxe (?); Roscoe sale, 1816, part of
lot 85, as Fra Bartolommeo, "A
Saint, full robed. Bistre. FINE/ 5h
2½w", bt. Ford 10s. 6d. (along with
Florentine School WAG1995.255);
C.R. Blundell
WAG1995.100

Identified by Chris Fischer as a
copy after a study in the Louvre
(inv. RF5549) for a figure for the
Last Judgement (C. Fischer, *Fra
Bartolommeo et son atelier: Dessins et
peintures des collections francaises*,
exh. cat., Paris, Louvre, 1994,
p. 43, cat. 41).

MARCANTONIO BASSETTI
Verona 1588–1630 Verona
*Pharoah's daughter with the infant
Moses and two companions* (?)
145 × 195 mm, oil on brown tinted
paper
Inscribed in ink on drawing, lower
right corner *Bassetti*
Provenance: Unidentified collector's
stamp with no. 135 written in ink
within it; 'Pseudo-Crozat' (L474);
Henry Blundell (?), no. 19, attr. to
Bassin
Exhibition: Venice 1980, no. 52,
entitled *Tre donne al lavoro e rovine*
WAG1995.92

Possibly an illustration to a biblical
parable of Christ as the leaven
bread.

**AFTER MARCANTONIO
BASSETTI**
*St Jerome's vision of the Last
Judgement with the Trinity seated on
clouds and the death of a female saint*
303 × 225 mm, pen and brown ink
and wash
Inscribed on drawing in brown ink
Tintoretto; in black ink, lower right
corner *JSB* (unknown collector?)
Provenance: Roscoe sale, 1816, lot
255, as Tintoretto, "St Jerome
alarmed in the midst of his
devotions by the Vision of the last
Judgement; a most spirited sketch
of numerous figures/ 12h 8½w", bt.
Slater £1. 15s.; C.R. Blundell,
valued at £1. 4s. in 1841
WAG1995.72 (see overleaf)

WAG 1995.100

159

ATTR. DOMENICO
BECCAFUMI
Cortine 1484–1551 Siena
*Studies of two partially nude bearded
men seated*
281 × 398 mm, red chalk
Inscribed in ink on mount, lower
right corner *Andrea del Sarto*; in
pencil on mount, lower right corner
28; in ink on back of mount, at top
N.30. Typed labels with Gronau's
attribution to Andrea del Sarto and
Popham's attribution as an early
work by Francesco Salviati, and a
pencilled attribution, *by Giuseppe
Porta* (?)

Provenance: Jonathan Richardson
Senior (L2184); Benjamin West
(L419; in pencil *West Florentine
School*); C.R. Blundell
WAG1995.363

Formerly attributed by Popham to
Francesco de' Rossi, called Salviati.
Perhaps related to Beccafumi's series
for the Palazzo Pubblico in Siena.

CIRCLE OF GIAN LORENZO
BERNINI
St Mark seated in clouds
283 × 185 mm, pen and brown ink
brown wash heightened with white,
oxidized, on yellow paper

Inscribed on reverse in brown ink
cut off at top *N 3[?]0–15–y 12[?]/h*;
followed by, in red ink *Lancret*; in
brown ink *No 41/ 2U.L.12*.
Remnants of 18th- to early 19th-
century wallpaper-tax wrapper on
back of mount
Pencil attribution initialled *AK[?]*:
18th c. Austrian?
Provenance: 'Pseudo-Crozat'
(L474); Henry Blundell (?)
WAG1995.241

Formerly Venetian School,
ca. 1700.

MANNER OF GIAN LORENZO
BERNINI
*The Virgin appearing to a monk
(St Bernard?)*
141 × 115 mm, pen and brown ink
and wash over black chalk
heightened with white
Inscribed in ink on mount *Cavalier
Bernin. F. Ecole florentine* (crossed
out and replaced by) *Romaine* (in
Saint-Morys's hand?)
Provenance: 'Pseudo-Crozat'
(L474); comte de Saint-Morys;
Henry Blundell (?)
WAG1995.154

Probably etched in 1793 by the
comte de Saint-Morys (see the
print in his style, WAG1995.155).

BARTOLOMEO BISCAINO
Genoa *ca.* 1632–1657 Genoa
Moses striking the rock
195 × 278 mm, red chalk
heightened with white on yellow-
brown paper within drawn frame
Inscribed in ink below drawn frame,

lower left corner *B. Biscaino*
Inscribed in ink on reverse *05 2* (?)
Secondary support backed with
remains of 18th- or early 19th-
century wallpaper-tax wrapper
Provenance: 'Pseudo-Crozat'
(L474); Henry Blundell (?), no. 40,
originally in Album I
Exhibitions: Edinburgh 1972,
no. 11, illus. p. 93
WAG1995.321

According to Mary Newcome there
is another study by Biscaino for the
same composition in reverse and
with slight variations in the Palazzo
Rosso, Genoa (inv. 1770).

AFTER ABRAHAM
BLOEMART
*The Rest on the Flight (The Holy
Family at the foot of a tree)*
235 × 175 mm, pen and brown ink
and brown wash heightened with
white (oxidized)
Inscribed in pencil on mount *A
Bloemart*; on reverse of drawing in
ink, lower left corner *A Bloemart/ b.
9/ 67/ Nº48*; in pencil, lower left
corner *h* (?). 'Roscoe' tissue paper
watermarked *JOHN HAYES/ 1814*;
on tissue paper in pencil *nº85/
CWB*
Provenance: C. Ploos van Amstel
(L3002, his inscription); Roscoe
sale, 1816, lot 470, as "Abraham
Bloemart's design for an engraving
in chiaroscuro", bt. Slater 9*s.* 6*d.*;
C.R. Blundell, valued at 8*s.* in 1841
Literature: Noted in *Catalogue of
Netherlandish and Flemish Drawings
in the Pierpont Morgan Collection*,
Princeton 1991, cat. 29, p. 18
WAG1995.295

Copy after the three-block chiaroscuro woodcut by Ludolph Büsinck (ca. 1590–1669) after the original drawing in the Pierpont Morgan Library (acc. no. I, 229). Büsinck engraved the Bloemart in reverse and did not follow its colour scheme of contrasting green and brown, substituting different shades of brown. The Liverpool drawing follows both the Büsinck colour scheme and its reversed direction.

ATTR. HENDRIK BLOEMART (?)
Utrecht 1601/02–1672/73 Utrecht
A merry company
162 × 202 mm, black chalk and light brown wash heightened with white (oxidized)
Provenance: 'Pseudo-Crozat'

(L474); Henry Blundell (?), no. 28, attr. "Chevl. Faccini"
WAG1995.142

Comparable in style, subject-matter and size to a Hendrik Bloemart, *Merry company*, Paris, Fondation Custodia, Collection F. Lugt, inv. J.4439, black chalk, pen and brown wash, 164 × 207 mm. The scene also compares with his painting dated 1632 (American private collection). Possibly representing Taste (M. Roethlisberger, *Abraham Bloemaert and his Sons. Paintings and Prints*, Dornspijk 1993, I, cats. H48, HD3, 2, H50–51).

BOLOGNESE SCHOOL
ca. 1600–1650
Study of the head of an elderly man
300 × 250 mm, black and white chalk on buff paper patched on both lower corners
Inscribed in ink on mount *Agostino Carracci*; in ink on reverse Richardson's number *DD30/ R/ the priest in the Communion of S. Jerome*; in ink at bottom of reverse of mount *l[?], Collectione Domini Johannis Sommers*; in ink at bottom, crossed out *Cholmondeley*
Provenance: Padre Sebastiano

Resta (*e. 49*); Lord John Somers; Jonathan Richardson Senior (L2184), sold 11 February 1746/47, lot 50, "Two Austin Carrat's head of the priest in the communion of St. Jerom, and the portrait of Mich. de Molinos", bt. Knapton £3. 15s.; George, 3rd Earl of Cholmondeley (1703–1770) (?), but no collector's mark; John Barnard (L1419), inscribed on the reverse *J:B N°:632/ 12 by 10*; Benjamin West (L419), possibly Christie's, 9 June, lot 74, "a head in black chalk by Ag. Carracci";
C.R. Blundell
Literature: Noted in J. Wood, 'Padre Resta as a Collector of Carracci Drawings', *Master Drawings*, XXXIV, no. 1, 1996, Appendix I, no. 44, n. 216
WAG1995.301

Wrongly identified by Resta and Richardson as being Agostino Carracci's drawing for the priest of his *Last Communion of St Jerome*.

WAG 1995.269

WAG 1995.304

WAG 1995.181

WAG 1995.350

WAG 1995.292

WAG 1995.117

MANNER OF BOTTICELLI
Standing youth with cloak hanging over his left shoulder
211 × 108 mm, pen and brown ink (crudely) heightened with white on ochre-tinted paper
Inscribed in ink on drawing *19*; and on mount by Richardson *f Botticelli/ Vas.* Typed label suggests dating *ca.* 1510–1520
Provenance: J. Richardson (no mark but Richardson's number *f32* on back of mount); Benjamin West (no collector's mark); C.R. Blundell
WAG1995.269

ATTR. GIACINTO BRANDI
Poli 1621–1691 Rome
The Temptation of St Anthony
263 × 200 mm, pen and brown ink
Provenance: Roscoe sale, 1816, lot 216, as Brandi, "Studies for a

picture of St. Jerome at prayer, attended by an Angel. Finely sketched/ 10½h 8w", bt. Slater 8s.; C.R. Blundell, valued at 8s. in 1841
WAG1995.350

Popham attribution to Venetian, School of Tintoretto (?). J. Stock to Luca Giordano. Compare also with Michele Pace, *St Jerome*, Cologne, Wallraf-Richartz, inv. Z2103
(R. Cocke, letter 13 March 1997).

ATTR. BENEDETTO BRANDIMARTE
fl. 1588–1592
Nine putti dancing a round in a landscape
198 × 310 mm, pen and brown ink and brown wash
Inscribed in ink on drawing *Brandimarte*; on back in pencil *Benedetto Brandimarte Lucchese v nel 1592/ Lanzi 1.224*
Provenance: Roscoe sale, 1816, part of lot 603, "Six in four sheets by

various Italian masters", bt. Slater 16s. (along with Donato Creti, Pier Francesco Cittadini, .281–282); C.R. Blundell
WAG1995.304

Derived from and in the same direction as Marcantonio Raimondi's engraving of *Children dancing with two amoretti* after Raphael (Bartsch 217).

CIRCLE OF ADRIAEN BROUWER
(?) 1605/06–1638 Antwerp
Four men at a table
132 × 205 mm, black chalk and brown wash
Inscribed on back in pencil *Adriaen Brouwer fine*; in ink *17 Mar* [?]*19–96*
Provenance: Roscoe sale, 1816, lot 518, as Brouwer, "Inside of a Tabaret, four boors regaling", bt. Slater 10s. 6d.; C.R. Blundell, valued at 8s. in 1841
WAG1995.292

ATTR. DENYS CALVAERT
Antwerp ca. 1540–1619 Bologna
Virgin and Child and an angel appearing to Sts Dominic and Francis
260 × 195 mm, black chalk, pen and brown ink, brown wash, heightened with white, partly oxidized
Provenance: 'Pseudo-Crozat' (L474); Henry Blundell (?), no. 4, Album II (319), as Annibale Carracci
WAG1995.181

Attributed to Calvaert by Julien Stock. Related to the altarpiece of *The Virgin appearing to Sts Francis and Dominic*, dated 1598 (Dresden, Gemäldegalerie Alte Meister), except that the figures have been reversed so that St Francis is in the foreground with his right hand to his breast and St Dominic in the background praying; some variations to the Child's pose.

WAG 1995.257

WAG 1995.279

WAG 1995.259

FOLLOWER OF LUCA
CAMBIASO
Sacrifice of Isaac
375 × 260 mm, pen and brown ink
and wash
Provenance: 'Pseudo-Crozat'
(L474); Henry Blundell (?), no. 53,
as Sebastiano Ricci
WAG1995.117

Another version, from the Santo
Varni collection, was sold in Paris,
Drouot, 16 June 1976, lot 42, pen
and ink without wash, 338 ×
255 mm (M. Newcome, letter 23
May 1996).

FOLLOWER OF LUCA
CAMBIASO
Venus with a looking-glass and Cupid
350 × 244 mm, pen and brown ink
Inscribed in ink on mount *Luca
Cambiaso*; and number *60*; on
reverse in ink a long inscription
quoting in Latin from Ovid:
*Dat facies animos____/ Scilicet à
speculis summuntus [?] imagine
fastus/ Nec nisi compositam se prius
illa videt./ Ovid. Amor
Amor II Ed.17/ Aut formosa fores [?]
minus, et minus improba! Says
Cupid/ H III Eleg. II*
Provenance: Jonathan Richardson
Junior (L2170); Sir Joshua
Reynolds (L2364); Roscoe sale,
1816, part of lot 133, bt. Slater
£1. 2s. (along with Follower of
Cambiaso, *Venus and dead Adonis*,
WAG1995.279); C.R. Blundell,
valued together at 16s. in 1841
WAG1995.257

Another version is in Stockholm
(NM 1591/1863, pen and brown
ink over black chalk, 333 × 233 mm
(P. Bjurström, *Drawings in Swedish
Public Collections*, Stockholm 1979,
cat. 343).

FOLLOWER OF LUCA
CAMBIASO
Venus supporting the dead Adonis
314 × 215 mm, pen and brown ink
Inscribed in ink on drawing *183*; in
ink on mount *Luca Cangiaso*; on
reverse in black chalk *I.n.y.11*; in
ink *L Cangiaso*; in red ink *P8*
Provenance: Roscoe sale, 1816, part
of lot 133, bt. Slater £1. 2s. (along
with "*Venus attiring*", .257);
C.R. Blundell, valued together at
16s. in 1841
WAG1995.279

WAG 1995.284

Two other versions exist, both with
a pair of dogs and a more involved
landscape: one in Stockholm
(NM 81/1973, pen and brown ink
over black chalk, 355 × 249 mm)
and another last seen Christie's,
London, 6 December 1988
(M. Newcome, letter 23 May
1996).

IMITATOR OF LUCA
CAMBIASO
Charity
350 × 270 mm, pen and brown ink
and brown wash
Inscribed in ink on drawing *An
undoubted original Luca Cangiassi or
Cambiaso*
Provenance: Thomas Howard, 2nd
Earl of Arundel (1585–1646) (?);
Roscoe sale, 1816, lot 134, "One, a
Charity; a Woman seated, with
three Children. Strong pen/ 14h.
11w./ From the Arundel
Collection", bt. Slater 17s.; C.R.
Blundell, valued at 12s. in 1841
WAG1995.259

An abbreviated version with
windmill visible but not the putti
carrying it, without wash (209 ×
173 mm) was illustrated in *Disegni
italiani e stranieri del Cinquecento e
del Seicento*, Milan, Stanza del
Borgo, 1969, cat. 11, as in a private
collection, Munich.

SIMONE CANTARINI
Oropezza 1612–1648 Verona
*The Madonna holding the Christ
Child; a sketch for a St Sebastian* (?)
105 × 160 mm, red chalk
Inscribed in ink on Ottley mount
Simone de Pesaro, Pittore

Provenance: W.Y. Ottley, sold
6 June 1814, part of lot 947, as
Simone da Pesaro, "a Madonna
and Child – red chalk; and a
Zingara, masterly pen"; Roscoe
sale, 1816, part of lot 412, bt. Slater
12s. (along with WAG1995.290 and
.339); C.R. Blundell, all valued at
12s. in 1841
WAG1995.284

The *St Sebastian* (?) figure may
relate to Cantarini's etching
(P. Bellini, *L'opera incisa di Simone
Cantarini*, Milan, 1980, cat. 25).

ATTR. SIMONE CANTARINI
Recto: *Draped female figure with
headdress*
Verso: *Study of an angel*
140 × 108 mm, recto: pen and
brown ink; verso: red chalk
Inscribed in ink below drawing
Simone Cantarino; in pencil on
mount *not good for much*; in ink on
mount *Simone Cantarini/ de Pesaro*
Provenance: Nathaniel Hone
(L2793); Roscoe sale, 1816, part of
lot 412, as Cantarini, "A Zingara or
Bohemian. Pen, do.", bt. Slater 12s.
(along with WAG1995.284 and
.339); C.R. Blundell, all valued at
12s. in 1841
WAG1995.290 (see overleaf)

According to a 1977 inventory of
the Weld collection the recto is after
Dürer.

WAG 1995.290

WAG 1995.339

WAG 1995.277

WAG 1995.365

WAG 1995.131

Copy after an Agostino Carracci
etching after an Annibale design
(D. De Grazia Bohlin, *Le stampe dei
Carracci con i disegni, le incisioni, le
copie, i dipinti connessi. Catalogo
critico*, Bologna 1984, no. 336a,
Annibale 16a).

AFTER AGOSTINO
CARRACCI
17th century
*Masks from a frieze in the Palazzo
Salem-Magnani, Bologna*
267 × 200 mm, red chalk
Inscribed in ink by Resta *Fr. Albano
della Sala de Magnani in Bologna
dipinta da Annibale Carracci prima de
reder [sic] a Roma*; on back in ink
BB.20; and in ink lower right corner
K; in pencil in centre *N°233*
Provenance: Padre Sebastiano
Resta (his inscription); Roscoe sale,
1816, lot 417, as Francesco Albani,
bt. Slater 10s.; C.R. Blundell
Literature: J. Wood, 'Resta's
collection of Carracci Drawings',
Master Drawings, XXXIV, no. 1,
1996, pp. 5–6, fig. 2, n. 29
WAG1995.277

WAG 1995.290 VERSO

ATTR. SIMONE CANTARINI
*Abraham and the three angels; two
angels taking a young man
heavenwards*
175 × 240 mm, black chalk
Illegible inscription in ink on verso
Provenance: Roscoe sale, 1816, part
of lot 412, bt. Slater 12s. (along
with .284 and .290); C.R. Blundell
WAG1995.339

AFTER DOMENICO
MARIA CANUTI
*St Teresa interceding to calm the
Divine Wrath*
448 × 326 mm, brush and brown
ink over red chalk
Inscribed on back in pencil lower
left corner *N°15*
Provenance: Benjamin West (no
collector's mark but inscribed on
mount in pencil *West*); C.R. Blundell
WAG1995.365

The altarpiece of this subject by
Canuti, datable *ca.* 1671, is

WAG 1995.306

presently in the church of Santa
Maria Lacrimosa degli Alemanni,
Bologna, and was formerly in the
Madonna di Stra' Maggiore
(S. Stagni, *Domenico Maria Canuti
Pittore*, Rimini 1988, no. 30,
pp. 168–69).

AFTER AGOSTINO
CARRACCI
17th century
*The Madonna and Child with a
superimposed outline of a plinth*
203 × 153 mm, oval, red chalk
Provenance: Jonathan Richardson
Junior (?) (?L2170); 'Pseudo-
Crozat' (L474); Henry Blundell (?)
WAG1995.131

A copy with variations of three
heads from the frieze around the
frescoed scenes of *The sacred exile*
and *The triumph of Romulus*. There
is a slightly larger (258 × 197 mm)
variant red-chalk copy, in a
different hand, attr. Agostino
Carracci, in the Albertina, Vienna,
inv. 2179. Attributed to Canuti by
Christie's.

CIRCLE OF ANNIBALE CARRACCI

Four studies of heads: a boy with frilled shirt and three youths pulling faces
216 × 300 mm, red chalk on buff paper heightened with white
Inscribed in ink on mount in right corner *Annibale Carracci*; in pencil above *not gen*[uine]
Provenance: Benjamin West (L419); C.R. Blundell
WAG1995.306

AFTER ANNIBALE CARRACCI

Copy from the Herrera Chapel: St Diego appearing to pilgrims at his tomb
248 × 390 mm, red chalk
Provenance: Henry Blundell (?), no. 47, as Carracci
WAG1995.65

FOLLOWER OF LUDOVICO CARRACCI

Latona threatened by the Lycian peasants in a river landscape
70 × 290 mm, pen and ink and brown wash on beige paper
Tissue paper with watermark
..TT & Co PATENT COPYING;
Inscribed in pencil on tissue *Nº20/ CWB*; in ink on mount *Lod.º Carracci.*; in pencil *doubtful*
Provenance: William Young Ottley, sold 6f. June. 1814, lot 1539, as

Lodovico Carracci, "a long slip landscape – the story of Latona – a harvest scene – fine pen and light wash"; Roscoe sale, 1816, part of lot 363, as Lodovico Carracci, "A Sketch of Several Figures; Men bathing &c 3h 11½w From Mr. Ottley's Collection"; C.R. Blundell
WAG1995.98

CARRACCI CIRCLE

early 17th century
The Madonna and Child
270 × 200 mm, black chalk
Inscribed in ink on mount lower right corner *3:3:0 Aug' Carats*
Provenance: Sir Peter Lely (L2092–4); B West (L419; inscribed in pencil *West Bolognese*); C.R. Blundell, as Agostino Caracci
WAG1995.107

CARRACCI SCHOOL

A seated cloaked cleric with a cap
330 × 235 mm, red chalk
Inscribed in ink lower right corner of mount *Annibale Carracci*; in pencil on mount *of the school but probably not genuine*
Provenance: Benjamin West (no collector's mark, inscribed in pencil on mount *West Bolognese*); C.R. Blundell
WAG1995.308

ATTR. ALESSANDRO CASOLINI

Mensano 1552/53–1607 Siena
Ecce Homo
115 × 98 mm, red chalk, pen and brown ink and brown wash
Provenance: Roscoe sale, 1816, part of lot 200, as Raffaellino da Reggio, bt. Slater 12*s.*(along with exh. cat. 44, Raffaellino da Reggio, and WAG1995.55); C.R. Blundell, valued along with two others at 12*s.*
WAG1995.54

ATTR. ALESSANDRO CASOLANI

Christ appearing to St Catherine of Siena (?)
131 × 100 mm, pen and brown ink and wash over red chalk
Provenance: Roscoe sale, 1816, part of lot 200, as Raffaellino da Reggio, "Christ with the Cross, appearing to the Virgin; pen and bistre/ 5h. 4w.", bt. Slater 12*s.* (along with WAG1995.54 and exh. cat. 44); C.R. Blundell
WAG1995.55

Possibly related to Casolani's *St Catherine with the Crucifix* in the Upper Oratory of the Casa di Santa Caterina, Siena.

WAG 1995.115

WAG 1995.150

WAG 1995.341

WAG 1995.198

WAG 1995.282

BERNARDO CASTELLO
Genoa 1557?–1629 Genoa
St Catherine delivered from martyrdom
397 × 200 mm, pen and brown ink and wash heightened with white (oxidized), squared with arched top
Provenance: Pseudo-Crozat (L474); Henry Blundell (?), no. 3, as Giordano
Popham attribution on mount *very possibly Bernardo Castelli*
WAG1995.115

Christie's attribution to circle of Orazio Samacchini. M. di Giampaolo agrees with Popham. For comparison see drawing attr. Bernardo Castello in the Pinacoteca Nazionale, Bologna (inv. 1742, Gernsheim photo no. 112 220) and the altarpiece painted 1619 of Castellino Castello (1578–1649) for the parish church of Sestri Levante (illus. *La pittura in Italia: il Seicento*, Milan 1989, II, p. 678).

CIRCLE OF GIOVANNI BENEDETTO CASTIGLIONE (?)
Christ on the cross with a Roman horseman and three figures
264 × 185 mm, pen and brown ink
Tissue-paper cover watermarked J Watt & Co. and inscribed in pencil *Valerio Castelli/ genoese School*
Inscribed in ink on lower edge of

drawing *n^i 21*; in pencil on back *Anibale Carracci* and other faint and illegible words and numbers in ink and pencil
Provenance: Roscoe sale, 1816, part of lot 147 as Castelli, bt. Slater 14s. (along with Castiglione, exh. cat. 17 and WAG1995.202, Merano); C.R. Blundell
WAG1995.198

Mary Newcome doubts the attribution to Castiglione or Castello.

FRANCESCO CAVAZZONE
Bologna 1559–after 1616 Bologna
St Catherine disputing with the grammarians before the Emperor Maxentius
235 × 162 mm, pen and brown ink and wash squared
Inscribed in pencil and partially erased on mount *Cavasoni*[?]
Provenance: Roscoe sale, 1816, lot 104, as Perino del Vaga, "St Helena avowing her adherence to Christianity fine pen and indian ink, Capital", bt. Slater 15s.; C.R. Blundell, valued at 12s. in 1841
Exhibition: *Drawing in Bologna 1500–1600*, London, Courtauld Institute, 1992, no.18
Literature: A. Ghirardi, 'Francesco Cavazzoni', *Fortunati*, II, 1986,

p. 854, illus. p. 858
WAG1995.341

Preparatory study for Cavazzoni's altarpiece painted *ca.* 1582 for the parish church at Castel San Pietro, Bologna. Attribution made before 1992 by Jürgen Winkelmann.

STUDIO OF GIUSEPPE CESARI
called Cavaliere d'Arpino
Perseus and Andromeda
200 × 160 mm, black and red chalk
Inscribed in ink on drawing lower right corner *4*; in pencil on mount *Cav d'Arpino*
Provenance: 'Pseudo-Crozat' (L474); Henry Blundell (?)
WAG1995.150

Attribution to Cesari's workshop, *ca.* 1630–40, by Professor Dr Herwarth Röttgen (letter 27 August 1997). Other versions in Venice, Accademia (inv. 239), related to painting in Providence RI, datable 1592–93, and in Vienna, Kunsthistorisches Museum, dated 1601 (*Il Cavaliere d'Arpino*, exhib. cat. by H. Röttgen, Rome, Palazzo Venezia, 1973, nos. 10, 32).

WAG 1995.167

WAG 1995.168

WAG 1995.116

WAG 1995.186

PIER FRANCESCO
CITTADINI
Milan 1613/16–1681 Bologna
*Genre scene (?): Drunken man being
pulled by women into a pool in which
there are two figures and a dog, people
playing quoits in the background*
197 × 128 mm, pen and brown ink
on blue paper
Inscribed on mount *Tutti tre di
Francesco Milanese* (in the hand of
an unknown Bolognese (?)
collector; see exh. cat. 47, Reni)
Provenance: Unknown Bolognese
(?) collector; Roscoe sale, 1816, as

part of lot 603, "Six in four sheets
by various Italian artists" (on same
sheet as Attr. Creti, .280–.281), bt.
Slater 16s.; C.R. Blundell
WAG1995.282

FOLLOWER OF PIETER
COECKE VAN AELST
*Three compositional studies for the
Miracles of Saint Anthony of Padua:
a young child declares the name of his
father; in devotion before a Madonna
and Child; attacking pagan antique
statues*
63 × 127 mm, 120 × 127 mm, pen
and brown ink and grey wash,
partly pricked for transfer (two
studies on one sheet)
Provenance: 'Pseudo-Crozat'
(L474); Henry Blundell (?)
WAG1995.167–168

MICHEL CORNEILLE
THE YOUNGER
Paris 1641–1708 Paris
Jupiter chasing a nymph (Semele?)
200 × 280 mm, red chalk
counterproof
Inscribed Popham attr. on mount to
J.B. Corneille "I think"
Provenance: 'Pseudo-Crozat'
(L474); Henry Blundell (?), no. 51,
as Ariosto del Franco
WAG1995.116

MICHEL CORNEILLE
THE YOUNGER
St John preaching in a forest
200 × 275 mm, pen and brown ink
Provenance: 'Pseudo-Crozat'
(L474); Henry Blundell (?), as
North Italian School
WAG1995.186

A copy after a drawing (Paris,
Louvre, inv. 25351) attributed to
Annibale Carracci in the 18th
century and then in the Cabinet du
Roi, when it was etched by the
comte de Caylus (no. 67 in the
British Museum Prints and
Drawings Dept. album, shelfmark
C.163 c.27).

WAG 1995.338

WAG 1995.183

MICHEL CORNEILLE
THE YOUNGER
after Agostino Carracci
St Francis receiving the Stigmata
190 × 276 mm, red chalk on buff
paper
Provenance: 'Pseudo-Crozat'
(L.474); Henry Blundell (?), no. 13,
as Ariosto del Franco (removed
from album in 1969)
Exhibitions: Edinburgh 1969,
no.18, pl. 29, attr. Domenico
Campagnola by J. Gere
WAG1995.338

Related to a print by Agostino
Carracci (D. De Grazia Bohlin, *Le
Stampe dei Carracci con i disegni, le
incisioni, le copie, i depinti connessi.
Catalogo critico*, Bologna 1984,
cat. 224).

SCHOOL OF CREMONA (?)
ca. 1510?
*Study for an altarpiece: Madonna
and Child with a bishop saint, a
knight, St Sebastian (?), St Roch and
two monastic donors*
290 × 251 mm, pen and brown ink
and wash heightened with white
(oxidized), greatly torn, stained and
patched
Inscribed on drawing in pencil
lower left corner *Raphael d'Urbin*; in
pencil on mount *Raphael*
Provenance: 'Pseudo-Crozat'
(L.474); Henry Blundell (?)
WAG1995.183

DONATO CRETI (?)
Cremona 1671–1749 Bologna
Tancred recognizing Clorinda
127 mm diam., roundel, pen and
grey ink on greenish paper
Inscribed in pencil on back *Per
Francesco Cittadini/ detto il Milanese*.
On the same sheet as .281–.82,
inscribed *Tutti tre di Francesco
Milanese*
Provenance: Roscoe sale, 1816, lot
217, as Niccolo Berettoni, "Venus
lamenting the death of Adonis pen
and bistre an oval", bt. Esdaile £2.;
C.R. Blundell
WAG1995.280

DONATO CRETI (?)
Esther and Ahasuerus (?)
123 mm diam, roundel, pen and
grey ink on greenish paper
On same sheet as WAG1995.280
and .282, inscribed *Tutti tre di
Francesco Milanese* in the hand of an
unknown Bolognese (?) collector,
see Reni, exh. cat. 47 and Tiarini,
WAG1995.333–.337
Provenance: Unknown Bolognese
(?) collector; Roscoe sale, 1816,
part of lot 603, "Six in four sheets
by various Italian artists", bt. Slater
16s.; C.R. Blundell
WAG1995.281

ATTR. CIRCLE OF CRETI
Seated female figure holding a book
109 × 84 mm, pen and brown ink
Inscribed by Pouncey *period of I
Oliver* (?)
Provenance: Roscoe sale, 1816, part
of lot 335, as Parmigianino, "Six,
various subjects/ From Lanckrinck's,
Richardson's and other Collections"

WAG 1995.280

WAG 1995.281

(along with attr. Annibale Carracci,
exh. cat. 15, and Roman School
WAG1995.58, Italo–Flemish School
.71 and after Parmigianino .296),
bt. Slater £1. 9s.; C.R. Blundell, all
valued at £1. 4s. in the 1841
WAG1995.57

GIOVANNI BATTISTA
CROMER
ca. 1667–1750 Padua
*Laban searching for his household
idols*
Verso: *Sketch of women begging
mercy from an enthroned man*
295 × 220 mm, recto: black chalk,
pen and brown ink and grey wash;
verso: black chalk
Inscribed in ink on recto and

WAG 1995.57

crossed out *G[Z?]anoni*; replaced in chalk with *Gio. Batta Cromer/ Padovano*; inscribed in ink on verso many times over as if practising a signature *Gio Batta. Cromer; Al ... Illsmo Sig Mio ...*
Provenance: Roscoe sale, 1816, lot 296, as Gio. Bat. Cromer, "d. about 1750 an Historical Sketch. Pen and indian ink./ 12h. 8½", bt. Slater 5s.; C.R. Blundell, valued at 4s. in 1841
WAG1995.218

ATTR. GIOVANNI BATTISTA CROSATO
ca. 1685/6–1758 Venice
Venus reclining with Cupid at her feet and putti and satyrs in a landscape
165 × 215 mm, pen and grey ink and purplish wash within framing lines
Inscribed in ink below framing lines *Giambatista Crosato Veneziano*
Provenance: Unidentified Venetian known as 'The Reliable Venetian Collector' (L3005c–d), his attribution on drawing; 'Pseudo-

Crozat' (L474); Henry Blundell (?), no. 57, as Baptista Veneziano
WAG1995.158

ABRAHAM VAN DIEPENBECK
's-Hertogenbosch 1596–
1675 Antwerp
St Catherine of Siena receiving the Crown of Thorns from the Virgin and Christ witnessed by Sts Peter, Paul, John the Evangelist, and King David and another nun
94 × 152 mm, pen and brown ink and brown wash heightened with white (oxidized)
Provenance: Joseph van Haecken (L2516, his mark on mount, possibly one of 48 Diepenbeck drawings sold in 4 separate lots in Langford sale, 11f. February 1750/51); 'Pseudo-Crozat' (L474); Henry Blundell (?)
WAG1995.140

A copy (?) after the drawing (in better condition) of exactly the same composition, *The Mystic Marriage of St Catherine of Siena*, but for a small female head added behind the back of the nun in background, in Rotterdam, Boymans-van Beuningen, inv. Diepenbeck 4, pen and ink with white heightening (93 × 154 mm, Gernsheim photo no. 29 756).

GASPARE DIZIANI
Belluno 1689–1767 Venice
The martyrdom of St Sebastian (?)
243 × 190 mm, pen and brown ink and wash over red chalk within a framing arch (upper corners cut)
Inscribed in ink on the drawing *Gasparo Diziani Bellunese*
Provenance: Unknown Venetian known as 'The Reliable Venetian Collector' (L3005 c–d), his inscription on drawing; 'Pseudo-Crozat' (L474); Henry Blundell (?), no. 24
WAG1995.153

AFTER CARLO DOLCI (?)
St John the Evangelist with the eagle seated on a cloud
328 × 224 mm, red and black chalk within a drawn oval
Inscribed on mount in pencil *Carlo Dolci*, followed in ink by *gen. W.*; also inscribed in pencil *Giovan Bellino*; on verso in pale brown ink top left corner *6g J.C* (?); in centre

G. Bellino| Udney's| sale; bottom
edge centre a number *3* under a
triangle; in pencil in a different
hand *Gentile Bellino born 1421|*
Venice died 1470 – he was Titian's
master
Provenance: R. Udny (L2248),
monogram on mount; Roscoe sale,
1816, part of lot 235, bt. Ford £1.
as Giovanni Bellini (along with
"Two, portrait of Giovanni Bellini,
taken after his death ... from the
Collection of Greffier Fagel [.84];
Cat. No.32 ... St Matthew in
Adoration; black and red chalk,
oval./ 12h 9w"); C.R. Blundell,
valued together at 12*s.* in 1841
WAG1995.68

WAG 1995.68

WAG 1995.217

ATTR. DOMENICHINO
(Domenico Zampieri)
Bologna 1581–1641 Naples
Landscape with figures and horseman
210 × 305 mm, black chalk
Watermark on mount: fleur-de-lys
in large circle (?) with crown
Inscribed in black chalk on drawing
30; in ink on mount *J:B|*
Domenichino; in pencil *genuine*; and
on back at bottom edge *ch*
Provenance: Jonathan Richardson
Senior (L2184), with his shelfmark
R12| K2| EE10| X26| O; sold,
possibly London 2 February
1746/47, lot 56, "Four Han Carats
academies, Domenichino landscape
&c.", bt. Penny £2. 14*s.* 6*d.*, or
9 February, lot 53, "Two
landscapes Gaspar Poussin and
Dominiquin", bt. Fairfax 15*s.* 6*d.*;
John Barnard (L1419), with his
attribution to Domenichino and
number *JB Nº:639* – 12 by 8½, sold
possibly London 22 February 1787
lot 17, "Two Landscapes,
Dominichino and F. Bolognese";
Benjamin West (no mark, inscribed
in pencil on mount *West Bolognese*,
possibly one of "seven landscapes
by Domenichino", sold Christie's,
12 June 1820, lot 96); C.R. Blundell
WAG1995.217

Spear expressed reservations about
Domenichino's authorship from a
photograph (letter 15 April 1996).

ATTR. EDWARD DUBOIS
Antwerp 1619–1696 London
Study after two antique female heads
89 × 142 mm, brown wash on
yellowy–brown paper with white
heightening

Provenance: 'Pseudo-Crozat'
(L474); Henry Blundell (?), no. 15,
as Lebrun
WAG1995.162

EDWARD DUBOIS (?)
OR SIMON DUBOIS
Antwerp 1632–1708 London
Figure- and compositional studies
partly copied from Guercino, Raising
of Tabitha
204 × 287 mm, brown wash
heightened with white and red wash
on yellowy-buff paper
Inscribed in ink on drawing top
right corner *g*
Secondary support backed with
blue paper stamped with paper tax
stamp
Provenance: 'Pseudo-Crozat'
(L474); Henry Blundell (?), no. 5,
as Guercino (possibly originally in
album along with .162)
WAG1995.297

Attribution to Dubois made by
J. Stock. The group of seven figures
in the upper right corner are all
taken in reverse from Guercino's
St Peter raising Tabitha, ca. 1618, in
the Pitti Palace, Florence.

AFTER DÜRER
Portrait of the artist's father
120 × 80 mm, pen and brown ink
Inscribed in pencil on drawing
Albert Durer
Provenance: Roscoe sale, 1816, part
of lot 605, bt. Slater £1. (with
South German School (?) .328;
Figino, .101; Attr. Parmigianino,
.253); C.R. Blundell, all valued at
12*s.* in 1841

WAG 1995.162

WAG 1995.297

WAG1995.240

A copy after a Dürer School
woodcut (F.W.H. Hollstein,
German Engravings, Etchings and
Woodcuts ca. 1400–1700, VII,
p. 273).

DUTCH SCHOOL
late 16th century
A young man holding a bow
270 × 170 mm, pen and brown ink
and wash on brownish paper
Inscribed in pencil on the mount
lower right corner *Biderbacke*(?)

Provenance: Pseudo-Crozat
(L474); Henry Blundell (?)
WAG1995.136

EMILIAN SCHOOL (?)
ca. 1600
The Mystic Marriage of St Catherine
290 × 240 mm, pen and brown ink
and brown wash heightened with
white and squared
Inscribed on mount *Maratti*; in
pencil on mount *very good perhaps
genuine/ almost too good for B*[?];
pencilled attr. by J. Gere *Biagio
Pupini?*
Provenance: Jonathan Richardson
Junior (L2170); Roscoe sale, 1816,
lot 195 as Federigo Barocci, "A
beautiful and highly finished
drawing, in bistre", bt. Ford
£4. 6s.; C.R. Blundell, as Barocci,
valued at £3. 3s. in 1841
WAG1995.86

GIOVAN AMBROGIO FIGINO
Milan 1548–1608 Milan
Study of the left leg of a man
132 × 65 mm, black chalk
Typed attribution to *Florentine
School 16th cent.*
Provenance: Probably part of
Roscoe sale (?), 1816, lot 605, bt.
Slater £1. (along with After Dürer
WAG1995.240, after Parmigianino,
.253 and South (?) German School,
.328); C.R. Blundell
WAG1995.101

Close to a Figino *Study of a left leg*
in Christ Church, Oxford (inv.
0201), with a Ridolfi album
provenance (J. Byam Shaw,
*Drawings by Old Masters at Christ
Church, Oxford*, Oxford 1976,
cat. 1172).

FLEMISH SCHOOL (?)
late 17th century
*Head and shoulders of a bearded
monk*
275 × 235 mm, coloured chalks
Provenance: Unknown
Inscribed on back in pencil *Sketch
by De Lonj*[?]*aike*[?]*)*
WAG1995.190

Formerly attributed to French
School.

WAG 1995.240

WAG 1995.136

FLORENTINE SCHOOL
late 15th century
*Standing male figure in profile to left
holding paper*
216 × 80 mm, black chalk
heightened with white on grey
paper
Inscribed in ink across top of
drawing and an erased attribution
lower left corner
Typed label suggests Filippino Lippi
Provenance: Roscoe sale, 1816, part
of lot 15, as Masaccio, "Man
standing with a paper in his hand.
Black chalk on blue paper", bt.
Slater 16s. (along with Domenico
Ghirlandaio workshop, exh. cat.
30); C.R. Blundell, together valued
at 12s. in 1841
WAG1995.268

WAG 1995.86

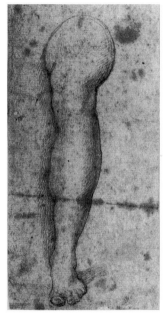

WAG 1995.101

WAG 1995.190

FLORENTINE SCHOOL
ca. 1500–1550
Pietà
95 × 75 mm, pen and brown ink
over black chalk heightened with
white
Inscribed in ink on mount *Study for
a picture formerly at Viterbo, now*

WAG 1995.268

WAG 1995.349

Lord Clive's[?] *see*[?] *Vasari in Fra
Sebastiano*; in lower right corner
collector's mark *V*[or *W*]*R*; on
backing card in pencil *Collection
Lestevenon*; in pencil on front of
secondary mount underneath
Florentine *not gen. W*
Provenance: J Richardson Senior
(L2183) with his shelf mark on
back *S.54/ C* [or] *E*; unknown
collector initials V or WR; W. A.
Lestevenon (?); Benjmain West (no
collector's mark but pencil
annotation *West Florentine* on

171

WAG 1995.255

WAG 1995.374

WAG 1995.319

WAG 1995.185

WAG 1995.163

secondary mount); C.R. Blundell, possibly one of "Three studies from West's collection", valued at £1. 12s. in 1841
On same sheet of card as Italian School (?) 17th century, .348
WAG1995.349

W.A. Lestevenon bought from the Dukes of Bracciano a collection of drawings that included 25 by Michelangelo which were given to the Teylers Museum Haarlem; they were reproduced and commented on by Baron F. de Marcuard in 1901 (F. von Marcuard, *Die Zeichnungen Michelangelos in Museum Teyler zu Haarlem*, Munich 1901).

FLORENTINE SCHOOL
ca. 1540?
Sts Andrew and Peter and a bishop
321 × 224 mm, red chalk
Inscribed in black chalk on drawing, lower left corner *Bartolomeo*; in ink on mount *Fra Bartolomeo*; and in pencil *doubtful but good*; on back in ink at bottom *Price*; in pencil *2660G*
Provenance: Jonathan Richardson Senior (L2184), with attribution to Fra Bartolommeo, possibly 5 February 1746/47, lot 39, "Two drawings Polidore Raphael's whole cartoon of the slaughter of the innocents, Fran. Bartolomeo three saints &c.", bt. Trevor £4. 14s. 6d.; John Barnard, no. 435, 12¾ by 9; Roscoe sale, 1816, lot 85, as Fra Bartolomeo, "a superb design but much injured", bt. Ford 10s. 6d. (along with After Bartolommeo, WAG1995.100); C.R. Blundell, valued at 16s. in 1841
WAG1995.255

FLORENTINE SCHOOL (?)
late 16th century
The Lamentation
352 × 460 mm, pen and brown ink and brown wash heightened with white
Inscribed in ink on mount in centre *Giacomo da Pontormo*
Provenance: John Barnard (L1420; no. 538, with an inscription relating to Pontormo on the back: *of Florence he studied under Michael Angelo Buonaroti/ & imitated his manner. He died Anno 1558 aged 65* – initialled *J:B*), possibly sold 22 February 1787, lot 72, "A Dead Christ by Pontormo"; Benjamin West (no collector's mark); C.R. Blundell
WAG1995.374

Popham thought it close to Francesco Salviati. Formerly attributed to Roman School *ca.* 1580. Composition resembles the *Deposition* by Luca Penni (Florence *ca.* 1500–1556 Paris), Chicago Art Institute, inv. 1922.905 (S.F. McCullogh and L.M. Giles, *Italian Drawings before 1600 in the Chicago Institute of Arts*, Chicago 1997, cat. 240).

ATTR. DONATO DA FORMELLO
The Birth of the Virgin?
205 × 253 mm, pen and brown ink and blue wash
Inscribed in ink on drawing *Donato di formello; l.26*

Provenance: Padre Sebastiano Resta; Lord John Somers (l.26); 'Pseudo-Crozat' (L474); Henry Blundell (?), as "Donta di Torretto" (misreading of inscription)
WAG1995.185

BATTISTA FRANCO
Venice *ca.* 1510–1561 Venice
The Holy Family
142 × 124 mm, pen and brown ink
Inscribed comment or name on mount erased; pencil comment on mount *genuine*
Provenance: Roscoe sale, 1816, part of lot 362, as Ludovico Carracci, "The Holy Family. Fine pen./ 6h. 5w.", bt. Slater 10s. 6d. (along with exh. cat. 14, now attr. Annibale Carracci); C.R. Blundell, together valued at 8s. in 1841
Exhibition: Venice 1980, no. 24, as Battista Franco
WAG1995.319

ATTR. BATTISTA FRANCO (?)
A dancing Bacchante
213 × 142 mm, pen and brown ink and wash silhouetted against brown paper

172

WAG 1995.125

WAG 1995.121

Inscribed in ink on mount lower right corner *Gambini*
Provenance: 'Pseudo-Crozat' (L474); Henry Blundell (?)
WAG1995.163

Formerly Circle of Girolamo da Carpi. Popham suggested Battista Franco. Anne Lauder helped identify it as a copy after a figure in Raphael's Vatican Loggie scene of *The Israelites gathering manna* (N. Dacos, *Le loggie di Raffaello*, Rome 1977, fig. 101), and suggested that it could be an early drawing by Franco when in Rome in the late 1530s (letter 10 February 1997). Girolamo da Carpi also drew the same figure on a sheet of the Rosenbach Album in Philadelphia (N.W. Canedy, *The Roman Sketchbook of Girolamo da Carpi*, London and Leiden 1976, p. 60, R.101, pl. 13).

MANNER OF BATTISTA FRANCO (?)
A seated goddess Roma holding a Palladium, the Wolf of Rome with the infants Romulus and Remus, two victories and two crouching putti
206 × 256 mm, pen and brown ink and very light traces of wash
Provenance: 'Pseudo-Crozat' (L474); Henry Blundell (?)
WAG1995.125

Copied from either the left side of Polidoro da Caravaggio's *soprapporta* façade for the Palazzo Gaddi, Rome, painted before 1527, or from Perino del Vaga's larger copy drawing made after 1538, in the Detroit Institute of Arts (1966.398). Two other anonymous 16th-century drawings after this section of Polidoro's façade are preserved in Paris and in the Biblioteca Reale, Turin (*Italian,*

French, English and Spanish Drawings and Watercolours: 16th through 18th Centuries in the Detroit Institute of Arts, New York 1992, cat. 13. Information from Anne Lauder, letter 3 November 1997).

FRENCH SCHOOL
17th century
The burning of Troy and the flight of Aeneas
262 × 390 mm, pen and brown ink
Provenance: 'Pseudo-Crozat' (L474); Henry Blundell (?)
WAG1995.121

FRENCH SCHOOL
17th century
Rebecca and Eleazer at the well
260 × 370 mm, black chalk heightened with white on brown paper
'Roscoe' tissue-paper mount watermarked *John Hayes/ 1814*

Inscribed in chalk *Poussin*
Provenance: Jonathan Richardson Junior (L2170); Roscoe sale, 1816, part of lot 569, as Poussin, "Rachel giving the servant of Jacob water to drink", bt. Slater 16s. (along with WAG1995.219); C.R. Blundell, valued together at 16s. in 1841
WAG1995.67

Formerly attributed to Circle of Nicolas Poussin.

FRENCH SCHOOL
17th century
The physician Erasistratus discovers the love of Antiochus for his mother Stratonice
185 × 203 mm, black chalk, brown wash heightened with white on brown paper
Provenance: John Talman (?; no mark but inscribed on back in pencil *ex collect. J. Tahlm...*); Sir Joshua Reynolds (?; no mark);

WAG 1995.67

WAG 1995.219

WAG 1995.108

WAG 1995.187

WAG 1995.157

WAG 1995.124

Roscoe sale, 1816, part of lot 569, as Poussin, bt Slater 16s. (along with WAG1995.67); C.R. Blundell, as *Antiochus and Stratonice*, valued as above, 1841
WAG1995.219

Formerly attributed to Circle of Nicolas Poussin. Both drawings appear to be by same hand as produced the Koenigs Collection *Plague in Athens*, pen and brown ink with grey wash heightened with white bodycolour on brown paper, 382 × 251 mm, formerly Spencer collection (*Five Centuries of European Drawings: the former collection of Franz Koenigs*, exhib. cat., Moscow, Pushkin Museum, 1995, cat. 201).

FRENCH SCHOOL (?)
ca. 1748–?1800
Copy after a portrait by Maurice-Quentin de La Tour of Jacques Dumont, called Le Romain
230 × 180 mm, black and red chalk
Provenance: Unknown;

WAG 1995.174

C.R. Blundell
WAG1995.108

For the original pastel portrait by Maurice-Quentin de La Tour of *Jacques Dumont, called Le Romain*, shown at the Salon of 1748, see G. Monnier, *Pastels XVIIIᵉᵐᵉ et XVIIIᵉᵐᵉ siècles*, exh. cat., Paris, Louvre, Cabinet des Dessins, 1972, no. 64. The Liverpool drawing is a copy with slight variations.

ATTR. ANTON DOMENICO GABBIANI
Florence 1652–1726 Florence
Study of a cupid
131 × 88 mm, pen and black ink, irregular fragment
Illegible attribution lower left corner on backing *Romano* [?]
Provenance: 'Pseudo-Crozat' (L474); comte de Saint-Morys (?); Henry Blundell (?)
WAG1995.157

A reproductive etched copy of the drawing in the Weld-Blundell collection by the comte de Saint Morys (?)(WAG1995.132) attributes the drawing to Domenico Gabbiani. Gabbiani produced many copies after cherubs and putti in the 18th century (Florence, Uffizi, album 4287–4359F, all of which are in chalk). Possibly after a Raphael putto in the Villa Farnesina frescos (see *Raphael Invenit: Stampe da*

Raffaello nelle collezioni dell'Istituto Nazionale per la Grafica, 1985, p. 632, as reproduced by Girard Audran (1670–1703).

GENOESE SCHOOL
ca. 1650
The Adoration of the Magi
171 × 248 mm, pen and brown ink brown wash
Inscribed in pencil on mount *Bassano*
Provenance: 'Pseudo-Crozat' (L474); Henry Blundell (?)
WAG1995.187

GENOESE SCHOOL
17th century
The Rest on the Flight into Egypt
180 × 250 mm, pen and brown ink
Provenance: 'Pseudo-Crozat' (L474); Henry Blundell (?), no. 30, as "Spinnetto", Album I (258)
WAG1995.124

Popham's attribution Genoese, 17th century. Christie's attribution Pseudo-Borzone. Possibly Carlo Antonio Tavella (1668–1736).

GENOESE SCHOOL
early 18th century
Study of a girl seated between baskets and another female head
150 × 189 mm, pen and brown ink and wash
Inscribed in pencil on drawing *2ᶜ*; on edge of mount in ink *Guercino*, crossed out and replaced by other illegible names in pencil; in ink lower right corner in letters *b.s/ j*
Provenance: 'Pseudo-Crozat' (L474); Henry Blundell (?)
WAG1995.174

Possibly from a drawing manual.

SOUTH GERMAN SCHOOL
ca. 1500?
Head and shoulders of a woman wearing an elaborate headdress
75 × 85 mm, silverpoint on prepared grey ground washed with pink, cheeks, lips and nose touched with pink chalk. Paper patched and reworked (?) in lower left corner
Inscribed in ink on mount top right corner *605*; in pencil on mount *not genuine/ but good of Albert D: time*
Provenance: Probably Roscoe sale, 1816, part of lot 605, as by "an

Inscribed on mount in in pencil *one of the best and most interesting?/ not by G but perhaps by Filippino Lippi/ but in rather a harder manner/ drawn at the end of the 15th cent/ at the period of transition.* Another typed label *This drawing cannot be much earlier than 1505–10 and appears to be close to Cosimo Roselli*
On mount Popham's typed attribution as a contemporary and accurate copy of Ghirlandaio's painting in the gallery at Volterra, (Palazzo dei Priori) and note to the effect that the drawing was lent to Popham at the British Museum between 27 June and 29 October 1949
Provenance: Roscoe sale, 1816, lot 48 as a "Capital drawing by Ghirlandaio", bt. Slater 15*s.*; C.R. Blundell, valued 12*s.* in 1841
WAG1995.285

ATTR. ANTONIO GIONIMA
Venice 1697–1732 Bologna
The rape of Deianira
285 × 210 mm, brush and brown ink with a thin strip added on left
Inscribed in ink on mount *Aug°
Caracci*; in pencil, lower right corner an attribution to *?A. Gionima* initialled *RABD*
Provenance: Robert Udney

early German master", bt. Slater £1. (along with Figino, .101; After Dürer, .240; and Attr. Parmigianino, .253); C.R. Blundell, all four valued at 12*s.* in 1841
WAG1995.328

The suggestion that it might be by a Southern German master was made by Dr Stephanie Buck (letter, 16 July 1996).

SOUTH GERMAN SCHOOL
ca. 1525
The Holy Trinity in glory surrounded by a choir of angels

285 × 185 mm, pen and brown ink, arched top. Formerly folded into eight sections
Album page inscribed in pencil (?)*Metre...l Sper....*
Provenance: 'Pseudo-Crozat' (L474); Henry Blundell (?)
WAG1995.147

AFTER DOMENICO GHIRLANDAIO
16th century
Christ seated on clouds surrounded by angels and five saints below
330 × 218 mm, pen and brown ink and brown wash, arched top

(L2248), sold 4–10 May 1803 as Anibal Carracci, part of lot 108, "the Rape of Dejanira, masterly sketch in bistre", bt. 4*s.* 6*d.* by P[hilipe?]; Roscoe sale, 1816, lot 373, as Agostino Carracci, bt. Slater 18*s.*; C.R. Blundell, valued at 15*s.* in 1841
WAG1995.203

Mario di Giampaolo agrees with the Gionoma attribution (in conversation, 30 October 1997). Formerly attributed to Elisabetta Sirani.

WAG 1995.88

WAG 1995.250

NICOLOSIO GRANELLO

Genoa *ca.* 1500–*ca.* 1560 Genoa
*Christ driving the money changers
from the temple*
405 × 280 mm, pen and brown ink
and wash
Inscribed on mount in pencil *G.B.
Gaulli/ detto Bacicchio*; 2
Typed label by Popham *Not Gaulli.
Genoese or Venetian XVI cent.*
Provenance: John George, 2nd Earl
Spencer (L8019), sold T. Philipe,
10f. June 1811, lot 118, attr.
Cambiaso, "Christ driving the
buyers and sellers out of the temple
– spirited pen and bistre, broad
wash", bought in to R[oscoe or
Reserve?] 10*s.* 6*d.*; Roscoe sale,
1816, lot 229, as Gio. Battista
Gaulli called Baciccio, bt. Slater £1.;
C.R. Blundell, valued at £1. 6*s.*,
along with a "Gaulli Nativity"
(Verona School, .89)
Literature: Noted in Larry Turcic,
review of 'Le Dessin à gênes du
XVIe au XVIIe siècle', *Master
Drawings*, XXIII–XXIV, 1968, p. 244,
n. 19, pl. 54b, as Granello
WAG1995.88

Mary Newcome agrees with Larry
Turcic's attribution of the drawing
to Granello (letter, 23 May 1996).

FOLLOWER OF GIOVANNI
FRANCESCO GRIMALDI (?)

*Landscape with a tall tree, bushes and
distant hills*
240 × 365 mm, pen and brown ink
and brown wash
Attr. to Grimaldi by Waagen on
mount
Provenance: Benjamin West (no
collector's stamp but inscribed in
pencil on mount *West Bolognese*);

WAG 1995.51

WAG 1995.51 VERSO

WAG 1995.146

C.R. Blundell
WAG1995.250

WAG 1995.275

ATTR. GUERCINO

(Giovanni Francesco Barbieri)
Recto: *Studies of a man's turbanned
head with an open mouth and a boy's
head in profile*
Verso: *Four studies of hands*
280 × 185 mm, black oiled chalk

heightened with white on grey-
brown paper
Watermark on mount Pv (?)
Inscribed in ink on mount *Guercino*;
in pencil on mount ...[?] *genuine*
Provenance: Benjamin West (L419;
inscribed in pencil on mount *West
Bolognese*); C.R. Blundell
WAG1995.51

CIRCLE OF GUERCINO

Venus in Vulcan's Forge
235 × 192 mm, pen and brown ink
and grey wash
Inscribed in ink on mount *Guercino*
Provenance: 'Pseudo-Crozat'
(L474); Henry Blundell (?)
WAG1995.146

AFTER GUERCINO (ATTR.)

Study of the head of a young boy
243 × 185 mm, black chalk
heightened with white on faded
blue paper
Inscribed in ink on mount
Domenichino
Provenance: Benjamin West (L419;
inscribed in pencil *West Bolognese
School*); C.R. Blundell
Literature: Noted in N. Turner and
C. Plazzotta, *Drawings by Guercino
from British Collections*, exh. cat.,
London, British Museum, 1991, no.
81, p. 277
WAG1995.275

An "indifferent" copy after a
drawing in the British Museum
(1946–7–13–83) in oiled charcoal
touched with white chalk on rough
buff coloured paper, 402 ×
276 mm, attributed to Guercino.

GIOVANNI GUERRA

Modena 1544–1618 Rome
*A man (St Paul?) reading out from a
scroll surrounded by a crowd with
tents in the background*
110 × 107 mm, pen and brown ink
and brown wash
Provenance: Roscoe sale, 1816, lot
351, as Bartolommeo Cesi, "Two,
Historical Subjects; pen and bistre",
bt. Slater 10*s.* (along with .61);
C.R. Blundell, valued at 8*s.* in 1841
WAG1995.60

Attributed to Guerra by John Gere
and Julien Stock.

WAG 1995.60

WAG 1995.61

WAG 1995.212

WAG 1995.114

WAG 1995.213

GIOVANNI GUERRA
*An apostle (St Paul?) preaching to the
multitude*
110 × 115 mm, pen and brown ink
and wash
Provenance: Roscoe sale, 1816, part
of lot 351, as Bartolommeo Cesi, bt.
Slater 10s. (along with .60);
C.R. Blundell, as above
WAG1995.61

Both Guerra drawings are possibly
related to his *Life of St Paul*, in the
Ecole des Beaux-Arts, Paris, Musée
des Beaux-Arts, Poitiers (inv. 2554,
fol. 5, and inv. 890–326, 890–327;
see C. Monbeig Goguel, 'Giovanni
Guerra da Modena', *Arte Illustrata*,
VII, 1974, pp. 164ff., figs. 7, 18) and
Metropolitan Museum, New York
(inv. 1978.376; J. Bean, *15th and
16th Century Italian Drawings in the
Metropolitan Museum of Art*, New
York 1982, no. 104).

GIOVANNI GUERRA
Procession of pilgrims
182 × 264 mm, pen and brown ink,
brown wash
Tissue-paper cover watermarked
J Watt & Co.
Inscribed in gold lettering on mount
L: Spada; on back in ink lower right
corner *Lionel Spada/ n°65*. An
erased collector's mark (?) in lower
right corner of drawing
Provenance: Roscoe sale, 1816, part
of lot 423, as Lionello Spada, "A
Sovereign stripped and conveyed to
prison, in a procession of ecclesias-
tics. VERY CURIOUS & FINE",
bt. Slater 15s. (along with
WAG1995.213); C.R. Blundell,
both valued at 12s. in 1841
WAG1995.212

Attributed to Guerra by John Gere.
Possibly related to Guerra's *Life of
San Gemigniano*, patron saint of
Modena (see *Libro di immagini con
storie di San Geminiano*, Modena,
Archivio Storico, exhibited in *Libri
di immagini, disegni e incisioni di
Giovanni Guerra*, Modena, Palazzo
dei Musei, 1978, cat. 6).

GIOVANNI GUERRA
*Military commander giving audience
to two ambassadors in his camp
(outside Bologna?)*
180 × 261 mm, pen and brown ink
and wash
Inscribed on mount in gold lettering
L: Spada
Collector's mark (?) erased in lower
right corner
Provenance: Roscoe sale, 1816, part
of lot 423, as Spada, "a
Commander giving audience to
Ambassadors in his camp", bt.
Slater 15s. (along with .212);
C.R. Blundell, as above
WAG1995.213

GILES HUSSEY
Marnhull 1710–1788 Beeston
A centaur tamed by Cupid
355 × 265 mm, red chalk
Provenance: 'Pseudo-Crozat'
(L474); Henry Blundell (?), no. 65,
as Hussey
WAG1995.114

Either a copy after the restored
antique statue formerly in the
gardens of Cardinal Scipione
Borghese's Palazzo del Borgo,
Rome (as engraved in *Raccolta di*

WAG 1995.138

WAG 1995.169

WAG 1995.73

WAG 1995.123

WAG 1995.97

WAG 1995.239

statue antiche e moderne, 1704, pl.
LXXII), or a 'reconstruction' of one
of the 2nd-century BC grey marble
Centaurs (minus cupid but
supported by a tree-trunk) by
Aristeias and Papias, discovered at
Hadrian's Villa at Tivoli in 1736
when Hussey was in Rome, and
now in the Capitoline Museum
(*Masterpieces of the Capitoline
Museum*, Rome 1996, pp. 30–31),
which was engraved by
Dequevauvillier after a drawing by
Vauthier (see Warburg Institute
photo files).

ITALIAN SCHOOL
16th century
Study of an Evangelist
90 × 70 mm, oval, pen and brown
ink, attached to the same sheet on
which there is an etched
reproduction of the drawing
(WAG1995.139)
Provenance: 'Pseudo-Crozat'
(L474); comte de Saint-Morys, as
Beccafumi; Henry Blundell (?)
WAG1995.138

The drawing must have been in
London by 21 May 1793, when it
was etched for the comte de Saint-
Morys's *Disegni originali d'eccelenti
pittori incisi ed imitati nella loro
grandezza col. parte 1*. Rejected as
Beccafumi by Popham.

ITALIAN SCHOOL
16th century
Cupid and a putto
126 × 83 mm, red chalk, irregularly
cut paper
Inscribed on paper repair *Raphaelo*
Provenance: J. Richardson Senior
(L2183); 'Pseudo-Crozat' (L474);
Henry Blundell (?)
WAG1995.169

According to Christie's thought to
have an Arundel provenance.

178

ITALIAN SCHOOL
late 16th century
St Ursula and her companions
222 × 310 mm, pen and brown ink
and wash heightened with white
(oxidized)
Provenance: Unknown, possibly
Roscoe sale, 1816, lot 291, as
Claudio Ridolfi, "the Empress
S Helena embarking with her
attendants on a voyage for the
promoting of Christianity. Pen and
bistre 9h 12w", bt. either Martin or
Slater 12s. (according to William
Ford's annotated copy of the sale
catalogue in British Museum);
C.R. Blundell, as Ridolfi, valued at
8s. in 1841
WAG1995.123

ITALIAN SCHOOL (?)
16th century
*Apollo and eight Muses with musical
instruments seated around a fountain*
98 × 157 mm (mount size), pen and
brown ink and wash fragment
patched around all edges
Inscribed in ink on mount
*Baldassare Peruzzi/ di Siena, Pitti e
Arch*
Provenance: William Young Ottley,
sold 14 June 1814, lot 939; Roscoe
sale, 1816, part of lot 93, as Peruzzi,
"Four [subjects] three on one Leaf,
viz. ... Apollo and the Muses on
Mount Parnassus/ From Mr.
Ottley's Collection", bt. Slater 17s.
(along with exh. cat. 42 and
Peruzzi, .244); C.R. Blundell,
valued at 13s. in 1841
WAG1995.97

ITALIAN SCHOOL
ca. 1600?
*Four Evangelists with Sts Peter and
Paul seated at a table*
197 × 203 mm, pen and brown ink
Inscribed in ink on backing card
*Lodovico Carracci/ The four
Evangelists with S. Peter &/ S. Paul*;
in pencil *genuine & v good; 8 (?)
Square*
Provenance: Roscoe sale, 1816, lot
357, as Lodovico Carracci, "The
four Evangelists with their symbols;
fine pen/ 8sq.", bt. Slater; C.R.
Blundell, valued at 9s. in 1841
WAG1995.73

WAG 1995.348

ITALIAN SCHOOL
17th century
*Christ blessing and holding the orb
(Salvator Mundi)*
187 × 126 mm, black chalk on
faded blue paper heightened with
white, squared
Watermark on mount cut off by
edge of mount: fleur-de-lys W (and
L?)
Inscribed in ink on mount, lower
right corner *dominichino*; and in
pencil <u>very fine</u> *of the Bolognese
School*
Provenance: Benjamin West (L419;
inscribed in pencil on mount *West
Bolognese*); C.R. Blundell
WAG1995.239

ITALIAN SCHOOL (?)
17th century
*Study of the head of a man in great
agitation*
155 × 130 mm, red chalk
Provenance: Nathaniel Hone
(L2793); Sir Joshua Reynolds
(L2364); Benjamin West (?; no
collector's stamp); C.R. Blundell,
possibly one of the "Three Studies
from West's collection", as
Michelangelo, valued at £1. 12s.
in 1841
On same sheet of card as .349,
Florentine School *ca.* 1500–1550
WAG1995.348

Formerly attributed to Neapolitan
School.

WAG 1995.161

WAG 1995.267

ITALIAN SCHOOL (?)
ca. 1700
Venus and Cupid (?)
104 × 155 mm, pen and brown ink
and wash within an ink framing line
Inscribed in ink on mount
Giminiani
Provenance: 'Pseudo-Crozat'
(L474); Henry Blundell (?)
WAG1995.161

ITALIAN SCHOOL
18th century
*A Bacchanalian procession of monks
towards a temple*
360 × 510 mm, pen and brown ink
with grey and brown washes
Inscribed on mount by Roscoe (?) *I
BEONI*; in pencil on backing card
not genuine
Provenance: Roscoe sale, 1816, lot
381, attr. Annibale Carracci, bt.
Slater 14s.; C.R. Blundell, as
Agostino Carracci, valued at 12s.
in 1841
WAG1995.267

Attributed by Christie's to Pier
Leone Ghezzi.

ITALIAN SCHOOL (?)
ca. 1790–1800
A Roman sarcophagus: Phaeton imploring Helius to lend him his chariot
112 × 360 mm, pen and grey ink and wash with fractures (?) on the original sculpture indicated in red chalk
Provenance: Henry Blundell
WAG1995.122

The sarcophagus, from the 2nd century AD, was part of Henry Blundell's collection of antique statuary at Ince Blundell (Ince. 523, Liverpool Museum; see J. Fejfer and E. Southworth, *The Ince Blundell Collection of Classical Sculpture*, I: *The Portraits*, London 1991, p. 14, fig. 3). Blundell purchased the sarcophagus twice, once *ca.* 1790 for £10 from the Villa d'Este, after which he had it cleaned of the mineral salts which disfigured it, and was made to give it to the pope in return for five marble-topped tables; and secondly for £260 from a Christie's sale in 1800 of works pillaged from papal apartments by French troops *Account* 1803, pp. 179–80, Appendix p. 310).

ATTR. ITALO-FLEMISH SCHOOL
ca. 1600
Figures in a Venetian (?) city street
162 × 138 mm, pen and brown ink
Notes on mount: Popham did not agree with Parmigianino attribution. J. Stock suggests Biliverti.
Provenance: Prosper Henry Lankrink (L2090); Wiliam Young Ottley (L2664); Roscoe sale, 1816, part of lot 335, as Parmigianino, "Six, various subjects/ From Lanckrinck's, Richardson's and other collections", bt. Slater £1. 9s. (along with attr. Annibale Carracci, exh. cat. 15 and Roman School, .58, .57, attr. Creti circle, .296 After Parmigianino); C.R. Blundell, all valued at £1. 4s. in 1841
WAG1995.71

ATTR. PIETER VAN LAER
Haarlem 1599–1642? Haarlem
A group of seven men, three seated, four standing
88 × 190 mm, pen and brown ink and brown wash on blue paper
Provenance: 'Pseudo-Crozat' (L474); comte de Saint-Morys (?); Henry Blundell (?)
WAG1995.143

A related etched partial copy possibly by the comte de Saint-Morys is WAG1995.144

AFTER JAN DE LAIRESSE
Agamemnon and Iphigenia
Verso: *Agamemnon*
256 × 384 mm, recto: grey wash and brown ink, markings for squaring up; verso: black chalk
Inscribed in ink in Dutch *de duik hier*[?] *van komt int klijn van het Schilderboek V. G. D. Larresse*; on back lower right corner *932*
Provenance: Unknown Dutch collection; Roscoe sale, 1816, lot 512, as Lairesse, bt. Slater 7s. 6d.; C.R. Blundell, valued at 6s. in 1841
WAG1995.266

In reverse and enlarged from the print by Gillem van der Gouwen (1673–?) after Jan de Lairesse on p. 133 of Gérard de Lairesse, *Groot Schilderboek*, Haarlem 1707. The illustrations for the *Groot Schilderboek* were done by Jan de Lairesse under the control of Gérard but they were redrawn for engraving by Philips Tideman (1657–1705) and Otmar Elliger (1666–1732) (A. Roy, *Gérard de Lairesse*, Paris 1992, pp. 55, 133).

CIRCLE OF GIOVANNI LANFRANCO
Sts Peter and Paul with an angel holding an escutcheon
Verso: *Studies of a nude male figure, limbs and a foot*
215 × 180 mm, recto: pen and brown ink and wash; verso: red chalk
Inscribed in ink on verso *441*; in pencil on mount *Mola*; in pencil on backing *?after drawing attr. to/ Bernini in Fachsenfeld/ Collection – see Catalogue/ H. Macandrew Oct.74.* Other attributions on tissue paper include *Giovanni Lanfranco/ Tiepolo* (?)
Provenance: 'Pseudo-Crozat' (L474); Nathaniel Hone (L2793);

WAG 1995.122

WAG 1995.143

WAG 1995.266

Roscoe sale, 1816, part of lot 419, as Giovanni Lanfranco, "Design for the Papal Arms, supported by an Angel and attended by St Peter and St Paul/ 9h 7w / From Count Caylus's and Mr. Hone's Collection", bt. Slater 14s.; C.R. Blundell, as Elisabetta Sirani, valued at 12s. in 1841, along with Attr. Mola (?) WAG1995.214
WAG1995.210

Nicholas Turner suggested that the penmanship and washes were more characteristic of Pier Francesco Mola (1612–1666) (letter, 26 November, 1996). Richard Cocke thought it was typical of the pen-and-wash style of Mola's follower Giovanni Battista Pace (born *ca.* 1640–45, active 1660s) (letter, 28 February 1997; see Cocke, 'The

WAG 1995.71

Drawings of Michele and Giovanni Battista Pace', *Master Drawings*, XXIX, 1991, pp. 347–84).

WAG 1995.210

WAG 1995.273

WAG 1995.182

WAG 1995.210 VERSO

WAG 1995.166

WAG 1995.216

VALENTIN LEFEVRE
Brussels 1642–1680/82 Brussels
Female figure carrying an infant
150 × 73 mm, pen and brown ink
and brown wash, squared, fragment
patched at top
Watermark on mount: large
crowned circle hidden by drawing
Inscribed in ink on mount *Paolo
Veronese*; and in pencil *genuine*
Provenance: Sir Joshua Reynolds
(L2364); Benjamin West (no
collector's stamp; inscribed in
pencil on mount *West Venetian*);
C.R. Blundell
Literature: U. Ruggieri, 'Drawings
by Valentin Lefèvre', *Master
Drawings*, XXVI, 1988, no. 35, pl. 19
WAG1995.216

Identified by Ruggieri as a fragment
of a preliminary study for a figure
at the right of a *Presentation in the
Temple* which reflects an unknown
composition by Paolo Veronese and
relates to two other examples of the
subject, in Munich, Staatliche
Graphische Sammlung inv. Z1452
and formerly in the collection of
Baron Speck von Sternberg
Lutzchena, both as Veronese.

AFTER LEONARDO (?)
*Eleven heads, mostly caricatures in
profile*
165 × 190 mm, pen and light-
brown ink on pinky-buff paper
Inscribed in ink *Lionardo da vinci*;
typed label suggests *Possibly a 17th
centy. copy. The head of youth looking
down on the right suggests Van Dyck.*
Inscribed in pencil on card backing
some probably genuine; in pencil on
mount lower left corner *A true
drawing very fine*; on reverse of

mount in ink *Old Masters*; in pencil
very good drawing
Unattached tissue paper J WATT
& Cº PATENT COPYING;
inscribed in pencil *Lionardo da
Vinci/ Florentine School*
Provenance: Roscoe sale, 1816, part
of lot 56, as "Lionardo da Vinci",
bt. Slater for £1. (along with
WAG1995.274, now After
Parmigianino, *Profile of a youth*);
C.R. Blundell, together valued at
16s. in 1841
WAG1995.273·

MANNER OF PAOLO
LOMAZZO
Sts Francis and Stephen
225 × 242 mm, black chalk, pen
and brown ink and wash heightened
with white on blue paper, squared
in black chalk
Inscribed in ink in lower right
corner *100*
Provenance: 'Pseudo-Crozat'
(L474); Henry Blundell (?), no. 12,
as Ludovico Carracci
WAG1995.182

Popham attribution to Pier
Francesco Morazzone.

LOMBARD SCHOOL
ca. 1580?
Study of an angel
175 × 95 mm, black chalk and grey
wash heightened with white,
squared in red chalk on green paper
Provenance: 'Pseudo-Crozat'
(L474); Henry Blundell (?)
WAG1995.166

WAG 1995.291

WAG 1995.327

WAG 1995.53

LOMBARD SCHOOL (?)
16th century
An evangelist writing with an angel
85 × 137 mm, grisaille heightened
with gold on green prepared paper
(damaged) with ink framing lines
Provenance: Alfonso IV d'Este,
Duke of Modena (L106; collector's
mark in top right corner), sold (?)
1796; Roscoe sale, 1816, part of lot
363 as "Lodovico Carracci an
Evangelist writing. A grand idea, in
bistre,/ heightened with gold./ 3½h
5½w" bt. Slater £1. 7s. along with
Attr. Lodovico Carracci, .98; C.R.
Blundell, valued £1.5s in 1841
WAG1995.291

Confirmed attribution on mount to
Ludovico Carracci by Julien Stock
in 1974. Formerly Ferrarese School,
St John the Evangelist.

LOMBARD SCHOOL (?)
16th century
*Design for the decoration of an
arcaded loggia with trompe-l'oeil nude
figures*
Verso: *Studies of a nude torso*
224 × 390 mm, recto: pen and
brown ink and wash; verso: black
chalk
Lengthy inscription on the back in
pencil relating it to Palazzo Farnese
(Alexander Farnese crowned by
Victory) from a description of
Rome published in 1779 (see
Roscoe sale, 1816, entry); label with
attribution to *Roman School –
Vignola* on mount
Provenance: Roscoe sale, 1816, lot
80, as Michelangelo, "the Interior
of the Great Hall in the Palazzo
Farnese at Rome, with three
Groups of Figures in Niches,
resembling the style of
Michelangolo"; and thus noticed in

the *Descrittione della città di Roma*,
1779, II, p.204: "*Nella gran Sala (del
Pallazzo Farnese) vi sono &c. ed un
gruppo grande di Alessandro Farnese
coronato dalla Vittoria, con la
Fiandria dinanzi a lui inginochiata
ed il fiume Escaut* [Scheldt]
*incatenato sotto i suoi piedi 9h.
15½w.*", bt. Ford for £1. 2s.; C.R.
Blundell as "Michelangelo Interior
of the Palazzo Farnese", valued at
10s. in 1841
WAG1995.327

Popham tentatively suggested Lelio
Orsi and believed it to be definitely
North Italian.

FOLLOWER OF CARLO MARATTA
Moses and the gathering of manna (?)
265 × 412 mm, black chalk
heightened with white on blue-grey
paper
Inscribed on drawing in ink in
Resta's hand *L'ebbi dal med°. e lo
crede a/ di Carlo, ma io non lo credo*;
in ink on mount under framing
lines *Luca Giordano*
Provenance: Padre Sebastiano
Resta; J. Richardson Junior
(L2170), with an attribution to
Giordano; Benjamin West (L419);
C.R. Blundell
WAG1995.53

Formerly attributed to Roman
School, late 17th century, as
St Peter and the daughter of Jairus.

MARCO DA FAENZA
(Marco Marchetti)
Faenza 1526–*ca.* 1588 Faenza
*Design for a vaulted chapel or aisle
chapel with Sts Peter and Paul, the
Virgin and Child, and four
Evangelists in pendentives*

341 × 192 mm, pen and brown ink
and brown wash
Inscribed in ink on mount *Giacomo
Sansovino*; on back in Italian
attribution to Niccolò Tribolo, pupil
of Sansovino; at top in red ink *P.8.*
Provenance: J. Richardson Junior
(no collector's mark, with his
attribution to Sansovino); Roscoe
sale, 1816, part of lot 95, as
Sansovino, "Interior and Cieling of
a Hall, with Statues and
Decorations. Pen and bistre./ 13½h.
8w./ From Richardson junr.'s
Collection", bt. Ford £1. (along
with WAG1995.272, now Attr.
Domenico Fontana, *Design for a
papal monument*); C.R. Blundell,
valued at 16s. in 1841
WAG1995.271

Attribution to Marco da Faenza due
to Popham and Gere. Alessandro
Cecchi suggested that it might be
related to a proposal by Marco for a
chapel in the Palazzo Vecchio,
Florence (in conversation, June
1997).

WAG 1995.271

ATTR. MASTELLETTA
(Giovanni Andrea Donducci)
Bologna 1575–1655 Bologna
*Study for an altarpiece with five
female saints: Sts Lucy, Agatha,
Cecilia, Catherine and Agnes (?)*
255 × 175 mm, pen and brown ink
and brown wash heightened with

WAG 1995.300

WAG 1995.176

WAG 1995.204

WAG 1995.110

WAG 1995.202

WAG 1995.204 VERSO

gold on brown-grey prepared paper
Inscribed in ink on mount *Agostino Tassi*
Provenance: 'Pseudo-Crozat' (L.474); Henry Blundell (?), no. 8, as "Terri" (a misreading of Tassi?)
WAG1995.176

Formerly attributed to Ferrarese School, late 16th century. Reattribution to Mastelleta, who knew Tassi in Rome *ca.* 1610 (C.C. Malvasia, *Felsina pittrice* [1678], edn. Bologna 1841, II, pp. 67–71), suggested by Nicholas Turner (in conversation 15 August 1995).

CIRCLE OF GIOVAN MAURO DELLA ROVERE (?)
Angels making music seated on clouds
283 × 215 mm, brush and brown wash heightened with white on blue

paper within inscribed oval
Inscribed in ink on back attribution to F. Lippi; typed label says wrongly attr. Filippo Lippi; on mount comment by J. Gere
Lombard close to one or other of the della Rovere
Provenance: Roscoe sale, 1816, lot 35, as Filippino Lippi, "a Concert of Angels, on blue paper heightened. Capital./ 11½h. 9w.", bt. Ford £1.; C.R. Blundell, valued at 16s. in 1841
WAG1995.300

Hugo Chapman disagrees with the Della Rovere attribution.

ATTR. GIOVANNI BATTISTA MERANO
Genoa 1632–1698 Piacenza
Roundel of a triton fighting a centaur within a wreath (frontispiece to a collector's album?)
167 × 170mm (mount size 425 × 275mm); pen and brown ink
Inscribed in ink on mount *CAV: GIO: BATTISTA PAGGI/ GENOVESE/ Raccolta Ghirtleriana*
Provenance: Ghirtler (?), unknown Italian collector; Roscoe sale, 1816, lot 147, as Paggi, *Battle of Centaurs*

and Sea Monsters, in an ornamental circle, bt. Slater 14s. (along with Castiglione, exh. cat. 17, and Circle of Castiglione, *Christ on Cross*, .198)
WAG1995.202

Attribution to Merano made by Mary Newcome, who suggests it might have been a design for a stucco medallion *ca.* 1650s–60s (see M. Newcome, 'Giovanni Battista Merano in Liguria', *Paragone*, XXXIII, July 1982, no. 389, p. 23).

AFTER MICHELANGELO
16th century
The statue of Rachel
380 × 190 mm, black chalk, grey wash heightened with white on buff paper indented around figure
Provenance: 'Pseudo-Crozat' (L.474); Henry Blundell (?), no. 54, as Michelangelo
WAG1995.110

Popham believed that this drawing derived from the statue of *Leah* in San Pietro in Vincoli, Rome, but Paul Joannides correctly identified it as *Rachel*, finished in 1545 for the tomb of Pope Julius II. Few other known drawn copies after Rachel other than by Figino (P. Joannides, *Michelangelo and his Influence. Drawings from Windsor Castle*, exh. cat., Washington DC 1996, p. 139). Possibly drawn from the statue rather than the reduced statuette visible in the portrait by Alessandro Allori (1535–1607) of *Ortensia de' Bardi da Montauto* painted in 1559 (Uffizi, illus. S. Lechini Giovannoni, *Alessandro Allori*, 1991, no. 176)

AFTER MICHELANGELO
16th century
Studies of Joram and Jehosophat from the Sistine Chapel
Verso: *Study of an outstretched right arm of a man*
266 × 425 mm, recto: black chalk

WAG 1995.307

WAG 1995.214

WAG 1995.352

with colour notes in the form of letters *R, B, V*, on drapery. Verso: black chalk. Patched in three corners
Notes on mount *Jaffé suggests Rosso or possibly Pontormo as copyist Stock disagrees*
Provenance: Lamberto Gori; William Young Ottley (L2662), sold June 1814, lot 1761; Roscoe sale, 1816, lot 66, "Two Designs on one sheet for Groups in the Capella Sistina. A Charity &c. Black chalk, CAPITAL. Size 11 h. 17 w. From the Collection of Lamberto Gori, afterwards Mr Ottley's", bt. Slater £2. 14s.; C.R. Blundell
Same provenance also described on

tissue-paper cover
WAG1995.204

Colour notes suggest that it must have been drawn from the original, yet the pose of the right-hand child held by Jehosophat is different in the fresco and Joram does not hold a pen, which might suggest that the drawing might record *modelli* by Michelangelo (P. Joannides, letter 22 March 1996). Similar lettering as colour notes found on Ashmolean's black-chalk copy after *Jonah* from the Sistine Chapel (Parker 359, 402 × 281 mm).

AFTER MICHELANGELO
16th century
Christ on the cross with the Virgin and St John with angels
455 × 303 mm, black chalk. Angels drawn in very faintly in black chalk. Patched in top corners and at sides
Inscribed in ink on drawing *k.52*; in ink on mount *Michelangelo*; on back in ink a lengthy inscription transcribed from Resta's inventory *Michel Angelo/ Fatta per la Marchesa di Pescara allora habitante in Viterbo; Dama dilettante inamorata della Virtù di Mich. Angelo/ come lui della virtù de lei*; and a lengthy comment by Richardson Junior: *This is the Crucifix they show at Rome in the Palace Borghese as that for which the Porter was kill'd; the Story is well/ known but not Believ'd even here & indeed to see the Picture nobody can imagine any such thing, so farr from a strong Expression/ of a Dying Man that 'tis Tame & Spiritless, nor is it Good in other respects as may be seen in part by the Drawing/ but there is a greater want of harmony, & Contrast than is perceiv'd here, for the Angels over the heads of/ the two Sts. on each side of the Crucifix being but just touch'd out is some advantage to it, as is the want of Bright/ Lights like the Sun & Moon in the Eclipse wch in the Picture is very regularly plac'd over each Arm of Christ. The/ Figures are about a foot long. There is another like Crucifix of this Ma. at S. John lateran's Only without the Virgin/ & St John & that the Picture is somthing bigger. R.jun.*; along the bottom *E' Collectione D^m Domini Joh^s: Sommers*; in upper left corner *2j 2 ifi*
Provenance: Padre Sebastiano

Resta, sold between 1698 and 1702; Mons. Marchetti, Bishop of Arezzo; Lord John Somers (*k.52*); Jonathan Richardson Senior (L2184), shelfmark on verso *V.40/ M201/ Zp20 Zm 57 Za*; John Barnard (L1417–19), inv. 410; Roscoe sale, 1816, lot 76, bt. Slater £3. 15s.; C.R. Blundell
WAG1995.307

Paul Joannides suggested that this is more likely a copy after a *cartonetto* for the painting Michelangelo made for his servant Urbino *ca.* 1556, based on a drawing he had made for Vittoria Colonna *ca.* 1541, and later painted by Marcello Venusti, now Galleria Doria, Rome (letter 22 March 1996). The drawing is by neither Venusti nor Giulio Clovio, the possible copyist of the comparable Louvre drawing (inv. 843), but probably another 16th-century artist. Roscoe also owned another "Michelangelo", *Crucifixion*, lot 75, "Christ on the Cross, a Figure in the Clouds on each side of him, in atttitudes of Lamentation. Exquisitely finished in black chalk, and undoubtedly ... designed for the Marchesa di Pescara. 15½h. 10½w. From the Collection of C. Jennings, Esq. with the ancient Print by Niccolò Beatrizet, after the same." A drawing fitting this description was in Ottley's sale, 1814, lot 1591.

AFTER MICHELANGELO
The Adoration of the Brazen Serpent
370 × 562 mm, black chalk spandrel shaped in two halves on two separate sheets of paper on

which part of the design has been repeated, joined together and slightly misaligned. Very slight fragments of a 'Mariette' blue mount around edge of drawing paper
Inscribed in ink on back *Michael Angelo Original/ 1629*; in pencil *one of the angles of the Sistine Chapel/ v Vasari 229 Ed. Bot*
Provenance: Roscoe sale, 1816, lot 72, as Michelangelo, bt. Slater for 3 gns.; C.R. Blundell, valued at £2. 10*s*. in 1841
WAG1995.352

Roscoe's 'graingerized' proof copy (Liverpool Central Library) of his *Leo X*, 1805, ch. XXII, p. 242, is illustrated with a print of the Brazen Serpent spandrel and annotated "Copy of a drawing by Raffaello from a picture of Michelangelo in the ceiling of the Sistine Chapel at Rome from which it is supposed that he endeavoured to improve his style from the works of Michelangelo". The print seems to reproduce the left-hand three-quarters of Roscoe's drawing. J.H. Fuseli made a black-chalk copy of the lower right corner of the Sistine *Brazen Serpent* in *ca.* 1777–78. (G. Schiff, *Johann Heinrich Füssli*, Zurich 1973, no. 670, p. 112; P. Bjurström, *German Drawings in Swedish Public Collections*, Stockholm 1972, no. 522.)

ATTR. PIER FRANCESCO MOLA
Coldrerio 1612–1666 Rome
Christ walking on the waves
189 × 265 mm, pen and brown ink
Inscribed in ink on mount *Cav. Gio. Lanfranco*
Provenance: Roscoe sale, 1816, part of lot 419, as Giovanni Lanfranco, "Christ saving Peter; bold pen sketch/ 7h. 10½w", bt. Slater 14*s*. (along with Circle of Lanfranco, .210); C.R. Blundell, as Elisabetta Sirani, valued with .210 at 12*s*. in 1841
WAG1995.214

Attributed to Giovanni Battista Pace by Richard Cocke (letter, 27 February 1997).

IL MONCALVO (?)
(Guglielmo Caccia)
Montabone 1568–1625 Moncalvo
Loosely draped youth seated with profile to left
190 × 235 mm, pen and ink and brown wash
Inscribed in black chalk *Parmegiano*
Provenance: 'Pseudo-Crozat' (L474); Henry Blundell (?), no. 6, Parmigianino
WAG1995.118

Popham rejected Parmigianino attribution. Stock suggested Moncalvo.

ATTR. GIOVAN BATTISTA NALDINI (?)
after Franciabigio
Fiesole *ca.* 1537–1591 Florence
The return of Cicero in triumph
207 × 242 mm (image size 192 × 225 mm), red chalk
Note inscribed in pencil on old tissue-paper cover, possibly in Roscoe's hand *The Return of Cicero in allusion to the return of Cosimo de Medici*. Pencil comment on mount *not genuine – later period*
Provenance: Roscoe sale, 1816, lot 91, as Andrea del Sarto, "A sketch for the picture at Poggio Cajano, afterwards executed by Franciabigio", bt. Slater 19*s*.; C.R. Blundell, valued at 16*s*. in 1841
WAG1995.230

Attributed by Popham to Naldini. A copy (?) after the red-chalk drawing in the Uffizi (14441F, 209 × 251 mm, image size 192 × 226 mm) attributed by Pouncey to Francesco Salviati (*Philip Pouncey per Gli Uffizi: Disegni italiani di tre secoli*, exhib. cat., Florence, Uffizi, 1993, cat. 8) which is derived from the left side of the fresco by Franciabigio in the Great Hall at the Medici villa of Poggio a Caiano.

CIRCLE OF ADRIAEN VAN OSTADE
Two musicians and other figures
72 × 90 mm, pen and brown ink over lead pencil. Repaired along left hand strip
Provenance: 'Pseudo-Crozat' (L474); Henry Blundell (?)
WAG1995.170

Popham attribution to Adriaen; Gere (?) suggested Isaac.

PALMA IL GIOVANE
(Jacopo Negretti)
Venice 1544–1628 Venice
A man praying
100 × 82 mm, pen and brown ink over black chalk heightened with white on blue paper. In new mount
Provenance: Unknown
WAG1995.79

WAG 1995.80

WAG 1995.70

WAG 1995.177

WAG 1995.113

WAG 1995.355

PALMA IL GIOVANE
St Francis holding a skull
100 × 80 mm, pen and brown ink
heightened with white on blue
paper. In new mount
Provenance: Unknown
WAG1995.80

Both this and WAG1995. 80 are
probably late Palma Giovane.

PALMA IL GIOVANE
*Sts Carlo Borromeo and Bernardino
adoring the Holy Trinity*
290 × 158 mm, pen and ink and
wash over black chalk, squared in
red and black chalk, with an
inscribed arch
Inscribed on back in ink *ID 278*
Provenance: Thomas Hudson
(L.2432); 'Pseudo-Crozat' (L474);
Henry Blundell (?), no. 23, as
Palma Vecchio
WAG1995.113

Preparatory study for the altarpiece
in the parochial church of Rovato,
Brescia, signed and dated *Jacobus
Palma F 1620* (S. Mason Rinaldi,
Palma il Giovane: L'opera completa,
Milan 1984, cat. 255, pp. 107,
445–46, fig. 705 (painting) and 706
(drawing, illustrated in reverse).

CIRCLE OF PALMA IL GIOVANE (?)
Martyrdom of St Lawrence
300 × 414 mm, pen and brown ink
and brown wash
Inscribed in ink on back *C/ f.º13
Nº11*
Provenance: Roscoe sale, 1816, lot
273, as Jacopo Palma senior, bt.
Slater £1. 9s.; C.R Blundell, valued
at £1. in 1841
WAG1995.70

Attribution to Circle of Palma by
Pouncey. The composition is
similar to a reversed and adapted

form of Palma Giovane's
Martyrdom of St Lawrence for San
Giacomo dall'Orio, Venice, *ca.*
1581–82 (Mason Rinaldi 1984, cat.
391, fig. 61).

FOLLOWER OF PALMA IL GIOVANE
Study of St John the Baptist
266 × 190 mm, pen and brown ink
and brown wash on blue paper
Inscribed in ink on drawing, lower
left corner the figures *f2/9*–; on
mount in ink *Tintoretto*
Provenance: 'Pseudo–Crozat'
(L474); Henry Blundell (?), no. 7,
as Tintoretto
WAG1995.177

The figure may have been intended
for a *Baptism of Christ*, although no
figure in this pose appears in any of
Palma Giovane's paintings or
compositional drawings for the
subject. A figure of Christ in this
pose appears in the preparatory
study for Palma's *Christ in glory
blessing Doge Renier Zen* (Mason
Rinaldi 1984, cat. 519, fig. 88).

ATTR. BERNARDINO DA PARENZA
Parenzo 1437–1531 Vicenza
*Fragment of a design for a Madonna
(?) enthroned with five prophets and
four putti reading at the base*
106 × 270 mm, pen and brown ink
on vellum cut irregularly on top and
left side
Old backing had attribution to
Cimabue on reverse. Present
attribution made by J. Byam Shaw
in 1942
Provenance: 'Pseudo-Crozat'
(L474); Henry Blundell (?)
Exhibitions: Venice 1982, no. 2, as
Bernardo Parentino
WAG1995.355

Comparison with the musical
cherubs in the painted *Musicians
between antique fragments*, Berlin,
illustrated in A. di Niccolò Salmazo,
Bernardino da Parenza, Padua 1989,
suggests that the drawing is unlikely
to be by Bernardino.

ATTR. PARMIGIANINO
(Francesco Mazzola)
Parma 1503–1540 Casalmaggiore
Proportions of the female figure
115 × 42 mm, pen and brown ink,
irregularly shaped fragment
Framed in an unusual mount with a
raised design in green and gilt
Inscribed in ink on mount *Albert
Durer*; inscribed in pencil on mount
by Waagen (?) *very pretty*
Provenance: Roscoe sale, 1816, part
of lot 605, as Dürer, bt. Slater £1.
(along with Figino, .101, German
School, .328, and After Dürer,
.240); Henry Blundell (?)
WAG1995.253

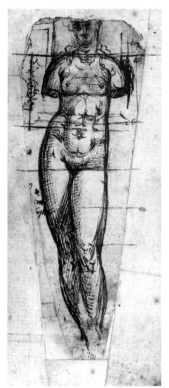

WAG 1995.253

WAG 1995.133

WAG 1995.159

WAG 1995.296

WAG 1995.274

WAG 1995.126

Popham thought it was by Parmigianino and related to similar drawings in Parma, possibly referring to Galleria Nazionale, Parma, inv. 510/4 (Gernsheim photo 119526).

MANNER OF PARMIGIANINO

Seated Prophet with a cherub (?)
110 × 100 mm, pen and brown ink and wash heightened with white on pink prepared paper
Provenance: 'Pseudo-Crozat' (L474); Henry Blundell (?)
WAG1995.133

AFTER PARMIGIANINO

Studies of three standing men, one writing, and three heads, two of putti
176 × 136 mm, pen and brown ink and brown wash (standing figures) red chalk (heads)
Inscribed in ink on drawing *Parmixiano*; in ink on mount *Parmigiano*; in ink lower right corner *N° 56*
Provenance: John Barnard (L1420), with his measurements cut off by left edge of mount; Robert Udny (L2248), possibly Philipe sale, 4–10 May 1803, lot 294, "Six various, mostly pen designs, some with bistre, one red chalk"; Roscoe sale, 1816, probably part of lot 335, as Parmigiano, "Six, various subjects/ From Lanckrinck's, Richardson's and other Collections", bt. Slater £1. 9s. (along with Attr. Annibale Carracci, exh. cat. 15, and Roman School, .58, Attr. Creti circle, .57, Attr. Italo-Flemish School, .71)
WAG1995.296

A close copy with very slight variations (lower cherubs' eyes open rather than closed) after the Parmigianino drawing in the Uffizi, inv. 13583F recto (see A. E. Popham, *Catalogue of the Drawings of Parmigianino*, New Haven 1971, no. 102, recto, pl. 129, pen and wash, 185 × 142mm).

AFTER PARMIGIANINO

Seated philosopher
107 × 74 mm, pen and brown ink and wash
Inscribed on tablet in drawing *O 15/.A*
Provenance: 'Pseudo-Crozat' (L474); comte de Saint-Morys (?); Henry Blundell (?)
WAG1995.159

Drawing in the same direction and almost same size (105 × 73 mm) as the etching by Master F.P. (see *The Illustrated Bartsch*, ed. Henri Zerner, XXXII, New York 1979, p. 31, no. 19 (24). The original Parmigianino drawing in the opposite direction and without the tablet shown in the Weld-Blundell drawing is at Chatsworth (inv. 795A, pen and brown ink and brown wash on a yellowish ground heightened with white, 102 × 72 mm, Popham 1971, no. 724, pl. 175, pp. 16–17). There is an etched reproduction of WAG1995.159 possibly for the comte de Saint-Morys in the Weld-Blundell collection (WAG1995.360).

AFTER PARMIGIANINO (?)

Profile head of a youth
201 × 145 mm, pen and brown ink
Inscribed on back at top *Bon° 1 Par°*; at lower left corner in brown ink *4621*; at lower left corner in red ink *Lot 205*
Provenance: Sir Joshua Reynolds (L2364); Roscoe sale, 1816, part of lot 56, as Leonardo, bt. Slater £1. (along with After Leonardo, .273); C.R. Blundell, together valued at 16s. in 1841
WAG1995.274

GIUSEPPE PASSERI

Rome 1654–1714 Rome
Six figures adoring the Holy Sacrament
330 × 245 mm, pen and brown ink and wash over red chalk heightened with white
Inscribed in red ink on mount *Giuseppe Passari*; at top in pencil *no. 5*
Provenance: Roscoe sale, 1816, lot 213, as Passeri, bt. Slater 13s.; C.R. Blundell, valued at 9s. in 1841
WAG1995.126

Attribution to Passeri confirmed by Dr Dieter Graf (letter 12 December 1997).

WAG 1995.229

WAG 1995.209

WAG 1995.207

CIRCLE OF GIUSEPPE PASSERI (?)

Christ before Pilate

326 × 298 mm, pen and brown ink and brown wash heightened with white (oxidized), lightly squared
Watermark on mount: D & Co. Blauw, countermark of a double Z within a shield
Inscribed in ink on mount *Marco Cardisco, detto il Calabrese*; on reverse in ink a Latin quotation from Matthew 27.24 regarding Pilate washing his hands *Lumens Aquam lavit manus, curam turba, dicens Innocens sum a Sanguine Justi huius*; and in same hand at bottom *Marco Cardisco, detto il Calabrese, Fiori nel 1536, Questo è il disegno Originali per gli Quadro da lui depinto nella Chiesa S Agostino in Napoli/ Gi/2*; in pencil on reverse lower right corner *No –8–*
Provenance: Thomas Hudson (L.2432), possibly Langford sale, 24 March 1779, lot 31, "Two by Calabrese &c. sold £3.10s."; Benjamin West (without mark); C.R. Blundell
WAG1995.229

Pouncey attributed it as 17th-century Neapolitan School (?). Marco Cardisco's altarpiece for Sant'Agostino in Naples, painted in 1530, was of *St Augustine disputing with the heretics* (now in the Museo Nazionale, Rome).

ATTR. PERINO DEL VAGA

(Piero Buonaccorsi)
Florence *ca.* 1500–1547 Rome
Studies for four scenes from the story of Neptune

210 × 275 mm, pen and brown ink and very slight wash (upper rank), black chalk (lower rank)
Tissue-paper cover watermark of Watt & Co, with pencil attribution *Perin del Vaga* and at bottom *N°50/ CWB*
Provenance: Roscoe sale, 1816, part of lot 102, as Perino, "Sketches of Figures &c – 3 compartments", bt. Ford 8s. 6d.; C.R. Blundell, valued at 8s. along with .207
WAG1995.209

ATTR. FOLLOWER OF PERINO DEL VAGA

Design for a frieze: two panels showing Noah's Ark and the Flood flanked by figures of Faith, Hope and Charity

205 × 394 mm, pen and brown ink, brown wash heightened with white (oxidized) on thin greenish-blue paper
Tissue-paper cover inscribed in pencil *No.45 CWB* and attribution *Perino del Vaga Flor*
Provenance: Roscoe sale, 1816, part of lot 102, as Perino, "Design of a Façade of an Interior, with Sculptures and Pictures. pen and bistre heightened/ 7h 15w", bt. Ford 8s. 6d.; C.R. Blundell, valued at 8s. with .209 in 1841
WAG1995.207

BALDASSARE PERUZZI

Siena 1481–1536 Rome
Half-draped figure of Penelope in mourning (after the antique)
Verso: *Schematic ground-plan of a columned vestibule*

132 × 90 mm, pen and brown ink
Provenance: William Young Ottley, 6 June 1814, lot 939; Roscoe sale, 1816, part of lot 93 (sold along with Peruzzi, exh. cat. 42, Italian School, .97 and Attr. Sodoma, .50), bt. Slater 17s.; C.R. Blundell, valued at 13s. in 1841
Exhibition: Edinburgh 1969, no. 66, pl. 15
Literature: C.L. Frommel, *Baldassare Peruzzi als Maler und Zeichner, Beiheft zum römischen Jahrbuch für Kunstgeschichte*, XI, 1967–68, p. 152, cat. 111, fig. XCIIb
WAG1995.244

Recto identified by Ruth Rubinstein as a drawing of the headless figure of Penelope in mourning in the Louvre (letter 4 October 1996; Warburg Institute photo files: 'Editions Tel', Musée du Louvre, III, pl. 215B) but also comparable to the figure of *Penelope mourning* between her housekeeper Eurykleia and two other women on a 1st-century BC terracotta in the British Museum, London, of which Cassiano dal Pozzo had a drawing made in the 17th century (D.609, ex Townley, illustrated in Pierre Grimal, *The Dictionary of Classical Mythology*, trans. A.R. Maxwell-Hyslop, 1986, p. 355. The type is fairly common: see H. Hiller, *Archäologische Anzeiger*, 1972, pp. 47–67; Ian Jenkins, 'Newly discovered drawings from the Museo Cartaceo in the British Museum', *Cassiano dal Pozzo: Atti del Seminario Internazionale di Studi*, ed. F. Solinas, Naples 1987, p. 154 fol. 34.). The verso was identified by Christoph Frommel as possibly a first idea for the entrance vestibule of the Palazzo Massimo alle Colonne in Rome, on which Peruzzi began to work *ca.* 1532 (C. Frommel, in conversation, June 1997).

AFTER GIAMBATTISTA PIAZZETTA

ca. 1740
Four young men in an interior
210 × 275 mm, oil on paper (grisaille)
Inscribed in ink *Invenzione di Giambatista Piazzetta*; on back in ink *C _?120*
Provenance: Unknown Venetian known as the 'Reliable Venetian Collector' (L3005c–d); 'Pseudo-Crozat' (L474); H. Blundell (?)
Exhibition: Venice, 1980, no. 68
WAG1995.95

According to Stock a contemporary copy of Piazzetta's illustration to page 181 of Book V, *Reflections Générales sur les Agitations de Melancton et sur l'Etat de la Reforme*, of J.B. Bossuet, *Hisoire des Variations ...* (*Oeuvres* II, 1738), for which the original preparatory drawing in chalk is in the Biblioteca Reale, Turin.

AFTER POLIDORO DA CARAVAGGIO

An antique sacrifice, from the Milesi façade
222 × 293 mm, pen and brown ink and brown wash heightened with white (oxidized) on faded blue-green paper
Inscribed on back in ink in (Latin?) *pictor vasos*[?]
Provenance: Roscoe sale, 1816, part of lot 191, as Polidoro, "a Christian compelled to Worship Idols", bt. Ford £1. 17s. (along with .313); C.R. Blundell, together valued at £1. 12s. in 1841
WAG1995.312

Copied from Polidoro's façade of the Milesi Palace, via della Maschera d'Oro, Rome showing the central portion of the *Story of Niobe, ca.* 1526–27. For the various engravings after the façade see P. Pouncey and J. Gere, *Raphael and his Circle*, exh. cat., London, British Museum, 1962, cat. 225.

AFTER POLIDORO DA CARAVAGGIO

The slaying of Niobe and her children, from the Milesi façade
225 × 265 mm, pen and brown ink and brown wash heightened with white (oxidized) on faded blue-green paper (as WAG1995.312)
Inscribed on back at top in ink *Polidore*, followed by a cross with crosses on each arm. On back of mount in lower left corner in red *30*
Provenance: Giov. Matteo Marchetti (?), Bishop of Arezzo (L2911; his mark (?) on back of mount); Roscoe sale, 1816, part of lot 191, bt. Ford £1. 17s. (along with .312); C.R. Blundell, as above
WAG1995.313

The *Story of Niobe* was the most celebrated and one of the most frequently copied of Polidoro's Roman narrative friezes, located below the first-floor windows on the façade of the Palazzo Milesi on the via della Maschera d'Oro. For some other copies see J. Byam Shaw, *Italian Drawings from the Frits Lugt Collection*, Paris 1983, cat. 444; S. McCullogh, *Catalogue of Italian Drawings before 1600 in the Art Institute of Chicago*, Chicago 1997, cats. 587–91.

AFTER POLIDORO DA CARAVAGGIO

Two Roman tribunes and their dogs, from the Palazzo Milesi façade
405 × 274 mm, pen and brown ink heightened with white on blue-green paper
Inscribed in ink on mount lower right corner *Polidoro da Caravaggio*; on mount in pencil *not genuine*
Provenance: J Richardson Junior (L2170); Benjamin West (L419; inscribed in pencil *West Roman*); C.R. Blundell
WAG1995.351

A copy after the same figures without the background buildings is in the Victoria and Albert Museum, inv. CAI412.

AFTER GUGLIELMO DELLA PORTA
ca. 1600
Study for the tomb of Pope Paul III in St Peter's
325 × 195 mm, pen and brown ink and brown wash
Inscribed on mount in ink *Il Deposito di Paolo III in S. Pietro a Roma, F. Guglielmo della Porta –*; in pencil below *v. Lett. Pittruche 2.148*. Inscribed on back in brown ink *N.42/ Emineti Pauli III Monumento Statua Pauli anca Pontificio in Habitu expressa/ due inferiores Statua e Marmore sedentes ad Tumulum prolixe commendant/ Gulielmi a Porta Mediolanenius Peritiam, qui suo Sculpto non tantium finas/ Pontificis pauli Virtutes ad vivum expressit scilicet Prudentiam Justitiam/ sed in altera earum, Julia Pauli Sororis, in altera vero eiusdem Matris Effigiem/ ut affirmat Floravante Martinellus in sua Historia a Philippo Bonani.
p. 91/ Bonani's Print differs from this Drawing, for there the Monument has a more lofty/ appearance than here, and two Boy-Angels are sitting over the two angular Masques/ but no Pediment nor the Statues of Charity, Plenty on each side the Arms.*; below in brown ink *Il Deposito di Paolo III (Farnese) in S. Pietro in Vaticano, fatto con Staue di/ Marmo, e Bronzo sotto la Direttione di Michel Angelo Buinaroti da Fra/ Guglielmo della Porta; Opera sopra tutte considerabile – Nuovo Studio di Pittura/ Scoltura &c. nelle Chiese di Roma dell'Alb. Fil. Tito p.10.11 – Vide Vasari Parte III.b.p.256*
Provenance: Padre Sebastiano Resta (?) with Resta-type

inscription on back in Italian; Jonathan Richardson (?; no mark but inscription in Latin and English on back), possibly 24 January 1746/47, lot 44, "Four drawings Lionardo da Vinci and Guglielmo della Porta, bt. Dr. Chauncey £1. 12s.); Roscoe sale, 1816, part of lot 97, as Gulielmo della Porta, bt. Slater for £1. 1s. (along with After Venusti, .195); C.R. Blundell, valued at 8s. in 1841
WAG1995.52

Showing the tomb figures as they were *ca.* 1600, after the lower reclining figures had been covered by drapery in 1593 and before the upper figures were removed by Teodoro della Porta in 1602 (see W. Gramberg, 'Guglielmo della Portas Grabmal für Paul III Farnese in San Pietro Vaticano', *Römisches Jahrbuch fur Kunstgeschichte*, XXI, 1984, p. 280, cat. 3.Z.9, fig. 18).

AFTER GUGLIELMO DELLA PORTA WORKSHOP
The bust of a bishop
205 × 172 mm, pen and brown ink
Inscribed in ink on mount *titiano*; pencilled attribution on album *Venetian ca. 1500*, initialled *J.U.C.*
Provenance: 'Pseudo-Crozat' (L474); Henry Blundell (?), no. 50, as Titian
WAG1995.148

Formerly North Italian School, second half of the 16th century.

ATTR. CAMILLO PROCACCINI
Bologna *ca.* 1555–1629 Milan
Christ comforted and supported by two angels
135 × 107 mm, pen and brown ink and brown wash
Inscribed in ink on drawing above Spencer mark *70* (?); inscribed in pencil on mount *Camilo Procaccini*; on back of mount in ink at top *G/ N°25*; at bottom *N°633 proharino Camomillo Procaccino/ Born 1546ᵈ :1626*
'Roscoe' tissue-paper cover with J. Watt & Co. watermark inscribed in pencil *Camillo Procaccini/ Bolognese School*; in different hand below *N°9° CWB*
Provenance: Lanier (?; his star mark (?) above Spencer); John George, 2nd Earl Spencer (L1531

or 1532), sold 10 June 1811, lot 632, as Procaccino, "Christ standing between two angels", bt. P[hilipe] 10s.; Roscoe sale, 1816, lot 354, bt. Slater 9s.; C.R. Blundell, valued at 7s. in 1841
WAG1995.299

CIRCLE OF CAMILLO PROCACCINI
The Resurrection of Christ
375 × 280 mm, pen and brown ink and wash squared with red chalk
Inscribed in ink lower left corner *all'organo di Milᵒ*; in ink lower right corner *h.94*; in pencil on mount lower left corner *G. Romano*: in pencil on mount *not genuine probably by Vasari (?)*; on back of mount in pencil *Ulysses Aldrovandini*; and lower right corner *1–16–6* (?); Popham annotation *by another Milanese Cerano*
Provenance: Ulysse Aldrovandi (?); Padre Sebastiano Resta; Lord John Somers (*h.94*); J. Richardson (?; no collector's mark but his (?) shelfmark on back *N17/ N.160*); Roscoe sale, 1816, lot 184, as Giulio Romano, bt. Slater 15s.;

C.R. Blundell, as after Raphael (?), valued at 12s. in 1841
WAG1995.87

Believed wrongly by Resta to be for Procaccini's design for the organ shutters in Milan Cathedral.

ATTR. BIAGIO PUPINI
fl. 1511–51 Bologna
Sketches of two nymphs carrying a child and a rabbit on a garland, and a child, goat, open fireplace, oil-lamp and vase
140 × 183 mm, pen and brown ink and brown wash heightened with white on brown paper. Paper patched and toned in the lower left corner
Inscribed on lower edge of drawing in ink *Giulio Pippi il Romano*; on back in ink at top *H;/ f.°31 N=°45*; and in pencil *47*(within a circle) and *365*
Attributions on mount *Giovanni da Udine*; in separate hand initialled *RABD*; *Biagio Pupini*
Provenance: Roscoe sale, 1816, part of lot 181, as Giulio Romano, bt. Slater 12s. (along with Attr. Romano, .200 on same mount); C.R. Blundell
WAG1995.201

SCHOOL OF RAPHAEL
Nine putti dancing
100 × 184 mm, red chalk on octagonal shaped paper, badly foxed
Inscribed on mount in ink lower left corner *Raphael*
Attribution pencilled on mount *probably genuine Raffael/ VRU* (?)
Provenance: 'Pseudo-Crozat' (L474); comte de Saint-Morys (?); Henry Blundell (?), no. 33, as Raphael
WAG1995.151

Copied (?) from Marcantonio Raimondi's print after Raphael (Warburg Institute photo files). The drawing was in London by 20 December 1793, when it was etched for publication in the comte de Saint-Morys's *Disegni originali d'eccelenti pittori incisi ed imitati nella loro grandezza col. parte 1* (WAG1995.152 is a later impression of the print).

WAG 1995.91

AFTER RAPHAEL
The Holy Family with St Elizabeth, infant St John and two angels (The Madonna of Francis I)
215 × 165 mm, pen and brown ink and wash heightened with white
Popham annotation *a bad copy after part of Raphael's "Francis I" Madonna in the Louvre*
Provenance: 'Pseudo-Crozat' (L474); Walsh Porter (?), 1790? (according to Christie's valuation); Henry Blundell (?)
WAG1995.91

AFTER RAPHAEL
The Holy Family with St Elizabeth, infant St John and two angels (The Madonna of Francis I)
342 × 225 mm, black and red chalk
Inscribed in ink on mount lower right corner *Raphael*
Provenance: 'Pseudo-Crozat' (L474); Henry Blundell (?), no.1, as Raphael, valued with .91 at £4. 4s. in 1841
WAG1995.145

AFTER RAPHAEL
Epileptic boy, from the Vatican Transfiguration
380 × 218 mm, red chalk heightened with white (oxidized) on yellowish paper, arched top
Provenance: 'Pseudo-Crozat' (L474); Henry Blundell (?), no. 45, as Cristoforo Albani
WAG1995.111

WAG 1995.201

WAG 1995.151

WAG 1995.145

WAG 1995.111

WAG 1995.112

WAG 1995.242

WAG 1995.288

WAG 1995.243

AFTER RAPHAEL
*Scene from the Vatican Loggie:
Melchizedek and Abraham*
207 × 275 mm, black and red chalk
Inscribed in ink on drawing *142.n*
Provenance: Padre Sebastiano
Resta (?)/ Lord John Somers
(*142.n*); 'Pseudo-Crozat' (L474);
Henry Blundell (?), no. 58 as
"Crayer"
WAG1995.112

Popham rejected 'Crayer'
attribution and Resta provenance.
Jaffé accepted Resta provenance.
A copy after the fresco in the
Vatican Loggie in which
Melchizedek offers bread and wine
to Abraham (N. Dacos, *Le loggie di
Raffaello*, Rome 1977, section IV.1,
pp. 165–66, pl. XIX).

AFTER RAPHAEL
*The Holy Family with St Elizabeth
and St John*
242 × 195 mm, pen and brown ink
on brown tinted paper, arched top
Inscribed in ink on mount *Rafaelle
d'Urbino*; on back in brown ink a
lengthy description of the drawing
(not here transcribed) as related to
the painting commissioned by
Domenico Canigani *Seconda
maniera di Raffaelle uscito da Pietro
dovindo Pietro andar a Fiorenza
Rafaelle con alcuini giovanni anda/ a
Citta Castello ... lavorò p quelche
mese ...* [final sentence] *da Michel
Angelo cono grandezza e scoglienecto
maggiore che non haveva sotto Pietro
Perugino /cosi stama socitto sotto 'l
Disegno precedente a questo/ di M.
Angelo/.* Signed *P. Resta M.S.*,
followed by a long quote from
Vasari, vol. 1, pt. 3, ed. Fior, p. 601
Provenance: Padre Sebastiano
Resta; Jonathan Richardson Senior,

no collector's mark but his
shelfmark *DD.54/ Z39. Zn.5u P.43.
J[?]* and a lengthy inscription;
Benjamin West (L419);
C.R. Blundell
WAG1995.242

AFTER RAPHAEL
*The Madonna and Child with the
infant St John the Baptist (The Esterhazy Madonna)*
252 × 170 mm, pen and brown ink
brown wash
Inscribed on back of mount in
pencil *genuine, original Esterhazy
Vienna/ very precise record ...*; in a
different hand *an old copy of the
Uffizi drawing*, with a reference to
an illustration of the Uffizi drawing
in a Burlington House exhibition in
1930 (inv. 593E, see below).
Provenance: Roscoe sale, 1816, lot
166, bt. Slater £1. 15s.; C.R.
Blundell, valued at £1. 10s. in 1841
Literature: Noted in *L'officina della
maniera: Varietà e fierezza nell'arte
fiorentina del Cinquecento fra le due
repubbliche 1494–1530*, exhib. cat.,
Florence, Uffizi, 1996, p. 156,
cat. 42
WAG1995.288

An almost exact 'forgery',
reproducing even the paper folds in
the original and varying only in very
minor landscape details, of the
pounced drawing by Raphael in the
Uffizi no. 539E, paper size 285 ×
190 mm, image size 252 × 175 mm.

AFTER REMBRANDT
*Sarah complaining to Abraham about
Hagar*
179 × 280 mm, pen and brown ink

with three dark resinous stains
Inscribed on mount in pencil
genuine and v.good
'Roscoe' mount with tissue paper
watermarked John Hayes 1814
Provenance: Roscoe sale, 1816, part
of lot 499, as Rembrandt, "Two
historical. Pen.", bt. Slater 10s.
(along with .286); C.R. Blundell,
valued at 8s. in 1841
WAG1995.243

Weak copy after a drawing in
Bayonne, collection Bonnat, which
Benesch attributed to Rembrandt,
dating it to 1643–44 (O. Benesch,
Drawings of Rembrandt, London
1973, III, no. 549, fig. 680).

AFTER REMBRANDT
*Thetis urges Achilles to return to the
battle against Troy*
188 × 277 mm, pen and brown ink
and brown wash
Inscribed in pencil on mount *not
genuine of the school*
'Roscoe' tissue paper mount
annotated in pencil *Rembrandt/ 165/
CWB Title: Thetis asking Achilles to
renounce the fight* [sic]/ *about 1633/
Kd.Kst. II 569*
Provenance: Roscoe sale, 1816, part
of lot 499, bt. Slater 10s. (along
with .243); C.R. Blundell, as above
WAG1995.286

A poor copy, with various mistakes,
after a drawing by Rembrandt in
the Pierpont Morgan Library, New
York (previously Warwick Castle
collection), dated by Benesch to the
early 1640s (Benesch 1973, IV, no.
A.45, fig. 1049).

WAG 1995.286

WAG 1995.99

WAG 1995.69

WAG 1995.373

WAG 1995.58

IMITATOR OF REMBRANDT
Isaac witholding his blessing from Esau
185 × 240 mm, pen and brown ink with brown wash
Inscription in ink in lower left corner cut off ... *Rembrandt* ...
'Roscoe' tissue paper cover with John Hayes 1814 watermark with pencilled note *Rembrandt/ 110/ CWB*
Typed label relating it to a drawing *ca.* 1636 and a painting formerly belonging to Earl Brownlow
Provenance: Daniel Daulby, sold T. Vernon, Liverpool, 16 August 1799, lot 86 (2), Rembrandt, "Isaac blessing Jacob" (along with a "St Jerome in a cave"); Roscoe sale, 1816, lot 494, bt. Slater 10s. 6d.; C.R. Blundell, valued at 8s. in 1841
WAG1995.69

A copy to which wash has been added after a drawing formerly in the Parisian collection of E. Wauters, 161 × 201 mm (W.R. Valentiner, *Rembrandt Handzeichnungen*, Stuttgart, Berlin and Leipzig 1925, cat. 68).

AFTER ORAZIO RIMINALDI
The martyrdom of St Cecilia
543 × 352 mm, brush and brown ink heightened with white on buff paper
Provenance: Benjamin West (L419); C.R. Blundell
WAG1995.373

Copy of the altarpiece painted by Riminaldi in the early 1620s originally intended for the Pantheon but placed by the artist in the church of Santa Caterina, Pisa. In 1697 Grand Prince Ferdinando de' Medici removed it to the Pitti Palace, Florence.

ATTR. GIUSEPPE ROLLI
Bologna 1652–1727 Bologna
Study for a lunette: an apocalyptic vision of St John the Evangelist
206 × 298 mm, pen and brown ink and pale brown wash over black chalk
Tissue-paper cover watermarked J Watts & Co
Inscribed in ink on mount *Canuti*; on back in ink *Domenico Maria Canati, Bolognese, Disc. of Guido 1623 ... 1678. In Palazzo Popoli*
Provenance: J. Richardson junior (L2170); Roscoe sale, 1816, lot 426, as Domenico Maria Canuti, "St. John the apocalypse. Pen and bistre, FINE. / "And when I saw him I fell at his feet as one dead.", bt Slater 11s.; C.R. Blundell, valued at 12s. with exh. cat. 11
Literature: E. Feinblatt, 'Some Drawings by Giuseppe Rolli identified', *Master Drawings*, XXX, 1982, p. 26, pl. 30
WAG1995.99

ROMAN SCHOOL
ca. 1580
St Peter and five other saints or apostles and a kneeling figure
133 × 70 mm, pen and brown ink with brown wash, badly affected by fly blow
Provenance: Roscoe sale, 1816, part of lot 335, as Parmigianino, "Six, various subjects. From Lanckrinck's, Richardson's and

WAG 1995.231

WAG 1995.236

WAG 1995.237

other Collections", bt. Slater £1. 9s.
(along with Attr. Annibale Carracci,
exh. cat. 15, Attr. Creti Circle
WAG1995.57, Attr. Italo-Flemish
School, .71, and After Parmigianino,
.296); C.R. Blundell
WAG1995.58

A photograph of the drawing in
Witt Library files is annotated
anonymously N. Circignani
(Pomarancio).

ROMAN SCHOOL
16th century
*A pope investing a monk (?) with a
cardinal's hat*
335 × 274 mm, pen and brown ink
brown wash heightened with white
(oxidized)

WAG 1995.234

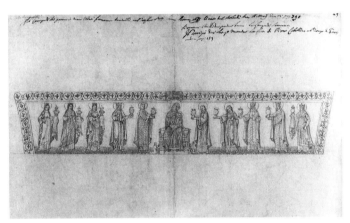

WAG 1995.235

Tissue-paper cover watermarked
J Watt & Co.
Provenance: Roscoe sale, 1816, lot
52, as Signorelli, bt. Slater 15s.;
C.R. Blundell, valued at 12s. in
1841
WAG1995.231

ROMAN SCHOOL
ca. 1600–30?
*Copy from Pietro Cavallini's mosaics
in Santa Maria in Trastevere: three
sections showing: The Annunciation
and Nativity; Dormition of the
Virgin; Adoration of the Kings and
Circumcision*
310 × 425 mm, red chalk
Inscribed on drawing in Resta's
hand *Portico di S Maria in
Trastevere/ Anche il portico di S
Maria Trastevere/ credo que posse
tutto depinto dal Cavallini/ ma
essendo stato imbiancato la pittura/
sono periti. Solamente è stato portato/
rispetto a cassa (?) SS. Nunziata e a
qualche/ abbia fe—ina (?) che dalla in*

*anima si reversa (?) essere opere del
nostro artifice – Bottari Jesuita (?) al
Vasari vol.1.10.16–*
Provenance: Part of a series
acquired for Monsignor Marchetti,
Bishop of Arezzo, by Padre
Sebastiano Resta; Lord John
Somers; Roscoe sale, 1816, lot 4, as
Roman School Early Masters, bt.
Slater 19s.; C.R. Blundell, valued at
16s. in 1841
Literature: A.E. Popham,
'Sebastiano Resta and his
Collections', *Old Master Drawings*,
XI, 1936, p. 5
WAG1995.234

ROMAN SCHOOL
ca. 1600–30
*Copy from Cavallini's mosaics in
Santa Maria in Trastevere: façade:
Queens bearing gifts to the Madonna
suckling the Child*
304 × 425 mm, red chalk
Inscribed in ink on drawing in
Resta's hand lower left corner

facciata di/S.ª Mª in trastevere; in ink
along top long inscription including
date (?) and page reference *pag.153*
in Resta's (?) hand; on old 'Roscoe'
tissue paper in pencil *from Mosaic
ceilings/ in Rome/ not properly
belonging to the Roman/ School but
placed here/ as curious [?]/ See
Roscoe's Cat/ Lot4*
Provenance: as above
WAG1995.235

ROMAN SCHOOL
ca. 1600–30
*Copy from Cavallini's mosaics in
Santa Maria in Trastevere: The Birth
of the Virgin (?)*
142 × 145 mm, red chalk
Inscribed in ink on drawing *49 tra
finestra di S. Maria Trastevere*; in
pencil on back *Pietro Cavallini
Nos.97–*
Provenance: as above
WAG1995.236

ROMAN SCHOOL
ca. 1600–30
*Copy from Cavallini's mosaics in
Santa Maria in Trastevere: The
Dormition of the Virgin*
140 × 145 mm, red chalk
Inscribed in ink on drawing *49 Tra
finestra in SM.ª in Trastevere*; in
pencil lower right corner *4*
Provenance: as above
WAG1995.237

Possibly part of the book of twenty-
four drawings by Agostino
Ciampelli (1565–1630), who
worked in Santa Maria Trastevere
in 1600, after early medieval
mosaics in churches of Rome which
Resta sent to Marchetti in 1700
(G. Warwick, 'The Formation and
Early Provenance of Padre
Sebastiano Resta's Drawing
Collection', *Master Drawings*, 1996,
XXXIV, p. 248, n. 60). The album
went to England but was not
recorded in Landsdowne 802 (see
Collector's Biographies) but sold in
British Museum Ms. Somers's sale,
1717, part 3, EE, lot 6. The whole
album was in Roscoe's collection.
Nine other drawings from the set
are in Edinburgh (National Gallery
of Scotland, D1050–1058) three of
which are also of Santa Maria in
Trastevere (D1054–D1056).

WAG 1995.318

WAG 1995.137

WAG 1995.179

ROMAN SCHOOL
17th century
A bishop seated in front of an altar surrounded by deacons and kneeling figures
266 × 252 mm, pen and brown ink and brown wash with several losses
Inscribed on back in red ink lower right corner *2^d Day/ Lot 22=*
Provenance: Benjamin West (no collector's mark; inscribed in pencil on mount *West*); C.R. Blundell
WAG1995.318

ROMAN SCHOOL
18th century
Four copies of Roman reliefs
140 × 203 mm, pen and brown ink on brown paper
Faint pencil notes in Italian under each scene including under top left *trionfo*
Provenance: 'Pseudo-Crozat' (L.474); Henry Blundell (?)
WAG1995.173

Top right and lower two scenes appear to derive from but not copy reliefs on the Arch of Constantine.

ATTR. GIULIO ROMANO
Rome 1485–1546 Mantua
Moses seated, holding the tablets
200 × 250 mm, pen and brown ink and wash over red chalk
Inscribed in ink on drawing top left corner *Z 30*, and an illegible name
Provenance: 'Pseudo-Crozat' (L.474); Henry Blundell (?), no.10, as F. Borghese
WAG1995.137

CIRCLE OF GIULIO ROMANO
Sketch of an eagle with outstretched wings
90 × 183 mm, pen and brown ink and brown wash
Inscribed in pencil below drawing *Giulio Romano*; Pouncey attr. *not Giulio*
Provenance: Sir Peter Lely (L.2092–94); Roscoe sale, 1816, part of lot 181, as Romano, bt. Slater 12s. (along with Attr. Bagio Pupini, .201); C.R. Blundell
WAG1995.200

MANNER OF GIULIO ROMANO
The martyrdom of St Lawrence
305 × 220 mm, pen and brown ink with brown wash heightened with white
Popham attribution to School of Giulio Romano
Provenance: 'Pseudo-Crozat' (L.474); Henry Blundell (?), no. 55, as Pompeo Battoni
WAG1995.179

WAG 1995.173

WAG 1995.200

JOHANN HEINRICH ROOS
Reipolskirchen 1631–
1685 Frankfurt
The Wrath of Ahasuerus
Verso: *Figure of Haman*
295 × 390 mm, recto: pen and
brown ink and grey wash over black
chalk, signed and dated in grey
wash *JHRoos fecit/ 1665*; verso: pen
and brown ink, inscribed in Dutch
and Latin in Gothic script *aut
mander mus*[?]/ *geerten heins ——
treint das*; followed by five lines of
illegible script
'Roscoe' tissue-paper cover
watermarked John Hayes/ 1814

Provenance: Roscoe sale, 1816, lot
513, bt. Slater 10s.; C.R. Blundell,
valued 8s. in 1841
WAG1995.309

FOLLOWER OF RUBENS
*Perseus petrifying Phineus and his
men with the Medusa shield*
140 × 180 mm, pen and brown ink
and wash over red chalk
Attribution in pencil on album page
Spagnoletto
Provenance: 'Pseudo-Crozat'
(L474); Henry Blundell (?)
WAG1995.165

AFTER RUBENS AND
VAN DYCK
The drunken Silenus with satyrs
315 × 300 mm, pen and brown ink
and wash over black chalk
Provenance: 'Pseudo-Crozat'
(L474); Henry Blundell (?), no. 56,
as Rubens
WAG1995.128

All the figures apart from the three
putti in the left foreground are
copied from *The drunken Silenus* in
Munich, Alte Pinakothek, datable to
ca. 1616–18. The putti are taken
from Van Dyck's version of the
same subject in Berlin, Staatliche
Museen, dated to *ca.* 1618–19. For
the style of the drawing see the
woodcut by Christoffel Jegher, *ca.*
1633–35 (illus. J.S. Held, *Rubens:
Selected Drawings*, rev. edn. Oxford
1986, p. 280, pl. 218, no. 212).

CIRCLE OF GEORGE PHILIP
RUGENDAS
Augsburg 1666–1741 Augsburg
*A fight between a cavalry officer and a
Turk*
285 × 295 mm, brush and black ink
heightened with white on slate-blue
paper
Inscribed in ink on drawing lower
right corner [?]*Johan_Z* [or]
dotra_z; on reverse of secondary
support in ink *611/* (?).*U.K. 13*
Provenance: 'Pseudo-Crozat'
(L474); Henry Blundell (?), no. 64,
as Wostermans
WAG1995.120

ATTR. NORTHERN
FOLLOWER OF FRANCESCO
SALVIATI
*St Catherine disputing with the
grammarians of Maxentius*
141 × 417 mm, pen and brown ink,
brown wash, heightened with white
(oxidized and overcleaned (?) in
one area) on greenish paper within
a ink-drawn frame
Inscribed on drawing in ink initials
[?]*oc*; in ink on mount by
Richardson Junior *Cecchino del
Salviati*; on reverse in ink
CHRISTIANA sum; on reverse in
pencil *San Elena*
Tissue-paper cover watermarked
J Watt & Co.
Provenance: J Richardson Junior
(L2170); Charles Rogers (L625),
Philipe sale, 20 April 1799, part of
lot 592 (along with a "Roman
triumph" now British Museum, inv.
Pp. 2–183, Salviati, *The Triumph of
Camillus*), and "a female figure";
Roscoe sale, 1816, lot 110, as
Francesco Salviati, "St. Helena
avowing herself a Christian before
the Emperor", bt. Slater 10s. 6d.;
C.R. Blundell, as Perino del Vaga,
valued at 12s. in 1841
WAG1995.59

WAG 1995.120

WAG 1995.59

WAG 1995.106

MANNER OF ANDREA DEL
SARTO
The Madonna and Child
240 × 140 mm, pen and brown ink
covered by blue wash
Inscribed in ink on drawing *Andrea
del Sarto*; mount annotated by Gere
??Beccafumi
Provenance: 'Pseudo-Crozat'
(L474); Henry Blundell (?), no. 16,
as Andrea del Sarto
WAG1995.178

CHRISTOPH SCHWARZ (?)
Munich *ca.* 1548–1592 Munich
Christ washing the apostles' feet
203 × 292 mm, grey ink and grey
wash heightened with white
(partially oxidized) on light
buff/brown paper. The secondary
support paper used as backing to
the drawing is a page from an
Italian account book starting "*Add
Ultimo Detto ...*", and is inscribed in
darker ink *Christoph Schwarz*.
Inscribed in pencil at bottom
N1343 and on verso of mount
N1276
Provenance: Benjamin West (no
collector's stamp; mount inscribed
in pencil *West*); C.R. Blundell, as
Lairesse, valued at 6s. (with .266)
WAG1995.106

WAG 1995.178

SIENESE SCHOOL
early 16th century
A group of four figures
180 × 146 mm, pen and brown ink
Popham typed annotation on album
not school of Raphael
Provenance: 'Pseudo-Crozat'
(L474); comte de Saint-Morys (?);
Henry Blundell (?)
WAG1995.134

The print (WAG1995.156) which
reproduces the drawing (in the
same style as those etched by the
comte de Saint-Morys in 1793–94)
is inscribed Domenico Sansovino.

WAG 1995.208

WAG 1995.134

SIENESE SCHOOL
mid 16th century
*Three studies of putti, from a
sarcophagus (?)*
302 × 210 mm, pen and brown ink
Watermark on mount: (?) simple
fleur-de-lys
Inscribed on drawing lower left
corner *mecarini*; in ink on back top
left corner *Book ≠/ n^il*; on back at
top *1284*; Popham annotation *not
Beccafumi nearer to Heemskerck*
Provenance: Benjamin West
(L419); C.R. Blundell
WAG1995.208

Dr Holm Bevers rejects the
attribution to Heemskerck (letter 14
August 1996). According to Dr
Ruth Rubinstein (letter 4 October
1996) the central figure is similar to
an amoretto supporting a garland
on his shoulder on the base of the
Triumphal Arch of Alfonso I of
Aragon, Naples.

SIENESE SCHOOL
late 16th century
The coronation of the Virgin with a young saint (?) kneeling in front of an altar below
495 × 336 mm, pen and brown ink and brown wash heightened with white, arched top
Inscribed on lower edge *Domenico Ghirlandaio*, and lower left corner *Domenico Cola da Siena*. Tissue-paper cover watermarked Watt & Co., inscribed in pencil *Domenico Ghirlandaio*; and in a different hand *good but of a later period*; below in pencil *No 95/ CWB*
Provenance: Three fleur-de-lys (L2781, 18th-century French mark, possibly Duke of Orleans); smudged mark, possibly 'Pseudo-Crozat' (?) (L474); Roscoe sale, 1816, lot 49, as Domenico Ghirlandaio, "the Coronation of the Virgin; a saint adoring at the altar below", bt. Ford £1. 10s.; C.R. Blundell, valued at £1. 4s. in 1841
WAG1995.74

Mario di Giampaolo suggests Bolognese School second half of the 16th century (in conversation, 30 October 1997),

CIRCLE OF ELISABETTA SIRANI
The Holy Family
280 × 210 mm, brown wash over black chalk on brownish paper within oval
Inscribed on back in pencil *Ludovico Carrache/ bought out Florence/ 489*; in ink top left corner: *147* (continental 7); and in centre: *C/[?]*; tissue-paper cover has comment in pencil that *too weak* for Agostino Carracci; attribution on mount initialled *RABD* to *?Sirani*
Provenance: Roscoe sale, 1816, lot 367, as Agostino Carracci, "The Virgin and Child. Broad wash, fine effect,/ oval./ 11h 8½w", bt. 12s. Slater; C.R. Blundell
WAG1995.265

FORMERLY ATTR. FRANS SNYDERS
Antwerp 1579–1657 Antwerp
Diana and her sleeping nymphs disturbed by satyrs
245 × 355 mm, pen and brown ink and grey wash over black chalk
Inscribed in ink on drawing *Rubens and Snyders were ... friends[?]/ Rymsdijk's Museum*; Popham agreed with Snyders probability
Provenance: 'Pseudo-Crozat' (L474); Jan van Rijmsdijk (L2167); Henry Blundell (?)
WAG1995.119

Very closely related to but not a full copy after a painting in Munich, Bayerische Staatsgemälde-sammlungen, inv. 344, of *Sleeping Diana*, formerly attributed to Rubens and Jan Brueghel, of which there is a painted copy, closer to the drawing, in an Italian private collection. For similar painted copies attributed to Jan van Boeckhorst see J. Müller Hofstede, 'Rubens und Jan Breughel *Diana und ihre Nymphen*', *Jahrbuch der Berliner Museen*, x, 1968, fig. 15 (Dr Konrad Renger, letter 22 September 1997).

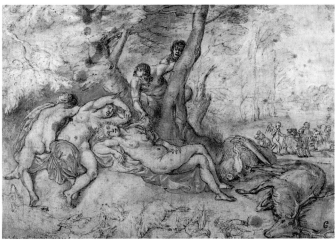

ATTR. IL SODOMA (?)
(Giovanni Antonio Bazzi)
Vercelli 1477–1549 Siena
The Virgin and Christ Child playing with a lamb
125 × 72 mm, silverpoint on pale green-grey prepared paper, with a faintly drawn sketch on the right for an infant St John (?)
Inscribed on mount in pen *Baldassare da Siena*; on mount in pencil *not genuine perhaps F[ran?]: Vanni*; on reverse in pencil *ROS.209(?)*; in brown ink *F.40*; typed label with Popham's comment *Not Peruzzi. Partial adaptation of Leonardo da Vinci's Virgin and Child with St Anne; probably Milanese about 1510*
Tissue-paper cover watermarked J Watt & Co, pencil inscription *Baldassare peruzzi/ from Richardson's Coll/ Florentine School*

Provenance: Jonathan Richardson (?; no collector's mark but his shelf-mark (?) *F.40*); Roscoe sale, 1816, part of lot 93, as Peruzzi, "The Virgin and Child, Christ playing with the Lamb/ 5h 3w/ From Richardson's Collection", bt. Slater 17s. (along with Peruzzi, exh. cat. 42, Peruzzi, WAG1995.244 and Italian School (formerly attr. Peruzzi), .97; C.R. Blundell
WAG1995.50

For a painted version of the design related to WAG1995.50 see the now destroyed *Madonna and Child with St Ann* by another Sienese artist, Andrea del Brescianino (*ca.* 1487–after 1525), in A. Hayum, *Sodoma*, Ann Arbor 1976, p. 25, fig. 38.

ATTR. HANS SPECKAERT, AFTER BATTISTA FONTANA (?)
Born Brussels, died 1577 Rome
Excited soldiers and men watching two men opening a tomb (?)
152 × 202 mm, pen and brown ink with brown and grey wash
Inscribed in ink on drawing *Batt Fontana fe/ 1565*; on back in pencil *The finding of the Cross/ Tavola di battista Fontana in S. Luca di Venezia/ S. Elena cinta (?) dalle sue dame di corte/ assiste al ritrovamente del salutifera/ croce – v. Lanzi 2–126–*; inscribed in in ink at top *I/ no 31*
Provenance: John George, 2nd Earl Spencer (L1530), sold Philipe 10 June 1811, lot 300, as Battista Fontana, "A historical design", bt. P[hilipe] 5s.; Roscoe sale, 1816, lot 290, as Battista Fontana, "the discovery of the Holy Cross, in the

presence of S. Helena the Empress; the design for his celebrated picture in the church of St. Luke, at Venice, particularly mentioned by Lanzi. The drawing is marked, 'Batt. Fontana fe. 1665 [*sic*]. pen and indian ink. Capital. 6h. 8w. From Lord Spencer's Collection.", bt. Slater 10s. 6d.: C.R. Blundell, valued at 8s. in 1841
WAG1995.343

The subject might derive from II Kings 13:21, which relates how a group of Israelites, being disturbed by Moabite raiders, hurriedly buried a man in the tomb of the Prophet Elisha, whereupon the man came miraculously to life (Dr Charles Dumas, in conversation, December 1997).

AFTER BARTHOLOMAEUS SPRANGER
Minerva and the Muses with a river-god
215 × 310 mm, pen and brown ink and brown wash over black chalk
Inscribed in pencil on mount *Esaias van der velde*; in ink on reverse *Rotteng[?]aemer/ 23*; in pencil on reverse *BB/ Bertel*
Provenance: Roscoe sale, 1816, lot 507, as Esaias Vande Velde (*sic*), "Apollo and the Muses; in front a River God with his urn Pen and bistre; fine. 9h. 12w.", bt. Slater 13s.; C.R. Blundell, as Esaias Van de Velde, "Apollo and his Muses", valued at 10s. in 1841
WAG1995.206

A copy after a Spranger composition recorded in a print by B. Dolendo (Thomas DaCosta Kaufmann, letter 30 March 1996), the original drawing for which is Besançon, Musée des Beaux Arts et d'Archéologie, inv. D.266.

ALESSANDRO TIARINI
Bologna 1577–1668 Bologna
The Mystic Marriage of St Catherine with St John the Baptist and other saints
100 × 75 mm, pen and brown ink and brown wash
Attribution on mount by Pouncey, Stock and Y. Tan Bunzl to Cigoli
Provenance: Roscoe sale, 1816, part of lot 303, as Correggio, "Virgin and Child, with St Cecilia; St John and St Jerome, in front. Pen and bistre./ 4h 3w/ This slight but highly curious drawing appears to be the first idea for his celebrated picture of the Virgin and St. Jerome, one of the finest productions of the art", bt. Slater for 12s. (with .62, now Attr. Carlo Urbino); C.R. Blundell
WAG1995.63

Formerly entitled *The Virgin and Child adored by four saints.*

ALESSANDRO TIARINI
The Madonna and Child enthroned with two saints and a bishop and children below
172 × 130 mm, black chalk and brown ink and wash heightened with white (oxidized)
Provenance: Possibly part of Roscoe sale, 1816, lot 428, as Tiarini, "Six historical, &c. on two sheets", bt. Slater 7s. 6d.; C.R. Blundell
Exhibition: Edinburgh 1969, no. 27, pl. 64, under J. Stock's attribution to Cigoli
WAG1995.78

ALESSANDRO TIARINI
The Madonna and Child adored by St Matthew and the Blessed Riniero with an angel
167 × 180 mm, black chalk and brown wash heightened with white on blue-grey paper within an inscribed lunette
Inscribed in ink on mount *del Tiarini*; on tissue-paper cover *Alessandro Tiarini/ Bolognese School*
Provenance: Roscoe sale, 1816, part of lot 428, "six historical &c. on two sheets", bt. Slater 7s. 6d.; C.R. Blundell
Literature: D. Benati, *Disegni Emiliani del Sei-Settecento*, Milan 1991, cat. 24, illus. pp. 100–01
WAG1995.211

A preliminary compositional sketch, minus the figure of St Carlo Borromeo, for the painting of *The Madonna and Child adored by Sts*

WAG 1995.211

WAG 1995.333

WAG 1995.336

WAG 1995.334

Matthew, Carlo Borromeo and the Blessed Riniero in Bologna Pinacoteca Nazionale, inv. 492, formerly owned by the Compagnia dei Salaroli, Bologna (C.C. Malvasia, *Felsina pittrice* [1678], edn. Bologna 1841, II, p. 132) and datable to *ca.* 1615–18.

ALESSANDRO TIARINI
Half-length figure of a woman wearing a veil
100 × 85 mm, black chalk heightened with white on grey/greenish-blue paper
Inscribed in ink on mount *Tutti quattro* [*sic*] *del Signor Tiarini* (there are in fact five drawings on the same mount made for the Edinburgh exhibition)
Provenance: Unknown Bolognese (?) collector (his inscription on mount, also found on Reni, exh. cat. 47, Creti, WAG1995.280–.282); Roscoe sale, 1816, part of lot 428, as Tiarini, "Six historical, &c. on two sheets", bt. Slater 7s. 6d. (with WAG1995.334–.337 on same mount and .211); C.R. Blundell
Exhibitions: Edinburgh 1972, no. 113, illus. p. 61 (with .334–.337)
WAG1995.333

ALESSANDRO TIARINI
Angel holding a vase of perfume
125 × 55 mm, pen and brown ink and brown wash over black chalk
Provenance: Roscoe sale, 1816, part of lot 428, as above, bt. Slater 7s. 6d.; C.R. Blundell
Exhibition: as WAG1995.333
Literature: Noted in Benati 1991, under no. 24; A. Bacchi and M. Mussini, *Il Santuario della Madonna della Ghiara a Reggio Emilia,* Turin 1996, pp. 119–20, figs. 70, 71
WAG1995.334

ALESSANDRO TIARINI
Angel holding a tazza of myrrh
125 × 57 mm, pen and brown ink and wash over black chalk
Provenance: Roscoe sale, 1816, part of lot 428, as above, bt. Slater 7s. 6d.; C.R. Blundell
Exhibition: as WAG1995.333
Literature: as WAG1995.334
WAG1995.336

Studies for two of the *Angels with Marian symbols* frescoed on the ceiling on either side of apse of the western arm of the Basilica della Ghiara, Reggio Emilia, which Tiarini painted *ca.* 1619.

ATTR. ALESSANDRO TIARINI
The Virgin and St Anne teaching the Christ Child to walk (?)
73 × 120 mm, black chalk with pen and brown ink and brown wash
Provenance: Unknown Bolognese (?) collector (as WAG1995.333); Roscoe sale, 1816, part of lot 428, as above, bt. Slater 7s. 6d.; C.R. Blundell
Exhibitions: As WAG1995.333
WAG1995.337

FOLLOWER OF PELLEGRINO TIBALDI
Design for a corner of a frieze: a seated nude youth
145 × 197 mm, pen and brown ink, brown wash heightened with white on blue paper
Various pencilled attributions to *Parmigianino; Farinato; nearer Tibaldi*
Provenance: 'Pseudo-Crozat' (L.474); Henry Blundell (?)
Literature: F.A. Gaudioso and E. Gaudioso, *Gli affreschi di Paolo III a Castel Sant'Angelo,* Rome 1981, II, cat. 109, p. 159, fig. 109, with attribution to a follower of Pellegrino Tibaldi
WAG1995.192

The figure corresponds to that of the young man on the left of the fictive frame surrounding the frescoed panel of *Alexander cutting the Gordian knot* in the Sala Paolina of the Castel Sant'Angelo.

AFTER TINTORETTO
Detail from the 'Paradiso' in the Doge's Palace, Venice
215 × 317 mm, red and black chalk
Inscribed in ink on drawing *Tintoreto*; in red chalk on drawing on left edge: *5 apostels*; on mount on back in ink lower right corner *N°.97*; on back in pencil another illegible inscription along top.
Attributions on mount: *probably genuine, and not Rubens*; a modern hand stating that Waagen suggested it was French 18th century in the manner of Watteau; *not Watteau, not French according to Dutch or Flemish inscription*, initialled *SRU* 'Roscoe' tissue-paper cover watermarked John Hayes/ 1814
Provenance: Robert Udny (L.2248), sold 4–10 May 1803, lot 393, as Rubens, "a sketch after Tintoretto,

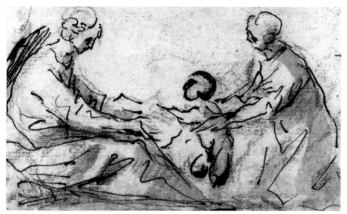

WAG 1995.337

WAG 1995.263

WAG 1995.192

WAG 1995.248

WAG 1995.260

in red and black chalk, from the sketch-book"; Roscoe sale, 1816, lot 473, as Rubens, bt. Slater 10s. 6d.; C.R. Blundell, valued at £2. in 1841 (with Rubens, exh. cats. 77, 78)
WAG1995.260

John Rowlands suggested an attribution to Pieter van Lint (1609–1690) (in conversation, 7 November 1996).

AFTER TINTORETTO
late 16th century
The Assumption of the Virgin
200 × 295 mm, pen and brown ink and brown wash heightened with white on brown prepared paper
Inscribed *Tintoret*; in ink on mount *il Tintoretto*; inscribed on back in red ink lower left corner *3rd day/ Lot 76*; in pencil lower right corner £7.7[?]
Provenance: Nicholas Lanier (L2885–86); Nicola Francesco Haym (L1970–72); Jonathan Richardson Senior (L2184) with his shelfmark *H.16/ K~o/ Zh.201/ Fa.24/ P*; Benjamin West (no collector's mark); C.R. Blundell
WAG1995.263

A copy with variations after Tintoretto's *Assumption* (1582–87) in the Scuola di San Rocco, Venice, with the addition of a bearded figure behind the two figures on the extreme right and the partial

erasure of the foreground figure next to the tomb.

AFTER TITIAN
Studies of heads from the Scuola del Santo, Padua
208 × 195 mm, red chalk
Inscribed in chalk very faintly on lower edge of drawing *Titiano.*
Corners cut
Typed label with attribution to Sebastiano del Piombo. Link to Scuola del Santo fresco made by Popham
Provenance: Roscoe sale, 1816, part of lot 238, as Giorgione, bt. Ford 19s. (along with "a pen sketch of four figures./ 7sq"); C.R. Blundell
WAG1995.248

WAG 1995.261

WAG 1995.256

WAG 1995.175

FLAMINIO TORRI
Bologna 1620–1661 Modena
The Virgin and Child in glory
254 × 180 mm, black chalk, oval
made up to rectangle with brown
wash
Watermark on mount: large fleur-
de-lys within crowned circle (?) and
countermark VI
Inscribed in ink on drawing
Annibale Carraci Bol; comments on
mount from W[aagen?]: *probably
too weak for A.C./ but of the school*;
attribution initialled *AES E
Sirani* (?)
Provenance: Unknown Venetian
(L3005 c–d) known as 'The
Reliable Venetian Collector' (his
attribution to Annibale Carracci);
Benjamin West (L419);

C.R. Blundell
WAG1995.261

Study for the lost picture by
Flaminio Torri of *The Madonna and
Child with Sts Jerome, Carlo
Borromeo, Nicola Tolentino and John
the Baptist* formerly in the Church
of the Carità, Bologna.

CIRCLE OF GIOVANNI
BATTISTA TROTTI
(IL MALOSSO)
Cremona 1556–1619 Parma
A seated female figure holding flowers
Verso: *Crowned female figure holding
a sceptre; study of an arm and a hand*
303 × 195 mm, recto: pen and
brown ink squared in black chalk;
verso: pen and brown ink (female
figure); graphite (arm and hand)
Inscribed in ink on recto *Zilotti*; in
chalk on drapery of the figure
colour notes *B G*; on verso at top
left corner *n.12192||*
Popham attribution to Trotti
Provenance: Roscoe sale, 1816, part
of lot 276, as Battista Zelotti, "A
Female Figure sitting. Pen./ 12h
10w", bt. Slater 9s. (along with
After Veronese .66); C.R. Blundell,
together valued at 8s. in 1841
WAG1995.256

The attribution to Circle of Trotti
made by Marco Tanzi (letter 7
October 1997), who suggests it is
by same hand as a *San Giovanni
Evangelista* in Cremona (inv. B.75;
see A. Puerari, *Museo Civico 'Ala
Ponzone' di Cremona. Raccolte
artistiche*, Cremona 1976, p. 147,
fig. 654).

ALESSANDRO TURCHI
(L'ORBETTO)
Verona 1578–1648 Rome
*The Virgin, St Joseph and angels
adoring the infant Christ*
355 × 258 mm, pen and brown ink
and wash over black chalk
Provenance: 'Pseudo-Crozat'
(L474); Henry Blundell (?), no. 2,
as Paul Veronese
WAG1995.175

Attributed to Turchi by Pouncey.
A preparatory drawing for the
altarpiece of the *Nativity* formerly
in the church of Santa Maria della
Neve, Verona, now in the Museo di
Castelvecchio, inv. 5739. (identified
by Giorgio Marini, Museo di
Castelvecchio, letter 8 October
1997).

AFTER ALESSANDRO
TURCHI
*The Virgin Mary, St Joseph and one
angel adoring the infant Christ*
322 × 272 mm, brush and brown
ink and wash
Provenance: Weld-Blundell
WAG1995.228

Poor and unfinished copy after
WAG1995.175

TUSCAN SCHOOL
late 16th century
*The Holy Family and two other
figures (Magi?)*
242 × 210 mm, pen and brown ink
and wash heightened with white
and squared with ink
Inscribed in pencil on mount
Taddeo Zucchero; in pencil top right
corner *L65*; Gere comment on
mount *not Taddeo*
Provenance: Benjamin West (L419;
inscribed in pencil on mount *West
Roman School*); C.R. Blundell
WAG1995.364

CARLO URBINO
Crema *ca.* 1510/20 – after 1585
Crema
*Psyche approaching Cupid asleep on a
baldaquin bed*
100 × 100 mm, pen and brown ink
Provenance: Jonathan Richardson
Senior (L2183); Sir Joshua
Reynolds (L2364); Roscoe sale,
1816, part of lot 303, as Correggio,
"Psyche with the Lamp attempts to
kill Cupid in his sleep", bt. Slater
12s. (along with Tiarini .63); C.R.
Blundell, valued at 10s. (with a
"Virgin and Child") in 1841
WAG1995.62

CIRCLE OF FRANCESCO
VANNI (?)
St Jerome contemplating the Cross
348 × 235 mm, red chalk
Provenance: 'Pseudo-Crozat'
(L474); Henry Blundell (?)
WAG1995.109

A copy after the drawing by Vanni
from which Agostino Carracci
produced an engraving (*The
Illustrated Bartsch*, XXXIX, New
York 1980, I, 74).

WAG 1995.364

WAG 1995.62

WAG 1995.228

WAG 1995.109

WAG 1995.84

WAG 1995.196

WAG 1995.96

VENETIAN SCHOOL (?)
16th century
Head of Giovanni Bellini on his deathbed
90 × 100 mm, coloured chalks with ink and wash
Inscribed in ink on drawing *Johan bellino veneto pictor/ quando era morto in cathalecto*; on back in ink *No.14; No.527*; in pencil *No.31*
Provenance: François Greffier Fagel, sold Philipe 20–25 May 1799, lot 32, for 15s.; Roscoe sale, 1816, part of lot 235, bt. Ford £1. (along with .68, After Carlo Dolci); C.R. Blundell, valued at 12s. in 1841
WAG1995.84

Though the crude colouring was probably added later the inscription may be in the hand of Peruzzi (see J. Fletcher, ' "*Fatto al Specchio*": Venetian Renaissance Attitudes to Self-portraiture', in *Imaging the Self in Renaissance Italy* (Fenway Court: Isabella Stewart Gardner Museum Bulletin), Boston 1990–91, p. 46 n. 12).

VENETIAN SCHOOL (?)
Abundance enthroned surrounded by Minerva, Justice (?) or Fortune (?), and other figures including a male amputee begging alms
143 × 225 mm, pen and brown ink and brown wash over black chalk, with an added strip of paper on left
Inscribed in pencil on mount *L Carracci*; pencil note on backing *not genuine*
Provenance: Roscoe sale, 1816, part of lot 363, "An Allegorical Piece/ 5½h. 9w.", (sold along with Lombard School (?), formerly Lodovico Carracci, WAG1995.291 and Attr. Ludovico Carracci, .98)
WAG1995.196

VENETIAN SCHOOL
18th century
Montano is prevented from sacrificing Mirtillo by Carino, his supposed father
267 × 190 mm, pen and brown ink and brown wash
Inscribed in ink on mount lower left corner *Murillo*; on back in ink description of the scene, quoting *Pastor Fido*, Act 5, Scene 4
Provenance: 'Pseudo-Crozat' (L474); Henry Blundell (?), no. 21, as Murillo
WAG1995.129

Scene from Battista Guarini's tragicomic pastoral work *Pastor Fido*, first published in 1590, which remained popular throughout Europe for the following 200 years.

WAG 1995.195

VENETO ARTIST (?)
ca. 1600–20
The Madonna and Child attended by St Catherine (?), two bishops (Sts Augustine and Ambrose?) and two children
250 × 180 mm, red chalk over pen and brown ink and wash
Inscribed on drawing in ink and crossed out *Palma 1622*
Provenance: R. Udney (L.2248), sold Scott and Philipe 4–9 May 1803, possibly part of lot 305, as Palma Giovine, "Madonna with saints … red chalk and bistre", bt. [?]otly[?] 6s.; Roscoe sale, 1816, part of lot 295, as Zanchi, bt. Slater

10s. 6d. (along with Attr. Zanchi, .94); C.R. Blundell, both valued at 8s. in 1841
Exhibitions: Venice 1980, no. 56, as Veneto mainland artist, *ca.* 1600–20
WAG1995.96

FOLLOWER OF MARCELLO VENUSTI
The Circumcision
228 × 183 mm, pen and brown ink and brown wash
Inscribed in ink *Marcello Venusti*
Tissue-paper cover watermarked J Watt & Co., inscribed in pencil *Marcello Venusti/ Nº25/ CWB*
Provenance: Roscoe sale, 1816, part of lot 97, as Venusti, "A Capital Drawing, highly finished in pen and bistre", bt. Slater £1. 1s. (with After Guglielmo della Porta, .52)
WAG1995.195

VERONA SCHOOL
ca. 1600
The Adoration of the Shepherds
425 × 305 mm, pen and brown ink and brown wash. Patched upper-right corner and washed over
Monogram in ink on drawing lower left corner *DB* or *CB*. Popham comment *not Gaulli but Venetian or Genoese 16th cent.*
Provenance: Unknown 17th-century art dealer (his monogram, G.K. Nagler, *Die Monogramisten*, Munich 1919, no. 989); Roscoe sale, 1816, lot 230, as Gio. Battista Gaulli, called Baciccio, "the Nativity with the Shepherds offering, sketched with the utmost freedom and effect, in bistre, and marked by the artist with his cypher", bt. Slater 17s.; C.R. Blundell, valued at £1. 6s. in 1841 (along with Granello, .88)
WAG1995.89

FOLLOWER OF PAOLO VERONESE
St George killing the dragon with four saints standing beside an arched opening or frame
120 × 85 mm, pen and brown ink and wash
Inscribed in ink on mount *del Signor Pietro Facini*
Provenance: Roscoe sale, 1816, part of lot 383 (?), as Pietro Facini, "Four Sketches of Historical Subjects./ Facini was the pupil afterwards the formidable rival of the Caracci, but died young. In vivacity and motion, his style/ resembles Tintoret; and with respect to his colouring,/ Agostino said that he mixed up his tints with human flesh.", bt. Slater 12s.; C.R. Blundell, valued at 10s. in 1841
WAG1995.81

AFTER PAOLO VERONESE
The Madonna and Child: study for a Presentation in the Temple
360 × 247 mm, black chalk on buff paper
Inscribed on drawing in ink partly cut off by lower edge *L 211* [?]; in pencil on mount lower left corner *Batista Zelotti/ Scuola Veneta Cp.2/ Contemporaneo ed Amico/ di paolo Veronese/ Lanzi 2.140*; and in centre of mount in pencil *Zilotti*
Tissue-paper cover watermarked J Watt & Co, with pencil attr. *Battista Zelotti/ Venetian School*
Provenance: "Pseudo Resta-Somers" (?), Italian collector; Roscoe sale, 1816, part of lot 276, as Zelotti, bt. Slater 9s. (along with Attr. Trotti, .256); C.R. Blundell, both valued at 8s. in 1841
WAG1995.66

Copy of the figure of the Virgin with the Christ Child from Veronese's *Presentation of Christ* for the organ shutters of San Sebastiano, Venice, 1558–60. The drawing is attributed to Giambattista Zelotti (Verona *ca.* 1526–1578 Mantua).

AFTER PAOLO VERONESE
The Judgement of Solomon
244 × 368 mm, black chalk, brown wash heightened with white (oxidized) on buff paper within dark brown framing border
Inscribed in ink on drawing *Paulo Veronese*; in red chalk on drawing

WAG 1995.66

WAG 1995.264

WAG 1995.276

WAG 1995.366

WAG 1995.367

WAG 1995.130

lower right corner *10*; in pencil on
mount *genuine*
Engraved: Bartolozzi, 14 March
1764, published T. Bradford, Fleet
Street; 3rd state published Jos.[h]
Read 10 March, 1791
Provenance: Roscoe sale, 1816, lot
265, as Attr. Veronese, "highly
finished ... This design has been
engraved by Bartolozzi.", bt. Slater
£1. 11*s*. 6*d*.; C.R. Blundell
WAG1995.264

A copy with variants after the
painting formerly in the Steuer
collection, Basle, formerly in the
collection of the Emperor of
Germany (?) and dated by
W. Suida to after 1580 (W. Suida,
'Notes sur Veronese', *Gazette des
Beaux-Arts*, I, 1938, p. 171, fig. 3).

FRANCISCO VIEIRA
(IL LUSITANO)
Lisbon 1699–1783 Lisbon
The martyrdom of St Lawrence
295 × 210 mm, pen and brown ink
and brown wash squared in black
chalk
Inscribed faintly in black chalk —
da Colona[?]; on back in ink *no 141*;
in pencil *Il Portuguese, Vieyra*
Provenance: Roscoe sale, 1816, lot
588, as Vieyra, "This picture was
painted by Vieyra with some
variations, and an etching from it
accompanies the drawing.", sold
Slater £1. (with an etching after a
related picture in lot 605 according
to inscription in sale catalogue);
C.R. Blundell
WAG1995.276

The drawing was etched as by
Francisco Vieira (undated) by
Gabriel Mathieu, who was working
in Rome in 1727 (impression of
print in British Museum, inv.
1860–14–4–35). Maria da
Trinidade Mexia Alves of the
Museu Nacional de Arte Antiga,

Lisbon, confirmed that the drawing
is not by Francisco Vieira Portuense
(1765–1805) (letter 17 March
1997).

MAERTEN DE VOS
Antwerp 1532–1603 Antwerp
*St Jerome, Archangel Michael and Sts
John the Baptist and Luke standing
in a landscape with their attributes*
225 × 313 mm, pen and brown ink
and brown wash
On same mount as .366.
Provenance: Benjamin West
(L419); C.R. Blundell
WAG1995.367

Carl Depauw believes this to be by
de Vos although he knows of no
related prints or paintings (letter 7
February 1997).

CIRCLE OF MAERTEN DE
VOS (?)
*Crucifixion with St John the Baptist
and St Dominic (?)*
312 × 250 mm, pen and brown ink
with grey wash. Paper has been cut
around central crucifix shape and
standing figures pasted back
together on to the same sheet
Inscribed in pencil at foot of mount
Maerten de Vos. On same mount as
.367
Provenance: Benjamin West
(L419); C.R. Blundell
WAG1995.366

Carl Depauw comments that
although the composition is close to
some de Vos schemes in execution
it cannot be regarded as by Maerten
de Vos (letter 7 February 1997).

CIRCLE OF MAERTEN DE
VOS (?)
*Title page for a collection of drawings
with female allegorical figures in front
of formal gardens*
135 × 260 mm, pen and brown ink
and wash
Inscribed in ink on oval inset
*Raccolta/ Di/ Disegni/ Dei/ Piu
Excellenti/ Pittori/ Di Diversi/ Paesi*
Provenance: Unknown Italian
collector; 'Pseudo-Crozat' (L474);
Henry Blundell (?)
WAG1995.130

AFTER ADRIAEN
VAN DER WERFF
*Shepherds and shepherdess in a
landscape*
277 × 340 mm, black chalk and
grey wash
Inscribed in chalk very faintly lower
left corner *chevalier/ A van der
Werff*; in ink on mount lower left
corner and top right corner *14/ 55*;
in pencil on mount *Adrian Van der
Werff/ his drawings are very rare.
3–3–*
Provenance: Roscoe sale, 1816, lot
510, as Adrian van der Werff,
"Nymphs dancing", bt. Slater 9s.;
C.R. Blundell, valued at 8s. in 1841
WAG1995.262

After a van der Werff drawing in
Rotterdam, Museum Boymans-van
Beuningen, inv. A.v.d. Werff 6 (in
black chalk, pen and grey wash,
317 × 404 mm, Gernsheim photo,
no. 37 172). Possibly a
counterproof of a counterproof.

ATTR. ANTONIO ZANCHI
Este 1631–1722 Venice
*St Anthony Abbot distributing his
wealth to the poor*
263 × 255 mm, pen and brown ink
and wash with small amounts of red
and black chalk
Inscribed in ink on paper below
image *Antonio Zanchi da Este*; in
faded ink *Santo Antonio Abate vende
tutta la sua facoltà a liberarsi di
questa a Poveri per Amor dato/ e
prende l'abito di Religioso*
Provenance: Unknown Venetian
called 'The Reliable Venetian
Collector' (L3005 c–d), attribution
to Antonio Zanchi; Sir Joshua
Reynolds (L2364); Roscoe sale,
1816, part of lot 295, as Zanchi, bt.
Slater 10s. 6d. (along with Attr.
Veneto Artist, .96); C.R. Blundell,
together valued at 8s.
Exhibition: Venice 1980, no. 59, as
Zanchi
WAG1995.94

FEDERICO ZUCCARO
After Correggio
Sant'Angelo in Vado 1540/41–
1609 Ancona
*A study of the Assumption of the
Virgin*
207 × 250 mm, black and red chalk
counterproof (?) on octagonal-
shaped paper
Popham comments on mount *a
counterproof copy by Zuccaro after the
Cupola at Parma Cathedral by
Correggio*. Pouncey agreed. Also
inscribed on mount in pencil *not
gen/ but good*
Provenance: Roscoe sale, 1816, lot
314, as Correggio, bt. Esdaile,
£2. 12s. 6d.; C.R. Blundell, valued
at £2. 2s. in 1841
WAG1995.56

Shows the same handling as two
black- and red-chalk drawings
attributed to Federico Zuccaro in
the National Gallery of Ireland,
Dublin, inv. 2063, 3287, of the
Virgin's attendants from Correggio's
Assumption of Virgin, Parma
Cathedral (but in reverse), both
203 × 273 mm.

CIRCLE OF TADDEO
ZUCCARO
*St Lawrence shows Emperor Decius
that the treasures of the Church are
the poor (?)*
272 × 235 mm, pen and brown ink
and brown wash heightened with
white on blue paper, lightly squared
Provenance: 'Pseudo-Crozat'
(L474); Henry Blundell (?), no. 49,
as Annibal Carracci
WAG1995.180

AFTER TADDEO ZUCCARO
Naval battle in a classical port
255 × 320 mm, pen and brown ink
and wash in an oval with fold line in
centre
Watermark on mount: fleur-de-lys
within crowned escutcheon with
arrow splitting letters LVC at
bottom, overlain with upper case
lettering HIVL[or I]LL[E]R on one
side and on other side overlain with
IHS
Inscribed in in brown ink on mount
Taddeo Zuccharo; in ink on back top
corner *79*
Provenance: Benjamin West (no
collector's mark); C.R. Blundell
WAG1995.317

One of at least ten copies of the
original Taddeo drawing now in the
Hermitage, St Petersburg, inv.
6516, for a maiolica plate
commissioned by the Duke of
Urbino, 1560–62 (see J. Gere,
'Taddeo Zuccaro as a Designer for
Maiolica', *Burlington Magazine*, CV,
1963, pp. 306ff.).

WAG 1995.262

WAG 1995.94

WAG 1995.56

WAG 1995.180

WAG 1995.317

Exh. cat. 10, Cantarini, *The Holy Family*

Exh. cat. 38, Palma Giovane, *Study for an Annunciation*

Exh. cat. 52, Sirani, *Self-portrait*

On drawing paper

On the drawing

On drawing paper

On backing sheet

On the mount/backing sheet

On support paper (with wash lines)

On the mount/backing sheet

CONCORDANCE

Only the last element is given of acquisition numbers commencing WAG1995.

.50	SODOMA	.122	ITALIAN SCHOOL	.206	SPRANGER	.280	CRETI
.51	GUERCINO	.123	ITALIAN SCHOOL	.207	PERINO	.281	CRETI
.52	DELLA PORTA	.124	GENOESE SCHOOL	.208	SIENESE SCHOOL	.282	CITTADINI
.53	MARATTA	.125	FRANCO	.209	PERINO	.283	exh. cat. 69
.54	CASOLINI	.126	PASSERI	.210	LANFRANCO	.284	CANTARINI
.55	CASOLANI	.128	RUBENS AND VAN	.211	TIARINI	.285	GHIRLANDAIO
.56	ZUCCARO		DYCK	.212	GUERRA	.286	REMBRANDT
.57	CRETI	.129	VENETIAN SCHOOL	.213	GUERRA	.287	exh. cat. 34
.58	ROMAN SCHOOL	.130	DE VOS	.214	MOLA	.288	RAPHAEL
.59	SALVIATI	.131	CARRACCI	.215	exh. cat. 78	.289	exh. cat. 80
.60	GUERRA	.133	PARMIGIANINO	.216	LEFÈVRE	.290	CANTARINI
.61	GUERRA	.134	SIENESE SCHOOL	.217	DOMENICHINO	.291	LOMBARD SCHOOL
.62	URBINO	.135	ASPERTINI	.218	CROMER	.292	BROUWER
.63	TIARINI	.136	DUTCH SCHOOL	.219	FRENCH SCHOOL	.293	exh. cat. 46
.64	exh. cat. 45	.137	ROMANO	.220	BARTOLI	.294	exh. cat. 26
.65	CARRACCI	.138	ITALIAN SCHOOL	.221	BARTOLI	.295	BLOEMART
.66	VERONESE	.140	VAN DIEPENBECK	.222	BARTOLI	.296	PARMIGIANINO
.67	FRENCH SCHOOL	.141	ATTR. ANTWERP	.223	BARTOLI	.297	DUBOIS (EDWARD
.68	DOLCI		SCHOOL	.224	BARTOLI		OR SIMON)
.69	REMBRANDT	.142	BLOEMART	.225	BARTOLI	.298	exh. cat. 24
.70	PALMA GIOVANE	.143	VAN LAER	.226	BARTOLI	.299	PROCACCINI
.71	ITALO-FLEMISH	.145	RAPHAEL	.227	BARTOLI	.300	DELLA ROVERE
	SCHOOL	.146	GUERCINO	.228	TURCHI	.301	BOLOGNESE
.72	BASSETTI	.147	SOUTH GERMAN	.229	PASSERI		SCHOOL
.73	ITALIAN SCHOOL		SCHOOL	.230	NALDINI	.302	exh. cat. 25
.74	SIENESE SCHOOL	.148	DELLA PORTA	.231	ROMAN SCHOOL	.303	exh. cat. 47
.75	exh. cat. 10	.150	CAVALIERE	.232	exh. cat. 14	.304	BRANDIMARTE
.76	exh. cat. 51		D'ARPINO	.233	exh. cat. 33	.305	exh. cat. 4
.77	exh. cat. 23	.151	SCHOOL OF	.234	ROMAN SCHOOL	.306	CARRACCI
.78	TIARINI		RAPHAEL	.235	ROMAN SCHOOL	.307	MICHELANGELO
.79	PALMA GIOVANE	.153	DIZIANI	.236	ROMAN SCHOOL	.308	CARRACCI SCHOOL
.80	PALMA GIOVANE	.154	BERNINI	.237	ROMAN SCHOOL	.309	ROOS
.81	VERONESE	.157	GABBIANI	.238	exh. cat. 7	.310	exh. cat. 20
.82	exh. cat. 30	.158	CROSATO	.239	ITALIAN SCHOOL	.311	exh. cat. 5
.83	exh. cat. 77	.159	MASTER F.P.	.240	DÜRER	.312	CARAVAGGIO
.84	VENETIAN SCHOOL	.161	ITALIAN SCHOOL	.241	BERNINI	.313	CARAVAGGIO
.85	exh. cat. 67	.162	DUBOIS	.242	RAPHAEL	.314	exh. cat. 61
.86	EMILIAN SCHOOL	.163	FRANCO	.243	REMBRANDT	.315	exh. cat. 48
.87	PROCACCINI	.165	RUBENS	.244	PERUZZI	.316	exh. cat. 59
.88	GRANELLO	.166	LOMBARD SCHOOL	.245	exh. cat. 42	.317	ZUCCARO
.89	VERONA SCHOOL	.167	VAN AELST	.246	exh. cat. 35	.318	ROMAN SCHOOL
.90	AGELLIO	.168	VAN AELST	.247	exh. cat. 76	.319	SEMOLEI
.91	RAPHAEL	.169	ITALIAN SCHOOL	.248	TITIAN	.320	exh. cat. 29
.92	BASSETTI	.170	VAN OSTADES	.249	exh. cat. 28	.321	BISCAINO
.93	exh. cat. 70	.171	exh. cat. 41	.250	GRIMALDI	.322	exh. cat. 2
.94	ZANCHI	.173	ROMAN SCHOOL	.251	exh. cat. 58	.323	exh. cat. 44
.95	PIAZETTA	.174	GENOESE SCHOOL	.252	exh. cat. 15	.324	exh. cat. 36
.96	VENETO ARTIST	.175	L'ORBETTO	.253	PARMIGIANINO	.325	exh. cat. 21
.97	ITALIAN SCHOOL	.176	MASTELLETTA	.254	exh. cat. 68	.326	exh. cat. 50
.98	CARRACCI	.177	GIOVANE	.255	FLORENTINE	.327	LOMBARD SCHOOL
.99	ATTR. GIUSEPPE	.178	DEL SARTO		SCHOOL	.328	SOUTH GERMAN
	ROLLI	.179	ROMANO	.256	MALOSSO		SCHOOL
.100	FRA BARTOLOMMEO	.180	ZUCCARO	.257	CAMBIASO	.329	exh. cat. 66
.101	FIGINO	.181	CALVAERT	.258	exh. cat. 8	.330	exh. cat. 3
.106	SCHWARZ	.182	LOMAZZO	.259	CAMBIASO	.331	exh. cat. 64
.107	CARRACCI	.183	CREMONA	.260	TINTORETTO	.332	exh. cat. 74
.108	FRENCH SCHOOL	.185	DA FORMELLO	.261	TORRI	.333	TIARINI
.109	VANNI	.186	CORNEILLE THE	.262	VAN DER WERFF	.334	TIARINI
.110	MICHELANGELO		YOUNGER	.263	TINTORETTO	.335	exh. cat. 55
.111	RAPHAEL	.187	GENOESE SCHOOL	.264	VERONESE	.336	TIARINI
.112	RAPHAEL	.190	FLEMISH SCHOOL	.265	SIRANI	.337	TIARINI
.113	PALMA GIOVANE	.191	exh. cat. 57	.266	DE LAIRESSE	.338	CORNEILLE THE
.114	HUSSEY	.192	TIBALDI	.267	ITALIAN SCHOOL		YOUNGER
.115	CASTELLO	.193	exh. cat. 12	.268	FLORENTINE	.339	CANTARINI
.116	CORNEILLE THE	.194	exh. cat. 13		SCHOOL	.340	exh. cat. 22
	YOUNGER	.195	VENUSTI	.269	BOTTICELLI	.341	CAVAZZONE
.117	CAMBIASO	.196	VENETIAN SCHOOL	.270	exh. cat. 18	.342	exh. cat. 62
.118	MONCALVO	.197	exh. cat. 17	.271	DA FAENZA	.343	SPECKAERT
.119	SNYDERS	.198	CASTIGLIONE	.272	exh. cat. 27	.344	exh. cat. 49
.120	RUGENDAS	.199	exh. cat. 11	.273	LEONARDO	.345	exh. cat. 52
.121	FRENCH SCHOOL	.200	ROMANO	.274	PARMIGIANINO	.346	exh. cat. 75
		.201	PUPINI	.275	GUERCINO	.347	exh. cat. 71
		.202	MERANO	.276	LUSITANO	.348	ITALIAN SCHOOL
		.203	GIONIMA	.277	CARRACCI	.349	FLORENTINE
		.204	MICHELANGELO	.278	exh. cat. 1		SCHOOL
		.205	exh. cat. 38	.279	CAMBIASO	.350	BRANDI

.351	CARAVAGGIO
.352	MICHELANGELO
.353	exh. cat. 16
.354	exh. cat. 60
.355	DA PARENZA
.356	exh. cat. 32
.357	exh. cat. 54
.358	exh. cat. 39
.359	exh. cat. 40
.360	exh. cat. 6
.361	exh. cat. 37
.362	exh. cat. 9
.363	BECCAFUMI
.364	TUSCAN SCHOOL
.365	CANUTI
.366	DE VOS
.367	DE VOS
.368	exh. cat. 72
.369	exh. cat. 73
.370	exh. cat. 31
.371	exh. cat. 79
.372	exh. cat. 63
.373	RIMINALDI
.374	FLORENTINE SCHOOL
.375	exh. cat. 65
.376	exh. cat. 53
.377	exh. cat. 56
.378	exh. cat. 19

WAG10843 exh. cat. 43